'So...
You Want To
Develop
Spirituallyؚ?'

Jenny Martin

'So...
You Want To
Develop
Spiritually?'

Published by:

Melissa Seymour Publishing

www.melissaseymour.co.uk

THE WONDER THAT IS LIFE

Table of Content

Introduction

This spiritual development course and method of teaching - step by step, month by month - was relayed to me by my spiritual guides over fifteen years ago and is a method I have used ever since.

After writing *'A Medium's Tale'* - my own spiritual journey - which for years had been persistently impressed upon me by spirit to write, I knew I had to write this one too!

How could I not share all that spirit had taught me and how could I not share all that I had shared with those who had patiently come to learn the lessons that I had learnt for myself? Surely, this tried and tested theory of how to achieve a better understanding of yourself and those who walk and work with you, would help countless others also venturing out on their own spiritual path?

Even after the initial 'Workshop' which always preceeded the year's course, I would be met with beaming smiles from some claiming to have found what they were looking for and often during the development course, others would profess, 'I feel I have come home!', eyes brimming with tears.

Then, not long after moving to Hereford late in 2011, I met two people within a couple of months of each other who both declared, 'I have been waiting for someone to teach me!' You will come to understand that, *"Spirit are great opportunists"* and *"When the pupil is ready, the teacher appears."*

I therefore realised that the best way to write a book on spiritual development was, of course, by example. All lessons were duly recorded, so the following pages are a true account of the interactive journey I took with these two wonderful angels and yes, I am indebted to them and to spirit for making all this possible.

I therefore hope you enjoy being present in our sitting rooms and listening to how two women from very different backgrounds found common ground by deciding to commit to a new chapter in their lives. Each of their short journeys with me would prove as exciting, wondrous and as enlightening as any story could be.

By learning how to communicate with those who truly love them, they both discovered the fruits and truths of the spirit world. They, and you, will never be the same again. Enjoy.

Jenny Martin

June 2014

AUTHOR'S NOTE: See page 394.

"Ancient is the one in me

that the spirit of this season

with its quiet murmur

calls.

Beyond, beneath the outer me

my wise old seer

looks out upon the dance with compassion

with a smile.

And the ancient one waits

for the young one to knock upon the door.

And both of them

are me."

The Essene Book of Days

A Spiritual Day: 'Workshop'

"You are an energy and so is everything else."

Jenny: 'Well, good morning!'

Grace & Bobbie: 'Good morning.'

J. 'It's lovely to have you both here. I have never had such a small workshop before but you know what they say, it's quality not quantity that counts! So I want to wish you both a lovely day and I definitely want you to feel at home and feel relaxed and think of this as your day off - it's your day today - and this is what you've decided to do so be completely and utterly selfish about it; just enjoy the day.

We will break for coffee and a two course lunch. We have lots of learning material and exercises to do so you'll probably both go home with a headache and, hopefully, we'll get to know one another better as we go along.'

G. 'I'm sure we will.'

J. 'So what I want to do first is start with an ice breaker and introduce ourselves so I'll start. I'm Jenny Martin, I live in Hereford. I have an autistic son who is 27, I'm retired now and, amongst other things, I'm a medium and have just started writing spiritual books; Bobbie?'

B. 'I'm Bobbie, I have two children. I live in a little, scruffy cottage but the area is absolutely beautiful. There's a tree which the council want to cut down and even though it's dead it's beautiful. I'm really interested in what you've got to teach.'

J. 'Excellent. Are you married?'

B. 'I am married, yes.'

J. 'Thank you. Grace?'

G. 'My name is Grace. I have two daughters, three grandchildren and one husband!' (We all laugh).

G. 'We've been married over forty years and I am really looking forward to today because he finds my spiritual work quite difficult to deal with. I live in a pretty little town and I like where I live and like the people. I also channel art from spirit. I am a little confused about this because I need to understand how this comes about.'

J. 'Thank you. OK, I need you both to pick up your pad and answer a question for me which is, 'Why are you here?' You're both very busy writing. So, Bobbie, let's first hear why you're here?'

B. 'I'm here to begin my journey towards a more spiritual path, to understand and to be able to communicate with my guides and helpers etc. To understand what they wish to show me, tell me and guide me so I can help others to find their true path in this lifetime.'

J. 'Oh that's lovely, that's lovely Bobbie. Grace, why are you here?'

G. 'I'm here to understand why me? Why has spirit chosen me? Someone who has never been trained as an artist to produce such wonderful drawings and paintings. Also to help me address these issues when talking to my family who see me as a wife, mother and grandma and to further my work with spirit.'

J. 'Lovely, thank you Grace. I champion the individual and adore how everyone is so different and it's something that I'm forever intrigued by. The longer I live, the more people I meet, the more work I do, it keeps coming up time and time again. Just hearing these two answers is testament to how amazing people are. I can ask one question and get two completely different answers. I love it. Thank you.

OK, it's time for you to know a little bit about me as we've never met before and I think it's very rude for me to have a day with you and you not know who is talking to you! First of all I'm deaf which in itself teaches you that you don't have to have your hearing in order to be clairaudient which I thought was quite a good way of introducing myself, so I lip read.

I've been deaf since I was eight when I got mumps and refused to wear a hearing aid so I'm good at lip reading, however, I have to work at tuning into people's voices, their tones and their accents so if someone mumbles and has an accent it's sheer agony for me as I have to work extremely hard to understand what they are saying.

As a child, both my parents regularly used to accuse me of being really selfish which when I think about that now, I can't believe as I don't think I'm a selfish person at all. My father would also regularly tell me to 'stop analysing' and I would think to myself, this is ridiculous telling me to stop analysing because this is the way I think!

I had very early on, what I now realise were quite profound thoughts. My childhood wasn't easy, was very stressful and hard going and I used to say to myself, 'We're not here to have a good time you know, it's bloody hard work!'

My mother died when I was fifteen and I used to lie in bed and think about death and even before this, when I was a child, I would think about dying and say to myself, 'When I die, the world will go on and on and on and on.' Then I would suddenly stop and exclaim, 'There must be more to life than this!' These two sayings I especially remember and, of course, when my mum died, these thoughts would reverberate in my mind and being older and having had that personal experience, I once again tried to make some sense of it all.

I would later learn so much which would answer so many questions and I remember, for example, trying to reason why a child dies whilst another person lives to an old age, it just doesn't make sense, does it? There are so many questions which I'm sure you have asked yourselves whether they've been conscious or subconscious ones.

So I became two people. I became the person that everyone expected me to be, the person my parents wanted me to be and who I thought I had to be and then there was my real self, which obviously I kept very, very private. I often think my own journey has parallels to a gay person coming out. I always knew I wasn't what I was purporting to be and all I really wanted was to be the real me but it was *really*, really hard.

I did have a lot of what we call 'psychic' experiences when I was young. I used to see faces everywhere. I used to see things floating around in my bedroom at night. I used to have very profound thoughts when I was young, like when I cut myself and drew blood, I thought this was something sacred. It was all very odd when I look back, for someone so young to think those things. Again, I just kept it all to myself. I didn't dare say anything because no-one was discussing anything remotely like what I was experiencing or thinking.

So I just carried on trying to find answers, trying to find someone like me I suppose and, much later, I did meet this guy who was well versed and travelled who had even received healing on the beaches in India and I thought, oh, maybe I can talk to him, surely he will understand? When I eventually asked him whether he saw things floating around at night he told me to go and have my eyes tested!

I thought I'm getting no-where but still I battled on and as luck would have it, my hairdresser was very interested in clairvoyant readings and her mother was quite psychic and when I went to have my hair cut, I was able to discuss things with her which, of course, was wonderful.

One day she was telling me about this amazing clairvoyant she had been to see in London and she was so excited about what she had been told, which was all very true and came to pass and she said, 'Jenny you should go!' So I went.

When I arrived I was presented with someone who was as big as I was small, as large as I was slight. This lady was Danish and I remember she said, 'Hello Daaling, come on in!' Well, that afternoon blew my mind because she brought my mum through who was a couture dressmaker and when she described what she was wearing these were clothes which only a well dressed person would wear.

The messages made me cry a lot. This was the first time I had experienced anything this authentic before and it was through this clairvoyant that I would be led to those who would become my spiritual family and consequently my spiritual mentors.

So the moral of this story is never underestimate who you meet, not even your hairdresser, because often people come along for a reason. I had no idea at the time, but now I am fully aware, that anybody you meet probably means something, no matter how little, but they need to cross your path and come into your life. So don't be in a hurry to turn people away because you might be turning away something that you may later regret. *"Nothing is ever for nothing."*

So my spiritual life began when I was 45. I now understand how important it is to have all your earlier life experiences. When people come to me and they're so young and they want to develop spiritually and I think, well, I don't know about this because they still have so much 'living' to do. *"Experience is the greatest teacher"* and if you haven't had experience of life, you also haven't learnt very much.

I know this may seem obvious but from a spiritual perspective you do need your life experiences, you need all your childhood experiences, all your youth experiences, they're not just co-incidences, they are very much there to shape you and for you learn from and to help with your future. So, I was just a very ordinary person who was starting my spiritual life just at the right time, in my mid forties, when I would have had the wealth of all my life's experiences behind me.

I am a natural healer, a trance medium, a rescue medium, an author. I did turn away physical mediumship which I could have done if I wanted but I made the decision that this wasn't right for me. So this is who is talking to you. Thank you for listening to that drawn out introduction but I know that there are some little gems hidden in there for you to think about. (Grace & Bobbie applaud).

That's the short version by the way! Right, there is no order for today's workshop. I know I have given you a programme but because spirit are working with me they can often say, 'Well, tell them about this or tell them about that.' and I may 'frog hop' from one thing to another.

OK, so what are we trying to achieve today, that's what you both want to know?

What I want to do first is to open a door. I want to open a door in your life and I want to open your eyes. I want to maybe take off your blinkers. People go around with what I call blinkers; they see but they don't see. I always give the example of two girls walking home from school. One of them is talking constantly, chat, chat, chat and in a world of her own whilst the other is silent but looking around, and I say to myself, what do you make of that?

The girl who is listening and looking around, she looks at a tree and recognises it's an oak tree by the shape of the leaves and as the leaves are starting to change colour she knows autumn is coming; she is *really* using her eyes. I will say to people look again, no, look again! No, *really* look again. That's what I mean by open your eyes. We've been blessed with our senses and we need to learn how to use them.

I also want to give you confirmation of what you already know. Well, you may think, well thanks a lot, but I think confirmation is very important because another thing I want to do is to give you corroboration of what you already know. We all think about things especially when people come here, they have reached a certain stage in their lives where they want to know more. They have been asking themselves questions again, consciously or subconsciously and today you will hopefully get some answers and you will think, I thought that or I knew that and that is *so* important.

Thoughts and hypotheses float around and often they don't set, they don't consolidate, so giving you confirmation and corroboration is a wonderful thing to have. It cements your own thoughts and brings about confidence in yourself. It is also one of the ways that spirit communicate with us.

I would love to touch your soul. It would certainly be a very big achievement for me so I might as well aim high!

I am going to try and answer some of your questions.

We're going to talk about you and hopefully make you feel as wanted, loved and special as you really are which comes back to me championing individuality. To me, we are *all* special, we are all loved, we are all like a flower - an individual flower - and the idea of returning to earth is to make you an even more beautiful flower. Don't cross pollinate with someone else's flower, just be you.

Be as unique as you really are and, without being dramatic, there is no-one in the whole universe quite like you! You are a one off and if everyone realised how unique they really were, I think people would like themselves more.

So as I said, I would like you to use your senses more. This isn't just for your own good but it works as a cycle. Whatever you put out, you get back, so if you use your senses more you are sending more things out to the universe and because of the *"Like attracts like"* law, you are returning all that to yourself. The *motive* is to give but there is always a reward.

Hopefully, today will be a step in the right direction for you and after today, you will hopefully be hungry to learn more and this will become a stepping stone for you. One thing is for sure, spirit want us to *"know our spiritual origin so we can achieve our spiritual destiny"* so we will be talking about spiritual origins today as well.

I just know that everyone who is supposed to be here is here. I never worry if I have two people or twenty-two people as I know that spirit have led people to hear what I have to say.

I am just a mouthpiece. I have just been given a role of sharing everything I have been taught with others and I take that very seriously. I also know that spirit would never waste my time. They would make sure that I am helping those who are ready to be helped, who are ready to learn, who are ready to take the next step and who want someone to guide them. What shall I do now? Where shall I go now?

There is a big truism that says, *"There is no such thing as time in spirit but spirit's time is perfect."* So I know, that even though there are just two of you here, it is well worth the effort today.'

G. 'I would like to write down what you said about time and spirit. Could you say that again?'

J. 'Yes. *"There is no such thing as time in spirit but spirit's time is perfect."*

OK, lastly, before we break for coffee, I need to say again that there is no order to today. I am not trying to teach you or convert you, I am just sharing what I know with you. It's very important you understand that. We all have our own path and right now we are all at a certain stage on that path.

I always say to people no matter what I'm doing whether it's a workshop or a course, take the bits you want, take the bits you need. My path has been *my* path. You have got yours to walk and to follow and the key is, if it sounds good, if it sounds right, it's normally right for you.

This brings me to another important point which I must make which is that everything I am sharing with you today I've already decided, 'Sounds good to me; I like that', but I have also put these principles to the test. I haven't been a 'yes' person and thought, OK, you say it, cool, that'll do me, I've challenged it. I've said, OK, I hear what you say, now I'm going to see if it works for me?

So, a lot of things I have been told or given I have personally put to the test to see whether they're workable, whether they're 'do-able', I haven't just taken things for granted. Funnily enough, my dad was really strong on this issue. He pummelled into me, don't take things for granted and it's one of the things he left for me, if you like, and it's no different with the spiritual teachings.

Today we're going to cover many things and you also need to understand that if there is anything that's offends your logic then I want to apologise for this now, even though I am just sharing information. Some people have pointed their beliefs so accurately that they are neither malleable nor flexible. They only want to hear what they *want* to hear so anything outside their comfort zone or box, or not under their heading, they don't want to hear!

I say this as I have had people attend my workshops who have been really offended by what I've said and I wasn't able to ask them, 'What are you doing here, if you're not ready to explore, to open your mind, to listen to what others have to say?' So it's like my insurance policy, I'm saying it now! However, it's extremely important that you make up your own mind about things. You must stick to your path; *"To thine own self be true."*

So, what are the hallmarks of a true teacher? I was told Simplicity, Humility and Love. *"Love is the hallmark of God and the trademark of all those who serve Him."* There is no point in anyone sharing or teaching something if their language is so complicated that no-one can understand them. Always simplify everything and make sure it's comprehensible. Make sure the people you are talking to understand what you are saying. Don't talk A-level stuff when you have O-Level students.

All spiritual truths are simple, *so* simple a child could understand, and it's for that reason that it *is* simple, so that children, who are so spiritual, can understand. It's not difficult, it's man who makes things complicated. They shouldn't then blame God for things which they have made complicated. OK?

So we're going to have a coffee break now. Hope you are happy with what's been said so far?'

G. 'Very much so because I'm dyslexic. I don't see or understand things as others do. I left school at fourteen and probably did my learning after I left school. I was never happy as I was the odd one out so simplicity is the key word for me.'

COFFEE BREAK...

G. & B. 'Yes.'

J. 'So every day we're given things to learn but we don't understand or see it as learning, we just think, what am I doing today? Within each day, if you actually stopped to think about it, there are lessons, there are gifts of learning being given to us, OK?

So never be afraid of putting someone first or giving to others; you won't be forgotten. We are told, *"No-one is ever forgotten, mistaken or left out."* All things are included, everything is necessary. One thing is just part of the whole.

The third truth which I thought was so profound and I have used it many times is, *"To lose yourself, is to find yourself."* In counselling, for instance, you listen to people talking about themselves, thinking about themselves *all* the time. It's a 'me, me, me culture' and they can't see the wood for the trees because they're completely wrapped up in themselves; there is no room for any movement at all.

Their whole life has been about themselves, it's 'chocker-block', full up, so there is no room for change. Their personal negativity is like a weed that has wrapped itself around their own flowering self and it is strangling them.

If you stop, if you think of others, if you make a space - you make a space to fill a space - and I always try and say, stop thinking about *you* and start thinking about somebody else. If you want to find yourself, you're going to have to forget 'self' and then self will reveal itself to you when the right time comes.

It's often hard for people to adjust to this way of thinking but I just say things like go and do some voluntary work. Stop the 'me, me, me' thing and start thinking of somebody else and you know what, something amazing happens when you start thinking of others, when you realise that there are many people a lot worse off than you.

However, you will also reap the rewards when you start thinking about others because by making a space for others, you will have filled your own and you will be surprised by the answers and by the results. So this truism about losing yourself in order to find yourself is quite a good one.

When I first realised that I had an opportunity to talk to people I said to myself, if I had just one opportunity to say something what would I say, what would it be, what would I grab with both hands? The one thing that changed me years ago was when I realised that we were all related, that we were all brothers and sisters, that we were all part of one enormous family and that God was our Father.

God doesn't look like Father Christmas and God isn't a man. To me, God is consciousness, God is the life force, you know, Star Wars and "May the force be with you!" To me, that is akin to God. But there is a hierarchy in spirit nevertheless and this explanation isn't something out of Greek mythology or from Disney's Hercules, there have been so many stories but I believed in this force.

In being alive, I was *really* immortal and so was everyone else and did they know this? And then the question, what made me live, what *was* my life force? The answer was this substance of existence, a small, minute piece of God which began its expression when I was conceived.

This life force would not only stay with me throughout my life here on earth but would stay with me for eternity because the creator of that force which fashioned the universe, who thought up how everything would work, would look like, would operate, would interact with each other, would affect one another, would progress, would learn, would teach - the whole 'shabang' - from the tiniest grain of sand to the largest erupting volcano, from the smallest flea to the biggest mammal on earth, all its inhabitants and all the planets in this vast cosmos, all this, was produced by this one power - which was God.

So how did the world begin? We hear about the 'big bang', don't we? I think the universe began as a thought. I think that this 'thought' took substance and just like the analogy of the oyster and the pearl, this substance, this 'thought energy' was irritated and constantly pushed around and irritated further and further. Just like what happened to that little piece of grit in the oyster, the thought energy was influenced so much by the surrounding energy that it produced the beginnings of matter and ultimately the planets - 'the pearl'. So I think that everything began with a thought which created substance.'

G. 'Because action always follows thought.'

J. 'Yes and also 'action/reaction.' To me, we as a human consciousness are just pure thought. So it was a massive thought or maybe it was just a little thought that turned into something massive?

Now, you think computers are amazing, well who developed the first brain then? If brains aren't computers then what are they? I feel that life is incredible. People forget and take for granted how amazing life is. How amazing is it that two people can have 'nookie' and produce a clone and that clone has all these facets including a computer brain in their head that allows them to work things out. I'm sorry but as far as I'm concerned, computers were not invented in the early twentieth century.

So that power, that almighty wisdom was my Father, was our Father, wasn't I lucky, wasn't I privileged? I really couldn't believe it when I had this euphoric moment and worked this out. So why isn't everyone happy? Don't they realise how lucky they are? We're infinite and our life now isn't just 'it'.

So going back to me and that little girl who thought there must be more to life than this - there was! In giving me a piece of Him, I could, if I wanted, help Him in creating a world worthy of Him. If He gives me this, surely I can give something back?

As I said earlier, my earth father taught me never to take anything for granted but until I understood who I really was, I had done, I had taken *life* for granted, no question about that!

So, think for a minute if you will, how come you are living? How come you are alive now? What is it that makes you operate, that makes you work, what makes you breathe? Well, it's my heart, when that stops I've had it!

OK, well what makes your heart beat then? It's the blood going round my body. OK, well what makes that work? It's the pump pumping the blood around the heart. Well, what makes *that* work? I don't know, it just does!

Listen, I'm no scientist, no biologist but you can keep going until you realise that there is something behind all this, something behind the mechanics of the bodily function and that, my friend, is that piece of Him, that is spirit, which animates not just humans but all life, the animals, the planets, nature, the wind, the sea, the seasons.

Now, quite few years ago I read something which blew my mind and I just want to share it with you now whilst we're talking about living things. I want to read to you something from Gardener's World and it says, "Compost is alive. In one gram of soil which is about a teaspoon, there are 25,000 species of bacteria, 10,000 species of fungi, 1,000 protozoa and 100 nematodes. Each of these has a role to play. Each one is contributing to the balance and health of the soil." Now if that 'don't blow your mind', I don't know what does. That is incredible! That is life which we take for granted.

As I said before, *"All life is one life"*, even the soil, especially the soil, especially our planet which is alive. Everything in the world is alive. Everything comes from the earth so everything has energy. The earth is a living thing so everything in this room, for instance, is alive, has energy even things which are man-made have origins from the earth and are made with elements from the earth so everything is moving, not just the earth itself but everything that we're looking at now is moving, has energy.

Let me explain about our earth's energies. The earth's energies are stodgy and heavy and are different from those in the realms of spirit where it is much lighter in vision and in weight. Because of centuries of negative thinking, materialism and the way man has carried out his thinking and doing, the earth has been getting denser and heavier with negativity which is causing a problem for the earth to regain its balance.

As I have just said, everything we see is actually moving, everything has energy and because of the earth's stodgy, dense and heavy negative energy, our planet appears to be still but it is not. You only need to think about space and how things fly around?'

G. 'Are we talking about gravity?'

J. 'Yes, but I want to explain this from a spiritual perspective too and I want you to appreciate that everything we see is a living thing, not just obvious things like wooden table and chairs. Even plastic, for example, has earthly components used in its production.

I'm now going to take you on a little journey to try and answer the questions, 'Who are we, why are we here, what happens when we die?' To my mind, if you don't think about this, then you're not walking a spiritual path. It's the fundamentals, like starting from the foundations, the foundations from whence we come.

To me, we all come back to earth to learn as the earth is a training ground. The earth is the hard school. As humans, we're not stupid, we all want the best for ourselves and the best place to learn is here on the earth plane. You can stay in spirit, you do not have to come back to earth to learn, however, your learning and progress in spirit would be a lot gentler, a lot slower but nah, nah, nah, we want to get on so we chose to come back here.

When we live in spirit, we reside within a soul group and that soul group is like our spiritual family. In choosing to come back here we actually agree why we need to come back. Remember I spoke earlier about teaching at a level that people will understand. People have evolutionary stages. Everybody is at a certain stage in their evolution.

Right now, I'm looking at two people who are at the sum total of all their incarnations. Everything they've learnt, everything that they've understood, everything that they are aware of is with them now, is within their consciousness but they have chosen to come back here to learn and achieve a bit more. Everyone has, otherwise they wouldn't be here and mummy and daddy helped make that happen!

To me, that's one of our jobs - to procreate - to allow those who are queuing up to come back to earth to learn. To give them the opportunities to continue their evolution.To get their spiritual O-Levels, to get their spiritual A-Levels or to achieve a spiritual degree.

We have to do this course on earth because we learn the theory in spirit but then we have to put that theory into practice to really understand it. The best place to practice is on the earth plane. Why, because you don't have that opportunity living with your spiritual family. Your spiritual family are people who have the same level of knowledge and understanding as you. Here on earth, you are rubbing shoulders with all kinds of people each with different knowledge, understanding and experiences; what a place to learn! I told you, you weren't stupid!

So it is in spirit that you decide what it is that you now need for your higher good. What are your next steps, what are your next tests? All these things are eventually agreed between you and your guides in your soul group within your spiritual family.

You then choose who are going to be your earthly parents, your family and where and when you will be born. You will work out your next spiritual journey and how long it will take you to achieve all your plans, how long it will take you to learn what I call your 'X,Y & Zees'.

You now know that your next stage is to experience and learn this, maybe to experience and maybe to also repay a debt and having worked all this out, you will have chosen how long you need to be on the earth plane. 74 years, 83, I can do this in 60 but whatever it is, it's all agreed beforehand with your spiritual family, with your guides, with your gatekeeper. Yes, we all have a gatekeeper.

We all have somebody who knows us *so* well and loves us *so* much and they elect to walk with you, agree to stay with you during the whole of your incarnation on earth. They agree to be your number one person which is incredible for someone to agree to do; that's love for you!

So you are born of the parents you have chosen. Why, because you know those two people, you know what they are like, you know what kind of life they are having, what spiritual path they are on and how this can affect you, teach you and help you with yours. Once again, you're not stupid.

However, spirit never does anything for one reason alone and your life will actually benefit your parents and family too. You in turn will give them the tools and lessons which *they* need for their own journey too. It's so clever.

In a family, they always say you never have two children alike. Have you ever wondered why? It's because we are all here to help and teach each other and where better to start learning than at home.

Have you had a lovely childhood? Not everyone has had a wonderful childhood and many pupils have looked at me in disbelief saying, 'No, I couldn't have chosen my father, no way!' 'Oh, but you did, because he taught you so much.' 'But he was awful!' they say. 'Yes, and didn't you learn a lot!' You don't just need to learn what's good and right but also what's not so good, maybe that especially so we choose the family who can teach us things, we all need opportunities to learn and experience.

As children we are learning things subconsciously, maybe parrot-fashion, we don't understand what we're learning, but in spirit, we have already worked out what we're going to learn and the choices that we will have to make. Our journey is mapped out with the opportunities which we need to help us along and to steer us on our chosen path.

Once we're on earth we don't remember any of this. How come we don't remember? Of course you don't remember, if you remembered, it would be like taking an exam when you already knew the answers. Absolutely pointless!

Coming back to the earth plane allows us to have our journey. It's a journey of discovery, a journey of self-discovery. Again, who am I, why am I here, what's all this is about? You have to discover it for yourself, that's the journey, that's the excitement. Excitement? Yes, it will be exciting if you are positive about it. If you look at things in the right way and if you take all the opportunities that come because they come for you. However, we don't remember that so it's like having to learn all over again in these restrictive earthly conditions.

OK, so we decide how long it's going to take us to do the X,Y, & Zees. I want to explain that when someone has finished their life and it comes to their time, it's their time. Believe me, it won't make any difference how good the surgeons are, how good the doctors are, it's their time. It's their chosen time and it's time to go home; it's not time to die.

And you have the funeral and people weep and spirit say, *"You may weep but we rejoice, a friend is coming Home."* Once you learn that life is infinite, that your life here is just a stage, a part of infinity, you will have a completely different outlook on life and the lives of others.

So you've passed away, it's your time - 89 years on the dot. So what happens then, do you go and meet Peter at the gate? No, of course you don't but you *are* met. Everyone is met. Every single person is met by somebody even if it's by their special dog or their favourite cow. You are met by someone who loves you, who then takes you 'over' to the 'other side', to your spiritual home. You never, ever 'die' alone. OK?

Once you have passed to the other side - and the other side can be like walking through a door - it is not terrifying, it is not painful. It is just like going through into the next room or if you are outdoors in the countryside maybe you'll walk over a bridge, maybe you'll cross a stream. Maybe you'll just cross a road because the person who is waiting for you is standing just across the way but it will be one of the most natural, enlightening experiences you will ever have.

So what happens when you get to the other side? Party time, definitely! I have been shown children scattering rose petals along a road lined with people waiting for someone to arrive home. Everyone in spirit knows you're coming home so celebrations are the order of the day but after that will come 'judgement' and not the judgement we've all heard about either.

You will have to judge yourself and how well you have managed your incarnation. You and your conscience will be the best judge of you. Being in spirit, you now come into the fullness of your consciousness and you understand and remember exactly why you needed to return to the earth plane. What it was you needed to learn, to do, to achieve and your life is played back to you in the same way as a tape or video recorder would be. Your whole life flashes before your eyes and you are able to perform your own judgement with honesty and clarity. Again, it is so clever.

And in judging yourself you realise what you have learnt, what you have achieved, that you have overcome things and what happens is that because your knowledge and understanding have increased so does the rate of your energy and so you now automatically vibrate faster than you did when you left for earth.

Because of the law of *"Like attracts like"* you will now dwell on a spiritual plane which equates with your new found vibration and energy rate and that plane of being will be with others who also vibrate at your new vibrational level, so your soul group may invariably change. Do you understand?'

G & B. 'Yes.'

J. 'So, we are energy first and foremost and that energy is God and that energy is Love so in effect, we are little Gods, little Loves.

Now your consciousness will invariably retain the traits of your personality and character when you come back to the earth plane. Sometimes you may also bring back 'gifts' which will help you achieve what you need to do in this lifetime. For example, Grace, you do drawing. Maybe in a past life, you were an artist and it starts to reveal itself at a certain juncture in your life.

Our soul is like a diamond and in essence, we come back to polish one or two facets of that diamond so that when we return home it is no longer dull but shines with knowledge and understanding.

There are two main Laws which I would like to discuss. The first is the Spiritual Law and the other the Natural Law. The Spiritual Law is simply to Love which is what life is all about and everything which has to do with anything comes back to love. The Natural Law, you may already have heard about, which is the Law of Cause and Effect and is known for its coin of phrase, *"As you sow, so you will reap."*

As I said, the Natural Law is one of perfect balance but everything has an order. For example, you cannot lie on your deathbed and say sorry for something you have done and expect to be automatically forgiven. Whatever negative action you have sown will have to be addressed, if not in this life, then in the next. You have to balance out right from wrong and all debts have to be repaid but remember you have an infinite amount of time to do this.

You cannot absolve your responsibilities. When I teach, I try and make people aware that if their conscience reminds them that they still haven't done this or they still need to do that, try and tie up all those loose ends and put things right in this lifetime; you won't regret it. Otherwise when your life flashes by and you judge yourself, you will realise that you never did get round to doing something which your conscience told you was necessary.

There is a saying that *"No-one is ever given anything that is too much for them"* so whatever you need to do to put things right you *do* have the power, the capability and the strength within you to complete the task otherwise you wouldn't have the problem in the first place. Again, *"Like attracts like."*

The spiritual laws of life include perfect compensation and retribution, again balance. For example, there are many doctors working in the world today who perhaps took away life in a previous incarnation and are back today in a profession which enables them to prolong life. They always knew they wanted to be a doctor.

When it comes to being a good human being, I personally feel that God doesn't measure this in terms of one's religion. To me, God doesn't demand anything of us and He doesn't mind what you attach yourself to or what you believe in. If being a Catholic or a Buddhist makes you a good person then isn't that wonderful!

The purpose of having an 'Almighty' and having 'almighty thoughts' is natural as that Godly energy is real and is what animates us. The God which many of us wish to serve and work with wants us to do our best and to do good by us and our fellow man. He doesn't judge us by our religion.

OK, before we move on I just want to say that although in our eyes man has been on a 'spiritual road' for a long time he hasn't, in fact, learnt very much at all. We are still fighting wars because religion still bans religion, because church still fights with church, sects have turned brother against brother and nation against nation.

We say that we will love our brother and serve our fellow man but how many of us actually do? So I think spirit do look upon us on earth and see very little progress at all, yet man is so arrogant in his thinking. He presumes that because we have come a long way technically that he is the most intelligent and superior of beings. I, personally, don't think so.

I am now going to talk a bit about our psychic gifts. *"The psychic is the tool for the spiritual."* If you looked up the word psychic in the dictionary it would say, "of or pertaining to extra-ordinary especially extra sensory and non-physical mental processes or thoughts". We all have senses. We were given them so that we could use them as much as we can to the best of our ability and for our higher good whether we want to pursue this area for ourselves or for our fellow man. What do they say, *"Seek and thou shalt find."* If you want something, go and search for it, seek it out.

Our mind, our consciousness, can also be used with other senses which are labelled psychic 'gifts' for use with clairvoyance, clairaudience, clairsentience, healing, psychometry, flower sentience, psychic art, etc. These are forms of expression fuelled from the spirit realms and fed through your mind to produce a communication dependent on your ability and understanding of what is around you.

Many people use tarot, playing cards, rune stones, crystals, etc. which are tools they believe they need in order to communicate with the spirit world. These individuals are using their own intuition, their thoughts and a percentage of spirit communication.

But if they wanted to, they could abandon these material possessions and just communicate direct with spirit; have a direct line to God. The conscious mind is the divine monitor, the channel for thought, the channel for communication - everyone has the ability to communicate. We all have minds, we all have senses and chakra points, we are all spirit inside our 'bodies' and we all have guides and helpers who are waiting to communicate with us and hoping that one day we will acknowledge their communication with us.

I talked earlier about the 'stodginess' of the earth and over time all the materialism and wrong thinking and wrong doing of man has caused the earth to become heavier and heavier. It has also caused man's spirituality to recede more and become less of a priority in his life. If you think of times gone by, in Bible times when, let's say, Abel was coming across the plains with his flock to visit his cousin Joshua, he would exclaim to his family, 'Abel is coming, I know he's coming and bringing his sheep.' Now how did he know they were coming? Did Abel phone? (Grace and Bobbie laugh).

Did he email, did he text, did he fax?' (Grace and Bobbie are still laughing). He just *knew* because he was spiritually aware. Look at tribes; 'It's going to rain tomorrow.' or 'I'm going to ask for help.' or 'We are going to pray for a good harvest.'

Before commercialism, before materialism, before we got heavier and heavier into modernism, the spiritual was, if you like, lying on the top of our skin. We had a natural communication with the spiritual world; that was the way it was done. We knew there were Gods. It didn't matter what we called them, we knew there were people who were with us, who supported us, who helped us, who guided us, who loved us, who cared for us, what happened - what *has* happened?

Look how the tribes could read the skies, could read the stars, could read nature. They related and understood the spiritual laws, spiritual energies and they knew how they were *all* connected to mother earth and to a spiritual hierarchy. They didn't take life for granted. Their lives and everything around them was meaningful often sacred and they knew they were part of a bigger picture.

They wore their spirituality on the surface but then man became greedy and more needy and as this advanced and materialism took over so the spiritual took a back seat and regressed further and further away and those who still understood the spiritual and what it stood for were in the minority.

Everybody can develop spiritually. Everyone can use the power of thought to develop their psychic ability. Firstly, you must want to and by doing that, you are giving the people who want to communicate with you permission. I say people because your spiritual guides and helpers are still human beings, just because they are in spirit doesn't mean to say they are ethereal beings with wings and halos. They have been here just like you. They have been through arduous journeys on the earth plane just like you and have probably had several incarnations - just like you. They are now on the other side.

Living in spirit is obviously different as you are living in a different dimension to this one. They say that *"Spirit is just a thought away."* People think that spirit is up above us. Spirit isn't up, spirit is all around, energies are everywhere. We tend to look up but that's fine, it doesn't matter.

As I said before, the earth has a specific purpose and is the best place to learn.

Now I am going to stop talking and we're going to do some exercises before our lunch. It's a good time to do exercises because it's always better to work with spirit on an empty stomach. So I now want you both to relax and to close your eyes and if you can just empty your mind and fill it with nothing, absolutely nothing.

The first thing I want you to do; I have spoken about the guides and helpers who walk with us so firstly, I want you to ask *your* guide now to draw close to you and when you think that has happened, I want you to open your eyes. It maybe a feeling or a thought, they will use anyone of your senses.

Excellent. May I ask you Grace, how do you know your guide is with you?'

G. 'I have a feeling on my left side of closeness and also a feeling of something connecting with my thoughts.'

J. 'Thank you, Bobbie?'

B. 'On my right side and I felt something close on my shoulder.'

J. 'Lovely, well done. Close your eyes again. I want you to go to a special place - a special place for you. I want it to be the first place that comes into your head and when you're there, open your eyes. Well done, that was quick! Grace, where were you?'

G. 'A beautiful glade with a little stream with sunshine coming through the leaves.'

J. 'Lovely, Bobbie?'

B. 'A glade as well with a waterfall coming down and the sun shining through the trees.'

J. 'Amazing, you both got very similar places! OK. We're going to go through a sequence of events

J. 'OK, hope you are both feeling more refreshed?

Consciousness, the conscious mind, the spirit, the life force; what is it? To me, it's that which makes us live, it's what animates all things. There are different levels of consciousness for humans, for animals, for plants, for the planets but *"All life is one life."* There is no new truth, *"Truth has always been and always will be."* The same truths apply now as when they were maybe written in the Bible or in the fourteenth century, they are still the same. So truth has always been and always will be, like life itself.

One of the first 'spiritual truths' I was given was, *"Love, give and give again and all will be added onto you."* I can even remember where I was when I was given it. I was having lunch with my father in St. John's Wood, London and I was crossing a pedestrian crossing when I heard it. It was such an extraordinary thing to hear in such an ordinary place and I couldn't believe it. This truth is all about what I call the boomerang effect. The more you love, the more you will be loved. The more you give, the more will be given unto you, back to you. You get back what you put in, so to speak.

The second spiritual truth I was given was, *"The first shall be the last and the last shall be the first."* and I remember I decided to test this 'theory' out on the traffic. I wondered whether if I stopped to let somebody go in front of me when I was out driving whether I would still end up first or in the same place - would it work - and it was absolutely incredible.

Generally, drivers aren't used to 'politeness' on the road as arrogant or selfish drivers often compete for 'poll position'. So first, the look of surprise on their faces when I let them through followed by my own utter disbelief as I watched each vehicle invariably turn off to the right or the left which resulted in me still being left in the same place. It was like a game, but nevertheless it was still a test to see whether spirit were right, and it worked!

The rule here is. In your desire to give and by putting others first, it is *you* who will end up receiving. It is the law; an ancient version of 'what goes round comes round.'

G. 'Is that part of the universal law?'

J. 'Definitely. You will come to understand that there is perfect balance in everything. In every single thing that lives there is perfect balance. Just like we'll talk later about what happens when we die, everything is brought into balance. If you harm, you will be harmed. If you give, you will be given unto. It is the Law, and there are laws within laws within laws. Of course, I don't know all of them but the ones I *do* know are brilliant and they are enough for me. Balance reigns supreme in spirit, there is no doubt about that.'

G. 'Do you think that spirit tell us these things on a need to know basis?'

J. 'Yes and we will be talking about this again later but I think it's part of life's experiences as you go through your life. This 'Jiminy Cricket' conscience of ours is saying, well what do you think of that then? You either listen to it or choose to ignore it. We're being taught all the time. Every single day there are things for you, there are opportunities for you - it goes back to the school girls - one of them looking at things and the other ignoring everything. Be open to opportunities, they come for you.'

G. & B. 'Yes.'

J. 'Well done! Well done! OK. Let's close our eyes again. I want you to ask your guides a question and wait for the answer and when you've been given the answer, open your eyes. Now you don't have to reveal what the answer is unless you want to...... Did you ask a question, Grace?'

G. 'I did.'

J. 'Did you get an answer?'

G. 'I did and I can share it with you. I asked my guide why did she come to me and she said because my love is in the stars.'

J. 'Thank you. How did you get on Bobbie?'

B. 'My guide was male and I ask what was my purpose and the answer was simply to love.'

J. 'Oh lovely, that's lovely. OK. Now we're going to go on a little journey.'

Meditation 1.

Jenny: 'So sit back, relax and you have come to a stately home. You've parked the car and you are walking in the grounds. The sun is shining and there is an avenue of trees. You are walking along a path and suddenly to your left across a short green you see a high wall with a door in the middle. It's a wooden door with an iron ringed handle. I want you to walk towards the door, turn the handle and go inside. Close the door behind you and you will find yourself in a sunken garden.

It looks like a very well laid out topiary and cottage garden combined. It has a walkway all the way round it and right opposite the door you have just come in, on the other side of the garden, is another wooden door with a ring handle and to your left on the other side of the garden sits a bench.

The sun is shining onto this garden and it is busy with colour, with insects, with bees, with birds - this is an all singing, all dancing sunny garden; very busy. I want you to take a left and walk all the way round the outside of this sunken garden keeping to the wall so you're not going to fall down.

You do see the steps leading down to the sunken garden but keep to the path and pass the bench until you get to the door on the other side. Open the door with the iron handle, go through and close it behind you.

You are now in a big expanse of field which slopes down. To your left you can see what looks like a glass house and to your right, a small oasis of trees. The grass is quite short. I want you to walk towards the glass house on the left. It is very warm and the sun is beating down. It is lot quieter now than the sounds from the sunken garden and there is a very light breeze to relieve you of any heat.

Once you get to the glass house it begins to shade. Go through the main glass house door. It is all glass inside and in front of you is a circle, quite a large circle. Walk towards the circle and stand in the middle of it. If you look up above your head there is a column of glass.

Coloured energy starts to fall down the glass column. Light colours; light blues, light pinks, light yellows, light greens, all pastel colours are starting to fall over you. It's like they're washing you but they're healing colours and they're healing all the dross of the day away. Enjoy this shower of healing colours and healing love.

Now step out from under the shower and you'll see you are not wet but completely dry. We are going to leave the glass house now and make our way over to the oasis of trees. You're back in the sunshine and you're walking towards the trees. There are only about four of them but they are quite close together; big trees - they've been there a long time - and you start to hear the trickle of water.

As you get nearer you can see a babbling brook flowing between the trees. Very pretty. The stream makes a gurgling sound as it ripples over the stones and rocks. When you get there you can see it is clear as anything. It is a beautiful sight and now you can see the odd white butterfly.

All of a sudden you become aware of somebody in the distance. As they get nearer, you start to recognise who they are and you both smile at each other. You remember them and are so glad to see them. You now stand together holding hands and you communicate in love.

The time goes so quickly and you know that they are only with you for a short time. After a little while, it's time for them to leave. They say goodbye but as they turn to go they put something in your hand and cover it with your fingers. "Don't look at it now" they say, "look at it later; this is for you."

You hug and kiss them goodbye and thank them for coming. You know that you will see them again. You watch them walk away until they disappear. You then turn to look at the brook still babbling and gurgling and twinkling in the sunshine and you know it's time to go back up to the sunken garden.

You begin to ascend the slight hill feeling the short grass tickle your sandals. Up, up, up until you get to the wooden door. Turn the iron ring and open the door into the walled garden. Close it behind you. Once more you experience all the noises of the sunken garden.

Turn to your right and make your way towards the bench still in sunshine. You sit on the bench marvelling at what has just happened and thinking lovingly of your visitor, appreciating how they came to see you and then, you remember they put something in your hand. So open your hand and reveal the gift?

When you're ready to come round, open your eyes.

How was that?'

Grace: 'When I opened the door and saw the sunken garden there were three steps down which, of course, I went down! Then you told me go to my left so I quickly came back up but I had seen the path that went all the way round, passed the bench with the wooden door, very carefully closing it, putting my back to the door so I could look and see where I was.

I went to the glass house and the shower of colours of healing was very beneficial - I could feel it. Then I came back out and went across to the trees and I could see the little brook and the stones and the way the water sparkled and the person who came to me was my mother and yes, she gave me a gift which she put in my hand but I wasn't sad to see her go because I know I can go back there and talk to her anytime.

I came back the way I had gone and when I sat on the bench and opened my hand, it was my mother's gold wedding ring which I do have but she reminded me of something I need to do.'

J. 'Lovely, that was a really nice journey.'

G. 'The gardens were beautiful.'

J. 'Good, Bobbie, how did you get on?'

Bobbie: 'I went through the door and walked round the path, passed the bench and through the door. I could feel the grass, it was lovely and then I went to the glass house and went and stood under the column. The colours were beautiful and I just felt better and felt refreshed and then I came out of there and walked to the trees and could see the water and it was just so peaceful and this Indian came towards me.'

J. 'What sort of Indian?'

B. 'He had a full headdress and he was in white trousers and top and I have seen him before anyway and we held hands and he told me he was proud of me.'

J. '*Aah.*'

B. 'And he gave me a pure white feather.'

J. 'I *knew* you were going to say that!'

B. 'It was beautiful.'

J. 'Look, you're nearly in tears, that's lovely. OK. I'm going to now leave you to do some mental exercises together. This involves taking it in turns to choose a primary colour and you will then each guess which colour the other one is thinking of.

After that you're going to try some psychometry so you need to give one another a piece of your jewellery or your watch to read - a possession which you have worn for some time. Then before lunch we will ask our guides to draw away from our auras thus giving them a break too.'

LUNCH BREAK...

J. 'Right, we've had our lunch so I now want you to close your eyes and ask your guides to draw close again for our afternoon session. I know you're full up with food so don't go to sleep!

I'm going to first of all talk about the issue of being a sensitive and coping with being a sensitive. Why do I use the word sensitive; why don't I use the word psychic? That's because not all sensitives *are* psychic but all psychics are sensitive - you will have to pause and work that one out!

You can be sensitive to something but don't necessarily have to be psychic but all psychics are obviously sensitive because they wouldn't be able to pick up psychic emotions, feelings, communications, etc. Yes?

So what kinds of people are sensitive? Let me ask you both some questions. Have you ever walked into a house or a building and felt there was something not right, that it felt oppressive? You have! Well that's you being sensitive. What about, if people have come over to your house and you've felt well when they arrived but by the time they leave, you're absolutely exhausted! (Grace and Bobbie both laugh in recognition).

That means you're a sensitive. Do either of you have a sign on your back saying, "If you have a problem, I'm your man!" (Again, Grace and Bobbie laugh). Are you someone who people come to with their problems?'

B. 'Yes!'

J. 'There you go, three out of three. What about, do you ever hear voices but you don't know where it comes from?'

G. 'I think occasionally but definitely once for sure.'

J. 'Then you're also psychic. Have you seen shadows, lights, people?'

B. 'Yes.'

J. 'That's being a psychic as well as a sensitive. What about a smell, have you ever had a smell?' (Grace and Bobbie both confirm this).

G. 'Yes, not for years but there was a time when there was a very definite smell.'

J. 'Yes, that's a good one and did you know immediately what it meant?'

G. 'I used to smell violets. I was quite young and I did used to feel someone around me, an older lady but because I was quite young I just accepted it.'

J. 'What's your smell experience Bobbie?'

B. 'Freesias and I knew it was my mum because it was her favourite flowers.'

J. 'Oh really, one of mine was coal tar soap and I knew it was my grandma. What about feeling a physical presence? (Again, Grace and Bobbie confirm this). Yes, OK, so not only are you both sensitive but you're also psychic.

Some people have been aware since they were a child that they were sensitive and maybe psychic and didn't know what it all meant but just accepted things the way they were. Their childhood is often difficult. They realise that they are different from other people and they carry knowledge deep within them and these people are usually born sensitive and end up as natural mediums.

Then there are others who have sensitivity thrust upon them. We begin, for example, with children with imaginary friends but later there are elements that awaken their dormant sensitivity. For example, people who take drugs or who drink, their sensitivity is heightened, awakened. They may have depression, an illness, be in trauma, suffer bereavement and these things are like the gates which open which can activate new things to happen.

I personally feel that is exactly when these 'gates' are supposed to open. I am a *"Nothing is ever for nothing"* person and I also believe that *"There is no such thing as co-incidence, by chance or a mistake"*. I believe things happen for a reason, it's an opportunity and it's there for you and spirit hope you take it. Don't forget you decided these things before you came back. You decided that at this juncture in your life there would be an opportunity and you would take it and as I said this morning, you won't remember it.

Finally, we have those who aspire to sensitivity. Those who *want* to develop, those who make a conscious decision, 'I want to develop my psychic ability and a greater sensitivity to spiritual things.' So what do they do? They try a religion, they join an open circle in a spiritualist church, they get involved in séances or Ouija boards, which they do in ignorance or they come to things like this, they come to a workshop!

When people do this through religion, I want to mention that churches and the Christian Church, often label anything psychic as part of the occult. They are suspicious of psychic ability; it's unwholesome and should be avoided. The church often implies that the manifestation of spirit is also evil and they condemn communication with the dead.

It's strange because it's alright for them to communicate (Grace and Bobbie both laugh) but they don't allow anyone else to do it. 'No, no, no, He comes through me and then I give it to you.'

To me, that's not right, that's not a Father treating or loving all his children the same. When we come to Jesus manifesting himself after death, it's alright for Him to do it but no-one else can. Only he's allowed to do something like this, it just doesn't make sense to me, it's illogical. Why would God choose only one person? He wouldn't do that. He wouldn't love one person more than another. He wouldn't say, well you can return to earth but no one else can. It just doesn't sit well with me.

Funnily enough, the name Jesus was quite a common name in those biblical days and yet we only ever here about one. Another point was the fact that Jesus was seen after He had died. Now my theory is that the Nazareen did not physically rise from the dead; he rose spiritually. Remember I said that spiritual communication was common in those times, it was a natural form of communication so what we now call mediums were 'two a penny'. In biblical times there were probably physical mediums who witnessed his presence and were able to report their sightings, why not?

I also feel that the Nazareen died, not to save everyone from their sins but died quite deliberately by His own choice. He came back to do what he said he was going to do just like we have all come back to achieve the purpose of *our* incarnation. I feel he was very conscious of what he was doing - this is what I'm doing this time; this is my mission - and he died on the cross to show that the spiritual conquers over the physical.

He knew that there would be people who would see Him physically after his death. It was all planned and so he had to have a very public death. Such was the enormity of his message so equally he had to address as many people as possible again, *"Like attracts like"*. If he had just died somewhere insignificant, none of this would have happened. He had a message, a mission, he had something to prove and it had to be to the widest audience possible, yes?

The spiritual being is Life and transcends the physical. He showed by His own physical sacrifice that man is not just a physical body but a spiritual being and it is the spiritual which retains life and is his true inheritance and I believe that was the reason he died. He wanted people to understand that there is more than the physical, more than I get up, I go to work, I go to bed, I die and that's the end of it. He was hoping that if people realised that he lived on maybe they would come to the conclusion that *they* did too.'

G. 'It's a big jump though, isn't it?'

J. 'Yes, but it was necessary. Spirit are great opportunists and they will take the best opportunity they can to show man the right way. People will miss these opportunities many times and spirit will often shed a little tear but something like *this*! If you believe that we are pure energy, that we are God's child, that we are part of Him, have a piece of Him and that our infinity is our consciousness and that our thoughts continue when we 'die'?

If our thought is what lives on, then something as big as the crucifixion should make us think? Use the power that is given to you and, don't forget, the gift that our Father gives us is freedom of choice, freedom of will, so we do have a choice, so think about it?

We are supposed to use our thoughts. Earlier on, we were talking about the relationship between creativity and being sensitive and spiritual. It's thinking how can I create, how can I do this or that? It's using your thought, your power and that power extends as far as you want, it's infinite, you can keep going, yes?

It's like a spiritual path in a way but you don't realise that it's infinite, that it's never ending. Right now, all you know is that you've just climbed a row of mountains and you're *so* glad you've got to the top, but then what do you see? Oh no, there's another range of mountains! (Grace and Bobbie both laugh). You think it's finished, it's not, it's ongoing. It's like the seasons, it's like the ebb and flow of the tide, it's like night following day, it's continuous. It's not just for Christmas, it's forever and ever, Amen! (They're still laughing).

OK. We talked this morning about when you die and go home and pass over to the other side, to your real home which is the spiritual realms, however, there are other times when you 'go home' whilst living on the earth plane. You also go home every night when you're in bed!

Now that may seem shocking for people to hear but if you understand that you're an energy, an infinite energy, and if you have a flame which never goes out, even if you blow hard, even if there is a hurricane, that is your pure thought, that is your consciousness protected inside your body. Why does that infinite flame need to sit and do nothing whilst you're sleeping? It's illogical. Your physical body needs the sleep not your spirit energy.

The *real* 'you', your spirit, goes home every night even when in the womb. The spirit inside a foetus will naturally return home. It's our physical body - which *we* have chosen by the way - (Grace and Bobbie both laugh at this). Actually, I was horrified when I learnt this as I hate curly hair, why did I choose curly hair! But that was the whole point. You've got curly hair because we know you hate it. Well that's not fair. Yes it is, now you have to learn to like yourself! (Bobbie is in fits of laughter now).

Think about it. If everything in the garden is rosy nothing is happening and you're not learning anything are you? Life's got to 'rattle your sabre'. You've got to have a problem, something that riles you, that niggles you. You've got to have something to work towards, to achieve, a hurdle to overcome, an obstacle in your way that challenges you, that's moving forward. People complain but actually we're really lucky to have all these problems because those things are going to teach us and make us grow. That's the meat on the bone.

So coming back to 'returning home'. Even after you've been conceived and are in an embryonic stage, all the way through the pregnancy, your spirit will still go home. On the subject of embryos, there is something else I want to share with you and you may not like what I have to say. We are told that, *"Just as people are afraid to die so others are afraid to be born."* Some of the abortions and miscarriages which happen are, in fact, perpetrated by the newly incarnated spirit beings who change their minds.'

G. 'I didn't know that.'

J. 'I don't want to do it. I don't want to do it, I'm not ready.' That's fine as they have an infinite amount of time to return to the earth plane. Remember, freedom of choice, freedom of will reigns supreme on both sides. That was another cornerstone for me when I learnt that and, again, it made perfect sense. Like planning to jump from the top diving board, you think you can do it but once you're up there you realise you're not quite ready to do this. We always have the choice.

We're going to move on to something that I feel you already know about but usually when I see people for the first time I asked them, have you heard of chakras and chakra points? (Grace and Bobbie both confirm they have).

(Chakra diagram on pp 59)

J. You have, OK. Did you know that this eternal flame which is inside your body which I call spirit's temple means that you have to look after your body as well as your spirit? Your spirit is infinite, it will never die but it has to be protected. If you know that you have something that enlivens you that's inside you, wouldn't you want to look after it and keep it safe?

So that encouraged me and was one of the very, early decisions I made to become a vegetarian. I don't think I did it because I wanted to look after my flame because at 20, I didn't know anything about the 'flame of Spirit', I just wanted to look after myself and I thought why are we eating living things which have their own consciousness? To me, animals were just as eligible as I was to remain living here on earth.

When I was older I even extended this to picking flowers. I will not pick a flower from a garden, a field, anywhere. Why should I pick a living thing? OK, I *do* buy flowers as someone has already done the picking, but I myself, won't do it.

So you need to think about your body if you want to walk a spiritual path, you need to think about your 'temple' and how you look after yourself. You can't say, I'll do this but not that. It's a commitment, it's an understanding and an awareness. It's controversial but this is the way I feel. Any questions, so far?'

G. 'No.'

B. 'I'm frightened of spiders. I try not to hurt them but I don't like them.'

J. 'I know, the big ones I throw out. The little ones, the fruit flies, I'm not very patient with them!'

G. 'If you really don't like something you can't even touch it.'

J. 'Well, I don't touch it. I cover it with a glass and a piece of card and throw it outside. It's always your choice.'

I'm now going to talk about something that I think is quite important; the difference between the psychic and the spiritual. If you saw an advert for a psychic medium doing clairvoyance and another for a spiritual medium, would you know the difference? You probably wouldn't think there *was* a difference, however, there is a big difference and I want to explain what it is.

"The psychic is a tool for the spiritual." It is an aid but it has become the all, meaning that people just want psychic, psychic, psychic. To me, people are more interested in the quick fix of psychic gifts rather than being spiritually-minded or following a spiritual path.

The spiritual is when your motive is more pure, you have probably given this more thought and you have now made a conscious effort to walk a spiritual path. You realise, maybe unwittingly, that there is a difference between the psychic and the spiritual so let's look at some of the differences.

Let's say we have two mediums, one psychic and the other spiritual. For a start, the energy that a psychic medium will use to give you information will be gleaned from what is around them and the energy they draw from you. A spiritual medium will ask for that energy to be channelled from spirit, from their spiritual guides who draw close. They will not use *your* energy to get information. OK.

A psychic medium will draw energies from the earth to get information. A spiritual medium will go to the source and the information will be channelled through them. This is an infinite source and because it's infinite, it can never be drained. A psychic medium does not communicate with spirit, however, their information may be wonderful.

They could tell you about your house, your family, the number of the house you live in, your state of health, things that have happened to you and can show you avenues that are open to you, etc. but they get all this information from your spiritual aura, from your spiritual blueprint. It's there for them to see, it's the energy that you are projecting.

Whereas a spiritual medium will establish an energy link, a vibrational link with their spirit guides and through that link, they will get what information they need to impart but spirit will not use the person's energy; it will be direct, hot off the press, a direct line!

Because the psychic medium is using the energies from you and reading your aura, blueprint and spiritual fingerprint and drawing energies from around you, the information will often fade so they will have to be quick.

When you learn about auras you'll understand that they are forever changing, they change via your mood by what you're thinking so you can even have an aura change during one sitting, yes?

Spirit will utilise a spiritual medium's energy and the information they receive will be passed down by loved ones, friends and family in the spiritual realms and channelled through the medium's guide and it will be up to the spiritual medium to give out this information as they receive it.

With psychic mediums, although they appear very clever and highly advanced, they tire very easily whereas spiritual mediums can go on and on and on. Psychic mediums, for example, often do not lift their vibration, they are not sending out love, they are just reading, whereas with spiritual mediums, love is the force with which they work with so they are always working in that love energy.

A psychic medium will therefore have less refined information and they themselves probably don't develop as there is nothing to develop as they are just using the same method over and over again. You will never see a change in them or an improvement in what they do so they often don't progress.

Spiritually you can grow because you're guides are helping you, walking with you, working with you, guiding you, supporting you, healing you, loving you. They are encouraging you on your spiritual path. A psychic will think of themselves, what they have to do and perhaps their monetary gain. Their motive is completely different.'

G. 'Is it possible to slip between the spiritual to the psychic and back to the spiritual. Can you do that?'

J. 'Of course, but it's always thought driven. You choose how you do things, it's up to you how you live your life and it's your motive that predetermines your development. Some people who have a gift, an ability, use that gift predominantly for their own gain so their motives will prevent them from growing spiritually, something that someone who is doing this to serve and help others will attract naturally.

A psychic medium can be said to be reading from the same page all the time rather than finishing the chapter and moving on to the next. You only ever get out what you put in and everything comes down to love. You can have a gift but your motive to put others before yourself will help switch you from the psychic to the spiritual. If you're thinking of yourself and what you can gain personally from your 'gift' this will always get in the way of your progress.'

G. 'That has answered a really big question.'

J. 'I was just about to say that if psychic mediums do work and communicate with spirit guides, they are the ones they work with anyway. Your guides, as I mentioned earlier, do not have wings and halos, they are people just like you. They guide you because they are like you, they are similar to you, they want the same things as you. So a person who is, for example, egotistical, who is money driven, who sees their psychic gifts as a way to earn a living, will attract the guides who are also egotistical, money driven, are you with me? (Grace & Bobbie both confirm).

You have a conscience. You are always asking yourself questions and those questions are not necessarily your own, some of them are put there by those who walk and work with you to help you.

For instance, you're leaving the house, you get to the car and suddenly you think, I've left the light on, or the oven on or I forgot to lock the door or my diary, etc. You think that that's your own thoughts but invariably it isn't. It's your spirit guide reminding you and helping you, yes?

People are with you all the time and those spirit friends are similar to you. If you're learning a 'project', they will be the ones who help you with that project but ultimately, you will have to move on and learn another 'project'. How are you going to be eligible to move on to that next project unless you have given your best and achieved everything possible on the current one? It's like walking up stairs.

Some people will stay on the same tread for years because they don't see any reason to move. They haven't thought about anything else, they are not progressive, they have no ambition, they don't want to better themselves and if they do, it's for the wrong reasons which keeps them on the same step!

The people who normally come to me are the ones who have thought, I want to move on, I want to progress, I want to develop, there must be something more to life that this, I want to help others, I want to do better. That is development, that is progress, that is growth and with that comes new people in spirit to help you with that, yes?

By tapping into energy belonging to the earth, elemental energy it is sometimes called, you are draining it, you also have no need. Crystals, rune stones, etc, what good do they do?

There is much on the planet that man has abused. You see, contrary to what many believe, the earth is not our natural environment. Our natural environment is the world of spirit. Here we are guests. If you draw from spiritual energy you will have no need from this planet. The spiritual way would enhance the earth's energies for spiritual energy replaces and replenishes our planet.

Remember you *are* a spiritual being. Your true power is spiritual power which is love and positive thought, not earthly material. If man turns away from this and accesses the power of the planet which can be accessed by negativity, he is draining it. He is little more than a spiritual thief because he replaces nothing. Whereas, if you access spiritual power from God, the Great Spirit, this is inexhaustible, this is infinite, this replenishes and heals. On its own, the planet cannot replenish its energies fast enough so you are helping to balance the earth's energies when you use spiritual power.

The earth is actually home to the animals. We humans are guests here but we also have a purpose because, being more evolved, we are here to look after and help those less fortunate than ourselves which include animals.

As we move into the middle of the afternoon, I want to mention reincarnation and share some fascinating facts about its history.

The Egyptians were the first to teach that the human soul is immortal and that at death, the body enters into some other living thing before coming back to birth. They thought you had to pass through a 3,000 year cycle of being creatures of the land, sea and air before the soul would once more enter into a human body at birth. (Some of the early and later Greeks also used this doctrine). Here is a beautiful quote from an Egyptian fragment:-

"The soul passes from form to form;

and the mansions of her pilgrimage are manifold.

Thou puttest off thy bodies as raiment;

and as vesture dost thou fold them up.

Thou art from old, oh soul of man,

yea thou art from everlasting."

When I read this, it reminded me of what I have always been taught that *"The body is the garment of the soul."*

In the first century AD, a prominent Greek describes a near death experience of a compatriot. In the course of the story, he mentions the 'silver cord' which binds his companion to the physical plane, something which is often mentioned today. He wrote:-

"Your soul's cable is stretched down to your body to which it is anchored and allows no further upward slack or play... We know that the soul is indestructible and should think of its experience as like that of a bird in a cage. If it has been kept in a body for a long time and become tamed to this life as a result of all sorts of involvements and long habituation, it will alight back to a body again after birth and will never stop becoming entangled in the passions and chances of this world."

This is amazing considering we talk symbolically about a 'silver cord' today and how once it is cut you cannot remain on the earth plane. This piece of early Greek writing also reminds me of my own interpretation of the soul being trapped in a body which is continually searching and what it is searching for is actually itself, the soul is searching for personal recognition and peace within - a journey of self discovery.

At least 57 cultures share the idea of there being a spirit double. This belief is so strong amongst the Burmese people and so embedded in their culture that they defy their monks who deny the concept of reincarnation themselves. The Burmese believe, *"When a man dies, his soul remains; His 'I' has only changed its habitation."* Many children, the Burmese will tell you, remember their former lives and as they grow older, the memories die away.

Another one of their beliefs is, *"A man has a soul, and it passes from life to life, as a traveller from inn to inn, till at length it is ended in heaven. But not till he has attained heaven in his heart will he attain heaven in reality."* This is very true, when you can become at one with yourself, then you are at one with The Great Spirit.

Finally, the Zulus likened the soul with a body to having a spark, the spark of the universal spirit; I must also be a Zulu then!

Let's now sit back as I'm going to give you an exercise to do which is also a very good tip when you feel the need of a lift!

So close your eyes, relax and imagine a hot air balloon complete with wicker basket hovering over a sandy beach.

You are going to put in the basket all the things you don't want in your life. So think of all the people, places, things, memories, all the things that you no longer want in your life. The hurts, the problems, anything that is negative or causing you pain or a problem, or simply now obsolete - all your excess baggage!

Put each and every one of those things in the wicker basket. When they are all in, cut the ties which hold the balloon to the shore and watch the hot air balloon fly away. Keep watching as it gets smaller and smaller and recedes from view.

When it is out of sight, walk towards the sea and immerse yourself completely in the water submerging yourself and then come up again. Now walk out of the sea and onto the beach. You are now cleansed from this negativity and completely refreshed. When you are done open your eyes.

So this is something you can do whenever you feel it necessary.

Now, we are going to go on another journey, our last one today, so close your eyes and sit comfortably.'

Meditation 2.

Jenny: 'It is a beautiful sunny day and you have decided to take a walk. Walking along a country road you come to a 5-bar gate which borders a field. The field has longish grass and is scattered with nature's seasonal flowers all of different colours and shapes.

Now open the gate and shut it behind you. As you continue, you see that some of the flowers are taller than others, some poke their heads above the longish grass whilst others peep in between. The air is filled with buzzing and humming and you cannot think of a more perfect setting for a sunny day. There is green all around with the different shades of green fighting for predominance. Look at me! Look at me, they seem to say.

After a few moments you catch sight of a wood which is lining the edge of the field. As you walk towards it you decide that it is a wooded glen and you want to explore. It has been good weather all week so the ground is dry and coming into the glen, the shade is now comforting after walking in the hot sun. Your shoes stay clean as you walk over the dry twigs and bumps from the tree's roots. There are not very many flowers here, but lots of green ferns soften the tree trunks. The sun twinkles and pours its rays wherever it can and there is more silence here too amongst the shaded trees.

After a short while the trees get sparser and an opening reveals a fallen log which acts as a natural bench. Go straight over and sit on the log welcoming the return of sun's warmth which seems to wrap itself around your body like a golden cloak. You close your eyes and find yourself dozing off in the sunshine.

All of a sudden there is a bustling of leaves as the wind picks up a bit which disturbs your reverie and upon opening your eyes there now stands a person a little way in front of you. The person gives you an all-knowing smile and you immediately smile back. They ask whether they can sit next to you and their very welcomed company remains for what seems like an age but is really only for a few seconds with the sun still warming your face and shoulders, you both enjoy the exchanges which take place.

Then the wind picks up again and the bustle of leaves awaken you a second time and you find your visitor gone. There is nothing to show for what has taken place apart from something they left behind on the log. You pick it up and once again smile - they know you *so* well!

You notice the sun is now dipping behind the trees which means it's time to make your way back through the wooded glen and across the field which is not as warm as before. You get to the 5-bar gate and try and open it but your visitor's gift is still in your hand! Go through the gate, shut it behind you, you know your way home.

Now when you are ready you can open your eyes.

Did you enjoy that?'

Grace. 'Yes I did and it was very positive and I gained a great deal from it. I felt a great peace whilst waiting for my visitor to come and be with me. They did not come straight away, almost as if having to make up their mind that it was the right thing for both of us. I hoped for my mother and it was she who came.

She had already said that she would not be coming back to the earth plane so to have her come to me was wonderful. We sat not really saying anything to each other, our thoughts were linked together and that was enough. A great many things were laid to rest.

The gift she left me was her gold wedding ring and I am still holding it tightly in my hand!'

Bobbie: 'When I came to the field full of wild flowers there was a stile. I climbed the stile and admired the beautiful colours of the flowers and heard the birds singing and the bees buzzing. I climbed another stile leading into the wood and followed the lovely glade with ferns until I came to the fallen log resembling a bench.

From another path White Eagle appeared and came and sat beside me. We chatted about how my journey was progressing and he said not to rush things, to take it slowly. When he got up to leave, he left me a single feather. It was white with a black tip. He then gave me an owl which he said was for wisdom. The experience was almost surreal.'

Response To Spiritual Day Workshop

Grace's response...

Grace: I went with an agenda:-

Why has spirit chosen me? Someone who has no training as an artist but can produce such wonderful drawings and paintings.

To ask for help in understanding issues with my family and loved ones who see me as a wife, mother, grandma and I hope friend.

They do not see me as someone in service to spirit. Working for spirit is my chosen path and I have no wish to change.

During Jenny's Workshop/Spiritual Day, given with such love and kindness, I received understanding of where I stand and where I am going. My path stretched out before me. I now know that I can walk along it with complete confidence whatever the outcome. I also understand that others close to me within the physical world will require my attention whilst this takes place.

Living a life on the earth plane is not easy. It is not called the Earth School for nothing or the school of hard knocks as I call it!

All life's experiences make up one big picture for ourselves and others. Sometimes a large brush is needed for long firm strokes, other times a small brush for more delicate work.

You see, this is where the balance comes in. If you give so you receive in return. If you love selflessly, it will be returned to you tenfold and more.

Things have crossed my mind during today's workshop, things that I now understand to be of my own doing. I feel now that I can address these problems and by doing so move forward in my work for spirit. The workshop today has given me clarity, has removed fear for the future, has given me courage to look forward with a new confidence.

After 12 years of searching, my teacher arrived; so the pupil must be ready.

Dear Jenny, you have opened a door for me. Thank you and Bless you.

Bobbie's Response...

Bobbie: The first thing that struck me with Jenny is her welcoming, friendly approach. She made us feel at home immediately.

She is an excellent teacher, she puts everything forward in a straightforward way, none of this superior attitude that you find at a lot of development groups. She explains simply but fully. She has a lovely way with her. She makes you feel that you are as important as anyone else. She encourages you and is a true inspiration.

I feel lucky to have found her and to be able to call her my friend. Her belief in what she is teaching is quite infectious. She taught me more in one day than I had learnt in the 3 years previously.

Thank you so much Jenny for being such an inspiration. I look forward to my lessons with you. I feel you have so much to teach me.

Thank you for a lovely day and a lovely lunch. God bless you.

Month 1:
'Getting Started!'

"Our search to find true expression is everyone's journey through life."

Jenny: 'This is the first day of your development course and I want to ask you what you're expecting?'

Grace: 'To connect with that other world that I know is very close. I want to be able to understand the spiritual side of this life before I move on to understanding more spiritual things. I feel at my age that it's possible and I often look at it like this; I understand things but it is my version of things but it's not always the right way.

I appear to have that understanding but sometimes I'm quite lost and so, because of the way I came to this work, which was with no special preparation and not a great deal of guidance over the last 11 or 12 years, I landed in the middle and I think there are things I need to understand that perhaps I think I do but I don't.'

J. 'Well first of all, you know a lot more than you think. Secondly, you're not alone and you have had people working with you and teaching you and guiding you for as long as one can remember. Thirdly, we all get lost, we all need to know, we all need to understand and you're just the same as everybody else, on a journey, and the people that you meet along that journey you have met on purpose for reasons which will be revealed when the time comes.

We all ask to come back here to achieve certain things and those things can only be achieved in the physical world although we can still progress in spirit realms but it's more gently done there. Here on earth, which spirit call a 'hard school', it's the toughest but most effective way to learn because we are 'in the raw' so to speak. We're not protected as much but our progress is more effective.

I would say the earth is the best school there is and who wouldn't want to go to the best school? You want your children to go to the best school therefore God wants his children to go to the best school. OK?'

G. 'That's the nicest way I've heard it explained.'

J. 'The process of learning is an evolvement and just like all other living things, you can't rush progress, you can't rush learning, you can't rush awareness and understanding; *"The soul comes into its own at the right time."* However, I do know that those who have been led to me will need to hear what I have learnt and share what I know otherwise we wouldn't have been brought together, so I know that I am in the right place with you and we will journey together for as long as it's deemed necessary.

There is a spiritual way to understand friendship; that we're all here for each other for as long as we're needed. When we have done all that we're supposed to do then we have to move on. It's not cruel, it's what progress is all about. I say goodbye and other people come in and that's what life is about.

I may stay with you and have a different relationship with you, or I may stay with you and you will still need other things from me but I know that, for now, suffice to say, we're holding hands and we're going to do this together.

So now I am going to explain to you what I believe this course is all about.

It *is* the 'missing thing' you talked about earlier. To me, it's about affirmation, confirmation, reiteration. It's the feeling that you're not alone. It's confirmation that what you're doing and who you are is correct. It will make you feel confident. As you learn, so you will grow in understanding and you will also forge a relationship with those who, at the moment, already walk with you.

There are others who may always walk with you and some who will come and go as and when they are needed and through these relationships you get your strength, you get your confidence, you become more at peace and you will know, without a shadow of a doubt, that you're on the right road. You will make decisions better, you will feel like you're a knife cutting through butter and you will execute a lot of your activities with more surety because you can communicate with those who have been standing and working with you.

We're opening up a channel that you already have; I am seeing a tree trunk and you are the tree trunk but I am giving you branches. I am giving you branches which will then grow into other branches. You will get the blossom and you will get the fruit and hopefully by the end of this course, you will see what type of fruit you have borne.

We'll meet once a month. You will have work to do during each month. It's up to you how much work you do but as with everything in life, moderation is the key. Don't overdo it, don't do too little, don't do too much - just like the three bears - get it just right!

What we will be discussing today is the very foundation of your course. It is like what your tree is standing on, understanding what you're standing in and on and how to feed yourself so that your branches can grow. What we do today and funnily enough, also next month, is the most important part of the whole course. Some people find it easy, some find it difficult but we've got to start somewhere and just like building a wall, the foundations have got to be strong, sound and secure otherwise the whole thing will collapse.

So it's very important that you understand this month's work and therefore you must ask me questions if ever you don't understand. It doesn't matter how many questions as long as it's necessary. OK, I understand *exactly* what you're saying because sometimes a sentence may be a bit ambiguous so I need to know that you understand me.

I will give you notes every month and these notes are what spirit gave me 15 years ago and I haven't now so close your eyes. The first thing I want you to see is a door and when you see it, open your eyes. Grace, describe your door?'

G. 'A large wooden door with the timbers placed vertically and a round brass door handle.'

J. 'Was the door open or closed?'

G. 'It was closed.'

J. 'Thank you, Bobbie?'

B. 'Mine was a wooden door and it was dark wood and it just had a little bar and it was closed.'

J. 'Thank you, close your eyes again. I want you to see a gold object and when you see it, open your eyes. Grace?'

G. 'It's the knob of the door.'

J. 'Wow, that's different to what I'm used to! Bobbie?'

B. 'It was horns.'

J. 'Horns? Wow, amazing! Close your eyes again. I want you to see a house and when you see it, open your eyes. You opened your eyes in unison you two! Grace, your house?'

G. 'It's a white house, two storeys and a tall chimney. The chimney is of brick. Not quite on a hill but on a slope starting towards a hill and the sun is shining.

J. Thank you, Bobbie?'

B. 'It was a red brick house but it was almost like a doll's house and it was painted red brick. It was two storeys and it had little gables and a path coming down from the front door and it had a white little fence all the round.'

J. 'Excellent, close your eyes again. I want you to see a person or an animal. Someone is coming into your vision now. When they appear, open your eyes. Grace?'

G. 'It's a sheep.'

J. 'Bobbie?'

B. 'It's my mum and Dad.'

J. 'OK, close your eyes again. I want you to give the person or animal your gold object and tell them to go to the house, open the front door and put the object inside the hall and when you've done that, open your eyes........ Did they do it?

changed those notes. When I teach you and because I'm teaching you on your own, my guides will say to me, explain it this way, explain that way, tell her about this, tell her about that. Although I have my notes, I am also working with the people who are with me to ensure that you get the best of me, alright?

Your pad is for you to use if there are certain key things that you feel you want to write down but it will also be your year's course book where you'll do your so called 'homework' so you'll have everything in one place.

Everything I teach you is always corroborated again and again throughout the course. I will give you example after example so I don't want you to be concerned that you've got to get it right the first time - we're just beginning - and it will be like riding a bike or brushing your teeth or driving a car, it will become more and more automatic for you.

You're not going to get a certificate from me after this either! This is for you. I'll know how you're doing and you'll know how you're doing.

Every month I will share with you a new topic to add to the 'foundations'. This means that we are learning about things spiritually, holistically; that there is another branch, and another branch, and another branch, all for the one tree - you. You will find that you may have surprises, you may have corroboration of things you always knew deep down and it's so lovely to hear it again and you will think, yes, I knew I was right about that and that's so refreshing.

All the things I teach you are things we can relate to, things that happen in our daily lives, things that happen in the physical world we live in. There is no use just talking about 'spiritual' things because the physical is also the spiritual and this is what some people tend to forget, misinterpret or misunderstand; they seem to put the physical in one pocket and the spiritual in another. They don't realise it's one and the same - you will grow spiritually *through* your physical knowledge and experience.

The most important tool you have is your mind. Your mind is your power, your mind is your everlasting consciousness, your mind is that which leaves you when you die and goes on to a new life in spirit realms. So, you will hear me say, time and time again, that motive is the key because mind is king and body is servant.

Your mind decides what to do, what to say, how to do it, everything starts in your mind. So your mind is going to grow, it's where all the work will be done and just like all education, you have to learn it but you will also have to experience everything you learn in order to understand with certainty the knowledge imparted.

So you will find that we will discuss something and you will learn something. Then the next time I see you when I ask you what's been going on, you will be amazed that something that you have recently learned has actually happened and confronted you in the physical. This is to test whether you have understood what you've recently learnt! The proof is in the pudding!

It's all very well saying yeah, yeah, I know what you say, I've even got the certificate but have you actually gone out and done it? Have you put it into practice and put your skills to the test?

I always used to say, it's easy to help others by putting money in a tin but have you sat with them, have you given them your time, have you helped them? That is more worthy than money in a tin. That is why I will never do fundraising. I believe in hands-on helping, I believe that to serve is giving of your time. That's the *best* way to help others not just to put money in a tin. I can be quite cynical sometimes.

When I was a child I remember my parents used to go to different functions. All over the country there are functions, dinners, balls; all these glamorous things to raise money. Yes, money is needed but it's easy, it's easy to put money in a tin. Haven't you had a lovely meal? Haven't you had so much food and drink you're going to go pop? All you've have done is enjoyed yourself. Oh, and by the way, you've put some money in the pot as well.'

G. 'You've paid for the dinner.'

J. 'Yes, I feel quite strongly about that sort of thing but sometimes this is the only way I can teach by trying to give examples of what I mean.

We will not be meeting in August and December. This is not only so that *we* get a break but so that spirit, our spirit guides, *also* have a break. You're not doing this alone but with the help of your spirit guides so we need to think of them too. They certainly celebrate Christmas! I realise you will want to finish the course as quickly as possible but I hope you understand that we will probably have a rest during those two months.

I want to make another point which is that I don't want to take it for granted that you're going to like the course. If ever you feel, actually, it's not what I thought, it's not what I wanted, I feel uncomfortable; that's fine too. All you have to do is to say. You haven't committed yourself.

We will be doing this month by month so I'm not going to take it for granted that you're going to stay the course because there have been many people that have said, no, this isn't for me or I can't do this, this is not what I thought it was, I'd rather go and play badminton than do this, etc.'

G. 'You have to give everything a chance.'

J. 'But that is your choice, you choose. The ball is always in your court.'

G. 'But you may find, you may decide that I'm not someone you wish to teach?'

J. 'No, no, no, no.'

G. 'You would never do that?'

J. 'No, because I help all those whose hands are outstretched.'

G. 'Now I understand!'

J. 'OK, so we're now going to start off with the most important aspect of this course. I'm going to read this 'paper' to you. After each lesson, you will be given your own copy to keep so you can go over it yourself. These are my teaching notes but whilst I'm with you, whether it's today or anytime, you can always ask me to elaborate on any given subject.

You may not understand something completely until maybe the third month when suddenly it slots into place; Oh, I get it now, the main thing is that you use me and ask questions. I do not want you to be a yes sir, no sir, three bags full sir, person. I want you to only say yes, if you're sure that you understand what I mean. It's up to you to query, yes?

Ok, we're going to start with the first lesson which is 'Attunement'.

Attunement

Jenny: 'The reason for attunement is to facilitate the accession of your spirituality, your soul being, to a more highly evolved spirit, or, to simplify that; attunement allows higher evolved spirit to communicate with you.

Man was not meant to be cut off from the world of spirit.

Notice I say 'attunement' and *not* 'meditation'.

With meditation -   you look within, you go within

you learn to control your mental ability

you learn to control the flightiness of the mind

you come face to face with yourself.

This is *not* what we're doing.

With attunement - you lift yourself *out* of yourself

you open your chakras

you allow the Light within to reach out to the Light of Spirit.

Attunement means At-one-ment - at one with spirit.

So this is the most important activity that I will teach you and you can continue doing this after the course. This can be done for personal re-assurance and at the special times that you have with spirit.

Why attunement, why not development? With development you do not attune but with attunement, your own development takes place automatically; it automatically grows when you attune.

Through attunement you gain a greater understanding of your own spirituality.

You develop your instincts and inner knowledge which you will receive as and when you need to access it. Spirit once gave me an example of this which I named 'the grain hatch.'

When you grow spiritually you grow in steps, in pieces, like a ladder. When you put your foot on a rung of a ladder you are at a juncture, then you put your foot on the second rung of the ladder which is the second juncture. People think about the rails, the treads, the steps.

What I think about, what spirit think about and what this particular course concentrates on, is what is happening whilst getting you from one step to the next. It's the 'in-between' spaces that we're concerned about not the steps themselves because when you have reached the second step you suddenly understand the knowledge that you've been given. You have gone through the experience and you suddenly understand what this has been all about, what you have learnt, as well as what you have achieved. You had to experience it to learn it, to understand it as well as to achieve.

They say *"Experience is the greatest teacher."* You cannot understand something unless you have experienced it. Take the woman going to see her friend who's just had the most horrendous labour and given birth to a baby and the friend says to the new mother, 'Goodness me, I can well imagine what you've been through.' This visiting friend has never had a pregnancy, a labour nor given birth to a baby so how can she possibly imagine what her friend has gone through? She's not qualified, so you really have to experience something to understand it.'

Grace: 'That reminds me of an example. When people used to have someone pass over or lose someone they loved, I used to say I'm so sorry, I'm really sorry. And then I lost my father who was the first one close to me and sorry was such an empty word that I never used it again because it meant nothing compared to what was going on. Only then did I understand or have some idea of what loss was about.'

J. 'That's a good example. To me, knowledge is like grains of sand and your head is the grain hatch. When you open the hatch, the grains of sand, the grains of knowledge pour into your head, pour into your mind.

I've said that you will develop your instincts and inner knowledge which you will receive as and when you need to access it. That is when the grain hatch will open; the grains of knowledge will pour into your mind which will be at the right time and you will understand. If you received this knowledge earlier, you wouldn't have understood, you wouldn't have got there. Do you understand what I mean now?'

G. 'I do.'

J. 'As and when you are ready to receive it. It's a *very,* very important lesson because you can't push knowledge, I can't force you to learn, it's up to you to do that. I can't make you understand either. Only you can get to the stage where you now realise, I understand perfectly and that comes with time and experience and thinking, yes?

Spirit usually develops one sense at a time when you're attuning then puts it altogether at the end. You are developed, then it stops and plateaus when you consolidate and co-ordinate all that you have learnt. Again, it's like the steps; a rise then it plateaus, a rise and then it plateaus. When you plateau, you need to consolidate everything you have learnt.

In attunement, you are spiritually communicating, you are spiritually blending your thoughts, your consciousness, that which is really you with those of your spiritual guardians.

You attune to their vibration and they, in turn, attune to yours. By lifting your vibration, by raising your thought you are refining it, it becomes better. Refinement brings accuracy, refinement brings beauty, you refine your vibrational level. So when you're sitting attuning, it's like you've turned on the radio; you're sending out the frequencies and your guides and guardians are tuning into it and in turn, linking up with your frequencies to allow them to start working with you, OK?

In attunement you are spiritually uplifted, you are given healing, your spirit guides calm you and bring you peace. You'll come to understand that there is more to attunement than just connecting with your guides. I won't say it all now but think of it as an holistic treatment, an holistic experience. You will not get just one thing from attunement, OK?

Your spirit guides and helpers will use the time in your attunements to talk to you, particularly about things pertaining to your development. It is your learning period. It is in that time that you learn to trust one another. You listen to their advice, you then put it into practice. You find that it works and you *know* that what you are being told is right.

Allow spirit to lead; that is why they are called guides! They are there to guide you. What is the point of having a guide if you will not listen to their guidance? Learn to work with them.'

G. 'It's always so straight forward, isn't it?'

J. 'It's man who complicates things. All spiritual truths are simple.

In attunement there is no thought of self, no thought of achievement - only of oneness. At the moment of attunement, you become at one with spirit. If your attunement is seeking the highest of consciousness, you in turn become at one with the Great Spirit himself.

We commune in his Light and in his Love.

The more you attune quietly in your own home or in a circle, the more you will become aware of what is around you and the more you will be sensitive to that upliftment, that light, that beauty, that love which is there for you.

You will find the more you attune, the more your home will become a sanctuary because you are drawing from spiritual consciousness and spiritual love and everything this brings, it therefore enriches the place where you attune, OK?

For you see, that's what attunement is. It is not simply raising one's vibrations. Attunement is not simply getting ready to sit. Attunement is never communication. Attunement is blending. Attunement is coming together of spirit to spirit. Your spirituality is the spirit that lives and dwells in the spiritual realms. It is the coming together and the blending of souls.

This is also very important. When people meditate, what I call attune, they think they are drawing towards them high, ethereal beings to help them progress and develop. The fact of the matter is, that we only attract spirit of like mind so the more you grow the more you will draw towards you the higher beings as you can only attract those like yourself. And as you become more spiritually aware and your understanding grows so those who have the same increased understanding get drawn towards you, OK?'

G. 'Is it that like vibration that attracts the same vibration, it cannot be higher?'

J. 'Yes, for example, I talk about this *"Like attracts like"* vibration in *'A Medium's Tale'* regarding when we go home to spirit world. People who work with spirit can only work with those of a similar ilk because of their vibrational level and your vibrational energy equals how much you understand, there isn't any other way of measuring it.

You and I vibrate at certain levels. In wanting to learn more about spirit and how you can develop and achieve more things for yourself, you have to first start by linking up with those who walk and work with you. I can't teach you any other way to grow because I know that we're only half of the equation.

Also, we don't just come back here for ourselves, we come back for others too and we need our spiritual partners to help us with those achievements. In fact, our spiritual partners are also relying on us to achieve those experiences because they have to achieve them too! Eventually, you will come to understand that you develop not just for yourself but for your spiritual guides because you both have the same remit.'

G. 'This is one of the little things I was missing. I was busily trying to be spiritual and gaining spirituality but measuring it against people in this world but actually it's a partnership. It's such a little thing but when you understand that, you suddenly think, that's what it's about!'

J. 'That's why you can't rush things. I always say that growth is like painting by numbers. You can't see the full picture until you've used all the colours. Funnily enough, as a little girl, painting by numbers was one of my joys and now spirit use it to explain things to me, 'Yes, it's just like painting by numbers!'

It's also like a puzzle, you just need that last piece or pieces. You *think* you know but you're still missing some pieces. I completely understand what you're saying so there will be many of these little things that you can add to your puzzle; to your painting.'

G. 'We think we depend on them but they also depend on us to do our part because otherwise they're just waiting there. I understand they work with others besides us perhaps, but it must be so pleasing when they get recognition from us that we're working together.'

J. 'Definitely, that's why spirit are so pleased about us being here today. They're probably saying, 'Oh yes, it's so exciting, I think we're getting another one! Gold star! However, you've got to earn your gold star, I'm afraid.

So, attunement is blending. Attunement is coming together of spirit to spirit. It is the coming together and the blending of souls that are of like mind and on a like path. Attunement is a sharing of God's

Love. Attunement is wonderful. Never be afraid to spend time in attunement for much is gained and much is learned and much is achieved in those silent moments of sharing and of blending soul with soul.

I'm now going to talk a bit about protection which is one of the key things that I teach because if you want to grow, it comes at a price. Working with spirit isn't a game, it's very serious. It's a commitment where you have to understand that if you're going to grow into a more shining light, you have to protect that light from all those that clamber around it.

At the moment your 'light' is shining at a certain level but as you grow in understanding, it will be like turning the bunsen burner up and your spiritual light will get brighter and brighter so you will be seen by more and more people in spirit who will be attracted to you.

I cannot only teach you the good bits, I have to teach as much as possible for you to understand and you have to be prepared to work at your protection. It's like brushing your teeth or riding a bicycle. To start with it's a pain but in the end it will be 'easy-peasy' and you'll realise that to keep yourself safe is a pre-requisite of working with spirit.'

G. 'Can I write something? It's just something, how you put it. I've been told about protection and have been very careful with protection but when you explain it by saying 'protect your light' that is the difference; a different meaning.'

J. 'OK, so here is something about protection and closing down.'

Protection

We think and work in gold and golden light because it is the most protective in the spectrum simply because it is the colour of highly evolved spirit. One day all the colours of our aura will blend to one and become totally translucent like white or mother or pearl. Highly evolved spirit are also incandescent light but it is difficult to imagine this so to work in gold is the easiest way to protect oneself. It is also a reflective colour so anything of a lower vibration is reflected back - it cannot enter.

Always ask for protection and work in gold. Trust it because your fear will undo the work. This is the power of the mind again.'

G. 'That is a hard one.'

J. 'It's a hard one I know but this course is challenging. You will build your strength. I always say to my pupils, 'When I've finished with you, your channel will be like thick, smooth, shiny steel.' At the moment it's beautiful but it's not strong enough.

If you're going to work with spirit you need to be strong, you need to be confident, you need to be fearless, yes? It's no good saying, I want to do this and I want to do that if you're sloppy, indecisive, if you don't trust, if you have fear. Fear will undo *all* your good work so we will work on 'fear'; it's one of the lessons in this course.'

G. 'I've been so-called caught out by fear.'

J. 'Yes, but what you need to understand Grace is that all your experiences are good ones. I'm pleased you've been caught out because it's very necessary to understand, just like you said, to experience bereavement, you experienced being caught out, it's good, it helps you understand things better.

Trust your guides, trust yourself and trust in the knowledge that you work in a high vibration for gold is a high vibrational colour.

When closing down - something else I'll teach you - you must close your sub-conscious mind as well as your conscious one. The best way to close down is not to think about spirit at all, however, spirit are still with you doing their work.

Your gatekeeper commands the opening so they can always get through. What I mean by that is that I'm going to teach you to close down but there is an emergency space if ever your gatekeeper needs to come to your rescue. It doesn't interfere with you closing down. It's a small space between your physical body and the first of your vibrational bodies and it's into that space that your gatekeeper can gain access.

Again, this is only the start and I can explain more as we go along, however, we all have a gatekeeper. We all have somebody who has probably had the most amazing relationship with us and because of their enormous love for us, has agreed to walk this lifetime with us and be the person who is always there for us and will be the person who, in an emergency, will come to our rescue. This is who I call a gatekeeper.

Then there are spiritual guides, there are helpers, there are people who I call runners, there are loads of spiritual aids, people call them angels or faeries and they are ruled by love and it is love that draws them towards us. So *your* gatekeeper - you may have even been their gatekeeper when they were last on the earth plane. It's an incredible bonding and it's the most..... what a compliment, 'May I be your gatekeeper?'

You can imagine being in spirit realms and being asked permission and the tears rolling down your cheeks, 'Oh my goodness!' That *is* love for you. You may already know who your gatekeeper is or you may have an idea but it is through this course that we're really hoping they're going to shine through.'

G. 'It is my understanding that my gatekeeper brings me into this world, walks through this world with me and takes me home. Is that correct?'

J. 'Your gatekeeper walks with you and is there whenever you call them. Sometimes you share gatekeepers. People think they own them and they can get very possessive about them but just like guides, we share them.

Taking you home, I don't know. I would have thought your gatekeeper would be in the crowd when you return home but whether they will personally take you home, I'm not convinced. I would say, in fact, I'm positive that your gatekeeper will not take you home. He will be there but he will not be one you go to when you cross over, OK?'

G. 'You read various books and have various friends but simply to have someone there and having you tell me that there is a space they can slip into as he has done in my life. He has, because I have felt something stronger and with such love, more than I've known, when I have been in a place where I knew I couldn't manage alone so I knew he, my gatekeeper or someone was there.'

J. 'Excellent! You should always pull the gold through your psychic centres, your chakras, when closing down as this cleanses you as well as protects. I am going to teach you how to do that too.

You need to cleanse your aura after communication as you can pick up people's depression and if you are a healer, their headaches, aches and pains, etc.

Also, there are times in development because you are using certain centres, chakras, that mediums may suffer sore throats or a few general aches and pains, maybe mood swings because your aura and its vibrations are being refined, refinement of the particular centre spirit are working on.

Now, logically, if you're venturing into something different, you should expect sometimes to feel a bit different, 'Action/Reaction'. When you do something, you get something back. You have a headache, you take a tablet and then something changes, you no longer have that headache.

Years ago, I used to sell magnets for personal health and wellbeing and I used to tell my customers that they may initially experience some aches and pains, some tweaks or twinges, anything. All that is happening is that the magnets are finding which part of you it needs to work on and adjusting things accordingly and that's a very good analogy for attunement.

When you sit and you commune with your guides, the registering of your vibration with spirit linking up and with them working with you, could result in you feeling different things and you will think, 'Oh, I felt something then!' So what I'm trying to say here is that you're not a dummy, you're a living thing and you may feel all kinds of senses.

Once you've begun working on this course, there is always a possibility that any future ailments may be spiritual or may be physical. People tend to lump everything into the spiritual. They phone me up or email me about a medical problem and ask, 'Do you think this is spiritual?' I usually say, 'No, go to the doctor.' They often seem to think it's spirit's fault. But you will learn as you grow, that some things are indeed spiritual but this is all part of the growth, all part of the understanding, which is all part of the experience, isn't it? To understand that there is a possibility that it could be one or it could be another?

I remember I wrote in 'A Medium's Tale', I don't know whether you remember this? I was feeling absolutely awful and I was lying in bed and I asked spirit, 'What is this? Is this spiritual or is this physical, I don't know what's going on?' And suddenly a bug crawled onto my bed and I laughed, 'Oh, it's a bug, I've got a bug!' Spirit were trying to tell me, no, no, nothing spiritual, you've just got a bug!

You're growing and because different people do different work for spirit, we shall find out what you're going to be doing, whether you're going to have another string to your bow, whether you're going to improve even more with what you're doing now, I don't know, all will be revealed.

I said this was an holistic course, it covers a big boundary. Your net will hopefully be big to catch a lot of fish as we have to know about everything, we have to consider everything.

Closing Down

Some mediums have a lot of difficulty closing down - this is also what I'm going to teach you today - and sometimes this is because they have further to go, they have a higher vibration to reach. Closing down is a discipline. Disciplines are difficult, disciplines are hard. You'll just have to learn how to do it. You'll either find it easy or you won't, we'll have to see but finding gold to look at helps with the closing down procedure.

Also standing beneath a light when you close down - again I will explain about this - because you get the gold shimmer from the light and that helps you to feel that you are being protected when you close down. This will help you feel the light coming in and around you because what we are doing, creating gold, is creating light.

When you go to bed you are at your most vulnerable as you are on the brink of two worlds, the same when you wake. There is a moment between sleeping and waking when it is very easy for spirit to communicate. Some people when I first mention this say, yes, yes, I know about that; something happens just when I wake up or something happens just as I go to sleep and that is the reason why, because you are more susceptible at these times.

If you understand that your spirit leaves your body every night. Your physical body stays in the bed but your mind, which in essence is your spirit, always goes home. As you go to sleep, spirit will be saying, "OK, Grace will be here in a minute, won't be long!"..... you're tossing and turning a bit......'Shouldn't be long now, can you wait for her?' Obviously, you've got work to do in spirit so you can see there's a time when you haven't quite left your body yet; you're just about to go off!

The same when you're waking up and you return to your physical shell and as I said in *'A Medium's Tale'*, this will start happening from the moment of conception. You're a spirit inside a nucleus, inside a womb but you still go home. In fact, a nucleus doesn't know the difference when they're in the womb because they're more in spirit than in the womb having just begun their new chapter, yes?'

G. 'Yes, I'm smiling because it hasn't happened for quite a while now but I used to be woken up at about 6 o'clock for quite a while and somebody would shout in my ear, 'Grace!, Grace!' and I'd be awake. It happened not all the time but then it would be just a few weeks and suddenly again and it would be early just between five and six and I'd be actually looking for somebody and the only thing I could think of was that my mother used to call to me like that!'

J. 'Too right! Finally, all developing mediums will go through a period of great fatigue. Some people do, some people don't but again, if you're being worked on you may feel the difference. I always say, you're in charge of you, you're responsible for you so you have to listen to what's going on and act accordingly. If your body says that's enough, let's stop for five minutes, then stop. Re-charge your batteries.

OK, so that is the first lesson on attunement and here are the notes for you to keep. So what we're going to do now, you will need your pad because I'm going to teach you how to attune!'

How To Attune

Jenny: 'So, how to attune? First of all, you will need to decide in which room you are going to do your attunement. You will need a comfortable chair where your feet touch the ground; somewhere you will always sit. I'd rather this isn't in the bedroom - I don't really want you to attune in your bedroom.'

Grace: 'Where it feels right?'

J. 'Yes. OK, have you decided in which room you will attune?'

G. 'I usually sit in that room.' (Pointing to a room).

J. 'OK. Have you got a comfortable chair in there or can you bring one in?'

G. 'I have one there.'

J. 'OK, so we've got the room and we've got the chair. Now, I want you to do these attunements at least three times a week so you will also need to decide, looking at your weekly/monthly schedule, on which day and at what time you're going to be doing this as spirit really like to have a rough idea when you're going to sit each week.'

G. 'It's like an appointment!'

J. 'You have to book it! As I said, you share your guides so it's nice for them to know, 'I'm with Grace then.' Yes?

So, at least three times a week on the same day and at roughly the same time. Now the time; I don't want you to start attuning after quarter to ten at night, however, it doesn't matter how early you start. Also, your family need to give you privacy so they need to know when you need to be on your own.

I also want you to set aside at least twenty minutes for each attunement but as you progress, you may want to increase this but to start with, three times a week for twenty minutes each time is fine.

You will need your dedicated candle and to feel completely and utterly secluded and in solitude meaning no phones, no disturbances and not expecting anybody. If during one of your selected times, suddenly, someone is now going to call or deliver a parcel or whatever, then you'll just have to mentally say to your guides, I'm going to do this a bit later or earlier or whatever you decide to do. You just need to send the thoughts up as they'll hear what you're thinking. OK?

So attunement is all about sitting in the silence. We say a prayer to start with and a prayer to finish.

Your prayer needs to be really simple and genuine and your opening prayer has to include the following two requests:-

* You need to call your guides and ask them to draw close; to draw near to you.

* You need to ask them for protection before you start.

When you attune, you do nothing but go into a blank space - all these things I'm going to teach you now - and then at the end of your attunement, when you come round, you say another prayer, which I will also help you with; to close down.

OK, so when you start attuning you need to be in quite a restful state. I always say you can't attune between Eastenders and Coronation Street; it's not going to work. You can't rush attunement. When *I* decide to attune, I usually potter around the house for five minutes winding down because what I'm doing is trying to silence my mind. You've got to stop thinking about the shopping, the washing, the dinner, who you've got to phone and start emptying your mind and I do this by just pottering; 'preparing to sit'.'

G. 'Settling.'

J. 'Yes, because everything is to do with your mentality. I usually start by thinking don't worry about that, don't worry about that, do that later, forget it, forget it, forget it! I turn the phones off and just potter; that works for me.

So when you sit in your chair and get comfortable, I want you first to do some deep breathing. Now the way I want you to breathe is to take the first breath and from nothing, I want you to breathe to the highest you can go without hurting yourself. So you breathe in slowly, until you reach the plateau and then you breathe out through your mouth, again very slowly until it's all out.

So I want you do this three times. In a way, that is preparing for prayer. So you breathe as high as you can, you take your first breath slowly up, up, slowly, up, up, slowly up, up until you reach your plateau and then breathe out again, very, very slowly until it's all out. You do this three times. OK?

Now when I first started this, I could only breathe a little way up and now I can breathe up to here (Jenny points up high) - it's astonishing! I can go on and on and on and on, breathe and breathe and keep going and going. It's really amazing how much further I can breathe now considering what a lousy breather I was! So, what I'm saying is, that it *does* change. To start with you can breathe in so much but eventually you realise that your breathing can grow.

Next you need to say your prayer. I have a prayer here which I'll give you a copy of but this is something I wrote after I'd been attuning for about six months but you can use bits of it if you want to. You can, of course, change your prayer at any time. As long as the prayer is genuine, it doesn't matter what you say, but it must include asking your guides to draw close and also asking for protection.

Now with protection, whenever you ask for protection you need to work in gold and see a gold symbol above your head. Now, if I ask you now to see a gold object, can you visualise a gold object?'

G. 'Yes.'

J. 'Good! Now, if you're protecting yourself and your aura, you will always need to have a gold light shining above your head so can you choose a gold symbol of light or a gold shower with gold water drops, anything visual which you feel will symbolically protect you? I need you to decide this now. So what do you think is the easiest to visualise?'

G. 'A light.'

J. 'OK, a light. Will it just be light or will it be a candle, a bulb or a coach light? What sort of light, explain what light you're going to use?'

G. 'I see it as a globe, a golden globe and then I see the beams coming out from it.'

J. 'Lovely, so write that down. OK. A gold globe with beams coming out equals your protection symbol so whenever you ask for protection, which you are going to ask for a lot, you will need to automatically visualise this golden globe as this is the symbol you will be working with and I'm happy with a globe of light because it has functionality, strength and definition.

So to re-cap, what you're going to do when preparing for attunemnt is:- To go into your dedicated room three times a week at the same time and you're going to make sure you have the solitude. Light your candle before you start, wind down before you sit, breathe in three slow breaths, say your opening prayer and when you ask for protection, you're going to see your globe of light, OK?'

G. 'Yes.'

J. 'Now close your eyes and I want you to tell me if you can see a blank TV screen or a blank computer screen? The screen has nothing in it.'

G. 'Yes.'

J. 'Right, so when you start attuning, I want you to see a blank screen. Keep on looking at it and focus on the blankness and stay in this blankness and without realising it, you'll go into the screen so to speak - you'll just drift off. Which is why I say that if you potter around for five minutes before sitting to ease and slow down your mind, you're also preparing yourself and getting rid of all the 'riff raff' in your mind.

So by the time you light your candle, do your breathing, say your prayer and start looking into the blankness of your screen, you'll have facilitated the linking up with spirit much more quickly. Preparation for sitting is so worthwhile.

Now, if you were having difficulty 'going blank', there are some helpful tips. For example, think of a beautiful place, maybe somewhere that is particularly special for you. Then continue to fix your mind and focus on that beautiful place and once again, you will encourage spirit to link up with you and, in turn, you'll drift off.

When you say your opening prayer, I also want you to ask spirit to bring 'you round' after twenty minutes. It's like saying, "I need help from you to know when my attunement with you is over, can you give me a sign so I know when I have finished my attunement?" Yes?

When you speak with spirit it's like you're speaking to anybody - they're a person - just talk from your heart. Ask them whatever you want, they've known you for eons of time so you're not a stranger to them or to each other even though this is a new road for you now.

So, you will have your twenty minutes and then you'll 'come round' and you'll open your eyes. Spirit will give you a sign, like you'll jerk or feel a twitch or a dog will bark; it will be something. I don't know what your sign will be but I know you'll recognise it as time to open your eyes.

You will then have to say your closing prayer so you may need to write one down until you have the confidence to talk without it. Now this closing prayer should include:-

* Thanking your guides for drawing close.

* Thanking them for giving you all the protection you needed.

* Anything else you want to say.

Now, I'm going to teach you how to close down. Do you know your chakra points?'

G. 'I think I know where they are.'

J. 'I have a diagram for you. (See page 59) Here are the main chakra points. What you now have to do is choose a closing down symbol. This has to be very strong, for example, a great big heavy door or a metal safe door, a submarine hatch; anything where you go 'clunk' and the door shuts securely. A symbol which you're very sure will work automatically but also choose something that you'll find very easy to visualise.

Visualise a secure symbol now as you will need to close each and every one of these chakra points when you close down, the openings needs to be shut tight!'

G. 'I see a window but the thing is, I can see through it, so I'm going to go for a round safe door.'

J. 'Brilliant! Now looking at the chakra points on that sheet, the first being on the top of your head, link up all these individual points together like dot to dot, creating a pipe or tube as in plumbing! I now want you to imagine liquid gold pouring in from the opening at the top of your head and winding its way down through all the pipework, linking up all your chakras until it comes out of your - you know what! When it does, kick the remaining gold liquid into the air as though you're kicking a gold football.

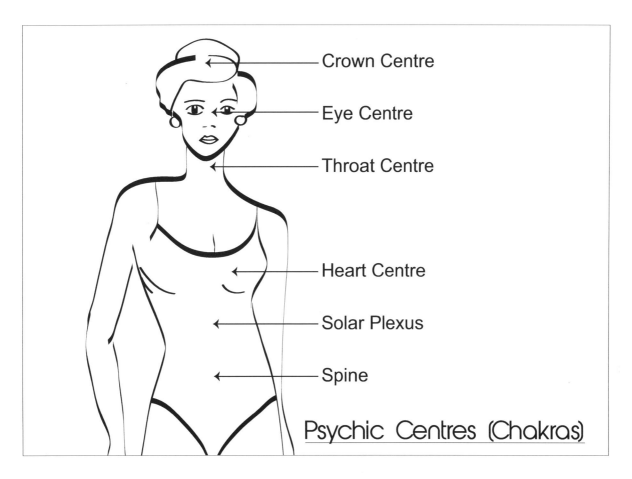

Crown Centre

Eye Centre

Throat Centre

Heart Centre

Solar Plexus

Spine

Psychic Centres (Chakras)

Now as the gold 'liquid' goes down and passes through each chakra point, immediately close each opening with your closing down symbol having cleansed each chakra point with the gold liquid. So the liquid starts to go in, you then cap off your top chakra with your safe door symbol, clunk, close, then your forehead chakra, clunk, close, now your throat chakra, then your heart chakra, your solar plexus and then your spine, all with the gold pouring through and then any gold liquid left over, you kick into the ether or else you'll have a puddle gold 'wee wee' on the floor!

OK, I now want you to do a practice run of closing down using your new closing down symbol - your round safe door - and having the gold liquid coming through whilst you're doing it. So close your eyes, start at the top of your head, shutting off each chakra; clunk, clunk, clunk, clunk, clunk, clunk and when it reaches the bottom, visually kick it out. Done, excellent, well done!'

G. 'That felt the best closing down I've ever done!'

J. 'Now you've got to open up now because we haven't finished. Opening up is easy, you only need to think of spirit and you're open. Closing down is the hard bit, you need to be disciplined but you will feel safe. Now I want you to write down on your pad all the other times you will have to close down! You need to close down at other times apart from after attunement, so you need to make a list.'

G. 'I need to think about this.'

J. 'It'll be in your head and it will be as quick as anything. Let me explain what you have to do and then you can tell me what the problem is?'

G. 'You've really caught me out now.'

J. 'Come on, don't worry, you need to write down all the other times you need to close down.

OK, I also want you to close down before you go to bed at night and I want you to do this either in the upstairs hall or the bathroom. I don't want you to close down in your bedroom; your bedroom is for sleeping. So, at night, when you ask your guides to help you close down all your chakra points, look up at the light in the hall or the bathroom - clunk, clunk, clunk. The ceiling light of the room will aid your closing down. It will only take a few seconds.

I *also* want you to close down whenever you leave the house.

I *also* don't want you to think or talk about spirit when you're in the car.

Also, when you're in a public place and people start talking about spiritual things, I want you to learn to close yourself down and ask for protection if needs be and suggest that you talk about this on the phone or when you get home. You need to start getting yourself into a good discipline of not talking about spiritual matters in public places.

Grace, you're not going to be able to do all this with a click of your fingers. The things I'm teaching you, you are now *learning* how to do them. This is all new and you will fall into a new routine. It's like the doctor has told you that you need to adopt a new eating/health regime which will be a good, safe, secure and disciplined routine and one which you will develop as naturally as brushing your teeth or riding a bike.

You can talk about spiritual things in the home as much as you want, talking to friends in the home or speaking on the phone because your home will become your spiritual sanctuary so, at home, you only have to close down after attunement and before going to bed. All the other times you're fine, you're being protected but when you go out of the house, a quick shut down and start getting into the habit of doing this.

It may be difficult at first but think of it as if you're switching off your light - your spiritual light - and you don't need to switch it on again as your chakras will open automatically when you think of spirit! Spiritual thoughts - draw them away - push these thoughts away when you're not at home.

When you're out shopping and you start thinking of your attunements or of spiritual things, push your thoughts and your spiritual guides away. Say, 'No, not now. We'll do it when we get home, I'll think about it when I get home.' You are half of the partnership remember. Your spiritual guides are eager to work with you. They are going to come in with 'stuff', with recommendations, advice, whatever, yes?

Because you're beginning this course and starting to communicate with them regularly, you may have to control them sometimes, saying no, when it's not the right time. 'No, I don't want to talk about it now.' You don't have to close down again but you may have to manage your guides.

Let's say you were having a meal with your husband and your guides come in and say something, it might be funny. You can say mentally, 'Oh thanks for that, now disappear, I don't want to speak to you now, talk to you later.'

G. 'Do I have to close down when I go into my garden?'

J. 'Good point, no, only when you leave your property. Your garden is part of your home. Spirituality and nature go hand in hand so gardens are spiritual places in their own right. You don't need to close down in the garden, that's unnecessary.'

G. 'What about if I go out to post a letter?'

J. 'No, that's only up the road, you'll be back very soon. If you're so specific, you'll drive yourself crazy! I know you want to get it right but you have to start somewhere. This is your first lesson and I have started to give you guidelines which you will formulate to suit you and your lifestyle. Eventually, please God, you'll learn to switch off. As I've already mentioned, the best way to close down is just not to think of spirit or spiritual things.

There's a lot going on now and your guides are all eager - busy, busy, busy - but we have to have a framework from which to start all this which is what we're doing today.

So, we've got the room, we've got the chair, we've got the candle, we've got switching off the phones or putting them on mute because you want to be alone and not disturbed. You need to have your five minutes or so to wind down. You need to get comfy in your chair so you feel really relaxed, maybe with cushions or a shawl or throw, if necessary.

Then when we start our attunement; we light the candle, we say our opening prayer including asking our guides to draw close, to give us all the protection we need. That's when you need to see and use your protection symbol above your head and you can also ask your guides to bring you round at whatever time you want. Then we go into the blank space.

When you come round, you need to say a closing prayer, thanking your guides for drawing close and giving you protection so you visualise your protection symbol again and ask them to help close down all your chakras. Visualise your closing down symbol and close off all your chakra points one by one with your round safe symbol whilst watching the gold liquid pour through the channel of chakra points and finally, kicking any surplus gold into the air. Finito!

After each attunement, I want you to write down on your pad all the things that happened to you whilst you were sitting because every time we get together we are going to go through what has happened in your attunements.

Now, to begin with, I will want to know *everything*. I will want to know what you felt when you were breathing and what parts of your body were affected as sometimes your connection with your guides start with your breathing. For example, 'The minute I start breathing out, I'm feeling this or that.' etc., so I want you to write down what you felt from the moment you started.

This is what happened when I said my prayer. Record anything that happens from start to finish. Anything you felt, anything you heard and anything you saw. That's clairsentience for feeling, clairaudience for hearing and clairvoyance for seeing. Will you do that?'

G. 'Yes.'

J. 'So that next time, when we start Month 2, we will start off with, 'How did you get on Grace?' Now the other things that we will also be talking about are any questions you have, the things that have happened during the previous month plus I'm going to ask about your sleep state, that is, what's been happening in your sleep? Maybe nothing but remember I said to you, they may test you, things which have been playing on your mind and also things may resolve themselves.

This is a new road now. I'm not being dramatic but in some way you're saying goodbye to the old Grace and hello to a new one. You're going to have proof of spirit by the things that happen in your life, the things you ask for are then received, the things which you have problems with which are then resolved. If you're with them, they're with you. That's the way it works. OK?

Now I'm going to give you a copy of my prayer (See page 63) but as I said earlier, it's just for guidance purposes. To begin with, make your prayer really simple and meaningful. OK?

One other thing about attunement, it's best done on an empty stomach.'

G. 'I can understand that.'

J. 'When I say empty, you can have a cup of tea and a biscuit but don't ever attune after a meal so make sure if you've eaten, you attune at least one and half to two hours minimum after this. I don't know the times you've decided to sit, I just need you to know, not on a full stomach.'

G. 'And I can choose my time earlier in the day? I quite often get up early, six-thirty, my husband goes to work, that would be my best time and I can be on my own.'

J. 'So that can be your new routine. You would have had a cup of tea but you wouldn't have had a meal, that's perfect! I don't have to talk about alcohol or smoking because I know you don't do either but, remember, if you're doing spiritual work, no alcohol beforehand.

So here is a copy of my notes for the first month of this development course which deals with attunement.'

Jenny's Prayer

'Father, hear me

Thank you for loving us, a love that is unconditional

Please give me all the protection I need

Here I am, how may I serve, guide me to the highest for my own good.

Please allow my guides, helpers, family and friends to draw close

All those who need to be here, please let them be here

And all the things that need to be done, please let they be done.

Help me to help others less fortunate than myself

To speak to them, to listen to them, to support them

To counsel them, to console them

To teach them, to heal them, to touch their soul

For we are all servants who seek but to serve.

Please lead so I can follow

Please tell me what you want me to do now

So I can fulfill the purpose of my incarnation

Please speak loudly so I can hear you

Please let me see you so I can give evidence of survival.

Amen.'

Month 2

"To find the peace within is one of man's greatest achievements."

Jenny: 'Well, you've returned for a second session? You're obviously a sucker for punishment as you want to carry on! No seriously, welcome back Grace.

I need to ask what's been happening to you since we last met but before we do that, we're going to start a new routine for when we meet in future. We're both going to 'light our lamps' at the top of our head as a way of telling our spirit guides that we're ready for them to draw close or as I always say - that we're now 'open for business'. So every time we get together to begin our monthly session, I will start by saying, let's light our lamps and ask our guides to draw close and then we can begin.

I, myself, just use a candle light for this. It can also be the same as your protection symbol, it can be anything. I've always done this, for as well as having this candle in front of us, spirit know we're open because we're discussing spiritual things.

Again, it's symbolic, it's something I adapted and it's always stayed with me. We close our eyes, we imagine the light above our head, we ask our guides to draw close and then we can begin.'

Grace: 'What I've written Jenny is, 'Light our lamps to let spirit know we're open for business.'

J. 'Everything I'm talking about and teaching you are things I've formulated with my spiritual guides but you may want to introduce your own way of doing things. Everything I'm teaching you is about a relationship and I'm therefore teaching you how to expand your own relationship with your spiritual guides.

It's like when I gave you the copy of my prayer, it's for guidance. I don't expect and I don't think you should use the whole of this for yourself but it's what *I* thought I should be saying after I had been attuning for a while but, at the beginning, my prayer was very limited.

I know when you are learning something you tend to take things as rote but you can't take 'spirituality' as rote because spirituality is yourself and the way you emanate, your own spiritual expression and, of course, your own spiritual partnership. So I don't need to say this again, you take what I have to say and make it your own. There is no one way to work with spirit.

So now let's start this session. How did you get on last month?'

G. 'I feel that I've progressed. I did lose some time as I was away in Scotland but I worked very hard to catch up. I have done 9 attunements and it's more or less the same time each morning for around 20 minutes.'

J. 'So let's hear your attunements.'

G. 'I've paid attention to what I first wrote down; The globe of golden light, the gold is reflective - I understand that. Fearless and strong that begins to grow. Fear nothing. Closing down means getting to it, pulling the gold through chakras. Action/reaction. Feeling different, very much so.

My first attunement was on 31 May. I've always had a problem with wanting to cough but that has lessened, not really happening anymore and it was a real problem.'

J. 'That in itself is some proof for you with a smile whilst saying, 'How come this is getting better? Thank you spirit!'

G. 'For the first time in many months I woke up with the feeling of strength. I have a lot of aches and pains but they are less. My first attunement this month went as follows:- Having settled myself in my chair, in my room in my home, I followed Jenny's instructions.

I noticed the sound of my breath which levelled out. This was followed by a stabbing pain under the middle of my left foot. It stopped after a minute or so when I realised that I continually shoot myself in the foot! I could feel the top of my head, my crown, becoming increasingly hot. This was to tell me that my protection was in place. Spirit knows me so well.

I felt many hands on my body keeping me safe. I thought that each pair, and they were in pairs, were relevant to certain organs in my body - healing. There was continuous conversation around me. I could understand but could not remember it as I tried to memorise it so I could write it down afterwards.'

J. 'Was this heard clairvoyantly, in your head, or heard outside?'

G. 'Clairvoyantly, so I was a little worried about trying to write it down and then a strong male voice said, *'Keep still and know I am with you.'* I felt myself become calm. I saw just at the end - with being a fusspot and trying to get things right - I realised that my screen had remained blank. Then there appeared to be a glow evolving slowly, it looked like eggs, blues and greens.

I then remembered from the earlier conversation that the man had told me to use my eyes and not my thoughts so I would not try to make things up to be more than they were. Length of attunement: 20 minutes.'

J. 'So can I ask you how did you 'know' you had to come round?'

G. 'It was just a natural ending. There was a clock in front of me and it was 20 minutes. I felt very pleased with myself and with spirit. It was proof that we were working together.'

J. 'You had quite a lot of proof that you were working together, didn't you? To get all that in the first one and you didn't know what to expect either, excellent start!'

G. 'I also did a little study. These were notes that I found myself writing as I sat down with my drink the next day. 'Jenny arrived just in time, when the pupil is ready the teacher appears. It has become apparent to me that I have broken a great many rules with my rushing and searching for answers.'

J. 'I wouldn't say broken, I would say that you're now looking at things in a different way. You see, there's no such thing as anything wrong, you just learn from everything you do. I always say 'the bad things' are the best things; it's an opportunity to correct things.'

G. 'You tend to remember the bad things more. My second attunement was on the Saturday. Again, I noticed the sound of my own breathing. The blank screen remained blank. I felt changes within my body. My shoulders were pushed and pulled back taking away much of the stiffness. There was work down within my chest area in the centre which faded away within seconds. Patience is the word I have been given. I feel this relates to the discomfort felt within my body. 'Be still and know we are with you' is my mantra. Length of attunement: 20 minutes.

I did write a small study later. It would seem that the moment my mind begins to think of spiritual matters in inappropriate places or at inappropriate times, there is a great clunk or bang like the hatch separating the two worlds have been slammed shut - my guides. I hear it and pay attention.

This is one more study - not an attunement - I felt it was incorrect.'

J. 'There's no such thing as incorrect. It's *you* who thrashes yourself!'

G. 'Well then, I've done 10 attunements - one extra! I have been on holiday in Scotland for four days and my spiritual education has not progressed to any great extent and yet I feel that some ground has been covered.'

J. 'That is rubbish, spirit are with you always. They told you *that* even when you were in Scotland!' (Grace laughs).

G. 'I have sat for 30 minutes this morning with my lighted candle. During my holiday, spirit had spoken to me as a question needed answering followed by the immediate closing of the hatch. I finished taking a golden shower to cleanse my aura to close down properly. The countryside in Scotland was covered by mile after mile of golden gorse, ribbons of gold everywhere.'

J. 'That sounds like a present; a feast for the eyes.'

G. '12 June, 7.45 to 8.15. I felt pressure in both of my ears, more so in the left, similar to what happens when flying and I expected my ears to pop but they did not. I find it a bit difficult to visualise a blank television screen so I'm now trying out a large empty crystal ball situated at eye level which feels better. I can see in my mind's eye a thin line connecting my ears which stretched through my head and seemed to be made of white light. It remained very steady and still, then the line switched to the vertical leaving my left ear and moving to the crown of my head. What was connected to my right ear now touched my throat. My throat opened and I could feel fresh air enter. The pressure was still in my ears.

After a very short time I began to notice a thin line of light brown, burnt orange, yellow, dark cream, they were level with my eyes some distance away and shaped very like bendy sunglasses. These lines of coloured light now stretched either side of my head and back into the distance. I felt a difference and my eyes opened and I was back in my chair. I closed down, protected, sent my prayer of thanks knowing that my day will go well.'

J. 'These colours, were they like a rainbow, one on top of another?'

G. 'Yes, but with a slight space in between.'

J. 'What you need to appreciate is that when I ask questions, I'm trying to understand what these things mean. You may probably think, 'Why does she want to know that?' but it all means something to me and the fact that there was a space between them also means something to me.'

G. 'I understand that, very fine but slightly wider than the line itself.'

J. 'Well that also means something to me. Spirit often communicate symbolically and they know you understand what they are trying to say. They don't actually say it, they show you and hopefully you will eventually understand what they are saying. You've already understood a lot of what they are trying to say, remember, 'You shoot yourself in the foot!'

You will instantly know what your guides mean by what they show you just like a wonderful relationship should be. Also, you now know they have a sense of humour, which is lovely.'

G. '15 June, 7.30 to 7.50 - these attunements are all a.m. I had a tingle in the heel of my right foot and my feet became very hot so I kicked off my house shoes. I felt myself being pulled backwards at a steady speed. There were huge clouds in the distance and the sun was shining upon them. Great mountains of white and gold were within the clouds but I kept having to look up to keep them in focus because I was in a sort of corridor made of dark grey mist and I could see, by looking back, that it ran below the white and golden clouds but I was in this corridor but I could also see the white and gold and I felt safe.

I then remembered that I had not taken my three deep breaths to begin my attunement and then I was no longer able to see any darkness or white and gold clouds, they were gone and I was in a different place.

The song, 'Over the sea to Skye' came into my mind, so I sang the first 2 lines in my head. Then I saw my granddaughter, with a scar running down her body. She was in her own bed recovering from an operation and I was bathing the scar with cool water and singing to her.

I 'came back' into the room just as the postman dropped post into the box by the door. Closing down and then resting with the thought that I am calmer and have more energy to carry out my daily tasks. Every time I attune, you have the energy to do whatever is needed for the day.'

J. 'Because spirit always leave some 'healing' energy for you. If you heal via the spiritual, you are never forgotten. As a healer, you're giving a service to other people so spirit always remembers *you* as well. I think I may have said that attuning encompasses loads of different things not just formulating a relationship with your guides but giving them time to be with you, but what they give you back is peace, strength, and healing.

People often under-estimate, including me, the value of attunement and as I'm telling you about it, I'm saying to myself that I have to make time for myself more and attune more!'

G. 'But to be doing something new is so exciting and wonderful that we have to remember how wonderful it is, even when we've moved on, because those first few times are something that it is difficult to repeat because of the feeling it leaves with you.'

J. 'Overwhelming. It's in a different league isn't it? But this is just the beginning Grace.'

G. 'I know I can't believe it! I have never felt more at peace in my whole life. I have felt peace but not this kind of peace. You feel that whatever life is going to throw at you, good or bad, it's going to be alright and that is wonderful, wonderful!

18 June. 7.55 to 8.15am. I sat and after a few moments could see a very large globe spinning to the right.'

J. 'This is the second time you've had the globe. I wonder what this means?'

G. 'I say globe but that is incorrect because at its top it was pointed, like an onion with a flat bottom.'

J. 'Like the Russian tops of buildings?'

G. 'Yes, it was covered in fine stripes of pale blue, lilac and pink going around it with a strip of soft brown every now and then.'

J. 'Are these stripes going down vertically or around it, horizontally?'

G. 'Around, horizontally. The globe, which looked to be suspended in space, then started to spin off to the left crossing my vision in the distance and moving across to the right coming to rest in its original position. Then I could see a great deal of yellow and gold - nothing to do with the globe now, that's gone. The colours were everywhere; golden material blowing in the breeze, the sand of the desert with a camel train in the distance, hot sun beating down upon me.'

J. 'You also felt this as well as seeing it?'

G. 'Yes, I could feel it. The thought came to my mind, why am I seeing all these colours? I thought back to the blue in the pointed globe and my throat seemed to swell. Perhaps a voice box, was my next thought? This settled down quickly and my throat became calm or I did. I'm not sure exactly why I had that or what it was about, it was simply there and I felt it. I felt the pressure in my ears which has happened in other attunements then my head fell back. Did I start to fall asleep? Then I was back in the room. It didn't feel like going to sleep.'

J. 'People often complain or admit this, saying I'm really sorry but I fell asleep and I always tell them, no, you did not fall asleep, you think you were asleep but you were not. Some of them are convinced. Sometimes they do the whole attunement and think they've been asleep!'

G. '20 June. 7.25 to 7.45 a.m. I used my own words for the opening prayer - up until now I have used Jenny's - which made me smile when you said, you need to start your own prayer. I remembered my three deep breaths in and out. At the beginning of my attunement I felt myself travel. I could see this mostly with my left eye even though both of my eyes were closed and I felt very tall. It took longer to settle into the attunement. Shapes and thoughts kept drifting across my mind and vision. Spirit was with me, helping and protecting.'

J. 'How did you know this?'

G. 'Their faces are so beautiful. I saw them. Long, slim but of perfect proportion.'

J. 'You saw their faces?'

G. 'Yes.'

J. 'So what did you see, *just* their faces?'

G. 'Yes, they were clear enough to see. They were drifting one into the other but their faces were there. I can't tell you more but there was more than one, at least three and they almost superimposed themselves onto one another at a very regular pace. They held an oval mirror up so I could see the reflection of my own face; a little sad but also at peace was what I saw within my reflection. Then I was bathed in a golden and yellow light.

They spoke to me answering a question, a question that I must have asked. I knew at the time that I would not remember this conversation; it was just at the back of my mind so I knew I must be patient. I just felt that a question had been asked and had now been answered. It was just there but I couldn't remember asking it but it now left me with peace that all is well. Whatever has gone on is as it should be.'

J. 'There are many times when something which has needed answering suddenly drops in. You may have not realised that you even asked the question. It may have been a mentally rhetorical question to you but spirit heard it. You have been given an answer to a question that you forgot you had asked!'

G. 'I had lost something. I lost it on the 22nd. It was a piece of paper and I needed it and then suddenly I knew where it was. It was under the mat where I had put it to flatten it! The answer just arrived with no pre-thought whatsoever. It was something of that nature.

I have been closing down and shutting off my chakras with a loud bang to make sure I was closed. When I reached my heart today, I was told that I could now close with a soft click and I found this much easier!'

J. 'Spirit knows best, however, we all *love* your enthusiasm!'

G. '21 June 7.30 to 7.50 am. I protected, grounded and waited. I have lost to some extent the energy gained from my four days away in Scotland, therefore, it crossed my mind to ask for help from spirit. My question was, because I never have enough length of time during the day to re-charge, could they assist me in gaining some rest and energy in the short periods of time that occasionally come my way?

I saw myself in a beam of golden light then the gold began to slide off showing a pyramid shape made of clear glass, plastic or some transparent material. The gold slid off slowly but smoothly and I could see myself standing within it dressed in a gold garment. Then I saw myself standing in a network of golden bars the shape of these bars were set out in a sort of star but the pyramid shape was still there.'

J. 'Like the Star of David?'

G. 'Yes, boundaries, it was all about boundaries and I must set them myself. Time to close down. I wrote another study. I went to a show in a community centre two days ago. I paid £25 and set up a table - my first one. I know what you said about places like these. It wasn't a Mind, Body & Spirit Fair just a community hall where we had lots of tables. I had already booked this and I knew what you said to me and never said anything to you as I thought I'd think on it.'

J. 'Was this about charging? What is it exactly that I talked about that you are referring to now? Was it something from my book, *'A Medium's Tale'*, that I said?'

G. 'It was about 'changing a worry into a concern.' You also said something to me before you left last time. It was almost like a throwaway but I picked up on it because it looks like I've been worried.

If there is something that comes up that's perhaps too far down the road to change, I think on it. I don't say anything, I put it in my mind and as the day goes by, I come to a conclusion. I think about it and I adjust it and come to a decision and I usually say when I've come to my conclusion, what do you think about this?

I went to the show on the 17th. I paid £25 and it was my first table for my paintings. I was protected and the day went well. There were three tarot card readers and their tables were in the four corners of the room, the fourth corner had the door in it. The room was large and airy and there was plenty of space and a nice energy most of the time.

People and customers do bring their own stuff with them. I felt well when I left but by Monday morning, not so good. It got worse as the day progressed and although I did my usual amount of work for the day, I struggled.

Today is Tuesday and I have improved but it is not as it should be. What is going on? Boundaries are needed and this was on the 19th and then, on the 21st I had this thought and I knew that besides protection, we also need our boundaries. People we trust and know, it doesn't stop people from approaching you, it kind of filters stuff out. As well as protection, sometimes you need these energy lines which also act as a filter.'

J. 'You think we need more than the normal protection?'

G. 'I think a lot of us do. I feel a lot of us do.'

J. 'Did you also ask your guides to protect you whilst you were there?'

G. 'I can't remember, I got very nervous because I was actually doing something different - something new. I was just trying to hold it all together.'

J. 'But I think you're to be congratulated on doing something new, because every new experience is massive, it's what we're here to do. We're here to push ourselves, to have new experiences, to find the confidence and courage to take that next step, maybe to go out of our comfort zone because every experience teaches us things.'

G. 'I was well out of my comfort zone.'

J. 'I know, that's why I'm congratulating you!'

G. 'I didn't go to sell, I went to see what interest people would have in what I did. I tested the market. I only had two things that I was happy to sell.'

J. 'I want to ask you something about your attunements? When you do the deep breathing, do you notice or feel anything change, say, to your limbs, your hands, your feet anywhere in your body?'

G. 'Yes, I feel lighter.'

J. 'Something else I would like to mention about attunement. If you have difficulty 'going blank' - being or staring into the 'nothingness', the blackness - and a lot of people do - I always suggest that you think of a special place instead. Some people can't visualise a 'blank screen' and so have trouble getting their attunements off the ground. So I say, OK, if you can't 'go blank', do you have a special place and advise them to just focus on that and then you will drift off and get 'taken' into attunement.'

G. 'I've got two more. 26 June. I opened up, did my breathing, said my prayer and sat. It seems that my mind is on overdrive. There is always a voice that overrides all others talking to me in my head with great love. It is usually a man but not all of the time but deep, firm and gentle.

My mind was not settled so the only thing to do was to go with what I had. I felt that when the voice speaks to me and I cannot remember what is said, that is how it is meant to be, the conversation will come back to me when needed.

In my collection of paintings is one which I have named 'Soul Group' and it has been very much in my thoughts the last few days, why? That remains to be seen. I watched my blank screen and finally it sprang to life. I saw a deep red sky and walking along the skyline were animals, all kinds from the dawn of time.

As I watched, this changed to become brightly dressed people from medieval times but still following in a kind of procession. As I watched I heard the words, *'You can stand and watch or run and join in.'* followed by, *'When we stand still, we cease.'*

I put down my pad and my pen. The pen rolled onto the ground at great speed as if pushed and a stern but kind voice said, *'Pick up your pen before leaving.'* I remembered to close down because I was about to leave the room without doing so. Thank you spirit! It just brought me back and I knew that I was done.

And my last attunement which was this morning. Alongside my pad, I've put, the globe does not work for me. You remember, I replaced the screen with a globe?

7.40 to 8 o'clock a.m. It has taken me until today to find my blank screen without a struggle. My hands became very hot and then I saw my soul group picture yet again with all of the faces looking back at me. When I returned their gaze, everyone in the picture turned one by one to look away.

The children, Elsie and Molly, were the last ones to turn but I did not feel left out or alone but felt more at one with them as though they were directing me to look with them into the far distance. Where we were looking or at what, was not revealed. I felt the sun and light on my closed eyelids, the air became lighter and breathing became very comfortable.

Then I felt the air change and become heavy, it was like trying to breathe through treacle. I could feel my lungs begin to struggle and then the air changed yet again and became the air that I know and use every day. As I continued to watch my screen, a hand pulled back a kind of curtain and an Arab face looked at me.

It was a man I knew very well. He looked about 50 years old this time. He is my scribe and helps me with my artwork. Then he became a young man again and we walked into his house with his beautiful white horse following behind, the reins draped over his shoulder and he has a name but I can't quite say it. He didn't need to hold the reins, the horse would just follow.

The first courtyard is the stable which is open to the sky and is sheltered from the sun by palms and other kinds of trees. The second part is a beautiful garden which is also sheltered by trees. The house begins after this and is built on a higher level with white steps just inside the entrance. Once inside, the floor is of large cream stone and covered in carpets of various colours with small tables and cushions for sitting.

There is one more level with stairs leading to it. Up here is darker with many small latticed windows looking out over the desert. This is the women's side. On the opposite side of this level is the sleeping quarters for the men. The servants sleep downstairs so as to make an early start each morning. I find myself back in my chair and on my feet are pretty golden slippers; a gift from spirit.'

J. 'Did you see these slippers clairvoyantly?'

G. 'Yes and I could also see the spelling of his name as I've asked. His surname was either Salliman or Sulliman. I could never quite work out as I see it as a spelling but I can't quite see all the letters. His first name is ISIAH and it's a shortened version of Isaiah. I looked it up but it's not said quite that way but it means God is salvation or salvation of God and it's believed to be from the Hebrew.

From past conversations with this man, there were four of them, two sons and two daughters and he went away on a quest or a crusade.......' (Grace goes on to explain about him, his family and their own relationship).

J. 'Is that all your attunements? Good. What I also need to ask you is how has your sleep state been? Have you been woken up or had any unusual dreams? You've had an immense amount in your first month so I don't really expect anything.'

G. 'I don't recall anything. My sleep is easier, more comfortable and I wake up more refreshed. When I've done my attunements in the morning, I really don't think of spiritual matters. I honestly think that I was never switched off but things are different because of what I now know.'

J. 'You're seeing the difference now because your understanding allows you to have a place for this and the time for that.'

G. 'Of all things, and it's all been wonderful, but this course has been something which has changed my life!'

J. 'What about anything in your life that you feel that you've had problems with or things that you were hoping to resolve? Is there anything that you feel is starting to work your way or is beginning to be accomplished?'

G. 'My husband, even though he jokes and laughs he is so much more considerate and so much more supportive in this work, so much more and it's happened in the last month. I haven't told him anything about this. I don't tell him that I'm sitting - it's not necessary - but he appears to be more understanding of spiritual matters.'

J. 'Really, that's great and that surprises you?'

G. 'Very much so.'

J. 'But maybe he's noticed a change in you?'

G. 'I'm sure that's the case. I have confidence now, confidence in myself. I have the confidence to take the next step and if it doesn't work, it doesn't matter, I'm calmer.'

J. 'That's a hell of a lot in a month, don't you think?'

G. 'Well now we're talking about it, I guess it is!'

J. 'OK, I'm going to give you some 'tools' before we carry on with the next lesson. I say tools, they're aids and you need to write them down. I always say to people at the start of this course, I'm giving you an empty tool box and the things that I give you, share with you, are like tools for you to put in your 'tool box'.

So this month I want to give you some more tools. When you close down at night - only at night - and you ask spirit for protection and close down all your chakras, I would also like you to finish by asking your guides to:-

   * Seal the top of your head with a golden cross.

So you've closed down, the liquid has gone all the way through, yes? So the last thing you do is ask them to seal the top of your head with a golden cross and you should then visualise a golden cross at the crown of your head which also seals the crown chakra closed and then also ask your guides to:-

   * Cloak you in protection.

So what I say to spirit when closing down at night is; 'Please seal the top of my head with a golden cross and cloak me in protection' and when you see the cloak, I want it to be a gold one made of satin or something shiny which reflects off any negativity.

When I first started adding this extra protection at night, I chose a gold velvet cloak. I soon realised that this wasn't reflecting anything, in fact, it was doing the opposite, absorbing everything, so I swapped velvet for satin as it was a shinier material. Even if you wanted this to be gold foil, it doesn't matter as long as the cloak's shiny and reflective.

That's the first new thing I want you to do when you go to bed in future. I'm also going to give you two more tools. One is a quick way of closing down and another is a quick way of getting energy.

So let's start with a quick way to close down. Let's say you were at your stand at a Fair and suddenly someone arrived at your table and you didn't feel good at all. There are times when you want to close down or ask for protection really quickly without anyone knowing.'

G. 'Absolutely!'

J. 'So here are some options, they're all symbolic:-

    * Imagine all your chakras points are represented by the end points of an umbrella. Now quickly shut the umbrella bringing all the end points of the umbrella closed tight into the solar plexus chakra of your stomach and cap it off with your usual closing down symbol, which for you is the submarine hatch.

    * Another protection symbol is a golden egg - like the Russian Faberge Eggs - they're very thick. So you can step into one of these golden eggs and bring the top down over you and clasp it shut to protect yourself.

    * The third choice is a bit flimsy for my liking but can be equally effective if you chose this, which is a gold sleeping bag. You step into the sleeping bag and zip it up completely with you inside so, once again, you are protected.

All these three can be done mentally and in a jiffy and can be used in cases of 'emergency'. You ask your guides, 'Please protect me, NOW!' using your emergency protection symbol. So have a think and decide which one would work for you as your 'quick closing-down routine' and stick with that.'

G. 'Always remember the symbol at the end?'

J. 'No, you're thinking, I've got to close down now! You don't want to close down the long way which is going through all your chakras points with the gold liquid so you just think, I've got to close down quickly.

You already know which is your 'quick closing down symbol' for this so you mentally use it straight away whilst asking your guides for protection and to close you down; you're asking *and* doing at the same time. (To me, the sleeping bag option takes a bit longer.) So, that's a quick way to close down.

Now let's say you were really tired for some reason and needed reviving, this is a quick way to get energy:-

* Stand underneath a light or look out of the window at the sun and ask spirit to replace your energy.

Years ago, I used to get really tired at work so I would go into the toilet and look up at the ceiling light and ask spirit to replace my energy and then close down the quick way afterwards. I've always used the umbrella symbol myself. Looking at the sun is also a wonderful way to renew your energy.

You may already be in the garden or you can look up at the sun through a window. Stand and look at it whilst asking your guides, 'Please can you replace my energy.' I don't have to remind you to only do this in private otherwise people are going to think what the hell is she doing if you go and do this in the middle of a supermarket!

Right one more thing. You now close down at night and seal the top of your head with a golden cross and cloak yourself in protection, yes? There is going to come a time when you'll be working in your sleep because that is part of progress, part of development; you are probably already doing this but are unaware of it. You 'go home' every night just like everyone else - you remember, it's only our body which needs to rest - but it will get to a stage where you *know* you're working in your sleep.'

G. 'Is that astral flying?'

J. 'Astral travelling - no, not necessarily, so what you also need to do when closing down at night is to start asking for your energy to be replaced in the morning. What I usually do before going to bed at night is to say to spirit, 'If you want to use me tonight, please replace my energy in the morning.'

So to recap. When I close down at night, I also thank spirit for everything that's happened that day. I send out love and healing thoughts to anyone I want and I say to spirit, if you want to use me tonight, please replace my energy in the morning as invariably they will use me in my sleep. Then after that, I close down and finish by sealing the top of my head with a golden cross and cloaking myself in protection, so I'm covering all aspects; everything.

Everyone is just an energy so you have to respect that energy and this course is all about learning to use your energy more efficiently and more proficiently, yes? Our energy is the same as God's energy but a lot less, if you like! So it's all part of the growth, the development, the knowing who you are and learning to work with spirit and setting some good ground rules.

As I've said before Grace, you've just begun this. You're not expected to take it up and run with it straight away because I'll be repeating and repeating things.'

G. 'I'll forget things; I know I will.'

J. 'I'm in your shoes. I've been doing this a long time and my guides will also *ask me* to reiterate things as they know what it is you need reminding. It will come up in what you say, it will come up in what I say whilst I'm listening to my guides.

I'm now going to say that you're very fortunate that you're doing this course on your own. In another way, you're not so fortunate because you're not benefitting from group work which enables you to share and learn and benefit from other people and the experiences they have had. Again, it doesn't matter. This was the way it was always meant to be - me teaching you on your own.

So this is what we're going to do today. I told you that Month 1 'Attunement' is the most important aspect of the whole course and if you didn't learn anything else, this would be valuable to you.

I also said that attunement is the foundation upon which you're going to grow and because this is *so* important, I extend this subject to the second month as well to make sure that everything is watertight, to give you a chance to go over the material and to re-enforce the importance of attunement and the implications of using it in your life. It's very important that we get this right so, we continue on the subject of attunement.'

Attunement II

Jenny: 'All mediums, all healers, all people who want to help others, who want to serve, walk the same road and yet walk a different road. This may seem like a paradox but it is not. For you see with each person who takes up the challenge of service there is an army of guides and helpers behind them.

For each person who answers their own call which pours out from within their soul, is not alone. Each person has with him or her, those who have chosen to serve with them. Those guides and helpers have their own individual way of working so no two mediums, healers, carers, servants, call them what you will, will ever work exactly the same way.

No-one should say to you, you must work this way or it should be done like this or like that. You, as a developing medium, as an individual who is seeking to serve through developing mediumship; *you*, must forge a link with your guides and with your helpers from the spiritual realm.

They will teach you, *they* will show you the best way of working for you and for them. That is what attunement is all about. Not just sitting for development but attuning, finding the moment of peace to lift your thought and by lifting your thought, you lift your vibration.

In lifting your vibration, you reach out to meet those who work within the spiritual realms. They come close to you. Your vibration is refined. It is honed so that it blends peacefully, beautifully with the vibration of spirit. There should be no jarring, no distress. The coming of spirit within your vibration should be a gentle blending, a gentle melding. That is the purpose of attunement.

As you attune, as your helpers draw close, you become aware of their presence and aware of the things that they say to you. Now, how do you know that the words within your mind, the thought that comes, is spirit talking to you and not your own imagination or your own thought? How do you know that the picture that you see, that forms within your mind, is the picture that is sent by spirit and not the picture that you have imagined? How do you know?

Firstly, by trial and error. It is inevitable that when you start out upon this journey your thoughts will get muddled with those of spirit. Sometimes, the things you long to see, you will create and see. Sometimes it *is* your imagination.

Attunement enables you to calm the mind. You will never empty the mind but attunement enables you to calm the mind. You have to learn to trust the things that spirit send by telepathy, for it is in thought; it is mental mediumship. The things that spirit send by image and by word will be much stronger than your own thoughts. The thought sent by spirit is almost a shout within the mind. The picture 'drawn' by spirit is so detailed, so vivid, so strong that you can recall it to mind years after you have seen it - our own imagination fades. Your thoughts are muddled but when spirit talks through your mind, the mind is clear and the thoughts are fluent.

I said you have to learn to trust this. You will find that spirit will earn your trust. They will give you guidance and help that will prove accurate, true, strong and right for you.

Closing Down

It is irresponsible of you not to close down. Spirit protects you from the spiritual side of life, your job is to discipline your instrument on the physical side of life - your instrument refers to your body. Through that teamwork, spirit can then make you safe. Here is an example:-

> * If you go on holiday and ask the police to look after your house whilst you are away and then leave your doors and windows open, it makes the job of the police extremely difficult indeed, almost impossible. This is what happens when a medium or a sensitive refuses to take responsibility for closing themselves down.

When we ask spirit to close us down we visualise in the closing down process to give ourselves the re-assurance that it is done. It helps your discipline when your mind strays and starts thinking of spiritual matters.

It is also important to learn how to cleanse your aura for when you have a person who is 'open' all the time and has difficulty in closing down, their 'light' shines very brightly which attracts spiritual beings of all levels to it. Cleansing the aura through with gold 'liquid' whilst closing down, helps to push and repel away any spiritual entity of a lower vibration who may become attracted to the bright light of your aura and who wishes to draw close. Visualising and working in gold helps enormously in reflecting back any unwanted energy.

Also with healers who forget or who find it difficult to close down when they go out, they can take into their auras other people's backache, headaches, depressions, etc. and to cleanse the aura through with gold, again, repels those sensations. There have been people, including myself, who have been debilitated, who have thought they were seriously ill, simply because they were natural healers and couldn't close themselves down or didn't know how to cleanse their aura.

We have spirit to help us. However, there is a part that we are responsible for because we live within the earth's environment which is of a denser vibration than that of the spirit realms. There is a small space of energy which sits just outside our physical body which we are responsible for and which we have to always close down. You can never be 100% closed but you can be 95% and that helps spirit protect you.

Once you have control, you can face anything, do anything, go anywhere particularly when armed with the trust of spirit behind you but if you have no control over your instrument, then you *do* have a problem. You only have to look in our mental hospitals where on average, 75% of schizophrenics cannot control their instrument.

This form of spiritual work, development, mediumship, service, whatever form it takes - you don't have to be a medium to serve - demands commitment and discipline. It is not something done lightly. It is not something one does one week and then not for the next two or three.

To develop the psychic instrument, maybe to progress into mediumship, to eventually sit in a circle, demands discipline, demands commitment. No-one ever achieved anything without it. You only have to look at athletes or musicians to see how disciplined and committed they are to becoming the best at what they do.

Development

Development in attunement happens automatically but you do not work, you do not practice, you do not dictate. Spirit look after you and refine your vibration. They take charge of your development. All you have to do is to make yourself available.

During that time of attunement you will be uplifted, you will be taught, thoughts will come across your mind. You will think they are yours. Gradually you will begin to understand that it is your guide, your helper using thought communication to talk to you. You do not need to try and talk back, just listen to what is being said.

For others words are not important. Somehow you will absorb the knowledge and a question that was weighing heavily upon your heart when you sat to attune will get answered, not necessarily by words but by a knowing. You will have absorbed the knowledge.

Spirit works in different ways so do not limit them, expect the unexpected. Do not go into your mediumship or development with a fixed idea of what you want, how you want it or where you want to go with it. Sit, attune and give yourself over. Allow spirit to teach, allow spirit to lead. It is not in their interest to lead you astray. Remember, they are the other half of the partnership and have to achieve and fulfil their half of the bargain but only with your help can *they* succeed.

I feel there are a couple of explanations to add now. From the workshop you will remember I explained how we all come back to fulfil the purpose of our incarnation. We have already agreed with our friends and guides in spirit why we are returning and our life here gives us the opportunity to achieve all that we said. However, when people here find themselves interested in the spiritual, they may already have a fixed idea where they want to go, what they want to be and therefore may ignore the inner voices that are trying to lead them.

A medium may be gifted but unless they follow their conscience and the guidance they are being given, they may, in fact, come to a complete halt. Many mediums on church platforms, for example, may never progress. They see platform work as the pinnacle of their career when, in fact, they may well have agreed to another spiritual vocation. Attunement allows your guides to guide so you always know you are on the right path.

There is another point I would like to reiterate. People think their guides are exclusive to them when, in fact, we share guides and they may have also given up other personal benefits to be with you. In being the other half of the relationship, they are not just walking with you to help *you* achieve but they also have their own remit as well. In other words, your achievement is also theirs! It's just another incentive knowing that you are achieving things together. Life is never a one-sided opportunity.

You need patience and trust with spiritual development. You cannot be developed overnight. This has to be set out at intervals. You may find you are developing beautifully, then suddenly everything stops, there is nothing, everything has gone quiet. Do not panic. It simply means you have reached a plateau and everything is now being settled, consolidated and harmonised, then you will move on again.

The different rates of development are important. They are carefully judged by those in spirit who work with you. If you push and demand and seek to run faster than you should, you can, in fact, harm your development and eventually you will just come to a full stop and develop no further. Again, trust those who work with you.

When your guides ask you to slow down, rest or take time out, understand they do this to help you. This is a 'famous last words' where if you push it, you'll break it. Always remember - balance is the key. If you work really hard, you need to have an equal amount of rest or you'll burn yourself out; it's really just common sense.

Believe me, your guides are just as anxious as you for you to complete the development so that you may get on with the tasks ahead of you but everything has an order and a time scale; which is another paradox because you know, *"There is no such thing as time in spirit but spirit's time is perfect."*

Development can be tiring because vibrations are being adjusted and when vibrations are being adjusted and harmonised, everything is a little out of kilter and so mediums may feel tired and developing mediums may go through periods of great fatique.

So Grace, is there anything you would like me to go over, reiterate, or explain a bit more?'

Grace: 'No.'

J. 'So what we've done today is to give you some extra tools:-

* Sealing the top of your head with a golden cross and cloaking you in protection at night and asking spirit to replace your energy in the morning.

* Giving you quick ways to close down.

* Giving you quick ways to get energy.

So now sit back, relax, close your eyes because we're going to go on a little journey.'

Meditation 3.

Jenny: 'Think of a beautiful bright light all around you. In front of you is a road. It is a white road and dusty. I want you to walk along this road.

In the distance you can hear the sound of a waterfall. It is a beautiful sound. It calls to you. Walk towards the sound. In the distance you can now see the spray and the light dancing upon the water. Walk towards the waterfall. When you get there, step into it and allow the water to flow over you. Crystal clear, sparkling water cleansing all the dross of the everyday world from you. Enjoy the coolness, enjoy its brilliance. It is refreshing and invigorating.

It's now time to step out from under its flow. You notice you are not in the least bit wet! You shake off the drops which are like little crystals dancing in the sun. You feel the invigoration, you feel the upliftment and nothing discomforts you.

On the opposite side of the road there is a little table. On the table is a ewer and a goblet. The jug is filled with beautiful crystal water. Pour some water into your goblet and drink so that your inside is cleansed as well as the outside. Feel the coolness slacking your thirst. Now drain the goblet of water - this is the water of life.

Replace the goblet on the table and continue walking along your road and in front of you, you see a cave. It is a crystal cave. Walk into the cave. Oh, it is so beautiful, it is like a rainbow. A myriad of colours are in front of you but one colour predominates. It is an important colour for you. It is so irridescent, beautiful and shining. Although the crystals are coloured, they are not opaque, they are light, shining, beautiful colours of light.

Walk through the cave. You are now walking upwards. The crystal colours become golden in light the higher you climb. You come out onto a surface of a hill. Although a great landscape is before you, you stare at the continuation of a golden pillar of light. It comes up from the cave you have just climbed. Like an eagle you are borne up by this light. You are lifted and you fly higher and higher and higher. The light fans out into white and gold - beautiful, shining colours of light.

You are now aware of a person. You do not say anything, there is no need. You know this person and the person knows you. The bond between you is great. You take their hands and you stand joined in love and in light. Enjoy the communion, enjoy the love.

The fan of light now closes. You are again contained within the pillar of light. The person slowly, slowly fades from view although you know they are still there. You come slowly back down through the pillar of light. Down, down, down, down underneath the ground.

Walk back along the golden crystal road into the cavern. Back to the cavern of your crystal colour, still shining and beautiful. Come out of the cave and walk back along the road, passed the waterfall, passed the table with the jug and goblet.

In front of you there is a wall. In the wall there is a door. Go through the door. Close it behind you. You are home.

Grace, when you are ready, you may open your eyes.'

Month 3

"Suffering is part of the path, reveals many truths and is part of evolution."

Jenny: 'So, welcome back Bobbie.'

Bobbie: 'Thank you.'

J. 'Do you remember what we do before we start each session? We light our lamps before we begin. Do you remember what light you chose for this?'

B. 'Yes, a coach lamp.'

J. 'That's right. So what we're going to do, to start proceedings, is to close our eyes and then you visualise your coach lamp, lit, above your head and I myself use a candle flame and spirit know that we're going to start a session and that we're 'open for business'. They draw close to the light and when you've got your coach lamp lit, open your eyes and we can start. Great, so how have you been?'

B. 'Fine. Yesterday wasn't a good day. I didn't even write things down because I had a sore throat, a cough and I was trying to attune and I was cough, cough, coughing, so...'

J. 'So spirit were saying, don't bother!'

B. 'Yes, so I gave up the ghost!'

J. 'So you've had your first couple of weeks where you've been doing your attunements with your eyes closed. Has it been better?'

B. 'Yes!' (Bobbie laughs).

J. 'Good. I'll never forget you Bobbie. You're the only person who has ever done this course or started doing their attunements with their eyes open!' (We're both laughing).

B. 'In actual fact, I found it more difficult to begin with!'

J. 'I bet you did because you got yourself into the discipline but did you manage in the end?'

B. 'Yes.'

J. 'And really, it's almost as though if you do this the hardest way first anything else should be easy. So let's have a listen to your attunements.'

B. 'In my attunement this morning, my first one with my eyes closed, in my head I thought, this is like starting all over again from the beginning. Then in my head I heard, 'This is not a bad thing, you must learn to walk before you can run, have patience.' So I believe spirit is teaching me to have patience. I do tend to want things done, like yesterday so thank you spirit for pointing this out to me and I look forward to my next sitting.'

J. 'May I ask you how long that attunement was?'

B. 'Half an hour, they're all dead on half an hour and I know when I'm finished because I suddenly take a deep breath.'

J. 'Oh lovely and that means you're done, you're cooked! (We both laugh). Go on.'

B. 'Today in attunement I saw these white steps and pillars either side. I went up the steps into a room which seemed to be full of paintings but I was drawn to one in particular. It was of a lady in either a red or orange robe, I think it was red, with a child. Then I heard the word renaissance, then it was gone.

Then I thought of the word kleptomania! I have no idea what all that meant maybe it was my imagination, maybe not. We will find out, no doubt. Looking forward to my next time with spirit.'

J. 'OK, so what do you gauge from that attunement?'

B. 'I have no idea!'

J. 'Do you know what renaissance means?'

B. 'Yes, it's a type of painting, isn't it?'

J. 'No, not exactly it's usually connected with a period of revival but I am getting re-birth.'

B. 'Oh right!'

J. 'So, if you relate that to you. What I want you to learn is how to read what you're being given because I can't be with you always and the more I share things with you, the more you'll start to link in what these words and images are telling you. You're obviously clear about what is being said through your clairaudience but what is harder is trying to understand what the symbols and the pictures mean and that comes with relationship-building.

So if you hear a word, then look it up because we don't know the meaning of everything. So, to me, renaissance for you means a re-birth or reviving a previous situation and the place you found yourself in with the pillars, etc, was very regal, yes? And you also saw a picture of the Mother and Child, didn't you, which was the birth.'

B. 'Right, yes!'

J. 'And he was the King, he was looked upon then as a King. So you get the regal area you found yourself in with the pillars and the grand paintings. You were led to the picture of a re-birth and not just any re-birth, it was a special re-birth and I think that attunement was saying to you that you're not just anybody. You are special and you should understand that and spirit think that you're special - that's the way they see you - and finally, that you are also beginning something really special too!

I think the kleptomania thing was a floating thought but it is an example and a reminder that some of your thoughts come directly from spirit and some are from you and you need to learn to tell the difference especially since you want to grow spiritually. If you look at your past notes, this is explained.

This word popping in could also be contributing to your earlier attunement when you were told to be patient. I may be wrong but I feel that physically, you're fine but mentally you need to slow down a bit. Am I right?'

B. 'Yes.'

J. 'It's in your head. I think this is what spirit are saying. 'Starting again is no bad thing, you're going to be re-born again, you're somebody special, let's take our time with this, there's no hurry.' It's like the breathing. When you do your breathing, do your breathing nice and slow and calm yourself right down.'

B. 'I do feel, as soon as I start breathing, I start getting hot, I get really hot.'

J. 'Good, because that's one of the questions I wanted to ask you, what you felt in your attunement? Are there any areas you can pinpoint exactly which change?'

B. 'It starts from my feet and goes right up.'

J. 'Lovely, excellent, that good because you've got your feet on the ground so you're connecting with your earthly energies as well. That's brilliant, that's good to hear. OK, so you understand a little bit more about that attunement?'

B. 'Yes. Today my attunement seems much more intense. The feelings were more intense. I seem to be in a study and there was a man writing at a desk. He was in a white or cream outfit with gold embroidery and he was wearing a white wig. It was obviously a period in the past and I felt I was a young woman, perhaps 17 or 18.

The man was my father and my name was Elizabeth. He told me he had discussed my future with mama and they had found someone they felt was a suitable match for me. He then rang a bell that was on his desk and a gentleman came in. This man took my hand and said that he had been given permission from my father to ask me to accompany him to the Hunt's Ball. He was older but seemed pleasant enough.

The feelings I got from Elizabeth was acceptance and then I seemed to speed backwards and I was back sat in my chair. It was a strange experience. I don't know what it meant if anything, maybe Jenny can explain it to me. I look forward to my next sitting with spirit.'

J. 'That's nice.'

B. 'The main word there was acceptance.'

J. 'Yes, but I also think that this was an example of your 'gifts'. It was an example of the relationship you already have with your spirit guides that you can just *be* and be taken. When you're in attunement, you just forget everything which is why I teach you to go blank. Let spirit guide, let spirit lead. You know in my prayer I say, "Please lead so I can follow" so you just let them take over, they're teaching you.

You need to progress and build this relationship with them so you must give them the best possible conditions to do this. The more quiet you are, the more 'nothingness' there is, the more opportunity they have to communicate with you.

In the past, I have taught loads of people and when some of them were in attunement they would say, 'God bless my mum, God bless my dad, God bless my cat, please make sure.....' and I would say, for goodness sake, shut up! (Bobbie laughs). How can your guides come through if you're constantly talking, they can't get a word in edge ways you're so busy praying or asking, yes?

And attunement is when you find yourself at one with spirit and you can only do that in the silence, in the blankness, in the 'nothingness'. So you having this sort of regression type attunement and visit, I think it was all about acceptance as you say but I want to throw that word right open. Accepting *everything* in your life. Go beyond what we're doing.

I think spirit may be talking about accepting the whole journey and your past journeys because you got a glimpse into your past and I think they are using that to teach you about the present, yes?

But to me they were also showing you, look what you can do? Again, it's to do with being special - you have this ability, if you work with your spirit guides.

The other thing you'll come to understand is that spirit never say just *one* thing, they will say lots of things by saying or showing you just one thing. The best way I can demonstrate what I mean is when you look at a tarot card. It's one picture but it tells you *so* many things, there are so many meanings in the one card.

The tarot card might say, Vitality or Peace and you're just staring at the card but no, if you look over here, they are talking about this, over there, they are talking about that. And, oh, do you see what's she's wearing and what does that mean? Do you see what I'm saying?

Spirit want you to open your eyes in order to understand and appreciate the fullness of their communication, are you with me? And this all takes practice so the more attunements you have, the more you learn how your guides are communicating with you. It's about starting again just as the first attunement was.

But on the other hand it won't be too difficult because you've been with them and they've been with you for so long but it's all been under the surface. Now they are showing their true selves, it's now all above ground.'

B. 'Yes, I understand, thank you. This morning my attunement was tremendous. As soon as I started to take my deep breath I felt the heat, it just got hotter and hotter then as I got further into the attunement, I just felt as if I was getting taller and taller. I knew I was a man. This lasted for a while but I didn't find out what it was about.

Then I remember asking who my guide was that was with me always? I then saw this bright light and it seemed to get brighter and brighter and the next thing was, Jesus was there. He said he was always with me but I knew this as I had known this since I was very young. He then said it was time to leave. Then I opened my eyes and it was exactly half an hour. I felt so humble and blessed and I look forward to my next attunement.'

J. 'Well this is the second time you've had the Nazarene in your attunement and as you say, this goes back to your childhood. Are you able to share with me a bit of that childhood?'

B. 'I just felt He was always there. I went to Sunday school and obviously we learnt about Jesus but I felt I knew him anyway. It just seemed when they were talking and saying different things about him, I just felt, yes, I know that.'

J. 'There were no surprises. It was like confirmation of what you already knew even though you were a child?'

B. 'Yes, exactly and I always felt really used to Him. I've always said he's my friend.'

J. 'Have there been any incidences in your life where He's 'popped up'?'

B. 'Not that I can remember. I've always talked about Him. My mother used to say I was fanciful, stop daydreaming! I got that from my school as well, 'Barbara could achieve much more if she didn't daydream so much!' But to me some of the daydreams weren't daydreams anyway, they were real.'

J. 'So when you read bits and pieces in *A Medium's* Tale', where I discuss my past, you must have understood and connected? It's not something you consciously think about or expect; it's just there.'

B. 'Well to be honest, I was thinking of White Eagle and I thought it was White Eagle so I was surprised.'

J. 'So that really doesn't need explaining does it? Apart from the fact that I'm delighted you recorded what you felt in your attunement. Things like getting taller which is good as I like to know as much as possible so I can see what is happening to you so I can help you better. So the fact that I now know that you also get a sensation during your breathing is actually 'cool' as I've always had the same!

If there are any feelings which you get regularly, especially on the onset of your attunement, I'd like to hear about it as there may be something new that's going to be coming through.

I also want to take this opportunity to ask you to remember to write these things down. In my attunement, I am starting to feel this, or I am starting to get this, alright?'

B. 'Yes. This morning's attunement was very interesting. As soon as I started my deep breaths the heat started again but also at the same time, I felt tingling all over but most obviously in my hands and feet. I began to get the same feeling of growing much taller and broader. I could even feel my hands were not fat but much longer with long fingers.

I knew I was a man but felt a feeling of real gentleness. I could also feel facial hair. Then I became myself again and Jesus again stepped forward and told me, 'This is how we would work together for healing purposes.' He asked if I was comfortable working this way which I said yes, I was fine with it. He then said that when I was ready to begin healing on someone just to ask him to step forward to work with me and through me, it was that simple. I look forward to my next sitting.'

J. 'Ah, now that is interesting because you're getting exactly the same as me, the tingling in the hands and feet. Now, the man that you *feel,* I think, is the guide who is working with you, yes? I think you are that near to them, that you are taking on his personification which is the way it should be.

I believe, personally, that a gentleman guide is going to come - it's not always going to be the Nazarene - it's almost as though He knows how safe you feel with him so *he* wants to start the proceedings.'

B. 'OK and pave the way?'

J. 'Yes. Spirit always think of the person they are working with and the best way to introduce a new spirit guide into someone's aura especially in the 'early days' of this course. Spirit also don't want to frighten anyone so, initially, they often bring someone through that you know and feel safe with. It can be a parent, an animal even the Nazarene - spirit know who we feel at ease with. I am talking generally here to help you understand how things are often done.

Personally, I feel that the Nazarene is presenting Himself to you at the outset and is, in effect, starting you off, so to speak because you trust him. He's someone you know and I think that the spirit guide you are going to be working with, who has been working with you and has been for ages, is a man and he is going to start to come foward. This is just my opinion.'

B. 'That makes sense actually, it does make sense. This morning's attunement was, I suppose you would call it practising. Getting used to Jesus coming in and leaving so I would become more comfortable with it, which is just what you've been saying! It is a strange experience but not unpleasant, just strange. I don't think it is my imagination as I feel so real. I hope Jenny can give me some insight into this. I really enjoy my time with spirit.'

J. 'And when you see Him, how much of him do you see; just his face or what he is wearing?'

B. 'Yes, what he is wearing.'

J. 'And is this always the same?'

B. 'Yes.'

J. 'And what is it?'

B. 'It's just a white robe and yes, he always looks the same.'

J. 'OK. Has anything happened during the night, are you sleeping differently?'

B. 'No, I'm still not sleeping very well.'

J. 'Do you do your closing down?'

B. 'Yes.'

J. 'Do you use any of the 'tools' I've given you, like asking to replace your energy?'

B. 'Yes, because I don't feel so tired when I get up in the morning.'

J. 'Good, so that's proof, isn't it and the closing down?'

B. 'Yes, I ask them to place the cross and I can see it and I can feel the cloak.'

J. 'What material cloak have you chosen?'

B. 'Gold lame'.'

J. '*Gold lame*', very poash!'

B. 'Very poash, (Bobbie laughs) yes, but I love gold lame', I love all the lame' actually.'

J. 'Brilliant. What about in your life Bobbie because you know that this course is to do with everything and anything about you from now on?'

B. 'Yes. I went to church Sunday and I sat in church and funnily enough the reading was talking about Jesus and the medium said, I don't believe everything that's in the Bible but I believe in his philosophy and all the rest of it. He went on and on and what he could have said in ten sentences, it just dragged on and on and it must have been for about 20 minutes. He was saying the same things in a different way and I thought, you're losing people, they're getting bored and he was losing the message.'

J. 'It was diluting the message.'

B. 'It was. He was rambling on and I sat there and I thought, 'Why am I here?''

J. 'You keep saying this Bobbie. I just wondered whether - look I'm not telling you how to suck eggs - but I wondered whether you should meet your friend in a cafe rather than at church?'

B. 'Well, I have been thinking this a lot because I'm not really getting anything; I don't feel the need to go to church.'

J. 'No, you've been saying that for a while. I'm not surprised because this course heightens individuality. It makes you think about what's important. It makes you think about yourself and the way you want to go, who you want to be, what direction you want to follow?

I think what's happening to you is all 'par for the course' and I think, if I may say so, I think you are being tested. For example, 'You keep thinking it Bobbie, why don't you *do* it!'

B. 'Yes.'

J. 'You have to walk the talk so to speak otherwise you're not progressing.'

B. 'Exactly. It's being a hypocrite really.'

J. Yes a bit but it's up to you. I think you're being encouraged to be true to yourself and this is just one more reminder. So you'll have to decide what you are going to do? What about your home life?'

B. 'Well my husband has been poorly so it's been quite difficult.'

J. 'How have you been, yourself?'

B. 'Yes, I feel relaxed, things don't get me down so much now and I feel more serene and able to cope with whatever life throws at me really.'

J. 'Good, so you're getting strength and a bit more confident?'

B. 'Yes.'

J. 'Excellent, that's definitely a hallmark of this course. It's what I'm expecting to hear because you are going to change. From the minute you started this course you will never be the same Bobbie again. All learning changes you.

You can't unlearn, you can't say I didn't hear it, I haven't felt it, I haven't experienced it. It's like the tape recorder scenario. It's just adding and adding to your life's experiences whether they're in attunement, in church, in the home or whether you're walking in the woods. What you are feeling, all these things are altering you as a person and your energy is changing because you can't experience this and stay the same, alright?'

B. 'Yes, yes I understand.'

J. 'Well today we move on to healing but before we do that, I just want to check a couple of things. When you do your attunements, you understand it's better done on an empty stomach?'

B. 'Yes.'

J. 'So are your attunements done relatively at the same time?'

B. 'Yes.'

J. 'So you have a good habit going, where you sit, etc. Again, if you're going to walk a spiritual path, I need to mention that smoking and drinking are going to hinder your way.'

B. 'Yes, I don't drink anyway.'

J. 'You still smoke?'

B. 'Yes, I know.'

J. 'Well you know I have to mention it and you have to make a decision what to do about that. (Bobbie agrees). And you're using the tools I've given you, 'Use me tonight' or 'Let me sleep tonight' - are you doing that?'

B. 'Yes.'

J. 'If you're allowing spirit to work with you at night, meaning if you're *not* saying - 'Don't work with me, I want to sleep' - then you are going to experience things at night which will be for your higher good as experiences are always the ones spirit want you to have.

So we're going to talk about healing today.'

Healing

Jenny: 'Healing is one of the highest forms of mediumship. It demands total commitment.

The healer very often does not see the results of his mediumship and is unaware of what they have achieved.

Sometimes things are not what they seem. A healer might feel so successful that he or she has done well but, in fact, it is not regarded by spirit as being a success and sometimes, when a healer feels he has not achieved, not brought relief, spirit look and they see the greatest of achievement.

We have the example of a 'healer' at a hospital bedside giving healing, maybe to a child. The parents are around but the child dies. How does the healer feel? He feels he has failed miserably. But the child came and achieved all they had to achieve and the healer brought peace, the healer brought serenity and surrounded the family in love and shared their sorrow and gave them hope. To spirit, that is the greatest of achievement.

A healer is a dedicated medium. The healer thinks not of himself but only of the receiver of his healing. A healer is a medium because the word 'medium' means to be between, in the middle - in the middle of two worlds.

Those of you who are healers chose to be so before you were born. Like all forms of mediumship, the choice was made in spirit between you and your spirit guides. You cannot *learn* to heal. You can be taught the necessary requirements within your material world. You can be given certificates for your own particular purposes, for insurance cover for instance. You can be taught the ethics of healing but you cannot learn *how* to heal. You are either a healer or you are not or to re-phrase this better, you are either a healing channel or you are not.

It is to do with the instrument, the psychic instrument that you have. What makes one violin produce a more beautiful sound than another? The way it is formed, the way it is balanced. This is all decided before you come here. Your instrument is formed for your use as a healing channel. It is attuned to the vibration of the healing that comes through from spirit.

All mediumship works on the vibration of spirit and healing is no different. It is the vibration of energy that comes through to the recipient. The body, the psychic instrument, is formed and fashioned in such a manner that those healing energies may flow freely, unobstructed through to the recipient. Healers are born they are not made.

"If I cannot learn to be a healer what do I do?" Nothing! You attune. You sit in attunement. You lift your vibration, you blend with the spiritual guides and helpers that surround you. The more you attune, the more that vibration is blended, the more it becomes as one. You do nothing. It is spirit who works through you. It is spirit who channels that healing energy through you who really does the work.

The greatest healers are the ones who do nothing. The greatest healers are the ones who say, "Here I am, use me."

All spirit require is someone who presents themselves as an open channel, in love, in humility and with the desire to serve and those who do *that*, are capable of the greatest healing. You do not need all these extra bits and pieces to help you get healing energy.

All you need is trust. Trust the Power of Spirit because it comes from the Power of God for the healing energies that flow through are channelled from the Great Spirit Himself. The healer is part of the transformer. The energies are brought down and the vibrational energy adjusted so that it can flow through you and into the recipient. You need do nothing but attune and trust.

Healing one to one is better than distant healing. Sometimes with distant or absent healing, the person to whom the healing is being sent is antagonistic and that can make things very difficult because you are trying to break through a negative boundary. However, when a person is consciously or unconsciously willing or is accepting, then the healing is strong but spirit have to work a little harder to refine the energies through the 'transformer' in absent healing.

Many mediums heal the soul because 'love' is a healing vibration. Spirit can calm, they can bring a sense of peace without that person necessarily understanding why. Think? If you walk into a room, sometimes there is a sense of serenity within the room because it has been used for healing, or for circle, or for teaching but you can feel that serenity and it calms you down. That peace and calm is essential to healing.

The patient may not wish to share with you the depth or the hurt of their problems but spirit know. If you trust as you give healing, the peace, calm and serenity will be given and maybe in that light, the patient then feels they can talk.

Like with all spiritual work or attunement, you cannot rush and give healing. You must prepare yourself first, give yourself a chance to relax and be still in order to attune for healing. If you are with someone, wait a little, sit together, maybe in prayer or talk quietly to settle and bring about a feeling of calm.

If there is a problem in the workplace, for example, just send a little message to spirit saying, "Friends, help with this one please." Remember to close down afterwards. If the situation continues, then you can set a time and a place when the healing can be given. As with any mediumship, the conditions of work are important; we are talking about protection here.

It is better to give the healing within the home or the church so that the environment is conducive. Using spiritual energies in a public place is irresponsible and can cause problems. Healers must protect and safeguard their spiritual instrument for the physical effects of an undisciplined healer can be quite dreadful.

If you are walking a spiritual road then your healing ability will come through your attunement which will be refined. You will be able to sit with patient after patient and you should feel no fatigue and, if anything, perhaps a little refreshed for a little healing will always be left for you.

One more thing, healing is a gift from a Father to his children. Do not charge for what is given freely. What is freely given, freely give. Heal in love, heal in humility and you will find the fruits of your mediumship wondrous indeed.

This is just one of the pieces I am going to give you today. I am also going to give you two other papers to take home. One is a synopsis on healing which I wrote years ago and the other is a talk I gave on healing so you have three pieces here.

I also want to let you know that at the end of this course we will have a 'Question and Answer' session. I would like you to divide these questions into two types. The ones you need answers to straight away - the ones which may be holding you back in the course - and others which are of a more general nature and which can be asked later on.

So perhaps you would like to make a page at the back of your notebook for any questions which crop up for our future questions and answer session. OK?

So here are the three papers for you to read.'

Bobbie: 'I look forward to reading those.'

J. 'Have you any questions about what we've been doing so far, any queries, any questions about yourself?'

B. 'No, you've answered them! You've answered them as we've been going along.'

J. 'OK. Good. I think that's it Bobbie!'

B. 'That's brilliant, thank you. I've really enjoyed this morning.'

J. 'Good.'

Healing Synopsis

The object of healing is a very simple one; it is to touch the soul. So success in healing is determined by whether the recipient's soul has been stirred, has been moved, has been awakened. Without this lodgement, if there is only physical healing then the healing must be deemed a failure.

You have not failed. You have done your best but the patient may have missed an opportunity so shed a silent tear with spirit.

All gifts of the spirit, including healing, should be exercised to create an awareness of the divinity each person possesses so they become aware of the purpose of their earthly incarnation. This is the whole object behind every phase of mediumship.

Divine Power is available to those who are ready to receive it. Spirit's directives are to create awareness within individuals of who they *really* are and what they must do to fulfil their purpose; *"Spirit want us to know our spiritual origin so that we can achieve our spiritual destiny."*

The gift of healing is part of one of the faculties that lie within the spirit body. To be a healer you have to be accessible to the power of the spirit. Spirit Power which is from the Great Spirit - the life force, the dynamic, the vitality, the consciousness, the animation - will stream wherever it can find channels. All you can do, if you have the gift of receptivity, is to develop it by achieving a greater attainment and attunement. The power is infinite.

The amount you can receive depends upon your stage of evolution and development so your receptivity determines the limit of Spirit Power that flows through you. If you increase your capacity to receive, then greater spiritual power will flow through you and greater results will be obtained.

The cause of all sickness, illness and disease is disharmony. Health is when there is the right rhythm and balance between body, mind and spirit. Nearly all illness begins in the mind and the spirit, even accidents can have a mental and spiritual origin. So you, the healer receive Spirit Power which flows to the spirit; the consciousness of the patient. You are the battery, the stimulator; you re-charge the vitality that has been depleted. You clear the blockage, you get rid of the impediment and restore the balance. The rhythm is now in concert and harmony again.

The healing succeeds because you touched the spirit - their spirit - this is the vital point. It is not putting your hands on, near or around the body that does anything. This is only a means of contact which may or may not be necessary depending on the stage of attunement you have reached. However, your aim is to touch their spirit, to quicken it, to awaken the slumbering, dormant spirit so it begins expression which was always intended for it by the Natural Law, *and*, if you do that, then all the natural, self-recuperating processes of the body get to work and health begins to result.

You have performed your function because you have opened the channel for God, the Great Spirit, to flow through you and touch the God, the Great Spirit within the sufferer and brought him or her to an awareness; maybe for the first time.

This is what is involved in spiritual healing and therefore you have a great responsibility. You cannot have knowledge without the responsibility that knowledge brings. You cannot have a divine gift without the responsibility of seeing that you use it in the way that it is intended.

There is a difference between psychic faculties and spiritual gifts. You can be a psychic healer or a spiritual one. With the latter you have to order your life aright to achieve the highest ideal that is possible. You may have the gift but its unfoldment is your responsibility. The way you use it is your responsibility too because the possession of the gift makes you one of the ambassadors of the Great Spirit.

You are more a minister of the Great Spirit than any minister of any church or chapel. You are representing the Great Spirit because the Divine Power is flowing through you and that is a great responsibility. You must not sully it, you must not tarnish it, you must not dishonour it, corrupt it or attempt to use it for the wrong motives. You must only have the desire to serve and to reach out to the highest possible.

Spirit Power is the life force itself so describing how this power is created is very difficult as we are trying to describe non-material forces. It is infinite, animated, malleable and can take a myriad of shapes and be capable of an infinite number of permutations and combinations.

In spirit, they have the equivalent of our scientists, doctors and chemists forever blending aspects of this life force. To characterise it, always experimenting so it may be conditioned to the greatest possible extent through the instrument - the channel - whilst bearing in mind the nature of the complaint or ailment which is to receive the healing. It is an individual process for every sufferer who comes to the healer.

The aura of the patient will help these 'scientists, doctors and chemists' greatly because it will give a perfect picture of their mental and spiritual conditions which are responsible for the ailment in the first place which then determines the necessary blending. It is like a blending of their mental energies with the equivalent of what we call 'chemicals' which determine the force produced. The mind is used in the spirit world as the mind is the reality of building everything.

Again, in absent healing, it is the thought that is real. The moment you send out a loving thought, that thought creates a vibration, a wavelength, a reality which is then used in all absent healing. You are like a television set. The spirit vibration comes to you and you transform it into the semi-physical healing ray to the patient. You are the transformer using your spirit body.

Once a link has been made for absent healing, it is not necessary for it to be made again. Every link with the world of spirit is a magnetic one. Once made, it cannot be broken. It does not matter where you are when you make this link. The world of spirit has no geographical location. It is around and about us all the time. You are no nearer the Great Spirit in church or in a pit or in an aeroplane.

The power of the spirit works best when you are bright and happy, cheerful and receptive not when you are miserable, doubting, wavering and disturbing the atmosphere around you.

When healing, it helps tremendously if you can mentally visualise an image of perfect health because your thought is a reality. The more you think of perfect health, the closer you come towards attaining it. You should always strive for the ideal. You should always visualise the best. Never abandon hope but always radiate cheer and optimism. These are the conditions in which Spirit Power produces its best results.

It does not matter whether the healer can see the aura neither does it matter whether the healer is able to diagnose, the object of the healer is to heal. He has to make himself accessible - to be as perfect an instrument as he possibly can. He has to outlaw from his nature all the weaknesses that prevent him from being the perfect instrument and the more he does that, the greater will be the power which flows through him.

It is the life you live that qualifies the attunement you can have.

You do not have to be a medium to be a healer. The gift of the spirit is the gift of the spirit. You are born with it and it is your responsibility to develop it just as a child born with the gift of playing the piano has to develop it by practice and training. How to develop this gift? It is not necessary to sit in a circle - it may help.

It is developed by your motives and by the way you live your life. It is developed by the attempt to reach the highest standard of purity and perfection that is possible. It is helped by increasing your desire to heal as much as you possibly can.

The only way to develop self is to forget self. The more you think of others the better self you will become. There is no book that will tell you how to become a better healer. What you have to do is to desire to serve and order your life in this fashion. *"The Great Spirit has endowed me with a gift of healing. May I be worthy of it."* If you live your life according to that principle, the gift will automatically increase in its strength and stature.

You also do not need to depend on another healer to help you when you are ill. You can learn how to attune yourself to the healing power so that it can produce the result on you direct.

Just as you do not have to go to church to pray to the Great Spirit so you do not have to go to a healer to get healing for yourself if you can enable the power of the spirit to come direct to you. You must open your heart, your mind and your soul.

Worry and fear are negative forces which will lead to illness sooner or later. The soul that worries is out of harmony already. If your mind, body and spirit are in the right relationship, you do not have worries. Anyone who has knowledge of spiritual realities should not worry. There is nothing to worry about once you know you are an eternal being and nothing in the physical world can touch your soul.

There is no such thing as an incurable disease - every disease can be cured - there are only people who could be incurable. Healing is not as simple as it appears. It is not a question of just healing the physical ailment. There are other qualifications because there are laws within laws within laws that involve other and more profound issues. For example, there are soul qualities that have to be measured. What is the effect on the soul? What is the purpose? Why does the patient go to the healer? Has that patient reached the stage of spiritual evolution when his spirit can be awakened?

These are matters you cannot measure with your material yardstick but they are all involved in healing. Because you are handling the life force itself, for the time being you are partaking in the process of infinite creation which is why it is such a great responsibility.

Where the illness is capable of being healed and the results are not obtained, that patient has possibly not earned the spiritual right to be healed. This is in no way suggesting they are bad. You have to remember that you are not necessarily looking at the problem with the eyes of the spirit.

To us here on earth, suffering is terrible but to spirit, suffering can be divine. To us, disaster is the end but to spirit, it is sometimes the beginning of a new life. Therefore, earning the spiritual right to be healed has nothing to do with being a good or bad person but is based on a collective number of factors along the soul's spiritual path.

How long a healer takes working on their patient is irrelevant. *"By our fruits ye shall know us."* It is the results that matter. The healer should so live his life that he attains the greatest pitch of attunement, then the results will come.

Put your own house in order and spirit will do the rest. No call for help is ever refused. No power is ever withheld. Spirit always strives to serve. They refuse none and welcome all. The power of the spirit is there for all to receive its benefits. All they want are willing instruments to help its divine flow.

Finally, remember where physical or absent healing is followed by the patient's passing, it may be the greatest success you have achieved. If you have helped a soul in its passing, that is successful healing.

The object of healing is not to prolong physical life but to touch the spirit; that is what matters. Passing into the spirit world is not a tragedy. Remember, *"You may weep but we rejoice, a friend is coming home."*

Spirit healing is here to stay. It will not be dislodged. You can contribute your quota and a very important quota too. Let the power flow through you. Those you cannot help by contact, send them absent healing.

Always remember that you are a divine channel helping the Great Spirit in the infinite plan of evolution. It is wonderful work that you have to do but it is also a great responsibility.

Healing: 'A Talk'

When we think of healing, we think of hands, healing hands but if you think about it again, healing comes from the heart, the soul, the mind and from the healing guides who walk and work with us.

Healing is massive. I would like to fling the subject of 'healing' wide open to explain different aspects of healing and what it can mean to different people at different times in their lives.

To most people and quite understandably, healing means, 'making me better' and yes, of course, that is what the purpose of healing is. However, these people are referring to their physical body but, in the spirit world, from whence we come and to where we return, they have other ideas and views on this.

That is why we have to look at the question, "Why are we here?" If you agree with me that we are here to learn, then healing, is one avenue through which we can achieve this knowledge. Through the experience of healing, it will teach us some important lessons.

The first step, of course, is for people to actually ask or go for healing and for that, they are to be congratulated. They have just put themselves on the first step to health but again, I am not just talking about physical well-being here.

If we take the premise that we are all on a journey then asking or going for healing is a massive step in the right direction on our journey. Why?

To me, this comes back to our spiritual guides, those who walk with us, those who are trying to help us fulfil the purpose of our incarnation here on earth. Those who are trying to guide us on our pathway - now do a right at this crossroads, then turn left, etc. We all have a path and we all have crossroads in our lives. I am sure you have all felt this 'crossroads period' yourself and maybe even had more than one?

Your spirit guides know where this next path will lead. Who or what is further along your road for you to experience or for you to meet. *"All is for your higher good"* but taking that first step is essential, vital and of massive importance. You see, the experience of healing may not *just* be the *first* step but where this will lead and to whom it will lead.

The subject of healing is also a controversial one.

I run parallels with a spiritual person who doesn't believe or accept reincarnation or even people who think all women can have children. The *'right'* to be healed, I'm sorry, but not everyone has.

Some healers will assume their healing role in an almost 'fairy-tale' way; that all healing has a happy ending. All true healing *is* positive, believe you me, but it might not have the effect that you thought.

This brings us back to spiritual philosophy. For example, you may have a really lovely person who you want to help. They are not only lovely on the outside, they're also lovely 'inside' too, they're almost a saint in some people's eyes - too good to be true - and if anyone deserves healing and a positive outcome, they do.

But the healing doesn't 'work' and they continue to suffer much to their healer's utter dismay and astonishment.

So we need to look at suffering, don't we?

One of my earliest recollections as a child was me saying, 'We're not here to have a good time you know, it's bloody hard work.' However, it wasn't until many years later that I realised what this actually meant because we are all here to learn and if *"Experience is the greatest teacher"* we therefore have to *experience* as much as possible in order to learn, I mean *really* learn something.

A vast majority of these *experiences* involve suffering whether it be emotional, mental, physical, psychological and if, like me, you understand that we have already agreed why we're here, what we needed to come back to the earth plane to experience, learn and achieve then suffering - the experience - must *also* be part of the plan.

You're crazy! Why would anyone choose to suffer?

Because the spiritual benefits - what we experience in suffering - teaches us things we could never otherwise comprehend and our desire to progress spiritually, our desire to learn, understand and achieve all our spiritual goals, is surely paramount above all else. So this person, the one who was both lovely inside and out, had her own agenda to maintain and fulfil irrespective of the results of the healer's help *and* maybe, including the healer's help, but learning something unexpected from it nevertheless.

But all this in *no* way deflects the love, sincerity and desire of the healer to help, serve and heal this person. Even the healer will have learnt something too which, of course, was always the plan!

I have been told I am a natural healer. Apparently, I heal people just by talking to them. One of the most beautiful experiences I had was many years ago when I was interviewing a girl in my office and a blue ball of energy floated across the room right in front of me and then floated back again. *WOW!*, what was that?

I really had to control myself and not blurt out to this young lady what I had just seen. She did not register anything so I knew she had not seen it herself. I soon learnt that it was a message telling me that I was a healer and so I was *very* fortunate to have been given proof of this.

I can also recall having taken away a physical illness from two women in my life without the 'laying of hands'. Having already visited them, both had gone back to hospital to be told their symptoms had gone. The second time this happened, spirit told me beforehand that her symptoms were no longer there, so it was not a surprise when she told me herself but still a surprise that it was true!

On another note, think of the healing power of optimism and humour? Why do they say, "Laughter is the best medicine" so who do you think comedians are? They are healers to be sure. Think about it?

So why do people want to heal? Because they care, because they have empathy, because they want to make a difference, because they love their fellow man?

We are not healers *ourselves*, we are healers only by name. We cannot heal unless we call to that source and ask for it to be sent through us. As individuals, we are not healers, we are just a channel for healing - facilitators for the healing process.

If suffering is the experience, then pain, be it physical, mental or emotional or even spiritual, is the teaching. Through illness, we learn a multitude of different things. To me, ill health is one of the bastions of knowledge.

"Spirit are great opportunists" and through ill health we can learn so much not just about ourselves but from others, about others and about the world around us. Years ago I gave a doctor an opportunity to learn, achieve and grow just by refusing to go along with his initial plans to help me; which was a blanket solution for this particular problem. I wasn't conscious of what I was doing at the time but later, I saw the depth of my decision for both myself and for him. I encouraged him to go into unchartered waters - what would we all learn?

Healing can also be connecting with other positive energies. For example, you buy yourself flowers, you admire a plant, the sea air invigorates you, you love walking your dog in the woods, you smile at your cat sleeping peacefully by the fire, babies....ooooh! What do you think is happening here?

"All life is one life." Everything is spiritual energy. When you connect and embrace another living thing, be it the flowers in a vase, a plant in the garden, your cat sleeping or a cuddle with someone's dog or a baby, what is going on here, it's *love* isn't it?

Love is infinite and there is an infinite way of expressing it but it's *all* positive and it's *all* healing. It makes you happy, it makes you smile, it makes you feel good, it gives off an energy and that is the positive energy of love *and healing* - because that is what healing really is - just simply LOVING.

As I said earlier, I heal just by talking to people. It's nothing unique at all. How many of you have been speaking to someone who has a problem and they then say either to your face or maybe on the phone or even via email, 'I feel so much better now I've spoken to you!' *Why?*

Because they got it off their chest, possibly? Because they shared the load, maybe? Because you genuinely cared and empathised with them and you wanted to help? *Definitely!*

Like love, 'healing' can be hard. With healing you need to be firm, you need to be disciplined and healing can also be; being 'cruel to be kind'. Do you know, some of the best healing is saying *no* to someone because you know that will be the best 'medicine' for them?

Healing is also karmic. Those of you who have attended my workshops will remember me mentioning that many of the doctors working all over the world are unaware that they are fulfilling a karmic debt. Where in a previous incarnation they may have taken a life, they now need to redress the balance and help to prolong it - one of their reasons for returning to the earth plane - one of their raison d'etres. I believe my own deafness has connections to a karmic debt.

Healers are born, they are not made. But *everyone* is capable of the most wondrous healing. Hang on a minute! You just said that healers are born and not made and now you're saying we are *all* capable of healing? Yes, you *are!*

If you have children, do you love one more than the other? *No.* They are all given the same opportunities. Well, our Father loves us equally too and we are all given the same opportunities.

Yes, there are natural born healers whose strengths are rooted in this but we are all capable of giving healing, of giving love, aren't we?

Love - do you truly love? In order to be a good healer you have to practice. If you want to be a good artists or althlete, you have to practice, you have to train to be the best you can possibly be. Most people aspire to be the best at what they do but to be a good healer, to be the best you can possibly be, you also need to practice but *not* necessarily practice healing!

You have to practice with your *LIFE*.

Do you love? Of course I love! But do you know how to love to the best of your ability?

Love starts like everything else, in the mind. True love, like true compassion comes from pure thoughts. When I teach about love, I always compare the emotional with the spiritual; there is a big difference.

In order to be the best healer you possibly can and the best healing channel for spirit, you have to order your life aright by pure thinking and pure doing in order to allow pure energy to envelop you.

Love is all around. Appreciate what is around you because it is all living, all spiritual energy. We, as human beings, are just pure thought and as healers, we are therefore a channel for healing thought, healing energy. In order to be the best healer, you have to attract the best healing guides to work with you through your channel.

The law of *"Like attracts like"* works on healing just as with any other spiritual faculty. So the more you are pure of thought, the purer your healing will be as you will attract those pure healing thoughts via healing guides whose loving thoughts and spiritual energy are on a par with your own.

I am pretty basic when it comes to where the healing comes from. To me, it doesn't matter who you are, what methods you use, what you practice, healing is coming through your channel from your healing guides in spirit be they Japanese Reiki guides, North American Indian holy men, Aborigines or past doctors of medicine or the Great Spirit Himself. It's all from the same source - *love* - and our pure thoughts *are* pure love.

Also, what kind of healing works for people is not so much the methods employed but *who* is using those methods, *who* is giving and channelling it - the healer themselves - whether they practice acupuncture, reflexology, herbal medicine or Reiki, it makes no difference.

And then, there is the big issue......Is the recipient ready to receive it? Are they ready to be healed? Have they earnt it? *WHAT!*

Oh dear, am I ruining all this for you *or* am I making you think?

Not everybody has reached the stage in their lives where they are ready to be helped. You can't turn on the healing tap, it doesn't work like that. Is the recipient at a stage in their life's journey when the healing will 'work'? Is this patient really positive about this and about *you,* the healer, too? Have they learnt the lessons from their past and recent experiences?

I once knew a wonderful woman whom I used to visit regularly. Half of her life was battling with emphysema. I felt it was one of her life's lessons and maybe even a karmic debt. It got to the stage where each time I visited her she would ask for healing. I knew that I had already made the link with spirit when I first gave her healing but she constantly kept asking. I knew this was unnecessary as the healing link had been made but we all keep on requesting, don't we, and when you care about someone, you put them first.

The *experience* of healing is always necessary. They are being offered nourishment but is that enough and is it at the right time? Does the recipient understand what is happening here and are they at a stage in their illness and their lives where they have undergone enough experience and understanding to qualify for the experience of positive healing with a positive outcome?

And then there is the question....... what is *a positive outcome*? It is a collective issue we are dealing with here. Every experience allows you to learn so the more experiences you have, the more aware and learned you should be.

And what about trusting and believing in the healing?

The story of Jesus and the Roman centurion is a fantastic story of belief and trust. The centurion's trust was *so* implicit that he didn't even need the Nazarene to go to his house to heal his servant. He said, 'I know if you give the word it will be done.' *Wow!* What faith in someone and how much more positive can you be?

I did say the subject of healing was Massive!

Month 4

Jenny: 'OK Grace, get comfortable. We're now going to start our fourth session and, as usual, we're going to start by closing our eyes, lighting our lamps using the light you've chosen so our spirit guides know that we're 'open for business'. They can then draw close and watch over the proceedings. So when you've done that, open your eyes.

Remind me again please what light you use; what's your symbol?'

Grace: 'I have a round golden ball - a globe.'

J. 'OK, so I now need to know what's happened since I last saw you. Let's start with your attunements and then we'll go on to any other questions which I have to ask you so I can get a clear picture of what is happening with you.'

G. 'The last time we were together was at the beginning of August. This first attunement is in the early hours of the 8 August. I called it a visitation because it was too early to sit with spirit.'

J. 'Why do say it was too early to sit with spirit?'

G. 'It was the early hours and I wasn't in attunement, my eyes snapped open and the bedroom was in darkness. My head was turned towards my husband, if he was facing me or turned away, I could not tell. The room was very dark. What followed must have lasted seconds but as my eyes opened, I could see the head of a man supported by a long bendy neck between our pillows. He had slicked back hair, dark eyes and brows with a white face and neck. He smiled and began to wobble towards me.

My feeling was, this was not his first visit and the long neck reminded me of a snake. I did not like what I saw one bit. I let out a loud gasp and asked God to take him away so I could neither see him nor speak to him ever again.

He was gone in that instant. My husband spoke asking if I had been dreaming and I replied, yes, I had. Visiting the bathroom, I did not feel afraid just shocked. The time was 2.30am.'

J. 'May I just say something. What I want to say is that what you should have done first is ask for protection. I want you to get used to doing that first whenever something happens that you don't like. That should be your first thought; 'Protect me', yes? You ask spirit for protection, you see your protection symbol and you *know* it's done.'

G. 'Yes, I'll put that in and I've also written it in the margin. I was shocked so we need to, although we're shocked, be aware that there are certain things we must put in place.'

J. 'Yes, it's like action/reaction and because you're now growing, you've always had, like everyone else, a spiritual light within you but this development course encourages your light, that flame, to grow and the more the flame grows, the more you become accessible to what is around you. Things may not always be to your liking which is why I teach protection right at the beginning so it becomes automatic like brushing your teeth.

That's what I wanted to point out, the minute something untoward happens, it doesn't matter where you are, you can throw up that thought and ask your guides to protect you using your protection symbol and know, 'I'm safe!' Then you can do whatever you want to do.'

G. 'It's strange because I need you to tell me that. It's important that you tell me.'

J. 'Grace, I'm going to tell you everything I think you need to know.'

G. 'But since that time, I have become very good at throwing up protection when I'm not comfortable.'

J. 'Brilliant!'

G. 'I need to stop and make a note of things like this which are *so* important. Back in bed, I wondered about protection, re-enforcing my own and then my husbands'. I then thought of my higher self. I saw in my head a beautiful vision; a lady dressed in a gown of silvery white. Her head was covered but I knew she loved and cared for me very much. Then I went back to sleep. My teacher asked me what I thought of my visitor and with her guidance began to understand that more flexibility is required on my side, hence the bendy neck.'

J. 'Who is the teacher?'

G. 'It's you! What I have seen was a small part of what was to follow. Also, the lady will always keep me safe.

In the early hours of the 9th of August, the following night, it wasn't an attunement it was a dream but very real. I had moved house, still living in the area but more into the countryside. The front of the house was built of red brick with peach-coloured roses around the front door. A country cottage with pretty centred gardens situated by the edge of a lane.

Walking through the hall with a girl child of about ten who I feel was my daughter, we both passed through a door at the back to find a countryside very different to that at the front of the house. The air felt cleaner, sharper somehow. There was rough grass and this reached as far as a stream which was the boundary.

Looking down at the water it was clear and pure, sparkling in the sun which was set in a clear blue sky in front of very high rocky mountains. I could see a house on the far edge of the rough grass which continued on the other side of this very bendy, shiny brook so that it was rough grass both sides.

A dark haired lady came out of her back door and she waved and smiled but then went back in. I glimpsed a man in the doorway but the door was closed behind them both with a firm click. I turned to my daughter and said I could see the banks of the stream almost touched in places and maybe we should step over and introduce ourselves to the neighbours.

I was a little afraid that my little girl might slip so decided to leave the visit for the time being. Thinking that I could become lonely in this beautiful place, I remembered that all my friends and family already visit me and that I will always be protected and loved.'

J. 'OK, so what did you understand from that dream?'

G. 'That there are two sides to everything. Not to take for granted the first thing you see - look a little beyond. That I very much love the countryside, I love my solitude; it's important to me. The stream was sparkling and flowing; I have given a great deal of thought to letting my life flow more slowly than in the past.

I'm quite controlling of what I do and I think that sometimes that might put up an obstacle to things in my work with spirit and my life but I also know that you can't pick and choose. If you put into place a way of easing this blocking that I do, allowing life to flow, I will find a great deal of difference in the speed at which I move along.'

J. 'It need not take a lot. Think of a chess game where you just need to move one piece and the picture looks completely different. You won't know what the picture really is until you have all the pieces at your disposal. Our greatest asset is the power of our mind which is the infinity in us. So, think, think, don't just expect. Expecting is good for certain things but sometimes expecting things can attract only just that, when in fact, there is a lot more!

No matter where you are or who you're with, you never know who is really there, they represent the communication; what is being said. Also, what was between you - the stream - was only an illusion and you could have crossed it. Like you said, you blocking you, but what you are getting is excellent.

Now let's go back to the first one, the visitation. I want to talk about it and ask you what that's about? *"Nothing is ever for nothing"* especially from now on when you're being helped, developed, honed, yes? So everything that happens to you is telling you something - has a meaning.'

G. 'I also think that it was his bendy neck that made me jump, it was snake-like although there's flexibility in there.'

J. 'The snake has different meanings and can be interpreted in more than one way. There is a positive side to the snake as well as negative. It's like what we said before about which side of the coin you're looking at.'

G. 'It could also be telling me that there needs to be more flexibility between my husband and myself.'

J. 'Big one! Well done, well done.'

G. 'And something you said to me because we talked about it on the telephone, something you said to me made me just a little sad that I hadn't spoken to him, the intruder. It wasn't his face that made me afraid, it was his neck and that made me jump but I could have asked what he needed to tell me and I will do that in future, I wouldn't just go, 'OOOH, go away!'

J. 'But he knows that.'

G. 'Does he?'

J. 'Of course, whoever comes, comes to you for your higher good whether it's a challenge, an experience, for healing, for love. It's all positive and he did have a smile?'

G. 'He did.'

J. 'And it was a 'knowing' smile, like he knew how you were going to react but he had to come. It was important and you were ready to receive him also, weren't you?'

G. 'I was quite impolite though.'

J. 'But you were still ready, that's the Law. You're not going to get anything *ever* in your life unless you are ready to receive it - it's the Law - it runs through everything. *"No-one is ever given anything that is too much for them."* No-one is ever given anything that is too much for them to handle. This is something that will repeat itself throughout this course, time and time again. You get it because you need it. It's time for you to receive it.

So why did it happen? That's what we're teaching you and your relationship with your guides is allowing you to find the answers.

Now let's skip now to the third attunement.'

G. 'I just have to say, I have been tired, I have been exhausted, I have been lacking in energy but I have pushed through it being away for two weeks. Also, I've been thinking, I have come back with far more energy than I've had for some time. I have been in a lot of pain within my bones; that has gone.'

J. 'Wow!'

G. 'I'm seeing life differently. It's as though I've been asleep for the last twelve months and suddenly I woke up! I don't remember everything about the last twelve months and it's as though everything is new. Everything is there to try and taste, to explore, to be excited about and there's not that feeling of failure. Failure is just another way of learning and I'm approaching things and people in a different way.'

J. 'You feel more confident?'

G. 'Yes.'

J. 'That's a hallmark of this course. When you start to get stronger and things begin to make a bit more sense; with that comes the confidence. In the past you kept mulling things over and over again and again and getting nowhere; now you're starting to execute life and its challenges more. You question yourself more and funnily enough, this does often come at this juncture of the course as well.'

G. 'So you're not surprised?'

J. 'No, not at all.'

G. 'So I've not done many attunements Jenny.'

J. 'But, there is also something I want to mention and the irony of it is, that I normally have a rest in August and December and let spirit have a rest as well - they need a rest too - so I hope that makes you feel a bit better?'

G. 'It does - we all went on holiday! So I'm back now, so this is the 2 September. It lasted from 7 o'clock in the morning till 7.15. It was a Sunday morning, I suddenly woke up and came and sat quietly. It was some time since I sat with spirit. Something or someone called me and I knew it was time to return and sit with God.

I have been walking in a garden, walking upon short rough grass amongst tall pampas grasses which form a tall hedge each side of me. After a short time, the foliage on the right began to thin out and I could see a five-bar gate just outside of the garden. Behind and through the gate, I could see a field leading to who knows where. Stopping, I wondered, should I leave this path I was following and open the gate and pass through that interesting field? Interesting, because this path I am walking along is dark and on the other side of the gate is much more daylight and perhaps opportunities?

I ponder, not sure what I should be doing. Then a thought appeared as if by magic. Don't think, *feel!* My feeling is to stay in the garden, the gateway looks inviting but the gate is closed, closed to me. I continue my walk knowing I have made the right choice and I can now see just a little way in front and the path is opening out. I walk from the last of the tall dark hedges onto an open hill. Sheep are grazing and it is evening. The sky is alight with the oranges and golds of a sunset.

Below at the base of the hill is a small town already brightened by the odd street light. I stop at the top of the hill looking down and feel real peace. Then I hear my mother's voice calling to me. 'Grace, it's time for tea.' I'm home, all is well.'

J. 'Lovely, really lovely. What did you gauge from that?'

G. 'I gauged that my family were close by. My father was a shepherd and used to tend sheep. I thought about the sheep and they were grazing. I think I have this correct as it's a long time since my father told me? If sheep are grazing then there's a possible change in the weather but if they're sitting down, not doing very much and not in a particular rush, the weather will probably be constant. So I thought about that.'

J. 'So it equals change?'

G. 'There is change.'

J. 'Do you know what change means? Change equals growth.'

G. 'Elementary! I've always loved sunsets. I've always felt that a sunset, not a sunrise but a sunset is the thing that starts the day off, *not* the sunrise. Why, I don't know but there's always been a real love of sunsets. The morning is beautiful but you can lose yourself in a sunset. It illustrates to me the magnificence of possibly the way to heaven. I could walk into that sunset and just keep walking. Sunrises are very busy, sunsets are peaceful. They have the strength of the entire day behind them, a wonderful time to watch a sunset.'

J. 'What about the gate?'

G. 'The gate was closed to me and I found it interesting that I could stop because I'm very visual, I could stop and try a different way, stop and feel and then actually look and think *that* gate is closed. If I was meant to go that way, my feeling is that it would have been slightly open. So it was just a signpost to continue. Signposts come in different guises don't they?'

J. 'On the other hand, you could have said, well, a gate is there, what's the gate doing? Why it is there? So it would have been interesting if you'd have gone through the gate to see where it would have led? There is no right, there is no wrong. On your path you have freedom of choice, freedom of will and whether you would have gone through the gate or not, it wouldn't have made any difference, I promise you. It would have been what you would have discovered. Yes?'

G. 'So there is a possibility that of instead of choosing a new beginning, I stayed in the same place? But what if I had gone through that gate, I might have found myself in that field but how do you know it is the right choice?'

J. 'You don't know but spirit would have brought the next thing on. All I'm saying is that you have freedom of choice, freedom of will. There was an equal interpretation here, being, the gate was shut but on the other hand, the gate was there for you and you could have decided that the gate is here, it's here for a reason, I'm going to open it and go through it. They are both equal. There is no wrong thing to do.

It's to do with you and your relationship with your guides and what you feel your guides are communicating with you about. That was for *you,* whatever you get is for *you.* Rather than talk to you, they're showing you - symbolically.'

G. 'Isn't it great!'

J. 'Absolutely!'

G. 'I so love this journey. It's also about taking a journey.'

J. 'Always. We were born to have a journey and when we die, we carry on with our journey, it's an infinite journey. We're never alone wherever we are, on earth or in spirit, it's always a journey which is why change is growth because if you just stand still nothing is happening. You're on your path and if you don't move, you stand in the same place. Quite simple isn't it?'

G. 'Elementary! But I loved hearing my mother's voice calling, very comforting.'

J. 'You couldn't have asked for a more loving.... the proof in that is just *gorgeous.* She brought you into the world, you brought your children into the world, it's just an ongoing process - it's embryonic almost. These words are known in every language, wherever you hear it, people feel the same, 'Time for tea!' Comforting, loving, what more do you need to say?'

G. 'Nothing. Now this attunement is a little different because now we're back at work, this was the first time I could sit back in my usual time but it lasted only five minutes!

My screen opened slightly, the top and bottom pulling apart into a narrow slit showing light behind. This opened wide in a blink of an eye. I was aware of rushing towards a blue velvety sky with silver stars of all sizes. Looking across and slightly back, I could see they were flat, very much like cardboard cut-outs but how they shone, both front and back.

I was moving at great speed. I could see the bright path of my energy far in front of me winding and twisting between stars of various sizes. I was far bigger than anything, bigger than the stars, I was huge and standing in my own energy.

I left the stars behind and moved into an area of planets of all sizes but still much smaller than myself. I moved through them, moving them around, replacing some, adjusting others as I moved. Very busy, I never stopped. Such freedom I have seen and felt who I really am.'

J. 'So what do you make of that one? Does that say anything to you?'

G. 'It tells me that anything is possible. It tells me that I am pure energy and that I can move in ways that I had no idea was possible. I can do things that I never thought I could. I can move forward. I can take whatever comes my way. I will always be Grace, I will always be that human part of me but I'm also an energy. We all misinterpret sometimes what we're capable of but sometimes we're shown our own magnificence. We need to be aware of what a wonderful - it's not personal - because when you're pure energy, we're all part of the source.'

J. 'I agree. I got that you're free to do anything and that nothing is standing in your way. Normally, the stars and the planets are bigger than us but this was the other way round which was very much done on purpose to make you realise how big you were and there was nothing standing in your way.

If you really want to do something, it's possible. Even though you know it, most of the time they're just thoughts and words. It takes a brave person to action thoughts and turn them into reality and if they manage it, they prove what understanding they have. It was also time to emphasise the enormity of *free*dom of choice.

OK, let's talk about your holiday, did that all go according to plan? I'm asking you this because when you make a commitment to work with your guides, they are not just working, helping, supporting and guiding you during your attunements but throughout your daily life. So did anything happen during your holiday that was relevant to your path, your growth, your spirituality? For example, you may have thought, 'I know why this has happened?'

G. 'I went on holiday very tired, wracked with pain and if I may say, heading towards a depression.'

J. 'You didn't want to go?'

G. 'That is quite normal because I hate packing suitcases but we got there. All was well, easy journey, easy to get on board the ship and a nice cabin so everything was in place. I was tired, I was in pain.'

J. 'Did you ask spirit for help?'

G. 'I did a lot of thinking. My husband was also not well.'

J. 'So you had that concern as well?'

G. 'I did. I have not had a great deal of time to myself but I have got through it and I know spirit have been close to me. In fact, I've done an awful lot of talking out loud, nothing personal, more to do with life in general and about the people not caring, etc.'

J. 'Do you think that you are now experiencing an increase in sensitivity? Normally I would say that when you go on holiday, you close down, you don't attune - you have a spiritual holiday - but spirit are also great opportunists and they will carry on with your learning and experiences.

A holiday is something different and it brings into play aspects of your life you wouldn't normally have at home so even though you're not attuning you still get spirit coming in which is fine as long as it's contained and controlled by you - you don't go off and keep yourself open all the time.'

G. 'You told me before you left to close down for the holiday. Because I wasn't at home working, I had more time to think and I thought, why is it that I always feel so poorly in the mornings but by five or six o'clock in the evening, I feel something has lifted and I feel better? And then I thought I take my medicine in the morning and I don't feel well again until late afternoon and I suddenly decided to say to my husband, I'm not taking it tomorrow and let's see if I can get away with it for a couple of weeks?

I have come off it before, under the doctor's instructions, so the next day I didn't take the medication and by about four in the afternoon I was feeling better so I carried on and didn't take it the next day and by the evening of the second day I was pain free! I haven't been pain free for twelve months!

My mind seemed clear, my memory which has been muggy for months has come back. I could get enjoyment from life. Life is good. This is fun - what shall we do, where shall we go? Instead of I must sit down, I don't want to do this, what's the point? All gone! So I continued without the medication for the rest of the holiday!

My husband who wasn't well suddenly asked me for healing - he has *never* done that! But I gave him healing every morning and he felt the difference and this is now an ongoing thing. That in itself is a minor miracle!

I've been pain free and really enjoying myself and one morning we went up on the top deck for breakfast which is where you go and it had been raining overnight and the deck was like glass. We were walking when my feet went from underneath me and I landed flat on my back, however, the water must have cushioned me as in no way did I hurt anything as I slid.

The only thing was that when I fell, my head went back and cracked onto the deck. I slid and went flat on my back and never hurt anything. I had a headache for about three days, I watched my own finger and I could follow it and I took paracetamol!'

J. 'You also told me that you took the opportunity on holiday to say to your husband, no, I am not doing what you're doing because I will be the one who will suffer. Let's try another way? You decided to put yourself first for a change and it worked for both of you. So well done, that is a big step because you usually do everything together and you will often suffer the consequences in order to please him.

Do you remember what I said to you that sometimes all you have to do was to move one piece 'on the chess board'? It wasn't difficult, an opportunity presented itself and you took it. It's not a question of you being selfish, it was time for you to be responsible for yourself too.

If *you* suffer, you can't help him so there was a lot more to it than just saying the words and changing the routine. It was a big step and I really understand that and I applaud you and I know spirit does too.

OK, we're going to move on to the next part of the course.'

Fear And Negativity

Jenny: 'OK, so today the subject is all about fear and negativity.

Fear is negative just like, selfishness, conceitedness, miserly, anxiety, worry, jealousy, envy, cruelty, cupidity, gluttony, greed, sinister, pessimism, deceit, I could go on.

Negative is also - Can't, won't, impossible, etc.

The bottom line is that you will not be able to move on unless you obliterate fear and negativity. These are the traits which will always hold you back.

Ignorance breeds fear so the way to deal with fear itself is to learn, to understand, to accept the alternative, which is really to TRUST. Trust is one of my 'Biggies' along with ASKING, PROTECTION and DISCIPLINE.

Let us look at an example of fear:-

You are watching the TV. The music is haunting - 'Doop, de-doop, de-doop, de-doop!'

The camera draws nearer and nearer to a cupboard. Once again the music is scary - 'Doop, de-doop, de-doop, de-doop!'

Fear is building up inside you because you *think* there is something bad in the cupboard. If you thought there was nothing in the cupboard, you wouldn't be afraid.

The cupboard door *opens!* 'Ta Da!' It's empty! All that wasted negative energy.

But the truth is that negative energy is *real* and it can attract the negative back. You remember, *"Like attracts like"*.

Here is another example:-

Briony lived in fear all her life. I counselled her and we got to the bottom of it, why she was always afraid, the source of the problem. Briony now understands. She now realises what it was all about. She is no longer ignorant. She is no longer afraid. She has now answered her own question - the answer to her fear - so she is no longer afraid. So getting over your fear will often mean talking about this at length to establish the route of the problem.

The questions:- Will I be able, will I manage, will I fall, will I fail? Will I lose, will I get fired? This is ignorance breeding fear.

Here is another example:-

Jenny was about to do clairvoyance in church for the first time. She was really scared. She had never performed clairvoyance to a whole group of people before so she had to counsel herself and start to adopt a positive frame of mind.

She had known for years that this day would come. She knew this was a hurdle she had to overcome, something that she had to personally achieve. She knew she *had* to do it otherwise she wouldn't move on. She understood it all - there *was* no ignorance - so she *had* to TRUST. 'After all, you teach it Jenny, so you have to live it too!'

So, Jenny ended up dealing with the situation by giving *all* her worry *back* to spirit. 'OK, spirit, you think I can do it, you say I'm ready for this - prove it? I haven't got a clue how I'm going to do this clairvoyance but if you're telling me now is the time, I'm curious as to how I am going to manage this clairvoyance, I really am. I am waiting to see how *we* will do this?' Notice the 'royal *we*'.

Spirit and I will do this in partnership. I will put my complete and utter trust in spirit. So, fear and the overcoming of it, will often involve putting things to the test and, of course, this is spirit's proof to us, what do they say, *"By our fruits, you will know us."*

Trust is not achieved easily, it has to be earnt, not just by you but on both sides. Your guides have to earn *your* trust too. Remember, this course is all about the relationship and relationship building. Working with the spirit guides who walk with you in love. You don't love instantly do you, but love begets love.

So, in relationship building, putting things to the test is, I think, imperative. It's a kind of proof but it's also all part of the relationship, the confidence, the trust, the growth and the experience. For without an experience, you will never learn, you have to experience something to:-

Believe it. To trust it. To understand it and to build on it.

What do people fear? The dark, the dead, the unknown, the difficulties?

It makes me laugh when people profess to be so interested in psychic or spiritual phenomena but they don't want to have anything to do with what frightens them - which is usually psychic or spiritual phenomena - they just want the 'good bits'!

I cannot make you lose your fear only you can do that. I can give you loads of explanations and examples but only *you* can reach the stage where fear is no longer an issue.

OK. Let's talk about what used to frighten you but no longer does. Grace, what used to frighten you but no longer does?'

Grace: 'Being wrong about something, simply being wrong.'

J. 'Good answer. How about what you still fear, what still frightens you?'

G. 'I would say I fear the unknown. I fear what I do not understand.'

J. 'Fear is a state of mind, yes? Everything begins in the mind. Your mind, as I have said before, is the most powerful tool you possess and there are no limits to what it can affect because it is infinite. Because of the Law - *"Like attracts like"* - your mind will only grow, expand, develop, evolve when you are ready to receive more but as I have already stressed, you have to earn it. Almost all of your gifts are earnt, not just in this life but over many lifetimes.

One hears about balancing out the negativity with the positive. You will hear me encourage you time and time again to think and work in the positive because only then will the positive come back to you. It's the boomerang effect - what goes round comes round.

You create your own environment, you are in charge of you. As a medium, you have to find balance, you have to find harmony, you have to balance the physical with the spiritual because first and foremost you *are spiritual* but, you are a physical being. You have a physical body, you are part of the physical world but you are also a spiritual being.

It is the spiritual being which is the *real* you, who makes you who you *really* are. It is the spiritual who makes you laugh, who makes you cry, that loves, hopes, that dreams and achieves. The physical is merely the 'house'. You remember in the workshop I said that your spirit dwells in your body. The physical body is spirit's temple, the house where spirit lives so you cannot ignore your physical being. For if the physical being is ill, is tense, your head will ache, your stomach will be upset.

If you are under stress, the physical will not work as it should and if the physical being is depleted or impaired, it can have an effect on the spiritual by making you negative, by making you feel at odds with your surroundings and by making you feel exceedingly sorry for yourself! The two have to be in balance and if the spiritual is in tune, in harmony and in balance with its source, then it will also come into balance with the physical.

How many of us worry what next week will bring? How many people lie awake at night wondering just where the next penny will come from? How many worry about a promotion, about their children, how they will fare in the future? How many worry about family, about parents and their welfare?

If one is in tune with spirit, one can then go to spirit for help, for guidance and for upliftment. If one can trust that the love that is the driving force of *all* the universe is there for you, then one is coming in tune with spirit. Once you start to trust the force that is love, once you start to trust the world of spirit with which you work, you are on your way to coming into spiritual harmony.

Now, just think? If all your worry, all your concerns could be handed over, not abnegated - you do not abnegate your responsibilities - but if that worry, that concern, could be handed over, shared with those in the spiritual realm with whom you work, shared with those whose vista is a little wider, whose task it is to guide and help you on your earthly path, then would not the stress and the strain of your earthly life be lifted from your shoulders?

A medium has to learn to trust those with whom he or she works. It goes for anyone, you do not have to be a medium to learn to trust, but a medium especially.

Whom do you trust? We have learnt about attunement and vibrations. In your attunements you should lift yourself to the highest. You should say, 'Here I am, how may I serve. Show me the way?' Ask your spirit guides to help you overcome your fear, your difficulties and your ignorance. Do it together!

You do not have to walk this life alone. You never have to do anything in your own strength. Share the load, share the problems, share the difficulties.

Remember, spirit are just as human as we are and have had many incarnations just like us. They understand why you may be afraid or be fearful and they *do* want to help but you must ASK and you must let them help you too. But here is the rub; you must *do your bit too*, you must do *your* share. You are the physical end of the partnership, they are the spiritual half.

Life is not easy and the choices you have to make upon this earth are not easy ones but you *do* have the ability to discern between the negative and the positive. You *do* have the ability to rise above all the negative emotions and the negative environments.

You do have the ability to put aside the bitterness, the resentment and the hatred and to turn and give love where once was hate, upliftment where once was bitterness and enlightenment where once was resentment.

We need teachers who will teach a negative world to love. Healers who will manifest the Love of God through their healing. Communicators who can open the door that divides physical and spiritual life. We need mediums who do not just *talk* about love, about giving but who *live* it and who live the Law.

For you see, *all* that you sow you will reap. So, think and work in love and positivity and you will see your fear and negativity stripped away to reveal the glow that is your true spiritual self and your courage, strength and trust will be rewarded.

Finally, I have a little tip for you:-

If you can change 'worry' to 'concern', you are dealing with your worry or anxiety in a more constructive way which then becomes positive. So change all your worries to concerns and deal with them positively and then, they no longer become either a worry or a negative energy because you are working in positive thought by dealing with the problem in a positive way.'

G. 'Really good, that's really good! Really, really good. They're all good but that one just knocks it on the head, doesn't it?'

J. 'The more you learn, the clearer it becomes, the simpler it becomes, the more manageable it becomes. Remember you are not alone, remember to ask for help. What did the Nazarene say, 'Reach out and your hand will be taken. Ask and it will be given.'

G. 'Yes, and they're not just words. That is really, really uplifting, Jenny.'

J. 'OK, homework starts today! Oh, and I meant to ask you, what did you think of the healing synopsis paper I gave you?'

G. 'Yes, I have to be truthful; I read it before I went on holiday. I have not read it since but it fitted in with a lot of the things that I actually know about healing. I could resonate with everything that was down there and sometimes it was like reading my own words and thoughts.'

J. 'That's good and the Healing Talk, was that quite controversial?'

G. 'I liked that, I actually liked that a lot. They're all good but as they go along they get really better don't they?'

J. 'It would be nice to eventually have some questions from you as we have a session on questions and answers at the end of the course. The synopsis on healing or the talk on healing may throw up a question so any query or thoughts that come up from now on, please jot them down and we can try and answer them later on, OK?

I'll give you your homework now which is for next time I see you and you'll be getting homework at the end of each session from now on. I want you to write half a page on 'Attunement' and your understanding and interpretation of it. This must be straight from your head - no cheating or looking at your notes! I want to see what you've understood about attunement. That's it!'

Jenny: 'Well Bobbie, how have you been?'

Bobbie: 'OK, apart from being ill and I couldn't do my attunements because I was coughing and sneezing every time I sat so that was impossible but now I've got back into it.'

J. 'There's a saying that when you need a rest, if you don't heed, spirit will make you have a rest one way or another! Maybe you did need it but it doesn't do any harm. It gives you a chance to rest, get your health back and be all the better for it. I'm not saying being ill is a good thing but it does tell you things. It does tell you that you were run down, doesn't it? If you were healthy, you might not have caught it?'

B. 'Yes, you're right. It's the first one I've had for years.'

J. 'So, you were well due a rest and maybe now you're going to see the justice of it and also have a think, what was I doing that was too much or maybe I wasn't balanced enough? Balance is always needed for health - it is a litmus indicator for health.'

B. 'Yes, I think that's my trouble. I've had to keep going. I haven't spread things out.'

J. 'And as we get older, we're not able to do the things we used to do in the same amount of time and I think everybody needs to re-look at their lives periodically and decide what needs adjusting. Our conscience tells us there's something wrong and we probably ignore it, no, I've got to do this, no, I've got to do that, yes, and so we battle against the current.

However, there's another thing, *"Out of the bad comes the good"* - so maybe out of this comes something much better for you?'

B. 'What I've learnt?'

J. 'And that's why we're here - to learn!'

B. 'And the patience part as well.'

J. 'You're here to discover about yourself and how you fit into the scheme of things and then there's the old adage, if *you're* not healthy, then everything else falls apart! As women, we're often relied upon to keep the universe going!'

B. 'Yes!' (Bobbie laughs).

J. 'OK, so you have gone back to your attunements which is brilliant. Let's have a listen and see what's been happening?'

B. 'OK, where am I? This morning was my first successful attunement since I got my cough and cold. I was able to go into the silence without being disturbed by coughing and sneezing. It was wonderful to be able to get close to spirit again although I did not see an awful lot, what I did see and hear was tremendously moving. I was asked to look into my heart and my soul and what did I see? I saw a light and was told that this was my humanity. The more I filled this light with love and compassion, the brighter this light would shine. Although I did not see who was saying this, it came from a brilliant light which seemed to be coming down from above me.

I really can't say if I actually heard the words or just felt them. I felt so moved and humbled by them. I hope as time goes on I will be able to understand more what spirit wish me to do. At present I am just happy to be able to spend time learning from them.'

J. 'Wonderful, welcome home and welcome back, that's what I'm getting here. The other thing you need to know is that even though you don't sit, spirit are still with you. I'm a firm believer that spirit are great opportunists and they will do all the things that need to be done and especially, if you are on a true spiritual path, they are with you all the time.

Your guides are using you and encouraging you to experiences the things you need. *We* only see to the horizon but spirit can see far beyond that. Your spirit guides know what's coming up, they know what you need to be prepared for and I just feel that this particular attunement said many things, including what you said but I also feel a reassurance and the magnitude of who is with you needs to be reiterated.

Your guide isn't just any old person and *you're* not any old person either. You wouldn't have this type of attunement, you wouldn't have the content you did. Because of the law of *"Like attracts like"*, you only get the same as yourself, your guides are on a par with you. If your motive is of a certain ilk, that same ilk will work with you. It's the law, you can't shift or abnegate it, it's natural, that's how it works.

That attunement also tells you how much they think of you. It says lots of things. Again, remember what I have said, 'Look at it again, no, look at it again.' It's not just surface stuff, don't take things at face value, it goes deeper and deeper, yes?'

B. 'Yes, I felt I was being cuddled. It was lovely, yes, it was *really* nice. This morning's attunement went very well. I got the tingling and the heat again. I went into the silence and for a little while there was just quiet with noises in my right ear. Then I saw a badger coming towards me, then the badger was gone and then there was a moose coming towards me and then the moose went.

I then began to get the feeling of being taller and slimmer and almost regal. This time I was definitely a woman with rings around my neck and I could actually feel them. I don't know how but I just knew that I knew this lady. It was the same lady that I had drawn a few years ago. Her name is Mtombi.

I felt her say to me that she would show me how to walk tall and proud, to take pride in who and what I was. I later looked up the meanings of badger and moose and it tied up with what Mtombi had said to me about being proud. I look forward to learning more and being able to understand more of what spirit is teaching me.'

J. 'Just brilliant! I remember you showed me that drawing of yours.'

B. 'Yes and I could feel her and the rings next to my skin.'

J. 'Wonderful. Where did you look up the information for the badger and moose?'

B. 'I've got animal medicine cards.'

J. 'Aah, because I've got the book Animal Speak.'

B. 'Oh right!'

J. 'So we can look it up in Animal Speak as well. Well, that's interesting.'

B. 'Right, the next one is, this morning's attunement was very interesting. It didn't happen immediately but after I go into the silence, there is just a very extreme relaxation and then I get this strange feeling. I really can't describe it but I now recognise it. I do not feel apprehensive. I did at first but now I recognise the feeling, I know what is happening.

I feel it is so natural. I grew tall and thin again and knew that it was Mtombi. I felt that I was walking tall and feeling proud. She showed me that I should celebrate this beautiful world, my life, my attunements, even my mistakes, that I should celebrate it every single day. That life is a wonderful gift. Then she was gone. It was almost like a balloon going soft and down.

Then Jesus came and I grew tall again. I don't really know how I know who it is but I just know. He said that I was making good progress. I don't know what all this means but it will become clearer as time goes on, I'm sure. I do enjoy my attunements and look forward to the next time.'

J. 'Lovely. It's very heart-warming to hear that you have a certain feeling and a 'knowing'. When we have a relationship with our guides, they make themselves known in a certain way. Sometimes you can't express or relate what that feeling is, you just recognise it. And when you talked about a feeling - a certain feeling - and you're beginning to recognise that feeling but you can't describe it, to me, it is a hallmark of a guide or a 'calling card' of a guide.

When you begin a relationship with a spirit guide, they invariably need to tell you, 'I'm here.' They tell you, I'm here, I'm close, I'm near you in a certain way and how they present themselves is agreed between the two of you before you return here. You agreed all that before you came back.'

B. 'OK.'

J. 'So that is why you are not fearful, you just *know* it's something. You recognise it but you can't put your finger on it. I *know* this. This is a positive feeling which stands out from other things.'

B. 'It does, it *really* does.'

J. 'So hang on to that because it means something and it's almost as though your guide is saying, 'You know this feeling, don't you? We agreed this, didn't we?' Do you know what I'm saying?'

B. 'Yes, it's jogging my memory.'

J. 'Yes, in a way, so you keep these certain feelings, let's say they're 'calling cards' but it can be anything. It can be a smell, a feeling, a taste, a feeling somewhere on your body, it could be anything. It's like they're an icon on your desktop! You know who they are and what they relate to and they return every so often.

So I think that attunement was telling and reminding you that your guide will be coming through in that particular vein. We'll see but it did stand out in everything you said.'

B. 'Right, it's making me remember our agreement before I came back?'

J. 'You single out a particular feeling as it occurs immediately before something relevant happens and you say to yourself, I think this is the way you let me know you're here? When I feel this, I know it's you, yes?

This course concentrates on your relationships with your spiritual guides. This course is helping you to understand that you have people walking with you, working with you, supporting you, guiding you, loving you, etc, and they are there for always.

When I leave you and we go our separate ways, you'll have all this understanding behind you and you'll think, 'I *know* this is you' by the way they draw close; what you sensed before they entered your aura. You'll have one, two, three, however many guides and when you ask for help or when you want confirmation, these guides communicate with you in a language; a language using your senses.

Do you remember in the workshop I said we're all given senses, use them? We don't use them enough and this course makes you understand that you can use your senses more than you have done previously. They're all there, it's like they're getting old and dusty! They are beautiful and help you so much especially in your relationship with the spirit world, alright?'

B. 'Yes. This morning's attunement went very well although very little occurred. I do feel spirit with me. I felt supported and wrapped in love. It was the most beautiful feeling. I felt I was being nurtured. I am most grateful for this and I thanked spirit for knowing what I need even if *I* don't. Thank you spirit, I look forward to my next attunement.'

J. 'That's a feeling, clairsentience. You're using that sense.'

B. 'Yes, then the next one, this morning's attunement was very informative. I found myself on this lush grassy plateau. This young Indian girl came to me and told me that there is a time for everything. There is time for planting, a time for growth, a time for harvest and a time for rest. She then left me and I just sat and waited.

Although I did not see anyone, I heard the words, 'You have reached a plateau, now's a period of rest and contemplation on what you have learned this far. Enjoy this time of rest and enjoy your attunements. Everything is done in perfect timing.' Then I took a deep breath and I was back round. So I will take on board what spirit has told me and I will look back on what I have achieved and I look forward once again to hearing spirit's words of wisdom.'

J. 'It's really what we have been saying, isn't it!'

B. 'Yes! (Bobbie laughs). I thought that actually afterwards. Yes, I went back over it because I thought, well, they wanted me to contemplate so I went back over what had happened.'

J. 'In the early days of this course, I talk about 'plateauing'. If you look back, I think it's in Month 2, Attunement II, it says, 'You work then everything plateaus' and you actually had this in your attunement, it's great! And everything then has to be consolidated. It's like digesting a meal. You can't be eating, eating, eating. You have to wait and let food digest and then eat again and then wait.

You have to digest learning and then something will happen and you get tested and you think, I know why this is happening and you will feel you're being tested; 'I've learnt about this and now you're asking me to put it into practice.'

B. 'Right, yes, this morning my attunement was a wonderfully restful experience. I found myself on the beautiful lush plateau again. I was sat leaning against a beautiful old tree. Then a young fawn came to me followed by a lamb, then came a young rabbit and a young fox cub. The fawn came and licked my face and the rabbit settled down on my lap. The fox lay at my feet and then the lamb and the fawn lay down either side of me. A young owl flew into a branch above my head. It was so peaceful and lovely and then I heard a voice say, 'Just relax and enjoy this period of rest. Prepare yourself for the next climb.'

Then I noticed to my right, crags going up steeply - my next climb, I presume? Then I took a really big breath and I was sitting in my chair but it was actually not half an hour, it was twenty minutes so now I know that this is a rest period before I begin my next set of lessons so I will just enjoy this period of quiet contemplation. Thank you spirit for your love and guidance.'

J. 'So did you get anything else from that attunement? Do you think it was telling you anything else?'

B. 'What I thought because they were all young, I'm young as well. I'm new to the world and learning.'

J. 'Yes, I see where you're coming from. Well I got something which is 'when there's peace, the lion will lie down with the lamb.' Normally a fox will eat a lamb but they were both quite happy to be together. You wouldn't normally get that situation, would you, all animals happy to be by each other's side?

There is no doubt Bobbie that you have a 'heading' - a big connection to do with the outdoors, with nature, with animals - that's very much running through not just your veins but your spirituality. You're very much akin to this.

You probably get a lot of your strength and your peace from nature and animals therefore it's not surprising that you get an attunement like that where animals come to you in the most natural setting. It's like you're a personification of the love of nature and animals so you give out that natural energy and that natural energy responds back to you.'

B. 'Ah right, yes!'

J. 'So you saw that in your attunement as it's a *"Like attracts like"* but also the message was one of peace, I think, the fact that the fox and the lamb were just lying together, normally that doesn't happen. That stood out immediately to me - gosh, a fox and a lamb together!

The other thing, if you look at it, is that if children are taught certain things, certain spiritual truths when they are young, it would help them so much with their lives when they grew older. These animals were young and it's almost like a wish or a prayer - I wish life was like this.

There is so much work to be done here on the earth plane and so much spiritual work to be done and it crosses over all areas of life. You can start with the earth and work 'up' to the heavens, it's the full compass and it involves babies, the young, right through life up to old age and when we die.

It's the full spectrum isn't it and it's all needed and all necessary and everybody does their bit and that includes what you now bring and maybe what you will be bringing more and more as you develop. So yes, that was very, very lovely.'

B. 'And the one I've got to so far is, my attunement this morning was very informative. I am starting to feel spirit coming closer and I am beginning to feel different energies for different spirits and I hope that I will come to recognise the different energies. Although I don't think I see spirit as such, it's more of a knowing who is speaking to me.

Jesus came and said that I wanted to know what my purpose was. He said that my purpose primarily was to be a channel for healing energies. He said that there were many forms of healing, there is the body, the mind and the soul. Each one of these illnesses disrupts the balance but first I need to learn how not to take these illnesses onto myself before we can really commence in earnest. So there is a way for me to go yet before I can begin to fulfil my purpose.

He also brought a man forward who, in my mind, looked like Gandalf from Lord of the Rings but more rounded. I felt his energy different from Jesus. It was a very subtle difference and I look forward to my next attunement.'

J. 'Really interesting, yes? It's interesting because my gatekeeper looks like Gandalf.'

B. 'Oh really!'

J. 'Yes.'

B. 'Well that's strange.'

J. 'No, not really. I actually think that when the Nazarene spoke of not taking the illnesses upon yourself, this may refer to protection? It's like, how can a doctor stay healthy if he has to see all those ill patients? So you need to understand, for example, that if in the future, you have to see anyone who is poorly, then you have to protect yourself. That should be the first thing you think of.

Remember we said right at the beginning that you have to keep yourself well because people depend on you. Well this confirmation that you are going to be used for healing could be anything. It could be that spirit are going to use you more for healing at night or like myself, you will be healing just by talking to people but whatever it is, your healing capability is going to be increased for whatever is coming down the track.

I always teach personal responsibility. You have to do *your* bit too in keeping yourself healthy which comes back to what we said right at the beginning, about balance. (Bobbie laughs).

In fact, the Nararene also spoke about balance, didn't He, so he is reiterating what we were talking about and knowing you and what your capable of when that little voice inside you says, *Stop*! For God's sake stop! We're all talking about the same thing, aren't we? (Bobbie laughs again).

This course is all about learning about yourself so you take a bit from me, a bit from your guides - it's all for the pot. It's a wonderful confirmation for us that we're on the right track so I take that as something for me to know that I'm on the right track as well because I'm trying to help you, He's helping you, he's helping me!

So we're saying the same thing. Remember in the workshop, our spiritual day, when I said you need corroboration, you need confirmation, it makes you feel good because you know that everything is in good working order and you're on the right track. So yes, that is excellent.

So, to précis what's happened since I last saw you. You've been poorly but it's been a wonderful lesson, you've been taught *so* much in just a few weeks. You've been taught about illness. You've been taught about yourself, how you must re-look at yourself and not be so hard on yourself. And also isn't it wonderful to have that motivation that you're going to be working for spirit so that encourages you to look after yourself?

It's almost as though spirit are saying, 'You've got to be healthy otherwise we can't use you!' You're going to have to learn about protecting yourself, balancing yourself, not just working with your guides, you've got to work on yourself too, do you see that?'

B. 'Yes.'

J. 'And everybody's saying it! And, also, it's as though you *had* to be ill as it was part of your learning, very clever. What do we hear, *"Spirit are great opportunists!"*

B. 'They *do* know what's best for us, don't they?'

J. 'They do and it's always for our higher good, there's no doubt about that. You *did* need a rest but you also needed to learn from it and it was a perfect way to do it, a perfect experience to have *and* at this particular time too.

Spirit were aware you were here doing this course with me and, the icing on the cake, what have you *just* leant about - *healing* - you had just finished your healing lesson! It's really quite incredible the more you think about it.'

B. 'It is, yes.'

J. 'That's what I mean about go on, look again, go on, look again, no, look again! It's all to do with thinking and examining what you have experienced. When you have a relationship with your spirit guides, you will think you've thought of it all and then something else will pop into your head to do with the situation and you'll be laughing your head off because it's so incredible as everything all ties up together! It's incredible. *Very* clever, very clever, you will never ever stop being amazed by spirit's relationship with you.'

B. 'That's the word, isn't it - amazement.'

J. 'So, excellent month Bobbie, fab month! In fact, it's simply been turned around, simply awesome, incredible, do you see that now? I think there's far too much there and I would even start making a list of what you've learnt. It's all being crammed in but equally, it's all needed at this particular time for you.

Is there anything else to talk about, your sleep state, your life at home?'

B. 'I'm sleeping better.'

J. 'Well I think that's also because of all the healing you needed. Is there anything else you want to talk about?'

B. 'Absent healing. Is there any particular way of doing this or is it just a question of asking?'

J. 'Do you want to make this one of your questions for our Question & Answer session?'

B. 'Yes. I could do, I'll make a note of it.'

J. 'OK. I actually made a note to speak to you after our last session when we carried on talking about you being prepared for something. (Bobbie laughs).

We spoke about your husband's health and how you could help. I talked about being an example to others by just being '*you*'. How you think, what you do, what you say, you are, in effect, being an example to others.

We then moved on to you being in a testing period. We're all tested along our journey and I told you that spirit never do just one thing and I said that I felt that you were in a pivotal situation at the moment, yes? Remember you said you were dropping things and then you dropped your cigarette!

I wrote down; Bobbie wants to progress and develop spiritually and I said that often this involves being put to the test by giving you challenges. Bobbie said that she knew what this meant and said that it may mean giving up smoking? (Bobbie laughs). To which I agreed!

I wrote that if Bobbie could do that, she would not only be helping herself spiritually, as smoking is an impediment to spirit communication as with alcohol but, also, she could be setting an example to her husband by showing him that, 'If I can do it, you can do it.' I've also put here that Bobbie could be more disciplined with *herself* to help her poor health.

Now, Bobbie, I don't always do this as we're not allowed to tell people what to do, OK? We just leave it in their court and that's what I'm now going to do. Sometimes it's good to remind ourselves of what we were saying because a lot can happen in the space of us not seeing each other which is why I wanted to reiterate this point to you now.

The other thing that I wanted to ask you is whether you read any of the healing papers I gave you - the Healing Synopsis and the Healing Talk?'

B. 'Yes, they were very interesting actually and very helpful and I was thinking about you Jenny, I did have a fear. You know when my husband and I had all our financial problems and I just asked spirit to help and they did! I can't believe it and now I don't worry about it.'

J. 'Good, there's no point.'

B. 'Because it's negative and that will only come back. So now I know I'll be alright!'

Month 5

"When there is nothing more you can do, give love."

Jenny: 'Let's sit quietly Bobbie and then we'll 'light our lamps'. I've lit my candle. Our spirit guides will know we're open for business and then we're ready to begin. When you're ready open your eyes. So, how are we?'

Bobbie: 'Very well.'

J. 'Good and you've recovered magnificently and maybe you've got even more energy than you had before? You look really well.'

B. 'Yes, I feel well actually.'

J. 'Good, so what have you got to report on your attunements? Let's start with that first, have you been doing them?'

B. 'Yes, oh yes!'

J. 'That's good to hear, that's a positive start! Let's hear what's been happening?'

B. 'This morning's attunement was just a time of relaxation and rest. There was not much more to report. I just went into the silence onto the grassy plateau and just sat and relaxed. I came out in exactly half an hour.'

J. 'There's a very good saying, I don't know if I have mentioned this to you? *"When the least is happening, the most is happening."* Have I said that to you before?'

B. 'No.'

J. 'Often people get really worried; there are no lights, camera, action, nothing and I always re-assure them that when the least is happening in attunement, the most is happening so I am quite happy with 'nothing happening.'

B. 'This morning's attunement went very much as yesterday although nothing really occurred, I feel very rested and supported. And then the next one was, this morning's attunement began as before. I was sat on the grassy plateau looking towards the large crags to my right. After a little while, I felt myself getting much larger. This time I did not recognise the energy. I asked who it was and heard, 'I am Joseph of Aramathena.'

I asked why he had come and he said he was going to give me the strength I would need on my next

---

climb when the time came. I felt he was a tall, well built man. He had large hands. Then he was gone and the next thing, I was back around. I know, I know that name but I can't remember where I know it from, I must look it up.'

J. 'I'll tell you where it's from, it's from the Bible. Joseph of Arimathea was one of the San Hendry who were a group of Jewish hierarchy, religious elders who, it is told, contributed towards sentencing the Nazarene to his death.

However, there were a few in the San Hendry who understood more than the others and who were more lenient towards the Nazarene and touched by His teachings and who, for example, were saying, we have all been waiting and waiting for the Messiah so why shouldn't it be now? One of those was thought to be Joseph of Arimathea.

He is well documented in the Bible and there are also stories of him later helping Mary Magdalene. Now if you didn't know who he was and got his name from your attunement, that is proof that he is actually there with you which is absolutely incredible!'

B. 'It was very nice but the thing I did notice was his hands. He had big hands!'

J. 'But you also recognised that it wasn't an energy that you had felt before?'

B. 'No. Right, this morning's attunement was quite uneventful. I was again on the grassy plateau leaning against the beautiful tree. It is so peaceful and lovely here. I just relaxed and enjoyed the peace and solitude. I feel I am conserving my energy for the road ahead. The half an hour goes quickly then I am round back in my chair. I do look forward to my attunements.

Then, the next one was, this morning my attunement began as before. I was on the grassy plateau leaning against the same beautiful tree then the scene changed a little. From the crags on my right, in the middle, came a wonderful waterfall and although there was a great deal of water coming down, the pool into which it fell was as calm as a millpond. As I got to the edge of the pool, someone said, 'Enter the water and feel cleansed.' So I disrobed and entered the pool. I began to swim around, it felt wonderful, exhilarating.

Then I came out and I felt myself being wrapped in a large fluffy white towel but it was so soft, almost like cotton wool. Then I heard, 'The road ahead will not be an easy road but know you can return to this place at any time you need to. This is your own sacred place for you to be cleansed, rested and invigorated.'

Then I was round and back in my chair. I felt really good especially to know I can return to my beautiful place at any time I need to. I look forward to my next attunement.'

J. 'That was incredible, wasn't it and you saw and felt it so clearly?'

B. 'It was really nice, yes, it was beautiful.'

J. 'It's almost magical that you've been given this special place. You always said you liked waterfalls and I'm sure you didn't conjure it up yourself? As you said, the pool was calm and yet the downward torrent was rough so that didn't make sense so it had to be something that was being given to you. What does that tell you, does that tell you anything?'

B. 'It tells me that I need to rest.'

J. 'I want you to start trying to interpret the things you are being given. It's to do with the communication you have with your guides. I talk about this to Grace when she has an attunement. Try not to look at things as factual but read into the picture you are being shown.'

B. 'Right, work out what they are trying to tell you?'

J. 'Yes, this is very necessary. This is part of the growth, part of the development, part of your relationship; you get better and better at understanding what your guides are saying. There's a saying, *"Nothing is ever for nothing"* so whatever you're given *means* something. It's trying to tell you something, it's a message. Sometimes you don't need words, the picture tells the story so to speak, so you just need to look and see what is being shown and therefore what is being said, yes?

So let's just take the example of the waterfall. The waterfall was rushing down but the bottom of it - what it was falling into - was still. So just a little test here, I'm not giving you marks out of ten, I'm just trying to make your mind malleable - like dough. Pretend your mind is like a lump of dough and we're going to knead it, get the dough - your mind - used to being used so that's what I want to work on with you from now on.'

B. 'OK.'

J. 'I'm going to be horrid! (Bobbie laughs). I'm going to start asking you what you think, so let's start with the waterfall, what does that tell you?'

B. 'Well the waterfall is like the journey and then the pond being so still, that's the plateau we talked about being a period of rest.'

J. 'OK, so what does that equal; the rush and the stillness?'

B. 'Going forward then stopping, going forward then stopping.'

J. 'Yes, but to me, it also means balance. It's giving you balance - the rough and the smooth. Also, do you remember your guides recently spoke about your path being rough, being hard, about you being tested? The fact that the water doesn't crash into the sea, means you're going to come through all these tough challenges unscathed.

To me, you're being told that balance is your key and that however hard your journey is, you will be helped and arrive at the smoothness, you will solve your problems, you will overcome your obstacles, you will achieve your goals and all will be well. Do you see that, do you understand that?'

B. 'Yes.'

J. 'You're not just saying it?'

B. 'No, I *do* understand that.'

J. 'And the rest was self-explanatory, the fact that you've been given this almost sacred place. OK.'

B. 'Today's attunement was very much as before. I found myself on the grassy plateau sitting leaning up against the lovely old tree. I could hear the waterfall. I then went over to the still pool and bathed. I found the lovely fluffy towel and then I was back under the tree again. I felt cleansed and rested. Then I heard the words, 'Enjoy this period of rest, relaxation and rejuvenation' and then I was back in my chair.'

J. 'So it all comes back to the same thing that you're being prepared for something and you're going to have to work harder so it's like what we said in Month 2; you grow, then you plateau, you grow, then you plateau.

A plateau is not without its significance. The plateau is also work of a different kind where you're being nourished, strengthened, given all the armour, given all the tools, whatever you need for the next chapter.

This last two weeks of yours has been very much a reminder to take advantage of this quiet period, telling you to make the most of it but also teaching you why it is necessary. You can't just battle, battle, battle. You have to stop for food and drink, you have to stop to sleep, to rest - balance again. Balance comes up time and time again in so many things.'

B. 'That's really the key, isn't it, the key to everything?'

J. 'Yes, I think it's extremely important. In your life, you mustn't overdo it. You must pace yourself. You must understand your limitations, what you're not capable of. Try not to bite off more than you can chew. (Bobbie laughs).

Don't be silly and go beyond your capabilities. Accept yourself and this is very much what we're going to be talking about today so that's quite uncanny too!'

B. 'Oh right! You know when Joseph of Arimathea came? What I was thinking about was what you said at the beginning. People are getting nothing but something is happening. It's almost as if he came to say, that yes, it's still going on. It's like encouragement really.'

J. 'Don't ever dismiss 'nothing'. I think a lot of us expect too much of ourselves - I know I do - and I'm in a period of rest myself and I find it very hard and it's almost as though your attunements are for me, in a way! (Bobbie laughs again). To remind me to accept a rest period and to accept the way things are at the moment.

You will come to understand that spirit never do just *one* thing, they're *so* clever and again, it's the timing. You remember the saying, *"There's no such thing as time in spirit, but spirit's time is perfect."* It's very clever; you'll never cease to be amazed how clever spirit are.

What about your sleep state, is there any change there?'

B. 'I'm still sleeping well and feeling more refreshed when I get up in the morning, I'm not feeling so tired.'

J. 'Have you learnt anything new? For instance, is there anything in your physical life that you can single out as a lesson or something that your spirit guides are helping you with? Is there anything in your day to day life when this 'little voice' is saying something or you're chuckling with a 'knowing' at what is happening; for your higher good?'

B. 'I've been helping my neighbour next door with emotional problems. They've just been through a really rough patch and were going to break up and she's been coming round to me and I've been a shoulder to cry on and I hope I've helped her because she seems to be OK again now.'

J. 'Well I'm sure you're not her neighbour for nothing and I did ask during the workshop, do you have a sign on your back saying, "If you have any problems......."(Bobbie laughs) and you did laugh when I asked that!'

B. 'Yes.' (Still laughing).

J. 'So it's coming to pass! It's very rewarding especially if you can see the fruits of your labour and it's also a big compliment being asked to help someone.'

B. 'Yes.'

J. 'If you were an old battleaxe, I'm sure she wouldn't even venture through your front door! So she sees someone who she can confide in, who she can trust, who would take what she says seriously and wouldn't ridicule her in any way. So that's very good. I'm sure she's very grateful.'

B. 'She is.'

J. 'OK, did I give you any homework?'

B. 'Yes, my understanding of attunement. What I understand attunement to be is going into the silence, quietening the mind, regulating the breath. This allows spirit to draw close to you and to be able to communicate more easily without having to try and get through all the thoughts and plans that are going on in your head. You can then begin to get communication between yourself and your guides, helpers, family and friends. You can then build a close relationship with them thereby helping each other on your journeys for as spirit is teaching you, they too are learning so it is a sharing experience.

Spirit will help you, protect you and love you and you know that they will be with you always. Once you begin your journey with spirit, your outlook on everything changes and you are never the same again but it is a wonderful, fulfilling experience.'

J. 'Thank you for that. Well done! So I know now that there's no problems with your attunements, you're happy all round?'

B. 'Yes.'

J. 'Have I taught you a quick way to get energy? Look up at a light or the sun, I just want to double check I've done that?'

B. 'Yes, I find the sun works better.'

J. 'Oh good, you've already tried and the sun works better, brilliant! There's a note here that I've written about last time when we talked about fear and negativity. You understand that we create our own 'heaven' and our own 'hell' - symbolically, I mean?

What I've always tried to do is to make people understand that in being an energy, your ultimate aim is to have you always thinking positively about everything because then the positive comes back to you. So whatever you do, check your thinking. Ask yourself, am I looking at this in the right way?

It's like a coin. There are two sides to a coin, so maybe if you flip the coin over, you would then see things from a different viewpoint; a positive one, yes?'

B. 'Right.'

J. 'Life is one of contrasts. Everything has two ends of a spectrum. Night and day, fast and slow, etc. and you can't have one without the other. You can't learn anything until you know and understand it's opposite. You can't learn how to be good until you understand what being bad is, it's like a litmus test or a thermometer, a gauge in life.

You have to start off with something in order to learn something else from it. Things don't appear out of nothing. There has always been, there always will be, there is always something there for you to judge; what do I think of this?

Ultimately, I would like you to be able to think and work in the positive *all* the time. So when you come up against something or when someone says something, you've always got a positive response. It takes practice but the earlier you start doing it the better and you can test yourself.

For example, let's say your husband says something and you say something back and then your mind will automatically work out was that a positive reply? Was I using positive thought? You can also challenge other people's negative thinking with your own positive thoughts and words and if I could teach you one thing, that principle would be the best one because only good would come back to you. Remember the boomerang effect and *"Like attracts like."*

As far as spiritual relationships go, it works least well when you're in a negative frame of mind, when you're unhappy, which is ironic because we usually ask for help when we're unhappy!'

B. 'Yes, this is true!'

J. 'So it's like spirit are saying, 'Yes, we know you're unhappy but be positive that we're here' and as one thought cancels out the other, it's no longer a negative!

Now today, we're going to start a new subject. There's quite a lot here but it's all very meaty! So sit back, relax and listen.'

Love

Jenny: 'Today, I'm going to talk about a 4-letter word, no, it's not a swear word! It's what for hundred of thousands of years, poems have been written about, songs have been sung about. Books, plays and films have been written about.

It's what people have fought for, men and women have died for, people have sacrificed for. It's what makes the world go round. It's the agony and the ecstasy - it's *LOVE.*

I think you will agree that there are many kinds of love:-

The love for your children. The love for your parents, grandparents, brother, sister. The love of your home. The love of the countryside; of plants, flowers, trees, the water. The love of a special place or haven. The love of an animal or animals.

The love for your husband, wife; the love for your lover! The love of food, wine, of music, poetry or art. The love of the elements; the sun, the rain, lightning. The love of scent, of colour........I could go on.

And I find it amazing and fascinating that each and every one of these things we love, fosters a different type of the same thing.

Some people mistakenly believe that love is only an emotion which you experience sometimes. No, love is the first cause of all life. Love is light and heat and life itself.

That a child or baby's first instincts is to love. What they give out is a radiance of love that almost glows when you look at them and as they go through life, they will experience a myriad of different loves which they will have to wrestle with as well as embrace; will have to understand as well as question.

Love operates and is active on *every* plane of our being; from the lowest on earth to the highest in heaven. On the lowest of them, we only know it as a passion that sears, burns and consumes but on the highest plane, it creates and gives life.

I remember I once took my father into my confidence and then he questioned me saying, 'What is this thing *lurve*?' He had married three times and he was saying *THIS!* I was absolutely astonished and didn't believe him.

But despite the intensity of the most ardent type of love, there is much more where that came from. There is emotional love and *then*, there is *SPIRITUAL LOVE.* This is an even greater, denser and more profound and acute type of love. This is on a frequency that leaves emotional love fading into the distance.

We hear about the 'touching of souls'. To me, this is when we experience Divine Love and now realise the difference and the contrast to even the highest form of emotional love.

Unlike emotional love, spiritual love is never painful, is never destructive, is never cruel or hard to bear. Spiritual love is uplifting, enlightening, overwhelming and has a power to take your breath away - literally.

Like the great Light that came down from heaven and blinded Paul on the road to Damascus, it was a sudden illumination, a sudden overwhelming recognition of the reality of God's Life and God's Love.

But just like wanting your soul to be touched, you cannot ask for spiritual love. You cannot demand it or bargain for it. It only reveals itself when you are ready to receive it, in fact, when you have earnt it!

Spiritual love can present itself in different forms and in different ways as each individual, being on their own path, could link to the experience of Divine Love at any time on their life's journey. In due time, this experience will come to each and every one of us. The light will flood our being and all our gifts will be enhanced by the incoming of this divine fire, this magic, this creative Power which is Love.

This is the Power that initiates us to perform what people call miracles and which acts, not only upon the human mind and emotions but on matter itself; it will transform metal to gold.

You see, you only find the answers when you love. It's locked away within you and is the key which opens so many doors. Often, it's locked deep within you on purpose, not because it wants to be, but because you have actually placed it there! The more secretive a place you have hidden love, the harder and longer it takes to find but when you do find it - Wow!

On the other hand, love can be in such an obvious place that you keep missing it! You're so busy constructing major assault courses trying to find love - going down this road and that road and turning off here and there - when it's actually staring you in the face!

But often, the key to the path of spiritual love is through service. This is the ultimate goal of all bretheren following the path, who seek earnestly and without thought of self, to serve their fellow man.

To serve is to love, *"Service is the coin of spirit."*

So, cultivate the art of loving others and not yourself. Self-consciousness is darkness, your lower self must be put behind. Like a lighted candle, the wick burns brightly and little by little, the wax around the flame dissolves and burns away. In the same way, the flame of Divine Love, by degrees, consumes the lower self; it is transmuted and transformed.

Love transforms *all* life removing all that is ugly and unwanted.

However, for a great many of us, one of the hardest of loves to confront is the love of oneself. Part of loving is learning to love *yourself*, accepting yourself, liking yourself, coming to terms with yourself and who you are. Not fighting with yourself any more but recognising that there is a beauty of strength and love in *YOU*.

In a highly competitive world, loving yourself and publicly accepting who you are and what you stand for, can be one of the hardest steps you will have to confront. Some of us never have the courage and the mask we chose to wear, becomes the outer layer as well as the permanent feature behind which we privately retreat.

I often feel very sorry for these people as I know that one of the reasons we are here, on earth, is for our spirit to find *true* expression. I also know that you can't move on in life until you face yourself, accept yourself and love yourself. This is not being hedonistic in any way but being, *"To thine own self be true."*

One thing's for sure, once you know and experience spiritual love, perspectives change and what you once thought was love changes too as a new and unbelievably deeper form of 'spiritual' love is exposed. It wraps itself around you and now the parallels and comparisons to emotional love, become obvious.

Emotional love is now seen for what is *really* is, which is *not* the reality. Emotional love is like the shadow, whereas spiritual love is the sun and now you don't only know it, you can see it and feel it; you now bask in this new found love.

Love creates beauty on the spiritual plane. This is why those who have neglected to love others find themselves in a state of darkness, coldness and barrenness when they pass into the soul world.

Love illuminates your heart and life as well as your countenance so that light goes forth to others through your mind, through your emotions, through your speech and every action. Through your *whole* being, love flows out into the world to touch those who are lifeless, those who are dead - I mean spiritually dead.

Many of these 'spiritually dead' people are walking our streets particularly in the big cities but when you understand how to love, you will have the power to bring these souls to life and power to send light to illumine their darkness to heal their sick minds and bodies.

The Power of Love is the magical secret of life. When this love fills the heart, the heart centre glows with divine fire and radiates like the sun and can be seen by all those who recognise Divine Love.

"Love is the hallmark of God and is the trademark of all those who serve Him."

So, the next time you get turned onto emotion, remember, there's plenty more where that came from and a million times better!

As tireless campaigner, Bob Geldof was heard to say, 'Life without love is utterly pointless.' Now, if that's not a spiritual truth, I don't know what is?

So that was the first paper on Love. This month's new material is in three parts with 'Love II' being the second transcript.'

Love II

Jenny: 'Love cannot be demanded. You can give a certain kind of love that is born of respect. You can give an admiration that is born of fear but you cannot *demand* love because like calls to like. Love can only call and it is to *that* call, that man has the choice to respond.

Peace can only be found in the giving of love and true peace is found where true love is found, in the Great Spirit.

It is very difficult to give love to the unlovable. It is easy to love your friends. It is easy to forgive your neighbours. It is easy to forgive your family but to love the unlovable? To love a family member who is a troublemaker, to love the person in your street who is obnoxious and who will find fault with everyone, to love the filthy and depraved? To love the unlovable is very difficult.

How do you do it? Where do you find that spark of divinity within yourself that is born of the Great Spirit? First, you must desire to serve. For you see in the giving, you receive, in the serving, you are served.

If you have the courage to look inside yourself and see the negativity around you, the things you dislike about yourself; to face yourself as you truly are. When you have the courage to do *that*, then you have the courage to strip the negative things away.

The hatred, the bitterness, the feelings of self pity, the fear of living, the fear of the future; one by one they go so the *positive* things, that are born of the Great Spirit which is you, the *real* you, begin to shine and begin to glow.

Then, with this flame, your own spiritual light begins to grow and those spiritual helpers who work with you in spirit, can draw closer and closer so the help you ask for can be given more quickly, more easily because spirit find it difficult to communicate where there is strong negativity.

If your life here on earth is built on negativity, then it will be in the darkness of negativity that you will dwell in spirit. The lower levels of spirit where ignorant and stupid people, not evil people, because there is no such thing as evil, but where ignorant people have made their home. These people can return and cause havoc *but* only if you invite them and only if your anger and your bitterness allows a chink in your armour. Remember, *"Like attracts like."*

Because of the Law of Cause and Effect, *"What you sow, so you will reap"* - what you do, what you say, how you conduct yourself throughout your life, has an effect, not only on the here and now but in the spirit realm and the lives thereafter that you will lead. So, you have a choice?

If your life here is built on negativity then it will be in the darkness of negativity that you will dwell in spirit. *But*, if your life here is built on positive things, on love, on giving, on service - it doesn't matter whether you believe in God or go to church - you walk a spiritual road and you build in the realms of Light.

Negativity cannot survive in light and the positive cannot survive in darkness. Positivity dwells in light which is man's natural environment.

Now, here is something that I learnt along my journey and it has to do with loving the unlovable, however, I found putting this theory to the test quite hard at first. I found it hard if someone had been hurtful towards me, had been inhumane, had been cruel which I thought I didn't deserve so how do I respond? How do I return love to someone like that?

I then came up with an answer which was to feel sorry for them. To respond by feeling sorry for their ignorance because if they knew that what they were giving out would only come back to them, they wouldn't act like that in the first place, would they?

And if they knew that perhaps one day they would also have to judge themselves when their life on earth had finished, maybe even have to return to put right the wrong they had done, they would think twice before thinking and acting in such a negative fashion towards others?

So I am now giving this theory to you in the hope that it will help you on your own journey.'

Bobbie: 'Thank you.'

J. 'Now here is the last paper on love.'

Love III

Jenny: 'Why do you want to develop? Why do you want to personally enhance your psychic ability? Why do you want to be a medium?

The sad truth is that mediumship and spirituality do not always go hand in hand. They *should* do but often they do not.

What is the first task of a medium? To prove survival? That is the second task.

The *first* task of a medium is to manifest the Love of the Great Spirit. If you do not do *that*, you are failing in your task as a medium.

If you cannot manifest the Love of the Great Spirit, the love of which you are part, the love of which you were born, you are like an empty vessel, you are like a clanging gong; you make a lot of noise but do very little good.

In manifesting the Love of God:-

Yours should be the first hand outstretched when someone needs help. Yours should be the first voice raised to make peace when someone has argued and caused discord. Yours should also be the first voiced raised when spirituality is called into question and debased with psychic tools and when development is placed above it.

For love also means discipline. Love is not something that is just gentle. Love is firm, love is bold, love is courageous. Love stands up for what it knows to be right. Love stands in the Love of the Great Spirit.

A medium should be pure love. Yes, it is difficult but we must try, we must strive to be pure love.

You must teach by example. You must lead so others can follow.

Mediumship is not an easy road. Mediumship is hard, mediumship is difficult. People will take advantage of you. They will take advantage of your good nature and will take advantage of the love that you show.

If you chose to serve Him, you must reflect Him. If you chose to serve Him, you must come to know Him for, *"Only as you truly know Him, can you make Him truly known."*

That is why, if you cannot manifest love, you cannot teach love and our world will never change until man can show love for his fellow man.

If someone gives you bitterness and anger, return love, gentleness and hope. Don't respond negative with negative, respond positive to positive.

You are responsible for you. You are responsible for each other. You are responsible for your brother.

If you have knowledge, share it. If you have love, give it in abundance and let your mediumship be to that end.

If you live the law and give in love, remember the Law of Cause and Effect; *"What you sow, you will reap."* So if you sow in a positive manner then that's what will come back to your door.

If you live the spiritual way, you can teach it. Put things to the test and see for yourself. It will change your life and you will never look back but you *must* have the courage to put this teaching to the test.

As seekers of the spiritual truth, as seekers who wish to serve within spiritual light, spiritual love, to do that fully, we have to become at peace with that love, at peace with that light and at peace with that truth.

How many times have you heard that *"Love is the greatest power in all the universe"* however, everything that is associated with love in this world tends to devalue its true meaning.

You see, if you cannot work in love. If you cannot call to that essence of being which is you, which is born of the Great Spirit, which is therefore borne of that Power of Love. If you cannot call to *that,* you cannot work within the Power of Spirit, for the Power of Spirit *IS* Love - pure positive, infinite Love.

That is why as physical individuals, we have to strive to work and walk in love. To give love when we receive hatred. To give care when we receive neglect. To give understanding when we receive bitterness. To give upliftment when we receive resentment. To give hope when we are met with despair. It is not easy.

It is difficult to remember all this when you are suddenly faced with a personal dilemma and you have to make an instant decision so, you practice. You work at it like anything else in life. It has to be worked upon until it becomes second nature.

To live within the Power of Love, to work within the Power of Love, to understand what that Power means in our lives is not easy and yet, the remarkable thing is that when we *do* put it to the test - it works!

We find that no longer are we met with the resentments, the bitterness, the despair, the anguish but people's attitudes begin to change. Slowly, gently but they *do* begin to change. Instead of negative responses we are met with positive ones.

As a physical and spiritual being, as a developing medium showing love, caring for your fellow man and living the law, this goes *way* beyond any psychic abilities you may possess.

If you have knowledge, share it. If you have love, give it in abundance and let your mediumship be to that end.

Now before we finish for today Bobbie, I need to set you homework for next time. I want you to write half a page on healing and your own personal interpretation and understanding of it. I want this to come straight from your head, from your own thoughts, OK?'

Grace's Attunements At This Stage Of The Course...

Jenny: 'OK Grace, you remember what we do before we start our session?'

Grace: 'Yes, I do.'

J. 'We light our lamps so spirit know that we're beginning our session, that we're open for business so they can draw close. When your light is lit above your head, you can open your eyes and we can start; lovely. So, how have you been since I last saw you?'

G. 'My husband and I have been busy and have both had dental treatment. I've felt a lot more confident in what we're doing here. It wasn't for lack of teaching because it was finding my own way.'

J. 'The confidence started last time in what you were doing so it's just an ongoing process now finding confidence in other things.'

G. 'Yes.'

J. 'Confidence is like a tree, it's branching out in different directions. So shall we start with your attunements? You don't have to read every single one. What I want to do is find the different things that are happening to you but obviously where you want to read a particular one, that's fine, I will leave this with you to discuss and share with me the ones you want. OK.'

G. 'This was written on the 12 September but re-written the following day because it became confusing. I have begun to notice that when sitting in attunement I feel a difference. It is smoother, just a slight shift but a shift nevertheless. It feels much more comfortable. I am feeling the different energies, not always, but certainly more often.

In the early hours of the 9 August you probably remember, I had a dream of moving house further into the country. The house with a stream had two very different gardens. At the front, roses, very English and at the back mountains, Himalayan. Gentle with sunshine in the front but although sunny, a cool keen breeze at the back. I had company in that dream, my eldest daughter, Isabel.

Upon my second visit to this place, things were different. Many years had gone by. It was the future. It was later in the year and the darker evenings were drawing in. As I watched it was as if I was viewing through a telescope, very clear but some way off. The house had fallen into ruin, many stones from the walls were piled upon the ground. There was half of a chimney still standing, doors and windows had disappeared.

A woman was walking through and around the remains bending to pick up a stone then dropping it. Reaching for an autumn leaf looking down at her hand, touching the leaf, turning it over with care. She looked up and I could see it was my youngest daughter Francis by her face and bearing. She appeared to be in her late forties, early fifties. Then I understood, although I could still feel that cool wind blowing off the mountain at my back, I was now in a different dimension, no longer connected to the earth but still connected to my daughter by the love between us.

Francis looked up, her sad face breaking into a beautiful smile. She felt and knew that I was close. I watched a beam of golden light leave me and touch her. We are always joined by our love each to the other. Thanks be to God; that brings a tear.'

J. 'That was really beautiful. At the beginning I thought they were talking about balance, with the front and the back but I agree that what they were doing was illustrating the time frame so it was the future, and as you say, it doesn't matter where you are, it's the love that holds everything together and doesn't fade.'

G. 'Just so close and that to me is the most beautiful one I've had. It's funny you should mention balance because the next attunement is about balance!

17 September, 'Just Sitting' I've entitled it. When I have placed my golden ball above and over my crown so that my aura is cleansed of all the energies and dross gathered which is not needed or beneficial to my physical or spiritual self, I then feel the ball lock into place and I feel the difference as the golden light begins its job of cleansing my body or subtle bodies.

Yesterday was my youngest grand-daughter Poppy's christening. There were many people who, after the church service, gathered together in the local public house - many energies in a small place. Today I feel scattered and ungrounded and will now spend a few moments finding myself and locking into mother earth. I shall stand once again in my own power.

I'm back. I felt my roots lock in and saw the beam of light which is shaped like a spear, so slim and quick with a point at each end. One end to the earth and the other to the source of all that is holding me between the two worlds. My balance and power have been returned to me. Time to close down.'

J. 'So different that one?'

G. '19 September, 'The Dream' and my eyes opened at 5.20am.'

J. 'So this isn't an attunement?'

G. 'No, but I think it's important nevertheless. This is something which started in the early hours of 8 August - a continuation - unfinished business. I was staying in a house, not my own home but still a place I was familiar with, walking through, carrying some clothing in my arms. I heard a noise. Stopping in my tracks listening, I heard the sound of footsteps walking towards me. I was not truly afraid at that moment but because I had thought myself the only person in the building, I stood still waiting.

A man walked into view. He was of medium build and height, wearing a checked shirt, brown trousers, boots unlaced and a black jacket. His hair was dark, wavy and down to his collar. His face was the face of someone who spent much of their time out in the open. He spoke asking if, and I do not remember the name he used, but he appeared to know the person well, were they at home, he asked?

This strange, uninvited man spoke with a soft Irish accent. He was watching me, looking straight into my face but he was smiling all the time. I knew he was false. He was a thief by trade and had never respected women, taking what he wanted. I felt in danger but not afraid.

I told him he was not supposed to be here and that he needed to go to the light. As I spoke, a star-shaped portal of light opened just behind him. He turned and without a word, walked into it. The door closed, the light was gone and I woke up.'

J. 'That's great, that's lovely.'

G. 'That was the man who was on the wobbly neck.'

J. 'Really! Really?'

G. 'I knew him - by his smile - I knew that smile.'

J. 'That *is* interesting because I did think about that, but, because your first experience with him happened so early on in your course, I didn't want to mention it. I have a rule where I don't go ahead of myself and I don't - unless it's so blatantly obvious - discuss anything to do with rescue early on in the course. But I'm also not surprised either and it's definitely something which I expected you to be involved with whilst you're with me. So, it happened!

And you also handled it *so* well because you took one step at a time even though you didn't have much time, you took the time to decide what you were going to do. Although he looked nicer than he was before, you were still cool, calm and collected and carried out your duties perfectly so well done and there's a thank you!'

G. 'I never forgot him and I wasn't surprised that he came back. Here's the next one which was on 24 September. Whilst dusting and checking my art materials on Saturday, 22 September, it came into my mind to find some pencils to draw. I let my hand move amongst the pads of different sized and weighted paper until one of them felt correct and the same exercise followed with the pencils and the work began at once.

I have been unwell for the last twelve months and at the end of the twelfth month, I had a breakthrough. It was the medication causing this feeling and I stopped taking it. It has taken one more month for my mind to fully heal and spirit have waited for the right moment.

Within approximately fifteen minutes, I was gazing at the most beautiful of faces. The ever-interesting thing about this drawing is that in the half light, the eyes of this beautiful lady appear to open or sometimes close.

As I sat in attunement this very old soul spoke to me. She told me, she had taught many who do work for spirit and now she will teach and guide me. We stood together above the earth at its northern hemisphere as she explained that the earth works within the universe as a compass. We watched the stars moving across the sky. She touched my arm with the end of her fingers until I felt more balanced.

She said everyone has a beautiful soul no matter how the outer shell might appear. She said that was my lesson for the day and every day.'

J. 'Lovely, lots of things there. I was thinking on the way here, that it was time for you to ask for your guide and your teacher so you've already beaten me to it! So I'm pleased about that. And again, your earlier attunements feature the stars and it was as if she has been waiting in the wings, so to speak, that's what I connect with. Do you remember, you had an attunement where you were amongst the stars and you were very big?'

G. 'I do.'

J. 'Well, when you said you were in the night sky, I immediately went back to that attunement of yours so I feel that, yes, she was preparing. I also remember during our Workshop, the very first question you asked your guide was why did she come to you and her answer was connected to you and the stars.

She *knew* she would be coming back to you in this attunement and, I just want to say, that looking at this drawing, it is overwhelmingly beautiful and I could stare at it all day! Whoever is working with you, the two of you are doing a simply amazing job, so, excellent!'

G. 'Thank you.'

J. 'So how did you feel after that attunement?'

G. 'I felt very secure, very at peace. I got my trust; it's been a long wait.'

J. 'It may be a long wait to you, but believe me, you're 'galloping gourmet' as far as I'm concerned! You're having a very good run with this course and it's been hard for you at times with your health but you've overcome it all. Well done!'

G. 'Thank you. 25 September. This morning I continued my conversation with my lady, Sonja.'

J. 'Her name is Sonja?'

G. 'Yes, which in Hebrew means 'Wisdom'. I can now feel the difference in energies between my angel and her. Some fine tuning was carried out yesterday evening but was halted after the feeling of sea sickness. I did feel really sick for a day or so afterwards.'

J. 'When was this; in that attunement?'

G. 'Yes. On the drawing, I just felt - it wasn't unbalanced - it was just a slight 'swimmingness' and it was like an adjustment of energies.'

J. 'But it was also proof of her being there?'

G. 'Yes, the 'sea sickness' made me feel very uncomfortable throughout yesterday.'

J. 'When you were doing the drawing or when you were doing the attunement?'

G. 'When I was doing the attunement. I was shown a black velvet cushion upon which rested a beautiful long stemmed white rose. The cushion represented darkness and the rose was for light. Two opposites of the scales, if you like. Balance in all things is needed for without one we cannot see or feel the difference.

We walk in light and love and by doing this, we are at peace. We then gather to ourselves all things good and positive. We are at one with our soul and are therefore connected to the source.'

J. 'Do you feel these words were coming through her to you?'

G. 'Yes.'

J. 'Because they are profound and they flow well and proof of the way spirit teach you often includes this fluidity as well as the profoundness of the words.'

G. 'Yes, this is from her.'

J. 'Lovely.'

G. 'I haven't sat many this time, they've all been a bit....'

J. 'Powerful.'

G. 'I have two left. 28 September and it's entitled - and I now get a title! 'Call Upon the Host.' I cleansed then putting my symbol above my head, I waited. I asked for my angel and then my new guide. My guide has been standing in the wings for some time but has only been working and teaching me from the beginning of this week.

I was introduced to my angel at a healing meeting sometime ago. It was just before Christmas. We were each told to ask for our angel's name. I heard the word 'Ariel' very clearly in my head.

My angel stands on my right side always, Sonja, my guide, on my left. I felt them both touch my arms and knew this was going to be special. I saw Jesus dressed in a simple white robe, brown sandals, brown wavy hair touching his shoulders. Then He changed and became a baby in his mother's arms, then a toddler, then a young boy, again a boy but older, then a young man and then as I had seen him at the beginning.

He told me if I became troubled, to call upon the Host. I heard my voice say, 'I call upon the Host!' and in front of me were many angels singing. It was a melody, the like of which I had never heard before. It was both soft and loud, it was both gentle and strong. It had words and it had none, the rhythm changing into both quick and slow.

Then it and the angels were gone, the only one left was Jesus. He smiled and repeated His words, *"Call upon the Host and have faith."* My angel and my guide relaxed their grip, then both of them stepped away and were gone and I was back in my chair.'

J. 'Whoah! Unreal, unreal, gorgeous! So before we go any further, what did you gauge from that?'

G. 'I gauged strength. A strength that I have and a strength that is given to me, flows through me and I just need to call if ever I'm afraid or uncertain. I just have to ask.'

J. 'And that is what we teach here isn't it - that you must *ASK*?'

G. 'Yes, and not be afraid to ask and not think it's impolite or pushy or 'me, me, me' - you just ask and it's fine; it's alright.'

J. 'In our lesson on fear and negativity, I say that you're never alone, that you never have to do anything in your own strength and all you have to do is ask. So it's almost another reiteration of that but in a beautiful way. Can I ask you where your angel and your guide were holding you, you said a grip?'

G. 'They were each side of me, each holding one of my arms. The angel reached out furthest from me and gripped me there, just held me.'

J. 'So they each held you just above your elbow on the other side to which they were standing?'

G. 'Yes, they reached across themselves.'

J. 'So it was like the wings around your back but holding each arm?'

G. 'Yes.'

J. 'The other thing I want to correct you on is, at the beginning, when you said Sonja had *just* starting working with you?'

G. 'When I said it, I knew, I knew!' (Grace is laughing).

J. 'The guides who come forward do so because *now* is the time for them to reveal themselves but, in actual fact, they've been with you a long, long, time.'

G. 'As I said it, I knew but it was out of my mouth and I couldn't take it back! I did know.'

J. 'It's all good because we're discussing anything and everything. The whole picture has to be painted, every single colour has got to be known and just as spirit are opportunists, I am also a great opportunist. So spirit will say to me, you've got to tell her that, you've got to mention this, etc. etc. so I don't want to miss anything out and I know you don't want me to miss anything out either?'

G. 'Not at all and I have one more which is this morning, 5 October and this has got a heading as well and it's called 'Strengthening the Soul.'

Whilst sitting in this morning's attunement, I found myself looking at a large tree, an oak tree. It had been sliced very neatly from top to bottom leaving half of a vertical view of itself and I was looking at the inner part of the tree. The long trunk with its strands of growth running down the inside showing how many years it had been in the ground.

The wood was a light colour as was the sideways view of its branches. The tree was very still, no breeze ruffling its leaves almost like a cardboard cut-out but I knew it was real. I could not understand the lesson being placed before me so continued to look at this big tree with half of itself missing.

Then I knew. None of us are complete without the other half. Our soul is what completes us. Without it, we cannot continue to live, without it, we are as nothing.

Sometimes our soul becomes tired but never gives up but continues with its work of trying to keep us on track but it has its work cut out. We ask for help and it gives it selflessly but we never think to repay it for its devotion to us.

From this moment, my soul will be part of my thoughts, my prayers, my journey. I will give my soul thanks and love it every day for the rest of my life. It is part of me - my other half - my best friend and dear companion.'

J. 'Good. I'm also getting other things from that which I want to throw into the water. It could be the tree of life which is extremely symbolic and which refers to many things. We are like trees ourselves in that we have a core, we grow, we blossom, we bear fruit and, like the seasons, we shed our leaves - symbolically, etc. and so it's very much a massive icon.

Trees are so amazing because they help to nourish everyone in the world and we often take them for granted. We forget how wonderful they are here on earth, the rainforest for example, and they shade us from the sun or the storm so there's so much there.

I also got that the tree splitting in two relates to our relationship with our spirit guides. The fact that half of this relationship - us - is on the physical side of life and the other half - our guides - are in spirit.

It's as though the tree was cut in two to say, don't forget you're the physical half of this journey and even though you're the physical half, you still have everything - even though you're half - you have *all* you need.

However, the other half which is missing is, in fact, not! The missing part is your guides and helpers in spirit and even though you may not be able to see them, they are there nevertheless, yes?

So it was very symbolic with a spiritual journey, symbolic with your core being, you being in between two worlds and you serving spirit from the earth plane. So do you understand how I was thinking of those things as well?'

G. 'I do.'

J. 'If we had other people here with us today, they would put their own interpretation on it and although this was for you, we're always encouraged to take the blinkers off and see as wide a picture as we can because we *all* have something to contribute. I only know as much as *I* know. You know things that I *don't* know, etc, etc. So, once again, a lovely attunement. So you're looking very pleased with what you've had this time?'

G. 'Yes, I think my understanding is becoming more acute although I didn't see half of the physical and half of the spiritual, I see it now. The other thing was there were birds in this tree.'

J. 'And those birds are not necessarily birds, they can be guides, souls, whatever, in the guise of birds. OK, shall we have a listen to your homework now? This is the first homework I set you so remind me what I asked you to do?'

G. 'Write half a page on attunement and my understanding of it.'

J. 'Great. You didn't cheat, it all came from your head?'

G. 'All came from my head over a period of time, having a think, making a note, etc. I split it up AT... TUNE...MENT.

AT - at one with myself, with my feelings, to be at one with my thoughts, with mother earth and the universe. To blend with all energies, to blend my voice with those of others I will meet as my life progresses along my chosen path. To be at one with love, given and received.

TUNE - being in tune with the world. In harmony with myself and others. Being in tune with the beating of the world's pulse and that of the universe. Work in time with God and the angels. Hear the sound of my guide's voices leading and guiding me towards the light; always to the light.

MENT - all of this meant to bring me to the understanding of blending together of all that is. At one, in tune, all meant so that, in the fullness of time, I will return home to blend with the pure love which is the source.'

J. 'I don't think I've *ever* received a homework like that. No-one in the hundreds of people I've taught, has ever split it up like you've done. This is novel, fantastic and I thoroughly enjoyed listening to it. Well done, well done!

Now, I think I remember asking you last time what did you think of the healing synopsis and the talk and I think that one of the things I said was that you're going to start writing down any questions, am I right?'

G. 'Yes.'

J. 'Also, at this juncture in the course, I normally check that you have no problems with your attunement which you don't appear to have. You're all settled and happy with when you do it, where you do it, how you do it and what comes through?'

G. 'I am.'

J. 'One of the things I will be asking you - you *do* tell me - but I just want to put an accent on what you *feel*, yes? Often our spirit guides have something we call 'a calling card'. Now I wondered whether the sea sickness was the calling card of your lady Sonja because one of the ways you can identify who is near you is through what you feel.

I'll say it again at the end but I just wanted to say it whilst it's in my thoughts. You *do* tell me what you feel, you tell me about the gripping of your arms, you tell me about the sea sickness but sometimes when people work with spirit they have a sense that is stronger than anything else, be it clairvoyance, clairaudience or clairsentience.

At the moment, in getting to know you, you seem to have clairaudience, where you hear them, the clairvoyance, where you see what they're showing you and you *do* have the feelings as well, the clairsentience. However, in trying to help you along your path, I wanted to reiterate that it's also important for me to know as well.

Also, do you remember when I mentioned the 'bits in between.' The bits in between are sometimes the most important?'

G. 'The spaces in between?'

J. 'Yes, the structure and the way your guides are working with you. With you, I just feel I need to pay more attention to the spaces in between so please can you *also* pay attention to them as well and log anything down?'

G. 'Yes, I will.'

J. 'Everything's fine, I am not unhappy with anything, it's like we're moving up a gear, yes? Let's also think about the bits in between, for example, what I loved was how you spiritually benefitted from your recent holiday, the things that happened on holiday.

We thought nothing would happen but actually quite a lot happened. Earthly progress is personal progress which equals spiritual understanding, if you think about what happened?

I normally ask people what happens in their sleep state and you're now having things in your sleep already which is fantastic. Again, as you grow, spirit are going to give you more and more experiences to deal with, like tests, but only when you're ready for them. You won't be given anything you're not ready to experience, OK?

So let's go up a gear now. This is month five, we're half way through the course, everything is going wonderfully well. I'm now thinking, OK, what else for Grace? So now I'm concentrating on the bits in between and I want to hear of anything that you're surprised about. Maybe something which has now been resolved, something that you never thought would happen, maybe a reaction from somebody else or a reaction from you?

Spirit works in your physical life not just in your attunements. This is how it will be for the rest of your life. You have made a commitment with spirit - I want to do this - I want to learn with you, I want to be with you, I want your help, your love, your support, I'm committed to you and I want you to be committed to me.

So things are not just going to happen in your sleep state or in your attunements are they? Things are going to happen in your *life* so I also want to hear of anything where you have thought, 'I know why that's happened.' You *will* pick up these 'bits in between' in your life.'

G. 'They *do* happen but if you ask me now to tell you, I would be hard pressed but I will pay attention.'

J. 'Because it's proof. It's proof of spirit's love and of them knowing you *SO* well and knowing the little things that mean such a lot to you. Do you remember when I said that you only have to move the chess piece one square and everything looks so different. I know there will be other things happening to you.

So we're moving on to our new material for this month and the subject we're going to be discussing today, would you believe it, is Love! (Grace laughs).

Can't get much bigger than that, so here we go.'

After Reading 'Love I, II & III' To Grace...

Jenny: 'So that is a big lesson on love?' All the fragments and bits and pieces - all the leaves hanging from the branches, all the branches hanging from the bow, the whole tree itself. There are so many facets of love, it's like splitting the atom, again and again and again. It is not something that you can take in all at once. It's massive but it's what we are all about and, if I may say so, it's actually who we are.

I've always said that we are all 'little gods', 'little loves.'

Grace: 'That's truthful words.'

J. 'So I will give you these notes.'

G. 'Thank you, thank you very much, that will keep me busy!'

J. 'I need to give you your homework for next time. Homework is to write half a page on your understanding of healing. How you interpret healing personally as well as healing on a universal stage. Whether it's personal to you or healing per se', it doesn't matter.

What you have to understand is that what I teach you is what was given to me years and years ago. I haven't waivered, I haven't changed it because there isn't any need and everyone is the same - a spirit - and spirit doesn't love one person more than the other.

What is fascinating is that everyone I meet is different and therefore I have a different journey with each of them. The journey I am having with you is unlike any other journey I've had with anyone else but it still doesn't mean that I give you anything different.

It's the responses which are different and the pattern, the mix that is you. I give out the same but I get back something different, the uniqueness of human nature. So even though you may have been on a certain journey, maybe you already know a lot about spirit, it doesn't matter, I still give you the same.'

G. 'I don't think anyone ever knows everything that needs to be known because things are constantly changing with each individual.'

J. 'What I'm referring to is that I know, for example, that healing isn't something new to you but I'm still going to give you the homework based on what I've taught you so far. Someone else may think, well as a healer, I really don't need this homework.'

G. 'I think I need it more than most, we mustn't become complacent. It's very easy to do when you've read numerous books over a number of years, there's always something new. It's very much you may have been a healer or someone who channels healing and have read a great many books, have spent a great deal of time thinking about it, practising it but there's always something different with each individual.

If one person, for example, breaks a leg then another person also breaks a leg, it's not the same leg therefore a different kind of healing may be required.'

J. 'And then they go to different people for healing.'

G. 'They do, it's a personal choice. They go for one type of healing or a different type of healing or they maybe the person who soldiers it out and will have no dealings with any of it and yet, still a miracle goes on somewhere.'

J. 'Now one of the things spirit prefer is working with you when you don't know it. It's an opportunity for them to work without any 'interference' if you like, so it's natural. Your spiritual guides will never stop working with you. They see the bigger picture, they know exactly where you're going, what you need, and because you've now responded by doing this course Grace, they are so excited!

People seem to think that because everything appears to be inactive, not pro-active, that our spiritual guides are not there which is absolute nonsense.'

G. 'I thought they were hiding almost giving me a period of re-generation, I can't explain it.'

J. 'On your side maybe but not on their side!'

G. 'I realised that they were still there and I knew they weren't going to give me anything more than I could do but they wouldn't let me drag my feet either. Whatever made me stop and think when I was on holiday, when it had been staring me in the face quite blatantly, that what I was taking, the medication, was causing my problem! Now that's a space between words because it was like a light bulb moment and I knew!'

J. 'It dropped in?'

G. 'Yes, very much.'

J. 'That's a hallmark of spiritual communication when something just drops into your mind.'

G. 'And I was away from home and I was having a quiet rest and I wasn't listening to them.'

J. 'I was making more the point that your guides never leave you. That they have an agenda, they have their work to do with you and it doesn't mean that you have to 'sit' for them to do their work. In fact, sometimes, if you're not sitting they can just get on with it, it's much easier that way.'

G. 'You know, I've never thought of it. Now there's a good 'light bulb' moment! So when I'm busy thinking well, I would really like to sit down and do something, they're working hard!'

J. 'Or, all the years prior to this course or when you've been poorly. I said to you before about the fact that your guides are 'half' of you and that they have a remit as well as you. They have a responsibility to you, to your progress, to your development and to your learning so they have an agenda as well.

They just don't sit and wait for you; 'Oh, c'mon, Grace is sitting now!' It doesn't work like that!'

G. (Grace is in stitches). 'I can see now!'

J. 'That's why I said about the lady, Sonja, not having just arrived in your life. It's very important that you understand that.

There's another point, in this month's 'Love' lesson, we talk about sharing what you know. Sharing your knowledge, sharing love, sharing everything and I was very aware years ago how possessive people were about their spiritual knowledge and yet I was always the opposite.

I knew that I had to share as much of my knowledge as possible and I'm saying that everything that you have done, or that you know, or that you have produced, you should share.

That's why I'm encouraging you to share your art work; make people happy. You have got a gift and it isn't for you alone, it's for you to share. I don't write for me, I write for other people to benefit. Don't you think people would get joy and pleasure from receiving something you've done and the fact it was done in a unique way?

OK, not everyone will understand this but a percentage of people will love it all the more because they know that your work was spiritually inspired, it was spirit driven. It's done in tandem with spirit - they'd love it, so think about this?'

G. 'I will, I will. It's this human side of us, to do something wonderful like that without any training. Firstly, you're very excited and you tell everyone and then you meet people who look at you oddly. They can't help it, they do and you're hurt and this wonderful thing you've had, you're a little bit more careful about talking about it.

Then you perhaps go on a little bit and that thought stays in your mind, perhaps I'll do this or perhaps I'll do that? But actually you're in service to spirit and you're there to share what spirit has given you.'

J. 'You'll come to understand that motive is everything. Your motive is your 'spiritual' thermometer, it's what spirit look at when they see you, when they look at your aura. You're motive colours your aura. So if your motive is pure, you remember earlier when we talked about making your love as pure as possible, only you can do that.

It's the way you think, it's what pulls you, what makes you who you are, what enlightens you, what enlivens you which is why you need to understand about spiritual love because there is another type of love apart from emotional love.

And especially if you're on a path of service. You begin to walk towards that spiritual love because you find more of it than what you thought was possible. You begin to get certain feelings and you've never had feelings of this genre before.'

G. 'I know.'

J. 'And it's on a different wavelength to what you've ever known and again, it's growth, it's understanding, it's holistic. Every time I talk, there's another thing, it's like the kneading of the dough again. 'Why don't you tell her about this, why don't you tell her about that.' It's like the meaning of love is getting bigger but it's also getting simpler?'

G. 'It's like tackling a food mixer. To begin with it's a huge thing you never think you're going to get the hang of but the more you experience using it, the more you understand it's benefits and so it's no longer that huge object you didn't understand and now you begin to love and cherish it and you both work so well together!'

J. 'Sounds just like a spiritual relationship to me and that's the key - it works for you!

The next step in life is always our own choice whatever the circumstance. However, we often limit ourselves even though there is no limit but sometimes we subconsciously choose to limit ourselves. We lack confidence and think negatively about ourselves and our abilities.

I think we're all here to help one another and to be there in those pivotal moments. I have always thought that people come into our lives for a reason and we often take them for granted by misunderstanding their role in our lives. We nearly always don't see the 'role' straight away but there always is one if we wait - we are all players on the earth's stage.

Sometimes people will come into our lives at a very pivotal time and spirit have been waiting for this particular juncture. I call it a network. Actually, I often view our life as a network or a grid with both horizontal and vertical lines and I always think that where these lines meet, where they cross, those are the juncture points when pivotal things in our lives are likely to occur.'

G. 'Do you know, I knew a lady about my age. She was a very gifted spiritual healer and she said to me one day, 'Do you know there's a universal web?' and I said what do you mean? She said, 'I can actually see it and it goes across and down but it also goes back and I can see people I know at certain places. I can see where my husband is in relation to where I am.'

J. 'Really, that's amazing!'

G. 'Whenever I see her I always ask her whether she can still see the universal web and she says yes and so I asked her, 'Where am I?' and she said, 'Oh, you're there!' That's awesome! Very wise, I thought. She was from the north of England and called everybody 'love'.'

J. 'Fascinating, I would sit and glean as much out of her as possible! Sometimes the most simplest of people are the ones with such amazing abilities.'

G. 'Oh no, she was an educated woman and still works. When she did her healing, she went into the finer points of knowing exactly where all these organs were but as well as healing the physical side, she also combined this with her spiritual knowledge.'

J. 'A perfect combination!'

Month 6

Jenny: 'Well Grace, how have you been since we last met?'

Grace: 'I've been doing a lot of thinking and seeing things in a different light. I think it's the accumulative knowledge from what we've done these past months. I feel different and I think I look different and I feel more confident.

I haven't done as many attunements but I've begun to notice the spaces in between. I've done my homework on healing and I have some attunements and I feel I've really moved forward, I feel I've really stepped up a gear - even after we had the spiritual day - it changed my perspective on things.'

J. 'Excellent! This course doesn't have an order although there is an order - a bit of a paradox - and there aren't any rules as to how the journey progresses once we start working together.

As you know, I need you to do the attunements because I need you to get to know your guides and the relationship you are having with them but also it helps *you* to understand and work out what's happening too! It gives you the practice you need to identify and work with your guides using the language with which they are communicating.

So attunements are very important, and if I might say, vital, in helping you to get to know you're guides better which, in turn, help you along life's journey. If you attune for the rest of your life, you don't need me to tell you when to do them. You do them when you feel you need to, when you're being pressured or when you seem to have a 'tap' on your shoulder - your guides saying, come on, I need to get together with you.

Development is holistic and it can take any road or progress outside of attunement. In fact, after a while attunement may become the minority and your life may become the majority; it depends on the individual. However, the two need each other in order to progress so I'm not at all concerned that you may have done less attunements this time.

What I am happy to hear is that you feel that you are making some progress and that your senses are working at a different rate, that you're 'reading' things differently about yourself and what is around you. So, it's great, I'm very pleased.

I have a saying, 'everything is for the pot'- it all goes in the pot! It doesn't matter whether it comes from attunements, your sleep state, your life or your spiritual relationship, it's all for *you*, to help you on your life's journey, isn't it?'

G. 'It is.'

J. 'So often people have apologised to me for not doing their attunements and I have to remind them that this course is for *them,* it is not for me, so there is no need to apologise. So let's start off then with your attunements and then I'll ask some other questions.'

G. 'This was on 9 October. On the morning of the 8 October, I sat, cleansed and placed my symbol above my head. I said my opening prayer, then asked for my angel and then my guide Sonja to stand by me; angel on my right, guide on my left.

When I had felt their energies touch me, I asked this question, 'What does my soul look like, what does the real me look like?' Slowly, there appeared upon 'my screen' the most beautiful lady. Every part of her was white, a soft, luminous white. I could just make out her features, they were almost mist-like as was her long delicate robes. She had a long veil on her head hanging down to her feet with the edges framing this exquisite face.

It was too much for me to take in so I asked to be allowed to close down. This morning I asked to see her again and this time we spoke. She is my soul, my higher self, that little bit of me left in heaven to await my return, so now our little band has a new member. We appear to consist of myself, my angel, my guide and my soul not forgetting our trusty charge hands - the source of all that is, was and will be forever.'

J. 'Tell me about this in more detail and what did you gauge from that?'

G. 'I gauged that I am more than I allow myself to be. There is this beautiful someone who is me, part of me, inside of me and she was so beautiful, because every part of her was beautiful - how she was, how she felt, how she gave love, forgiveness - all these things.

I couldn't believe inside each one of us is such a lovely being that looks out through our eyes, sees things through our eyes, feel things through our touch and that sometimes we forget that part of us but it's always there, always willing, wanting to be there.

We think of ourselves as two separate beings - this is me and there's my soul - but we need to be aware that we are one. We may look different whilst we're in this earth school but inside of us, we each have the most beautiful, exquisite soul that shows itself to us if we have the courage to ask.'

J. 'Do you feel the lady was your soul or the personification of your soul?'

G. 'Her energy was my soul. She showed herself to me so that I would understand that everything is beautiful. What you see, what you don't see - everything we do has a beauty to it even the things we're not proud of have a beauty to them because we eventually learn from them.'

J. 'OK, I understand exactly what you are saying and I agree but I also feel that the lady was the personification of what every person has a right to be. I feel that she was demonstrating, as you say, the length and the breadth and the depth of a soul.

Here is another point worth mentioning. Our spirit guides often cannot communicate exactly what they want to say because they are restricted by our own language; the English language.

Because the earth is not our real home - we *think* our life here is a reality as it is the only one we know - but it's not and so spirit are also constrained by that as well. They try *so* hard to give us as much information and guidance as possible within the parameters they can work with, which is why clairvoyance is so helpful because they can speak a thousand words by visually showing you something.

Remember in the workshop, our Spiritual Day, I asked you to look at a tarot card and I said, if you look again, you can see more, can't you? Do you know what I'm saying?'

G. 'Yes, I do.'

J. 'And that *IS* the relationship. The relationship allows you to look more and see more and split the atom and split it again and get more and more information from the same thing. On life's journey, the more you develop, the more you will see and the more you will understand.'

G. 'Yes, it's there, you just have to keep looking.'

J. 'You have to use *all* your senses. Again, in the workshop, I was stressing the use of senses because you look, you hear, you feel, you *know* - there's this knowing - you can't describe *that*! All we can say in our English language is, 'I don't know how, I just *know*' and I never ever 'poo-poo' it when someone says that because that '*knowing*' is formidable.'

G. 'It's so direct, it's there, it hits the spot and you know that it's correct, you just know.'

J. 'Now your consciousness, isn't 'up there'. Your consciousness is with you but your soul is massive. It's like your soul group. Your soul, to my mind, isn't an individual thing. I believe we come back to polish facets of 'our diamond', facets of our soul, yes?

So when we're here, as you have said, our personality is here, *we* are here but we're not complete because everything is energy. How can you say that this bit of energy is here and that bit of energy is there and that bit of energy is there - you can't - which is why it's all one.

However, the main thing that comes out of this attunement is the communication, your perception and you *asking*! Spirit praise you for wanting to know and they try and answer as best they can, but we will never know it all and learn it all because learning is infinite and even she, the beautiful lady, God bless her, *she* will tell you, '*I* don't know it all.'

Also, the lady in white maybe other things as well but you are presented with an answer and that answer is what you wanted and it told you and confirmed to you and corroborated many things, yes? What I most get from this attunement is that you know so much already. She came to you because she knows you and that to me is an indication of your evolvement because of the law of *"Like attracts like"* - you only get what you need, you cannot have anything more, because you haven't got there yet.

So that one attunement said so many things and I think it answered much more than your question, do you see where I'm coming from?'

G. 'I do, I do. I asked a question but I got so much more relating to the question.'

J. 'She also knew that we would talk about it and that I would proffer some more information. When I work with you, I am trying to ascertain who you are, what you need and where you fit in to the scheme of things; what can I give you whilst we're working together?

As a teacher, I will never give you more than I think you need and I would never give you something that is too complicated for you to understand; it would be a waste of time. So I think that was a formidable question and an amazing answer and I would also like to thank you for sharing it with me because that was a really useful attunement.'

G. 'It's my pleasure. This one was the 12 October. This week has been difficult, there has been little or no rest. After opening up and then saying my prayer, I felt my angel settle at my right side but I had to ask my guide Sonja three times before she stood upon my left side.

I sat in a different chair this morning but did my written work in the usual chair. I felt both my angel and Sonja take my hands, holding them tightly, I knew that something different was about to happen. I then felt a powerful and loving energy pressing me back into the chair. It didn't so much surround me as penetrate right through my very being.

I heard the words, 'You must rest more and frequently throughout the day.' I have been given some flexible silver armour. This can be worn whilst working and this will give me rest and strength to continue under pressure.'

J. 'First question; what made you sit in a different chair?'

G. 'I didn't feel particularly well but it didn't appear to be anything truly physical.'

J. 'Why did that make you change the chair?'

G. 'I don't know. I just wanted to be somewhere else almost as if I was thinking, there will be times when you don't feel well but you need support and you won't always be in the comfort of your own home. Let's see what happens if you're somewhere else?

The most I could do was move to the other room but I was feeling very, very tired physically. I had been doing a lot of, not physically work but work 'on this earth plane' if you like and I was just extremely tired and I did not want to not sit with spirit.'

J. 'I wonder what would have happened if you had sat in your normal chair?'

G. 'I have no idea!'

J. 'I don't understand because when you're with your guides you get everything you need anyway. You get the healing that is necessary. I just don't understand why you changed chairs and I'm just trying to draw it out of you what it was? You're doing the same thing, you're linking up but what difference does a chair make?'

G. 'None whatsoever, does it?'

J. 'The only thing I can say to you in defence of all this, is that years ago spirit told me specifically, 'we want you to sit in *this* chair' and I have always sat in it when doing my attunements or when working for spirit.'

G. 'I didn't feel comfortable but I still went there.'

J. 'It's crazy! It's as though you were denying yourself something almost as though you thought you didn't deserve to have a proper attunement in your normal place. It doesn't add up apart from you inadvertently putting something to the test.

But I think having said all this 'palaver', it doesn't matter, the message is the main thing. I think your conscience was telling you to rest anyway. You knew you had to rest and I think actually, that the lesson here is that you must listen to that small voice!'

G. 'I didn't!'

J. 'Remember, your spirit guides are with you all the time, not just when you sit in attunement but theirs can also be that small voice, yes? Again, it's part of your relationship with your guides.

OK, I'm now getting something else. You said that you had to ask three times before Sonja appeared but I'm hearing Sonja saying, 'I don't have to 'appear' to you to be with you, I'm always with you.' So I've just heard her say that.'

G. 'That makes me feel better.'

J. 'And, as a true pupil, Sonja wants you to learn that too. So you wouldn't have learnt that unless you would have had that attunement where you needed to ask her three times before she appeared! This attunement enabled Sonja to deliver this important message to you.'

G. 'She's always there.'

J. 'Exactly! So she doesn't have to be there in visual form - she wants you to know that - so that's nice too, isn't it?'

G. 'Yes.'

J. 'It's part of the 'trust' which, as you know, is very important in this course. I say that TRUST is one of my 'Biggies'. It's something you have to earn and if you look in your earlier notes, I think it's in Month 2, I talk about earning trust and your guides having to earn your trust too so it's like an affirmation. So although that was not very much, there was actually quite a lot there?'

G. 'There's more coming out of these one or two that I've done than a lot of them.'

J. 'So it's quality rather than quantity and we're also looking at the spaces in between!'

G. 'Absolutely! This is the following day, and with this attunement, I've got a heading; 'Feeling the difference.' I sat with my angel and my guide feeling their energies, each very different. I can speak to

God using my opening prayer telling him my thoughts and hopes. We have become more like minded and are speaking with much more understanding. Of course, he always knew me and any hanging back was on my side.

The whole of my attunement this morning consisted with me planning my day and what I should do to give myself more time for myself; strange but helpful. Spirit know that I have to have everything in place before giving myself over to them. More work on the above subjects will be needed.'

J. 'Well that's very unusual because it was almost like a contemplation attunement. You used your time in attunement to help yourself in the physical and again, very unusual but we are all given freedom of choice, freedom of will to decide what to do and how to think, so why not? So that is quite unusual for you to sit in attunement and say, right, I'm not going to attune per se', I'm going to work out what I need to do now?'

G. 'It is very physical - on the physical plane.'

J. 'But you could have done your attunement as normal and then when you have a cup of tea at four o'clock, you could have sat down and worked out your plan but you didn't, you combined the two. It doesn't matter because, as I said, it's all holistic, it all helps, it all helps you on your journey, it's all progress because the spiritual and the physical are one and the same.'

G. 'Which is blending, which is what attunement is. The following day, the 14 October, this is called, 'Seeing the bigger picture.' At the beginning of this morning's attunement, I found myself on one side of a mountain gorge. I was looking across to the other side upon where I could see animals grazing. I could not understand why the scenery before me seemed to be moving in one direction when I appeared to be travelling in the other?

It was very hot and the countryside looked like pictures I had seen in books about India. Close behind me I could hear the sound of a train; a small one, open-sided, rattling along the mountain track. It was as if I could see behind and in front at the same time.

Looking down, I could see the ground but it was approximately six feet below my shoes. On the right side of me I could see a pair of what appeared to be a man's bare feet. On the left, were a pair of dainty slippers sticking out below a blue gown. I was being held between my angel and my guide. There were two hands linked at my back and two more, one each side, holding my upper arms firmly; they were keeping me steady.

No-one spoke, we just watched the mountains, sky, animals and felt the sun and wind upon our faces; just observers. Of course, stand back and look at the bigger picture or, as in this case, hover! As soon as this thought entered my mind, I found myself back in my chair.'

J. 'Quite surreal just to see a pair of feet, was it a pair of feet or one foot?'

G. 'Two feet.'

J. 'Two but the feet on one side were bare whereas the feet on the other side had shoes.'

G. 'Yes or slippers.'

J. 'If we try and analyse what that meant, the feet, because, remember, *"Nothing is ever for nothing"* - it's like looking at a tarot card and seeing those bare feet one side and slippers on the other side. Just give me one interpretation?'

G. 'It made me laugh. I found it hilarious and that was the one thing that stuck out in my mind. I knew I was quite safe. I knew I was hovering; that I was being held up. I looked at this pair of feet and I actually laughed. I looked at the others so nicely presented and it was almost as if, it seemed to me, that spirit has humour?'

J. 'Oh, most definitely!'

G. 'That everything isn't dreadfully serious, they teach us by making us smile sometimes. We get hung up on our own selves, being serious, trying to get it right and we must get it right and we don't sometimes and I think they must find us hilarious sometimes and it's as if they were saying, 'C'mon Grace, lighten up!'

J. (Jenny laughs). 'Literally, I get that! I *do* get that, definitely and spirit also say they can communicate with you better when you're in a positive mood, when you're happy, when you're glad, when you laugh - again it's the positive to positive.'

G. 'Yes, I realise this.'

J. 'And maybe, I was just about to say, 'make light work.''

G. 'Very good!'

J. 'Your guides may want you to make more light work, meaning you're work doesn't have to be a drain or if you 'colour' it differently, it's still works underneath but with a different wash on it. Maybe they're saying, approach work in a more light-hearted manner?

I actually think and you have to be the judge of this, that maybe your guides are saying that you take your work too seriously especially at this stage in your life and maybe in your husband's life? That you have a choice which is either go barefooted or put shoes on, yes? You have a choice how to approach things, how to live, how to make decisions - to make choices?

They appreciate that everyone is in a material world, in a physical world but the way you handle life, the difference it makes, is phenomenal.'

G. 'It's true.'

J. 'And also, what you get back by thinking in a different way, it can make an incredible difference. As you know, I always use the analogy of a chess board where if you move just one piece, the whole board looks different and that can apply, not just to what you do but how you feel, how you perceive, what you want, your goals. At the end of the day, what is really important - your priorities - they will keep changing too as you get older and grow spiritually.

I think maybe, I don't know, because this message is for you, this is not for me, but the more I make you think, which is what your guides want you to do - they want you to be an expert thinker - because the more you think, the better your relationship will be with your spirit guides, yes?'

G. 'Yes.'

J. 'That is why when you're with me, I will give you, 'Well, maybe, they're saying this or maybe they want you to look at that?' Take the blinkers off, widen the vista, especially you Grace, at this point in your life, I think this is quite a valid argument, don't you?'

G. 'I do. It's been tumbling around in my head a bit, anyway.'

J. 'Yes, and that's what I was just about to say; you already *know* this!'

G. 'But I needed it to be put into words so I could just consolidate.'

J. 'I think you needed to be reminded and also it's a 'timing' thing. You know what they say about spirit's timing? *"There's no such thing as time in spirit, but spirit's time is perfect."* So I think they want you to look at the bigger picture now. Look at it and see if you can do this a different way - it could benefit everybody?'

G. 'I agree, I absolutely agree.'

J. 'And again, look how clever they are? Spirit talking to you and you are already getting to understand their way of communicating with you.'

G. 'Yes I am, a little. It's so smooth, you don't realise sometimes what you *do* know.'

J. 'But this vision, this clairvoyance in your attunement, was like a tarot card. That picture could have been on the back of a card and when you were at the workshop where you were analysing what does it mean, what does it mean for me, yes? And because of the attunement which preceded that one - Oh, spirit are *so* clever - they're actually giving you a bigger picture! Every attunement you have is adding something more to clarify one message, don't you see that?'

G. 'I do, it's building, it's pulling together all these pieces.'

J. 'And your spirit guides are doing this attunement by attunement. So I do think, for you personally, that you need to realise how important this is. I very much doubt it will be easy because these things never are, it's a test. That is how we progress - we have to be tested. Spirit know when we're ready for the test and it's almost as though they are being very nice to you and giving you clues saying - we're testing you now!

They are giving you attunement after attunement and they want you to put all the pieces together so I think this is a chat in your ear on the physical plane - this is the way they are talking to you. This is one of the ways your spirit guides communicate with you and you are naturally acclimatising to the way this is being done.

When we talk about getting the best back, it runs in harmony with spirit being able to help you more easily if you are in a positive frame of mind. You will hear me say time and time again, to think and work in the positive.'

G. 'Yes.'

J. 'This particular truth weaves itself in everything we do in our lives. We tend to compartmentalise things. We naturally think, Oh, this doesn't have anything to do with positivity but *everything* is woven into *you*, into your life, into your path, your journey, the things you have to make choices about. There isn't any compartmentalisation at *all* which is why, after hearing your attunements each month, I will always ask you about things in your life because I know that the physical and the spiritual are one and the same.

I've always tried to explain this particular theory symbolically with a ladder. One side of the ladder is your physicality, your physical life and the other side of the ladder is your spirituality, your spiritual journey. The rungs in between are the chapters in your life, the challenges along the way and the hurdles you have to overcome but it's all *one*; one ladder.

But the ladder is also synonymous with you - *you're* the ladder. You have sides to you, you live on the physical plane, you *are* a spiritual being. It's the spiritual which teaches you how to live your life aright and how to make the best choices for you and your family.

So with the knowledge and understanding that you glean from this development course, it will help you get the best out of your life and therefore your journey will become more successful and hopefully, you will achieve more but you're still learning. You will never *ever* stop learning from a minute incident to a massive choice, it all helps you. It's the building blocks, for example, which is why *everything* in life is important so don't take life for granted.

And you also had that in an earlier attunement; *everything* is to do with the *all* and it *all* must be positive. Ultimately, you will hear your own alarm bells ring when you make negative decisions or a negative thought starts creeping in and you will hear yourself say, this isn't helping me at *all*, yes?

Also, you will find a way to spread that understanding to others. By being an exemplar yourself, you are helping others because one of the best ways to help others is by being an example.'

G. 'To lead by example.'

J. 'You don't have to say anything, you don't have to do anything in particular - just *be*. Then the people who know you, who hear you, who watch you, they then have the choice to respond to what they hear, to what they see, to what they now realise and understand about you.

So as a spiritual being, you are also a living embodiment of spiritual knowledge and understanding helping others and it just gets bigger, doesn't it?'

G. 'It's enormous!'

J. 'I will leave you with a headache if I continue but I know you're ready to hear all these things.'

G. 'I am, I am!'

J. 'The last thing I want to do is to give you bits only to leave out other bits because you need to expand your *thinking* and I know this is beginning to happen. You are starting to increase your thinking; to look at yourself, your life, your family, where you are at? Where am I now, what do I want, am I happy with who I am, etc?

And you've already said that you feel that you're changing and that is what happens when you begin to have spiritual knowledge and understanding. You can't stay the same, so feeling different is proof of your growth, proof of your development and it's exciting!'

G. 'It's extremely exciting!' This is my last one and this was the 18 October, this is called 'Solace'. Had my talk with God. I got rather confused and somewhat overcome during our conversation but I am sure He understands. A thought came into my mind that now my earth mother and father are in spirit, busy doing other things, He is my only father, mother and therefore my main support. My angel and my guide stood either side of me and it is becoming a very natural feeling; we are a unit.

When we three had taken our positions and got comfortable, I felt a strong energy touch my body. It came in from the front and was very different. I asked it to stand in the light before me. I could see a huge angel dressed in full angel garments complete with wings. He spoke to me saying, 'We will give you solace.' Then he repeated the same words looking down at me with such kindness.

As I watched, he spread his wings and flew upwards beyond my vision. I then saw myself at the foot of three steps in a large room shaking the hand of Prince Charles! Then I was back in my chair.'

J. (Jenny is laughing). 'Don't worry, I get that too - things pop in - I've had Elvis Presley! (Grace is laughing now). OK, what do you deduce from that attunement?'

G. 'Well, it made me smile at the time and I debated whether to even write it down and said, no, I have to do everything. It just kind of felt like, well, that's a job well done, something of that kind as if I had done something that I should be proud of and was being congratulated. I was a little bit confused over that; however, it felt very good and it felt very positive.'

J. 'Yes and I'm now getting 'rewards' regarding your spiritual development so I think that possibly the energy you felt was a progressive energy, meaning we're now preparing you for something else.'

G. 'Ooh, gosh!'

J. 'I get that for a number of reasons. Number one, the 'Solace'. Spirit always say that they can work better with us when we're 'out the way', when we're having nothing to do with things. The silence and the stillness is a great help to spirit when working with us.

The fact that you felt energies which were different, was also a clue. I think the fact that you have already admitted that you feel different and we have discussed that you must have learnt things and that your understanding has grown. It's like a stairway and you're being prepared for the next thing; so that's my deduction.

Also the fact that he was such a beautiful, strong and wise being, it also tells you not to take this lightly.'

G. 'No, he was in full flight, such power. You felt you were being held by the safest pair of hands you ever could be and that no matter what, it was all going to be alright.'

J. 'OK, so what else did you want to discuss?'

G. 'You asked me to think about the spaces between things and their connections?'

J. 'Right, OK. I wanted you to be aware of the importance of this factor when you look at things in life. Some people look at the obvious but the spaces in between, I feel, are what *really* count because they often contain bigger messages and I felt that I needed to point this out to you at this stage of your development.'

G. 'Yes, I have started becoming more aware of what individual aspects of my life mean. I am thinking more and I am also very much aware of words coming into my head. It started off with the word 'solace' but I've also had ubiquitous and omnipresence! 'Solace' just arrived in my head. I couldn't spell it and had to look up the meaning.'

J. 'These words are coming in and, again, I think, this is proof to you that your relationship with your guides has turned up a notch. We all need confirmation of what is going on. You're starting to get words come in that you don't normally use, that you don't know how to spell and don't know the meaning of but when you look them up, you see how profound these words are.'

G. 'I couldn't believe it!'

J. 'This is all part of the relationship too. This is all part of your growth but it's also your spiritual guides wanting you to know how well the 'reception' is, yes?'

G. 'It's amazing. If I ever needed proof that, to me, was proof!'

J. 'Yes and it's very important for us 'little ones' here on the earth plane to have proof and spirit know that too as it also spurs you on.'

G. 'And they've started working on my husband a bit as well.'

J. 'Brilliant! Now I gave you homework?'

G. 'Yes, I had to write half a page on my understanding of healing, personal or on a larger scale.

My dictionary, which was printed when there was still a British Empire, tells me that to heal means to make whole, to cure, often to forgive, to grow sound. Healing means the process by which anything is healed or cured and health means wholeness or soundness of body and mind.

But real healing comes from the heart, just a feeling, the thought to help. In order for healing to work at its best, it is all about the intention to channel from spirit without thought of reward. Permission should be asked from whoever requires this help and, if it is not needed, it is dissipated and returned to the earth, nothing is ever wasted.

Healing can be a smile given to someone you pass in the street, you do not have to know them. It can be a cheery good morning given to someone who perhaps lives alone, family now scattered, living their own lives or they may have lost their husband or partner to spirit and are still recovering.

It can just be a touch of your hand on someone's shoulder giving comfort. To see someone's face smile back at you, to watch them stand up a little straighter, walk with a firmer step is a reward in itself. There has been a change, you have made a difference. You, yourself, will feel better, lighter, healed.'

J. 'Brilliant, absolutely brilliant! I loved the humility most of all. OK, let's move onto some new material.'

Astral Travel &
Working In Your Sleep

Jenny: 'Today I'm going to talk a bit about astral travelling and working in your sleep.

You have probably heard me say to you after recalling a particularly vivid, unusual or disturbing dream that it sounds as though you are working in your sleep. This can obviously produce a different experience for each individual so I am generalising here.

Firstly, you need to understand that you are never alone when this work takes place. Secondly, I have mentioned to you before in our Workshop that our spirit leaves our body when sleeping as it is only our physical body that needs to rest, our spirit is infinite - like an eternal flame - it never goes out or needs to rest.

However, when your spirit leaves your body during sleep and comes into the realm of spirit, you are always escorted by the guides who walk with you and work with you. It is important that you understand that because no-one should ever travel through the astrals alone and you *have* to travel through the astrals to get to the higher realms of spirit so no-one ever travels through the astrals without the aid of their spiritual guides and helpers.

You may hear some people say, 'Oh, I astral travel.' In fact, it is very dangerous to do so unless you are with your guides. They should always be with you and it should always be a controlled situation. When you travel in your sleep, you are always protected by your spirit guides as the astral plane can be a dangerous place due to the lower vibrations of spirit which often dwell there in darkness.

Existing on the astrals are people who have chosen ignorance even though a lot of them are very clever, very intelligent yet for varying reasons they have chosen what we call 'the left hand path' which is one of darkness.

These lost souls have caused immense harm and pain and damaged so many people's lives not for reasons of punishment but because that is what they have created for themselves. You may remember me saying that we create our own heaven and our own hell - even though there is no such thing as hell - but people can create their own hell with their constant negative thoughts and deeds. Their whole being is one full of anger, bitterness, hatred and vengeance and they live on those low, dark levels, yet even they have the right to ask for help.

There are different types of work which you can do in your sleep state. Those who are healers will be taken to give healing. Those who are 'teachers' go back to spirit to teach. They teach in halls of learning; my son does this.'

Grace: 'I've visited the halls of learning.'

J. 'Lovely. They teach in the higher planes of spirit often to their own soul group and what they teach is what they experience here on earth. What it is like to be in the physical, what it is like to go through the experience of being here because this helps those who dwell in the realms of spirit. It helps our spirit guides to guide and helps them give the right advice to those with whom they work here on the earth plane; it is still a partnership!

Then there are those of us who undertake what we call rescue work but for those living in spirit, they consider this a teaching process - an enlightening process. Higher evolved spirit do not go down to the lower regions of the astrals as their very bright 'light' - their highly evolved energy - will harm an ignorant soul so they are not allowed to go.

But mediums like yourself have given spirit permission to be used in your sleep state and go down to those darker realms because, being in a physical body, you are of a denser vibration and can therefore go lower than highly evolved spirit, making contact with those ignorant souls without your own light harming them.

However, you are never alone when you do this. You are linked and protected by your spirit guides and can go and enlighten and help those who have called for help.

Earlier on in the course, I encouraged you to ask spirit to replace your energies at night. When you go to bed, if you do not wish to be used in your sleep state, say so. You see, if you feel you are being used in your sleep state it is probably because you have already agreed this arrangement with your guides before you came back; you have already given your permission.

Therefore, before going to bed you should always say, 'If you want to use me tonight, please replace my energy in the morning.' Alternatively, if you do *not* want to be used at night say, 'Please do not use me tonight, I just want to sleep.' If you fail to mention anything, spirit will still think that they have your permission.

I am sure some people have woken up in the morning and felt like, excuse the pun, 'death warmed up!' You have probably been working very hard and have forgotten to ask for your energies to be replaced. So remember to ASK - famous last words!'

G. (Grace is in fits of laughter). 'Oh, that says something to me, now I know! Oh, and I do forget sometimes. No wonder I wake up at five o'clock thinking (Grace is still laughing) ......oh dear me!'

J. 'Simple, it's very simple, right?'

G. 'That was very, very - they *are* clever aren't they?'

J. 'Yep, they do know when to say things.'

G. 'Yes they do but they say it in such a nice way.'

J. 'So, your homework for this month will be, write half a page on fear and negativity and your interpretation and understanding of it.

Now usually at this juncture of the course, I talk a bit about me and my experiences not because I'm showing off or anything but we've started talking about astral travel and I want to give you some examples of astral travelling that I've had and how it affected me.

I never know what each person is going to experience spiritually. Therefore, the more knowledge you have of what can happen, it's like being forearmed, you're forewarned so I'm going to share with you some of the things that have happened to me in the hope that you will be able to relate to this now or in the future.

Remember in Month 5, the 'Love lessons' it says, 'If you have knowledge, share it and may your mediumship be to that end.' So that's what I want to do now.'

Examples of Astral Travelling & Physical Phenomena

Jenny: 'In order to teach you about astral travelling, I am going to share some of my experiences with you. I think this would be a good way to learn.

The astral travel experiences I have had, have all been in my sleep state and never in attunement but that doesn't mean to say that it can't happen in an attunement because it can.

This new experience started off one night in bed. I began to feel that I had been given an anaesthetic because I suddenly felt very numb. This was followed by a rush of energy. This rush of energy seemed to make me 'split in two' as I now felt that I was in two places but I was still me - one person.

I was going to begin a journey which I would later realise was called astral travelling. I was aware that I was still in my bed, *very* aware so it was like I was experiencing two different things at the same time.

I also remember in one of your recent attunements Grace where you experienced going backwards and forwards at the same time so, in a way, you may have actually experienced something like this already?

So my first astral travel experience began with my whole body suddenly going numb - all of it - my arms, my hands, my legs, my feet, my body. I was like was a dead weight and then, there came this rush of energy. That rush of energy is the 'travelling' bit, it's what sends you into an 'astral travel mode.'

So the first time I had this, I was propelled forwards and immediately found myself looking into the vastness of a summer's day in the countryside but I was actually looking down at the countryside below so this rush was making me fly - so I was flying!

I then thought, I must have changed into a bird so I was going with it and flying and, as you can imagine, it was absolutely unbelievable! I could see this glorious sun-filled countryside as far as the eye could see. I carried on flying for not that long really as I then ended up in a tree. I had stopped flying and was looking at a caterpillar sitting on a branch opposite me.

I then looked down at myself and saw that *I was also a caterpillar!* I thought this is absolutely crazy, how can that be? If I've just flown over the countryside and now I'm in a tree, looking at a caterpillar and I'm *also* a caterpillar, I've just got to accept everything - I'm not lying to myself - this was as real as anything I have experienced.

I obviously felt a right twit and couldn't understand any of it apart from the fact that I had enjoyed it so much! And then I was back, back in my bed and the moment was gone.'

Grace: 'Were you still in a sleep state?'

J. 'I was never in a sleep state, no, I was awake.'

G. 'Was it just that time between waking and sleeping?'

J. 'Good question, no, it was right in the middle of the night. It wasn't in between sleeping and waking or waking and sleeping.'

G. 'Did you wake up suddenly and then start to astral travel?'

J. 'No, I think I was aware of the change to my body as I began to feel numb and heavy or I may not have been sleeping and just lying there like a lemon wanting to go to sleep; it was a long time ago when I had that first experience.

However, since then, there have been many times when, unbeknown to me, I am due to work for spirit. I can't get to sleep, never realising it's because I'm needed by spirit to help them. Eventually, I say something like for God's sake I want to sleep and then, finally, I realise that I'm needed for a rescue or something and when it's all over I'm able to go to sleep!

When this particular incident happened all those years ago, it was my first astral travel experience and it was also at the beginning of my 'above the ground' spiritual journey; when I knew for certain that I was mediumistic.

When I told my mentor about the flying and the caterpillar the next day, I thought she would laugh at me for my stupid experience but she didn't laugh at all. She smiled and told me that in spiritual terms a medium is often betrayed as a butterfly so I immediately replied, 'So I've begun then?' I knew that the caterpillar would have to go into a cocoon to emerge as a butterfly, and she replied, 'Yes, you've begun.'

So it was also a personal message for me in the form of an astral travel experience; I had the new experience and a message as well! The fact that I had this experience the night before I was due to meet my mentor was something which would occur again and again with my own pupils as on a number of occasions one of them would say, you never guess what happened to me yesterday or last night?

This was a pattern I could identify with *so* well as it used to happen to me the night before I was due to meet my own mentor and now it was happening to them!

The next time I astral travelled was the night I had been to a funeral. This person was very dear to me and when his coffin was being taken down the aisle, my first thoughts were, I'm sorry everyone, he's not here, he's in 'spirit hospital'.

This young man had had a long illness and I had been taught that people who die after having had a long illness cannot immediately return to spirit. Their energies are so depleted that they would first need to go to spirit hospital; a name I thought was so cute.

These tired souls stay there until their energies have been maintained and reach the correct level so spirit hospital is like a spiritual staging post where you are treated before going on to your appropriate spiritual dimension.'

G. 'So you would be resting?'

J. 'I do not know what they do but this place has a function and in 'A Medium's Tale' I mention another example where a neighbour's husband had died, again after a long illness. He had been placed in a hospice where he had died and I remember spirit had told me that he had 'gone from one hospital to another'. This had made me laugh because I knew exactly what they meant - that his passing had been from a hospital on the earth plane to a hospital in spirit - and I remember thinking what a wonderful way to go.

So I was already in possession of this knowledge when I had my next experience. When I astral travelled the second time I had exactly the same symptoms; the feeling of being anaesthetized, of being completely and utterly heavy, unable to move or do anything.

I immediately thought, I know what's going to happen now, I'm going to astral travel again which, of course, is what I did because this was the way it worked; the procedure which would always precede my journeys. However, it doesn't mean that if you astral travel, you would necessarily follow the same process as me.

I have taught people who have told me they have astral travelled but I haven't always seen them experiencing the same 'procedure' as me. It is an individual experience but I guess it must incur an overall process as well.

So, in my second experience, after feeling numb and having the rush of energy where I 'split in two', I first saw what looked like the Parthenon in the distance. I then noticed there was a sign across two of the columns like when you see a 'Derelict - Keep Out' sign. Then the Parthenon started to come towards me and I remember thinking how is this possible? When I looked down I saw that I was on a 'dolly' - a small track similar to what they put cameras on in film making - and I realised, hang on a minute, I'm now being taken to the Parthenon!

I got nearer and nearer and was then taken through the heavy, thick columns and I found myself in this grey room. It was like being surrounded by grey mist or seeing through a grey veil, it was all grey like powder grey; it wasn't a morbid grey but misty and I could see through the mist.

The next thing I saw were two nuns who were dressed in light grey habits and grey wimples with white banding inside their wimples. I couldn't see their faces but one was standing nearer to me and the other one further away.

Then I noticed that the ground was sand, that very cool, soft sand that runs easily through your fingers and toes. I also noticed there were two fires in the ground which were circular in shape with flames coming up out of the circles; again one in the foreground and one in the background and I realised that these fires were lighting up the room.

There were also two small circular pools of water, again one near me and the other further away. I was just totally mesmerized by what I was looking at, I mean, it was incredible and then I heard the words, *'Yes, this is Spirit Hospital.'*

I immediately realised that I had only thought of this place earlier that afternoon at the funeral so to astral travel to spirit hospital that very same night must be to confirm that yes, you're right this is what it looks like! This, to little me, was phenomenal and in a league of its own, especially as I knew who was there.

It was incredibly personal and very special to me and again, spirit never do just one thing. They give you the experience, the confirmation that you're thinking correctly and not only that, this is what it looks like and yes, this is where your friend is! It was just layer upon layer. Amazing!

I had a couple of Princess Diana experiences but the one I want to explain, again, happened the night of a funeral. The night I watched Diana's funeral on the TV, the same thing happened. The numbness, the rush, the split, I knew exactly what was going to happen; Oh, I'm going to astral travel now, I wonder what's going to happen?

This time I was standing at the bank of a river. I could see a lush island in front of me in the middle of the lake. There was a rowing boat moored beside me and someone offered me their hand and I went to step into the boat but then my mind strayed to something else and everything went and I lost it!

I realised, there and then, that when you have a spiritual experience like this you have to stay 'in the moment'; don't look back, don't divert your thoughts, keep focused, 'travel' with it and see what happens.

If you're experiencing something in the spiritual you must not think 'in the physical' - as Jenny on the earth plane - because you're actually 'in the spiritual'. The minute you think of something about the physical, you're back in the physical.

Remember, everything is mental. Look how fickle, powerful and amazing the mind is. So I lost the journey and, of course, I was mortified. The only consolation I received was when Princess Diana was later buried on an island in the middle of a lake and I thought maybe that was the significance of it?

I didn't learn my lesson either as I had another astral travel experience after that where I was taken to a place that looked like Stonehenge. I saw the Nazarene standing by one of the tall stones with His arm around John the Baptist who was carrying a staff and all I could say - out loud - was, 'Oh my God, Oh my God, Oh my God' and I lost that experience too. So I was very, very cross with myself for not learning from my last mistake. I think I probably sulked for a whole week!

So there are some examples of astral travel but the main thing is for you to understand that if you're supposed to experience something, those experiences are for your higher good and you must try and not let them pass you by especially for a developing medium like yourself.

There are other forms of spirit communication where you experience physical manifestations. Again, I'm not going to go through all of the ones I've had as a lot of them are in 'A Medium's Tale' but, you may remember the example of the spider when I tried asking for proof from spirit?

A clairvoyant had encouraged me to ask for proof and when I finally decided to test this out in one of my attunements, I never actually thought I would get an answer. Although, in hindsight, the whole thing was a bit like a joke, it wasn't a joke to me as the proof turned out to be a big spider who, I later learned, was actually my Gatekeeper in animal form.

This was how I was introduced to him personally! He had presented himself to my mentor as a human the first time she and I met, however, after his first meeting with me as a spider, he reminded me in no uncertain terms that, 'You do not need to ask for proof. YOU, of all people, know we are here.' So a bit of stern talking balanced out his joke.

However, the whole incident formed part of our incredible relationship, part of our getting to know each other and part of me finding out he had a sense of humour. You know a relationship is 360 degrees, there are many sides to it so I learnt a lot about 'the spider' - my gatekeeper - in those early days.

Thereonafter, my gatekeeper would always show himself and appear as a spider especially when I was having a first experience like the first night I worked on the church platform. When the service was finished someone got out a ladder to get a big spider off the wall and so I thought, hey, he's been here! Again, "Nothing is ever for nothing" and I always say this.'

G. 'But it is so true.'

J. 'So, spirit's way of communicating can be in a multitude of ways and sometimes they can communicate with you by something physical. There is one story I do want to tell you about because I have something to show you.

I came home one Friday afternoon with my son Sam and as we were bringing the shopping into the house I saw something lying on the carpet just inside the lounge door. This piece of rock was about the size of a small box of matches. I looked over at the fireplace on the other side of the room and thought there was no way it could have fallen down the chimney and rolled right across the room to the door; it was physically impossible!

I then looked up at the ceiling in case the ceiling was coming down! However, my first thought was that it was something to do with spirit but I immediately thought there must be another explanation, so straight away, I put this thought to one side.

I had friends for lunch on the Sunday and before leaving I handed the object to Tony and asked him what he thought it was? He examined it for a bit and said it looked like chalk and then his wife exclaimed, 'Chalk, blackboard?'

When I returned to the lounge after bidding them goodbye, I immediately heard spirit say, 'You may be the pupil now but you will be the teacher' and this is what they left me, this piece of rock chalk. This was a present from spirit and a spiritual present is called 'an apport.'

G. 'I've always wanted to know what an apport is?'

J. 'Yes, so this is my present which I obviously cherish. I know it doesn't look very much and, of course, what had I been taught? - *"Always go with your first thoughts as they're usually the right ones."* So there was another spiritual truth thrown in for me to re-affirm! So Grace, you may be lucky enough to get an apport one day.'

G. 'We do dismiss things because we think it's impossible, improbable and we do put it to one side till something comes along which gives you a little nudge and says do we understand that?'

J. 'I think it is the law that everything is just as it should be and totally balanced and whatever you need, if you've earnt it, you get it. Do you remember in the 'Love' lesson I said that you can't demand or bargain for things, it's pointless, forget it. One has to earn everything and it's the universal Natural Law - Cause and Effect - and that works 360 degrees so if you need it, you have it.

It's all part of learning and I think one of the most important things is that as long as you realise that you're a unique person on a unique path, it's got nothing to do with anyone else what spirit are doing. People will say, oh I wish I was like you but what they don't understand is that we are all doing what we're supposed to be doing at this moment in time. It doesn't make one better than the other or one right and one wrong, life doesn't work like that. Spiritually, there is no competition in life.

It's to be expected as we don't know any other way being on the earth plane. However, we must all try and work things out for ourselves. Examine what others are doing, what are they saying? All this is necessary so you can work out what do *you* think, what do *you* feel, what do *you* think you should be doing or saying; we all learn from others.

That's the whole point of the path, the journey. We are all given freedom of choice, freedom of will to make the best decisions for ourselves. Sometimes it doesn't matter how many times you tell people this, they will always say, why can't I do this or why can't I be that but then this message just hasn't sunk in yet and they also don't love themselves enough to be an individual.

Another example where spirit have communicated with me in the physical is by giving me a flat tyre because they don't want me to go somewhere or by making things awkward because they want me to do something else.

Our spirit guides want us to *think*, why is this happening? Spirit can communicate with you in a physical way here on earth not just by using your psychic senses. This course is all about developing communication with your spiritual guides so at this juncture, I try and explain that this can take *any* form of communication, yes?

It can be via astral travelling, it can be through something physical in your life. It can be an experience you've had where you know it's a test, when spirit are saying, do you get it, do you understand what we're saying, can you 'read' this properly?

So there's a multitude of ways when communication takes place and communication doesn't just take place in your sleep state or when you're in attunement. It takes place here in your house, it can take place whilst you're out walking, driving, anywhere - so this is *really* the message I want to put over this month.

There are more examples in *'A Medium's Tale'* especially the experiences I have had in my car, where I have physically wrestled with spirit, received guidance when I got lost and been sent an extremely negative elemental which clung onto my windscreen. All these experiences have both communicated and taught me the lessons I needed to learn at the time.

And, as a result, I do tell *all* my pupils to be disciplined and not to think about spirit whilst driving in the car - always be closed down. Help yourself by listening to music.... or sing!

It's when we take our blinkers off that we understand that communication can happen at any time, in any fashion, whichever way our guides think is the best way to get their message across to us.

We have to learn to understand what our spirit guides are saying, what do they mean, what are they referring to and this all takes time. You're getting to know them more and more as the days and months go by and never forget that your first thoughts are normally the right ones!'

G. 'You have to be quite alert to catch that first thought as another one may follow very quickly.'

J. 'Yes, it may do but your 'Jiminy Cricket' will tell you, yes?'

G. 'Yes.'

J. 'Are there any questions?'

G. 'I've smiled a little bit because some of the things that have happened in my attunement are things that you have explained and I would have asked you but now I don't need to!'

J. 'Well spirit have a very good habit at providing answers you know! I just want to say before I forget, that the communication between you and your guides is learnt both ways not just by you; so they are also getting to know you better too!'

Bobbie's Attunements At This Stage Of The Course...

Jenny: 'Well Bobbie, it's lovely to see you.'

Bobbie: 'Yes, it's lovely to see you too.'

J. 'OK. Shall we start off with lighting our lamps to let spirit know we're here and then begin with your attunements, I'll ask some other questions later.'

B. 'Right, Tuesday, 6 November, this morning's attunement was quite eventful. I went into the silence and I found myself on the lush plateau. This time things changed a little. By the pool was a wooden seat so I went and sat on the seat.

I then became aware of a path going behind the waterfall and there seemed to be a cave so I followed the path and it did lead into a cave. I was expecting the cave to be dark but it was full of light. In the middle of the cave on the sandy ground was a ring of stones with a fire inside. White Eagle was sat there and beckoned for me to join him.

I sat beside him. It was very quiet apart from the crackling of the fire. Then I seemed to be pulled backwards and upwards. I was flown over different scenes. A native American camp with dancing going on round the fire and singing, then over deserts, then over forests. Then I came to this old wooden building with signposts nailed onto the walls but the writing was something I did not know.

I then saw a man who looked like Gandalf. He beckoned me to follow him along a passageway so I did. The next thing I remember was hearing someone say, 'Although the road of love and light was not an easy road, know that I would never walk the road alone. I would be guided, protected and loved all the way.' Then I was sat back at the side of the pool.

I then found myself very tall again. It was definitely male but I didn't recognise who it was so I asked but could not get an answer. So I called my gatekeeper who I know is called Yellow Wolf and asked him to take this energy away. Immediately I was back to myself.

I believe this happened to prove to me that I am protected from any energies that should not come forward or that I am uncomfortable with. I only have to ask my gatekeeper to help and he is there. Then I was back in my seat. Such a lot seemed to happen in half an hour. My sacred place seems to be expanding. I really look forward to my next attunement.'

J. 'There was much more there and the energy that drew close right at the end, you weren't comfortable with otherwise you wouldn't have told it to go away?'

B. 'No and they wouldn't tell me their name or who they were. I couldn't get anything.'

J. 'Can you describe what you felt? You may not remember as it was quite a while ago. Did you feel it or did you sense it... that it wasn't positive?'

B. 'Sensed it, I suppose, more than felt it. I just knew I didn't feel comfortable. With most of the energies that I've got now, I do recognise the energies and I feel safe.'

J. 'But what's going to happen when we progress a bit further and you're going to have to confront energies that you don't like, you *do* realise that don't you?'

B. 'Oh yes.'

J. 'I need to mention it because this is also your spiritual journey. Your guides actually said it was a journey but the journey encompasses everything especially all your challenges and all your tests.

For you to grow, you have to overcome challenges and you have to surmount difficulties so this energy at the end - that you wanted taken away - we will be watching because I think the next step, whenever it comes, will be for you to say to your guides, 'OK, I know you're with me, let the energy stay and help me deal with it. OK?'

B. 'Yes, right.'

J. 'I want you to know this now because I think you're ready to know it because it won't be long before we'll be dealing with this sort of thing. Now, may I ask how did you know it was White Eagle?'

B. 'I've seen him before. I believe in a previous life he was my father.'

J. 'Oh really, how did you deduce that?'

B. 'In a meditation and I was a young Indian girl in a village and White Eagle was my father.'

J. 'And how did you know it was White Eagle?'

B. 'I don't know, I just knew. It's odd really, I just... it's knowing.'

J. 'OK, I'm not going to contradict you there. There may have been something you recognised or he may have been wearing something when you first saw him .....he wouldn't have had a T shirt with White Eagle on it!'

B. 'No, no!' (Bobbie laughs).

J. 'And I know this sense of 'knowing' is very powerful but did someone tell you it was White Eagle?'

B. 'Yes, they did but I don't know who, I just heard.'

J. 'Was it another medium who told you?'

B. 'No.'

J. 'It was a voice that *you* heard?'

B. 'Yes.'

J. 'That's fine, that's much better. OK.'

B. 'I just heard the words this is White Eagle.'

J. 'Just like you heard I am Joseph of Arimathea but you heard Arimathena?'

B. 'Yes.'

J. 'So how old were you then, how many years ago was this?'

B. 'Oh, it was quite a few years ago yes, about 10 years ago now.'

J. 'So it looks as though your lush plateau is your starting point now maybe?'

B. 'I still seem to go there.'

J. 'Do you ask to go there - do you visualise it?'

B. 'Yes, I do visualise it now.'

J. 'Because in order to grow, you need to do other things too so we'll wait and see what all your other attunements are and if they all start off there, then I want you *not* to visualise it in future, OK?

Let your guides take you somewhere because you need as much proof and as much of a relationship as possible. We trust spirit implicitly so we hold out our hand and say, 'You lead and I'll follow.' We'll talk about this at the end but do you understand what I'm trying to do? I'm trying to get your spirit guides to *lead* rather than *you* say, OK, we'll start off on the plateau.'

B. 'OK, right, I'm with you, yes.'

J. 'The plateau is *always* yours but you don't have to start every attunement there and already they're taking you off to other places, aren't they? So it's almost as though spirit are saying to you, 'OK, OK, we'll start there - at the plateau - but *now* we have to go HERE! (Bobbie laughs).

Whereas we could have gone straight *there!* It's all part of the learning isn't it and it's no big problem but it's just that I'm here to try and explain things, maybe to point out to you and suggest why don't you do this? It's like expanding, giving you the length and breadth of the relationship. You already know you feel safe so you can just say, 'OK, where to?'

B. 'Yes.' (Bobbie is laughing).

J. 'I am trying to think whether there were any other messages in that attunement, what do you think?'

B. 'The signpost. Anyway, I think it fits in with what you were saying.'

J. 'Oh yes, the signpost and you couldn't read what it said. Did you recognise the language?'

B. 'No.'

J. 'It wasn't hieroglyphics or had letters of our language?'

B. 'No, I didn't recognise any of it.'

J. 'Excellent, well that tells us something too, doesn't it? Because to me, you wouldn't have been given that unless they thought well, come on, you know what this says. They - your guides - are not going to be dumb enough to put a sign up that you can't read! But it tells you that, at one time, you *could* read it, yes, and that was before you went into where?'

B. 'Another passageway.'

J. 'Was that before you saw Gandalf?'

B. 'Yes, the signpost and then Gandalf and that was when they told me I'd never walk the road alone no matter how difficult it was.'

J. 'OK. So there was White Eagle, there was Gandalf and then there was Yellow Wolf and obviously he's a Native American Indian and probably 'chummy, chummy, pally, pally' with White Eagle somewhere along the line.

I think we'll just take that for what it was; a 'what you see is what you get' attunement but I think the most interesting thing for me was at the end, the energy you didn't like so I'm pulling that up. OK, next one?'

B. 'This morning's attunement was peaceful, restful and although not a lot happened, I did feel the sense of spirit which I found very comforting. I know they were there supporting me and just before I came round, I cupped my hand and was presented with a beautiful lotus flower. I heard the words, 'Your journey is like a lotus flower as each petal opens. This is like a stage of your journey completed.' I felt that this can be almost like a calendar of my journey so I will keep the lotus flower in my 'tool box'. I am finding my attunements very rewarding even when little appears to be happening.'

J. 'Lovely and when you saw the lotus flower, how many petals were open?'

B. 'About three, there was still a lot to open.'

J. 'So maybe there was still two thirds left to open?'

B. 'Yes, there were quite a lot of petals on it. White with pink at the bottom, it was beautiful.'

J. 'So maybe the lotus flower represents your infinite journey because I don't think it's your current journey - I think you're quite a way through your existing journey, unless you've got a hell of a lot of work to do and they're opening them like no tomorrow! We shall see, won't we?' (Bobbie laughs).

Your clairaudience seems to be good. You hear these messages whether somebody specific is talking or if it's given you generally. Do you still sit for half an hour and do they still bring you round the same way?'

B. 'Yes.'

J. 'I was going to say to you, I don't know why, I have the feeling and I have to go with what I was getting during the week. I want you to attune for ten more minutes, would that be possible?'

B. 'Yes, that's fine.'

J. 'This is what I'm getting so I want to test it out so from next time, I'd like you to ask your guides to bring you round after forty minutes if you have the time. OK, let's have the next one.'

B. 'This morning's attunement began as usual then I began to get feelings of pure joy and happiness. This feeling persisted all the way through. I again found my hands cupped together and when I opened them butterflies emerged and were flittering all around me. They were very beautiful, all colours that shimmered in the sunlight. I seemed to be in a wood just strolling through.

Then I felt myself growing tall and straight and I know it was Mtombi. She said she would help me to find a joy in all things and all situations then I was back in my chair. The feeling of joy and happiness is being like a young child going on a trip. It was a wonderful feeling. Thank you spirit for your help on my journey, I know I am not alone, you walk beside me.'

J. 'So it was that sort of anticipation of a young child?'

B. 'Yes, it was.'

J. 'It's really good that you actually explained that. It's nice for me to share that feeling too. Describing a feeling is often very hard and so that pin points the feeling very nicely.

What was also very interesting is something which we're actually going to deal with today which is the butterfly so I'm not going to say any more because I've just realised that we're going to talk about it a bit later. So that's good timing, isn't it?'

B. 'Oh right!'

J. 'Very simple but another gift - you're getting gifts galore! Lots of lovely rewards but again, *"Nothing is ever for nothing."* The other thing I like is the fact that your guides are making you cup your hands which is another qualification of your relationship. When your spirit guides draw very close they can encourage you to do things like cupping your hands so this tells me how far your relationship has come. It's not just hearing or seeing or feeling; they are now taking over your limbs!'

B. 'Oh right!'

J. 'Which is excellent so I'm delighted to hear that and I want you to understand and be encouraged by it, OK? That hasn't happened before apart from the lotus flower and now the butterflies so they're actually steering your hands - *whoah* - very good!'

B. 'It's lovely isn't it?'

J. 'It is.'

B. 'Right. This morning's attunement began with the tingling and heat as normal. First of all there was just the silence and darkness then I began to grow tall again and I recognised the energy of Jesus. He told me that this is how we would work together for healing. He said that as we begin to work, I would remember more as we have worked together many times before. I look forward to working together then I shrunk back to my normal size.

I then asked who my guide was that was always with me and was shown someone who was very familiar to me from when I first started to meditate. He was an old Native American Indian, his name was White Eagle. I feel so comforted in his presence. He has a gentleness but also strength. I just know I feel great affection for him. He told me that we will be together always. (Bobbie is now struggling to hold back her tears but they fall anyway).

He told me that we will be together always and there will be others who will teach me things that I need to know but he will be there always to help me with teaching, understanding and interpretations of symbols. I feel so blessed for the love, support and guidance that spirit gives me.'

J. 'Aah, this is very nice because when spirit's love draws so close it makes us cry so he is obviously here so please don't worry about that. It's lovely that you appreciate this so much and I think this is what stands out so strong about you.

You know, in this modern world where a lot is about take, take, take, gimme, gimme, gimme; a disposable, quick-fire happiness with instant gratification, it's an absolute joy to see appreciation and so can you imagine how spirit feel to get that appreciation? It glows in your aura so they see your true self, your true motives, if you like and, you don't just say it, you actually glow with it?

And, as I said before, you only get what you put into it, you can't rig it. Do you remember when I talked about spiritual love, I said that you can't ask for it or bargain for it - it comes when you're ready to receive it - so there's a spiritual love here which is due and it's showing itself more and more the longer I get to know you.

The thing that concerns me is about this Jesus thing. I'm not 100% sure that it is Jesus per se'. If you think of God - the greatest Power in *all* the universe - in the spirit world there is a hierarchy, OK. There are those souls who have done all they possibly can and they eventually decide that they no longer want to come back to the earth plane.

As a higher evolved spirit serving God, their ultimate compassion would be to join with God in the oneness and having done that, they would never be able to return to the earth plane again. Now, that is the ultimate of choices and obviously an incredible decision to make but they make that decision with their own knowledge and understanding which is so massive; you *totally* understand what you're doing and you do it.

Then you get people in spirit who, for reasons of ignorance or circumstances, don't immediately pass over to spirit realms but reside on the astral plane - the next dimension from the earth plane - and then you get all the layers, the spiritual dimensions in between.

Now the Nazarene is receiving his wisdom from that immense oneness, that supreme, universal, spiritual wisdom and so all spirit guides have, what I can only describe as a family tree - they are all receiving messages from the ones above them - from the guides who dwell in a higher plane to themselves and so these messages get passed down plane by plane until it reaches one of us. So, in essence, the person we get our advice and guidance and support from is often getting it from higher up the chain, yes?'

B. 'Yes.'

J. 'And it's necessary for you to know this because I believe that you're not just working with the Nazarene but I feel you're working with many others as well. However, it's to Him that a great many are looking to for the healing and because it's all thought, it doesn't matter where it comes from as long as the quality is of the right essence, do you understand?

Now many years ago, I was told by a spirit guide, 'Names - what use are they, I've been many people, which name do you want?'

B. (Bobbie laughs). 'Yes, I can understand that.'

J. 'But here on the earth plane, we want to identify with someone specific.'

B. 'It makes us feel more comfortable.'

J. 'Yes, it's more tangible and for us living here who are limited by our energy here on earth, it's a bit juvenile to spirit, if you understand my meaning. However, I feel that *you* have got to the stage where you can see it collectively and as a 'oneness' and I think you're ready to understand that your guide gets his messages from his guide and so on but it all comes from that one massive source of knowledge and understanding.

Please understand, I am not 'poo-pooing' the Jesus 'thing' but I want to open it up. I want you to see other ways of seeing things. I think last time I said to you that it may be Him because he knows you feel secure with him.'

B. 'Yes.'

J. 'It may be someone who looks like him - it may be John the Baptist for all I know. There have been many seers and, of course, it's also like the unsung heroes. There have been *so* many people that we've never heard of who are sublime in their enlightenment but we wouldn't know them, they have no well-known names but to look at, they remind us of someone we *do* recognise.'

B. 'I understand what you're saying but obviously the energy feels nice.'

J. 'But what it does do, and I know I'm repeating myself, but it tells you what level you're at in your evolvement and I think that your guides are trying to communicate that you're not just any old person. *You* have had *many* incarnations which I think was what was said in that first attunement when you went to different places and also with the strange language on the signpost.

That's what I was getting there but, also, the quality of your love is such that this is the calibre of spiritual people who are working with you and I think that is the *most* important message out of everything. Do you understand?'

B. 'Yes. This morning my attunement began as normal with the tingling and the heat. I then found myself on the beautiful plateau. The trees seemed to have grown thicker and stronger. I went to the waterfall and looked into the still pond. I immersed and went into the crystal clear water and it felt wonderful. I felt so refreshed. I came out, found the fluffy white towel. It felt so soft and warm. Then I was dressed. I followed the path behind the waterfall into the cave. I could feel the sand between my toes. There was a fire burning in the centre.

I felt I had to walk down a passage which led to another cave which was very brightly lit by a golden orb in the centre. The orb was not on anything, it just seemed to hang there. There were steps leading up to it. They went all the way around it. I just knelt on the bottom step. Then the orb just went out and it was dark, so dark that I cannot describe how dark. Blackness, almost thick blackness and then I felt someone beside me. They said, 'Are you afraid?' I answered, 'No, I am not.' They said, 'Why are you not afraid?' and I said, 'Because I walk the path of the White Spirit, the path of Love and Light.'

Then the orb was shining brightly again. I turned and went back to the first cave and by the fire sat White Eagle. I went and sat by him. I asked him, 'Am I beginning my next part of my journey?' He said, 'Yes, but this part will be slower and more intense.' He gave me a pale blue candle. I lit it and it cast a lovely pale blue glow. I felt calmness and serenity. White Eagle said if I felt the need for this calming effect to just light it again. I thanked him and then I left the cave.

On the plateau, the sun was shining brightly. I looked up and asked for my energy to be replenished. I felt a surge of energy and then I was back in my chair.'

J. 'It's getting heavy isn't it?'

B. 'It is isn't it.'

J. 'I definitely think the light going out was a test and to me, it's a test for the work you're going to be doing in the future and I'm not going to disclose this at the moment. There are two things now that are linked to the future as far as I'm concerned. The fact that you had that bad energy before - that was a test- and another one when the light went out! You could have freaked and run away not that you could see where you were going! (Bobbie laughs).

I'm amazed that I don't have to work very hard with your attunements. Sometimes attunements are very symbolic and I have to work 'like the clappers' trying to work out what it all means but these attunements are very simple, very effective obviously. You're getting clairaudience in them as well, telling you why things are happening so it's almost as though you don't need me at all!'

B. 'Yes I do!'

J. 'Because they're very self-explanatory. Another gift, a blue candle! My word, you've got your serene place - the whole of it - then you had the lotus flower, then the butterflies and now the blue candle, anyone would think it's Christmas! And a lot of these you can use time and time again so they're gifts for life, aren't they? And also when, for example, you use your blue candle, you'll know that White Eagle can link up with you because that's from him.'

B. 'Right, OK.'

J. 'You do seem to have quite a few guides surrounding you as well which obviously makes you very secure and it's almost as though they've joined hands now and you're in the middle so you're getting it from 360 degrees; very lovely, OK.'

B. 'This morning's attunement began in the usual way, the tingling and then the heat then it was just the silence and darkness for a while. I then found myself back on the beautiful plateau. I was drawn to the pool. I stood looking at the waterfall for a while then I bathed in the pool. I came out, dried myself on the lovely fluffy towel. I feel so cleansed afterwards.

I then made my way to the cave behind the waterfall. In the centre of the cave was a fire. Sat by the fire was White Eagle. I went and sat beside him. I asked him about the 21 December and what it all meant? He said it was not the end of the world just the end of a cycle and the start of the New Year. He showed me myself in a big circle holding hands and said I should link with others to welcome in the new energies. I then found myself back in my chair and the attunement was finished.'

J. 'Funny that he's just mentioned a circle and we talked about a circle. Do you plan to sit?'

B. 'Yes, I think I will.'

J. 'Were you going to before or you will now?'

B. 'No, I will do now but I hadn't planned to.'

J. 'Well I'm going to sit so we can sit together and link up. I haven't asked you about your interpretation of this. Is there anything you want to say at the moment that we haven't discussed?'

B. 'To be honest I think they're quite..... There are a few things sometimes that I have to work at to try and understand.'

J. 'Is there something that you wanted to mention; about this attunement or the one before that? Is there anything you recognise, any interpretations that you want to throw in that we haven't talked about?'

B. 'No, not really because they explain it quite a lot even if it's not in words. What they show seems to explain the point they're trying to get across.'

J. 'Alright. I don't want you just to rely on me to tell you things, I want you to talk to me about what *you* think too.'

B. 'To work it out?'

J. 'Yes, that's very important. I'm only here *for* you, I'm not here to *tell* you.'

B. 'The thing about the trees getting thicker and stronger, I thought perhaps that was me?'

J. 'Yes, I agree with you, it was synonymous with you definitely. I got that straight away, oh well done for that!'

B. 'This one's quite a long one actually. This morning's attunement began as usual but quickly things unfolded. I was once again on the plateau. I went quickly to the pool and bathed. Came out, dried myself as usual and then came to the cave behind the waterfall. There was a fire again in the centre and White Eagle was sat there. He beckoned me to sit beside him. As I sat down I became aware of other natives sitting around the fire. Then we all had drums and we were drumming with our hands. Then the circle opened and a medicine man came in dancing around the fire and chanting. There then appeared in the circle a large elk. I thought at first it was a moose but was corrected and told it was an elk.

The elk turned and began leaving the circle. The medicine man motioned me to follow the elk. We went along a passageway and came out into the sunlight. We went down a steep path which seemed to be a huge forest. We then went up a really steep path until we were on a precipice overlooking the forest.

Suddenly, a golden eagle flew down and landed on my shoulder. I then became the eagle, flying over the forest and as I looked down it was like looking through binoculars. I then flew back to the passage entrance and as I landed, I was me again. It was the most surreal experience, absolutely wonderful!

I then went back along the passageway into the cave. White Eagle came towards me and said I should find out what messages I have learnt from the experience and I should look it up as it was important. So I will look it up in Jenny's book. I can't wait for my next attunement.'

J. 'OK. I got that he wanted you to interpret the journey as well as the elk and the eagle, what did you get? Did you look up elk and eagle?'

B. 'Yes. I think elk was about strength and in a way, I think this is what you said earlier on, it's a bit about discernment. Not to take everything at face value really and flying over like an eagle and seeing things like as if you were looking through binoculars - look closer.'

J. 'Looking at things subjectively rather than objectively and looking at things with wider.....'

B. 'With wider implications for you.'

J. 'Yes, often we tend to worry about things that really aren't worth the piece of paper they're written on. If we saw the wider view, our worries would fade into the distance or into insignificance; they're petty.'

B. 'Very.'

J. 'We often miss the plot and think of other things which take up a lot of our time and use up a lot of negative energy, etc, etc. Maybe you have reached the stage in your life where your priorities are changing?'

B. 'They are!'

J. 'And so you see things from a different perspective now, like the eagle seeing things, seeing the wider view and therefore you're no longer wasting time on things 'grovelling on the floor'; you're looking up, you're setting your sights higher so all these have a symbolic meaning.'

B. 'Right, yes, I can see that.'

J. 'And also, saying goodbye to the old Bobbie, soaring to new heights yes, there's a lot there really and all to do with growth, what's now important and maybe what to devote your time to? It may also be a little nudge to say, 'Do you remember you said you'd do this work?''

B. 'Right.'

J. 'And you want to be able to fulfil the purpose of your incarnation, don't you? Which is why you're doing this, isn't it?'

B. 'Yes, yes.'

J. 'So it's all wrapped up in a bow really, the whole box is full of it. It's saying different things but the meanings are the same. Do you get that too?'

B. 'Yes, I also think it's to do with strength but I don't think it refers to a physical strength more strength of character.'

J. 'Yes, and spiritual knowledge and understanding naturally leads to more strength of character. It also gives you peace, you feel stronger with more confidence. You also get peace so the things that used to worry you, bother you or concern you, no longer do.'

B. 'No they don't.'

J. 'So you're thinking on a different level now, good! Do you see why I don't want you to always go to your plateau?'

B. 'Yes, I'm understanding that now.'

J. 'I'm not saying that it hasn't been necessary, I'm just staying that I think you can try and put it to the test and say to your guides, 'OK, I'm just going to go blank, *you* can take me where you want us to go' rather than meet me at the plateau.'

B. 'Definitely. This morning my attunement began in the usual way. Nothing happened for a while then I got the most odd feeling. I felt a really strong energy surging throughout my body. It was a strange feeling but not uncomfortable. I can't explain it really, you would have to feel it to know what I mean.

I then began to shrink and became bent over, my head almost touching my chest. I felt very old, a woman definitely. I did not like the energy, I can't say why, I just felt really uncomfortable.

Then I began to grow tall, straight and strong. I was a male. I knew the energy and liked it. It was my gatekeeper, Yellow Wolf. He said that I should not be afraid as he would always be there to keep me safe from any energies that were not welcome. He was there to protect me. He told me he was of the Cree nation then he was gone.

Then I heard, well not exactly heard - just knew - I should link with others around the world to welcome in the new energy as this energy was a much stronger energy. It was coming to help more people to become Light Workers and that a stronger energy was needed at this time. Then I was back in my seat. So I will tune in at the correct time.'

J. 'Again, what did you get from that?'

B. 'That Yellow Wolf really wasn't going to let anyone hurt me, that he would be there to protect me.'

J. 'Do you know why?'

B. 'So that nobody can infiltrate, take over my body, he wouldn't let them; any negative energies.'

J. 'Because you will be working with negative energies.'

B. 'Yes I know.' (Bobbie laughs).

J. 'The thing is that the 'the old dear' was needing help and they were testing you just like the one you called away at the end. You need to get used to these negative energies because you will be helping them but you're going to be working with your spirit guides whilst you do that, so you'll be perfectly safe.'

B. 'Right, yes.'

J. 'I think it's to do with rescue. You're being prepared for rescue work, I'd put my money on it!'

B. 'So it's really to get me started?'

J. 'You've started feeling these negative energies and you have also had acknowledgement from your guides; 'Yes, we know you're getting these negative energies but we're with you so there's nothing to worry about.' It's the experience - it's for you.

This is the way they are doing things, this is the way they're working with you. They're letting you sample negative energy but at the same time they're standing next to you and saying, 'Did you feel that? We brought that in because we want you to feel it as you're going to have to get used to working with energies you don't like. Those energies belong to people who need help and we're going to help you help them.'

B. 'Right, yes, well that makes sense actually.'

J. 'That's the second time today you've read out something that is showing you negative energies. *"Nothing is ever for nothing."* Spirit are not saying, 'Oops, sorry, didn't mean to give you that!' (Bobbie laughs). It's happening on purpose.

Spirit are giving you negative energies to feel, saying 'You don't like that, do you, NO! Do you know why, because it's not very nice.' These are the people who need help.'

B. 'Yes, it makes sense, it makes absolute sense.'

J. 'Grace has been having her negative experiences; you're getting them this way. Everyone's on their own path, it's all to do with you as an individual. Whether you believe it or not, you agreed that this would be the way that it would be done and at this point of your journey. So yes, that was very good.

And to me, it's like dipping your big toe in the water. Your guides are being really gentle with you, aren't they? They're not leaving you for one split second, they're so solidly around you and letting you know so too. Anything else?'

B. 'Today's attunement began in the usual way. I went into the silence. I waited for things to unfold and although I felt spirit with me nothing really occurred. I get the feeling that I am still being taught to have patience, particularly with myself! I know this is one of my failings; I must work on this. Even though nothing happened I still feel that I am learning.'

J. 'Patience is very necessary - it's one of my 'biggies' - and, as I have told you before that when the least is happening, the most is happening. Next?'

B. 'I began my attunement in the same way. I went into the silence and was determined to have patience. I found myself under the lovely tree on the beautiful lush plateau. I went over to the pool and swam around in the clear water. It was so restful in the water, not cold at all. I came out, wrapped myself in the white fluffy towel then made my way along the path under the waterfall into the cave. The sand in the cave felt warm beneath my toes. In the centre was a fire and sat by the fire was White Eagle. I went and sat beside him. Then there were others sat around the fire and we all had drums and began drumming!

It was very slow drumming. A black bear appeared in the circle. He slowly ambled towards me and sat before me and allowed me to stroke his thick coat. He was gentle and I didn't feel at all afraid. The next thing was I was sat back in the chair. I have tried to think what this meant but as yet I still don't know. The only thing that comes to mind is strength.'

J. 'OK, so did you look up black bear?'

B. 'Yes. Actually it was about using all your resources and obviously strength is involved.'

J. 'Have you looked them up in Animal Speak or your cards?'

B. 'Your book.'

J. 'The Animal Speak book gives you quite a lot on each animal so you can pick out different aspects of each animal.'

B. 'Another bit was using - not wasting anything - they never waste anything and they also search for things.'

J. 'OK. Seek it out.'

B. 'Maybe they're saying I'm not seeking out the meanings properly?'

J. 'Yes, I agree. I think it may mean about being more in tune, about doing more thinking. A lot of the time spirit will say, don't go looking, let it come to you, we'll bring you what you need. I don't always agree with the physical 'seeking out' bit but what I do think seeking out applies to is seeking out the meaning of things.

You remember the saying *"Nothing is ever for nothing."* When things happen to you, don't just accept it, think about *why* it happened, is it telling you something? It's almost as though this attunement means working on your relationship with your guides more. Ask them more questions.

Don't accept them so much. Seek your guides out more in as much that the relationship you have is two-way. You *have* been asking questions which is good, however, if you're growing and having a new phase, I think your guides may want you to expand the relationship more. For example, when you're at home, you don't have to be in attunement to have a relationship with them, they can be with you whilst you're washing up!

I used to get the most from my guides when I was near water whether I was in the bathroom or by the kitchen sink; it was classic. I would get so much when I had water in front of me and I came to understand that and you're relationship is developing too now.'

B. 'I think that's probably what you've just said actually, I've just been doing this in attunement.'

J. 'And then switching off the light - so to speak?'

B. 'And that's not it?'

J. 'No! You've started this course and because you've been doing your attunements in your home, your home and your garden has become more of a spiritual sanctury now.'

B. 'Right. So I don't need to close down after I've done my attunements?'

J. 'Yes, you do as it's good practice, as it's a good discipline but things will still pop into your mind. Spirit will still talk to you, yes?'

B. 'Yes.'

J. 'I mean opening up is like the blinking of an eye, you only have to think of spirit and you're open and you are allowed to do this at home. You can relax your disciplines more at home because, like your body is spirit's temple, your home is your own spiritual temple, do you understand that? So maybe this is something that you haven't been aware of that you can actually talk to your guides and have a relationship with them outside of your attunements but still be in your home which you now know is your sacred place. So it looks as though you didn't know that?'

B. 'No.'

J. 'Well thank God we've discussed it! It reminds me of when you took things literally and started attuning with your eyes open and I didn't know this until a bit later! (Bobbie laughs). Well that is a massive thing we have discovered today!'

B. 'Yes, that's good!'

J. 'So you can talk to your guides at home and you can receive - so you can 'make calls and receive calls' - and it's free; it doesn't cost you anything! And even when you're in the garden and in the woods, yes? Attunement is like the concentration of the relationship.'

B. 'OK, yes.'

J. 'They never leave you, they've told you that, haven't they, they're always there. I mean you could be in a cafe and suddenly they'll drop something into your mind and you'll know it's them. You can just mentally say thank you and then switch off. You can't have them say, 'Oh God, we can only speak to Bobbie between eight and nine!' (Bobbie laughs). Your guides must get really frustrated!'

B. 'I was just thinking that actually, it's now patience with them!'

J. 'It doesn't matter because they're working with you even when you're not attuning. I think it's more the pleasure of being able to speak to them whenever you're at home. Whatever's coming through, whatever they put in, whatever's happening to you, maybe you giggle because something's happened and you know they've done it on purpose, yes?'

B. 'So it's just really acknowledging?'

J. 'It's just carrying on the relationship; just expanding it. Spirit are great opportunists so they'll do whatever, whenever. So next time the two of us get together you may say to me, 'Remember you told me this, well I was sitting in the garden.......'

B. 'I was putting the washing out!'

J. 'I can't tell you what's going to happen; it reveals itself when it's needed so it's showing itself today. Anymore? You don't have to read every attunement, just read the ones which you think are relevant or the ones you want to share, OK?'

B. 'We'll just take it as read that I'm in the cave again with White Eagle. We got up and I followed him along a passage. We came out on top of a hill - a cliff - and I could see like golden walls everywhere I looked. There was a lot of noise in my head like thousands of voices talking at once. White Eagle took my arm and guided me back to the cave. We sat again in front of the fire. He began to talk to me.

He explained that before we could begin to work I had to master protection. They would be there to protect me but it was important that I protected myself. He said the stronger our link got, the brighter it would shine and the more it would attract and that some spirits would be less desirable than others. He said that I needed to place myself in a bubble of silver light. My guides and helpers would use golden light.

As I sat there I felt myself growing again. I knew I was male but not old. I felt it was my nephew Jason. It did not last for very long, in fact, it was quite brief. I then heard the words, 'He is learning also.' Then I was back in my chair. I felt I have quite a way to go before I am ready for the work I have to do even though I am not sure what it is I am going to be doing. I am enjoying my journey.'

J. 'Excellent! Well that was very significant, wasn't it? You've got another present which was a protection present which is excellent because you will need that in your work on top of the other protection symbols that you already have so I would take heed about protection.

I don't know exactly why they're bringing it up, however, the deeper we go into the course, the more protection you will need but also, he talked about a bright light which was fascinating because that's what negative spirit are attracted to, so that was very interesting and reassuring.

And yes, I get the feeling that you need to roll your sleeves up girl and prepare for what's coming! The one thing we've discovered is that you can communicate anytime when you're at home or in the garden. Apart from that, I think everything else is going swimmingly. You seem to swim a lot anyway in the pool, hee, hee!'

B. 'Do you think I was a dolphin in a previous life!'

J. 'Nah, but seriously, it's cleansing and invigorating and also, years and years ago, for holy people, cleansing was very much a part of their spiritual regime. Have you heard of the Essenes?'

B. 'I think I've heard of them.'

J. 'They used to have dedicated pools in their communal dwellings and they would cleanse themselves regularly as part of their religious practice, similar to water used in a baptism ritual, I guess, so cleansing in water as part of enlightenment and purification has a part to play. OK, so your homework?'

B. 'Yes, I did it! What I understand attunement to be is going into the silence, quietening the mind, regulating the breath. This allows spirit to draw close to you and to be able to communicate more easily without having to try and get through all the thoughts and plans that are going on in your head. You can then begin to get communication between yourself and your guides, helpers, family and friends. You can then build a close relationship with them thereby helping each other on your journey for as spirit is teaching you, they too are learning so it is a sharing experience.

Spirit will help you, protect you and love you and you know that they will be with you always. Once you begin your journey with spirit, your outlook on everything changes and you are never the same again but it is a wonderful, fulfilling experience.'

J. 'Brilliant! All I would say is that your journey with spirit began this time when you were first conceived and has been continuing ever since. But your relationship takes on a whole new meaning once you begin to attune which brings your relationship with your guides into a league of its own - like a seed bursting and beginning new growth - and so spirit enjoy the experience more as communication is now a two-way affair and the bond grows even more.

OK, that was on attunement, what was the second homework I gave you, healing?'

B. 'Yes. To me, healing is being able to clear one's mind, to become a clear channel so the healers in the spirit world can work through you to deliver healing energies so you are an instrument for their energies. Again, it is a joint partnership. You and spirit working together as one for the benefit of those who seek healing so although you do not actually do the healing, your role is important for the spirit healers. The energies will guide you and inform you of anything you can do to aid in the healing process.

Again, it is a partnership that is not only beneficial for the person having the healing but also yourself, for you too will receive healing if needed, and, of course, spirit will know. I believe healing is a wonderful gift from spirit for all of us. Not only for the physical but for the emotional also. It is a privilege to be a channel for healing.'

J. 'Lovely. Right now we're going to move on to some new material and today we are discussing astral travelling and working in your sleep.'

Month 7

Jenny: 'Well, what can I say, welcome back Bobbie! I'm so pleased you're here.'

Bobbie: 'So am I!'

J. 'I just want to remind you that we need to close our eyes...'

B. 'And light our lamps.'

J. 'Yes, light our lamps. I'm sure all your guides are pushing to get into this room. I don't think you really need to ask them to be here, I think they're already here! Then we can begin. Great, so the 'wonderer' returns!'

B. 'Yes.' (Bobbie is laughing).

J. 'What I want to do just before we get back into our normal routine, I just thought we'd have a quick chat about the reasons you stopped. Are you able to share with me any of those reasons to help me understand?'

B. 'Yes, of course I can. We live in rented property, as you know, and we discovered that our landlord hadn't been paying the mortgage so it went into receivership. We had the landlord coming to us saying don't do this, don't do that, don't do the next thing, I will sort it all out. Then we had the receivers and they were saying that the worst scenario would be that we would have to leave.'

J. 'So it threw you off track but up until then were you attuning, was everything fine?'

B. 'Yes, apart from the one instance and that was when I went upstairs to make the bed and while I was making the bed, I suddenly had this; it wasn't a voice or anything else, it was this overwhelming feeling that I was going to be moving and I thought this is strange but I didn't give it a second thought.

I came downstairs, made a cup of tea, went into the living room and the mail had just come through the letterbox and in the mail was the letter from the receivers.'

J. 'Amazing, isn't it. You mentioned that after we linked up in December, you had nothing?'

B. 'Everything was fine when we linked up and then everything seemed to stop. I did start again on Saturday, 1 December last year.'

J. 'And what did you get?'

B. 'Nothing, nothing, nothing, nothing.'

J. 'So all your attunements were empty as well? So spirit were indicating that you need to stop.'

B. 'Yes.'

J. 'So that was your first clue that's something's amiss. What's going on, what's wrong, did you actually stop?'

B. 'I didn't stop actually until the 11 December which was my last one.'

J. 'What about the spiritual truth, *"When the least is happening, the most is happening*?"'

B. 'Well that is what I kept thinking all the way through. I thought mainly it was me, that I couldn't clear my mind and they couldn't get through so that's when I stopped.'

J. 'It must have been quite disconcerting for you because you didn't know what was going on? But then, when you *did* know, when you had proof of what was actually happening, in a way, it was very helpful, wasn't it because you now knew - that's why!'

B. 'Oh yes, this is why and because I *do* feel that there's always a reason. I always remember you saying, nothing is ever for nothing.'

J. 'So if that was the reason why you stopped, can I quickly ask you why have you now resumed?'

B. 'Well things have settled down a little bit and I miss it! There was a part of me missing.'

J. 'Aah, you can't have a better answer than that, not as far as I'm concerned so really you were pulled back?'

B. 'Yes in a way. I think that was my biggest reason, something is not finished.'

J. 'Unfinished business. Did you think about the course, think about having stopped it and what would it mean if you carried on and finished it, did those things go through your mind?'

B. 'Yes, I thought about all the different pros and cons actually but I just felt that I had something more to give.'

J. 'That is superb. OK. So we've caught up and you are now 'firing on all cylinders', if you like and back to the way you were?'

B. 'Yes, as much as possible, yes.'

J. 'Excellent! So welcome back and I'm thoroughly glad to have you back as not only did you miss it but we missed *you* because it hasn't felt right not having you with us and not carrying on and not being able to finish.

I, myself, felt as though I was standing on jelly a lot of the time and the jelly was moving here and there - Oh, what am I going to do! (Bobbie is laughing). OK, let's pretend that you never left so we're going to jump in and I'm going to say, how have you been and have you got any attunements to read and share with me?'

B. 'Yes I have. I'll start with the 21 December which is when I did it in the evening; should have been done in the morning.....'

J. 'No, no it didn't matter to spirit.'

B. 'Anyway, I sat to greet in the new energies. I was to link up with Jenny so I went into the silence and immediately felt the tingling and the heat. I asked my guides to help me to link up with Jenny and to greet the new energies. I felt White Eagle come close but I also saw 'Gandalf' as I call him so I felt that Jenny and myself had linked up.

After a little while, I felt a strong energy step forward and I heard the words, 'We have come to saturate this earth plane with love and energy. We feel it is sorely needed at this time.' I also felt two other energies. It felt quite intense but then it was gone. I know I did OK but I did get the words, 'The 28th we begin.' I believe this to mean I start my attunements again starting the 28 December so this I will do.

So I waited until the 28 December. This morning began my attunements after our Christmas spiritual holiday. It began with the familiar tingling and heat. I sat in the silence and waited. I felt the energies from the 21st step forward and I felt myself growing very tall and broad. I felt not only bodily strength but also a strong, I'll say, personality, for want of a better word. I asked for his name but he quite abruptly said that names weren't necessary as I would recognise his energy.

Then I shrank back to myself and he was gone. Then I grew again, this time I was again a male, tall and very slim, almost thin. This felt a much, more gentler energy. I asked for his name and I felt him smile he said, 'You may call me Isaac.' This energy was definitely not as forceful as the first one, then he was gone. I had the feeling there was another energy but this one did not step forward and then I was back in my chair after forty minutes passed.'

J. 'Forty minutes, brilliant! I think there was a hell of a lot there, I mean very encouraging. To think that you ended up stopping, I can't believe it! I had to laugh about the one who said about names because in the past I've always been greeted with, 'Name - which name do you want? I've had many names!'

But again, you've got a balance there. You've got the stern one and the gentle one which is lovely because we *do* need help of all kinds, don't we? For as we grow and new guides come in, which is obviously what is happening here, having these new energies coming in, you're *so* lucky to be able to recognise these energies. You're so lucky that they're coming in close enough for you to feel the change that is happening to you and to be able to decide, Oh no, this isn't Chunky, this is Fred! (Bobbie laughs).

Which is exactly how it should be because no two guides work the same way. The stern one will work with you in one way and Isaac will work with you in another but it doesn't mean that one is better than the other. They will each provide a different set of tools to support their teaching so that is brilliant, absolutely brilliant and as I said, I can't believe you stopped after that attunement, go on.'

B. 'This is the next day. This morning began in the now familiar way. Although I did feel that the heat was more intense, I felt the forceful energy step forward and I began to grow again. This does not bother me anymore as I seem to be getting used to it although it still feels strange.

I heard him say, 'I apologise for my abruptness. Had I realised that it is easier for you if you have a name so you may call me Daniel. It is a good name, it is as good a name as any other. Myself and many others have come at this time because there is much need for more loving energies. There is so much greed and hatred in your world it is upsetting the fine balance. We welcome all those who would work with us to restore the equilibrium. Thank you.' Then he was gone and I was sat back in my chair and the forty minutes had flown past.'

J. 'So he made his peace and you got a name?'

B. 'Yes, Daniel.'

J. 'OK. I think that's wonderful and you know, it's not surprising the words they say because we know it, don't we? We know how much work is needed and we know the way the world's going, it's not rocket science. When you're told, it does make you as sad as they feel?'

B. 'Yes, I was just going to say that to you actually. I just feel that they're very sad.'

J. 'Yes. OK, I'm not asking for your interpretation because a lot of these are self-explanatory.'

B. 'Tuesday, 1 January, 2013. I began my attunement this morning with anticipation. I went into the silence. I felt the tingling and the heat. I found it quite difficult to quiet my mind but I eventually managed it. I began to get flashing images going by really quickly of all different times and places. It was quite overwhelming. I don't know what that means, I'm sure. I will ask Jenny. When that stopped, I found myself in a huge white hall and in the centre was a tall brazier, I think?'

J. 'Was it like a black metal furnace?'

B. 'It was gold. It had pure white light coming from it. I then felt the presence of Isaac and Daniel who led me up to the brazier and Daniel took a metal torch kind of thing which he put into the bright white light, he handed it to me and told me to look at the light. He said that when I used my protection symbol not only to use gold but to use this pure light to cleanse.'

J. 'Like a shard of metal which he put in and took out again.'

B. 'And it was like white light coming from that. I thanked him very much and then I was back in my chair.'

J. 'That was wonderful Bobbie. I can identify with all these flashing images you spoke of. Sometimes - sorry, I'm laughing - I always used to call it 'Pathe' News' like what was shown in the cinema before the main film comes on!

It was when I sat in circle and it was just like, Oh, here we go and you're looking at all the things that cross your physic 'screen' and it was everything and anything. From all ages, all times, all histories and every time you saw something you would think, oh this is what it's about and then that would go and something else would appear and you would think, Oh, this is what it's about and that would go and this used to go on and on.

In the end, after months and months of this you think well, this has got to be Pathe' News because.... it's none of it! (Bobbie is laughing and laughing).

It's just like spirit are thinking well, we'll give you something to look at whilst we're busy behind the scenes so if you want to take that or not because it will save you a lot of grief trying to figure out what it is! You're identifying lots of things only to have each of them taken away so don't despair Bobbie. You can take what I've said if it helps?'

B. 'OK, so don't try and hang on to something in particular?'

J. 'No, don't despair if it comes and goes or if it's fast moving because that's one of the ways spirit can work with you. It's almost as though your clairvoyance is being massaged and anything that you're picking up clairvoyantly, even though you're not picking it up on purpose, you're just open and it's just coming in and going out.

It's like that game on TV with Bruce Forsyth with the conveyor belt. I don't remember what it was called, you know, cuddly toy, microwave; good game! It doesn't hanker for very long however, I'm pleased that I can identify with what is happening to you and what you're experiencing - even if it does drive you mad!'

B. (Bobbie is still laughing). 'And the next one was, this morning my attunement began as usual. Within a short time Daniel stepped forward. He told me I had become lazy. I was sitting around too much. It was not good for my physical health or my mental health. He said this was a new beginning for me and I had to grasp it with both hands, that I was not to let lethargy consume me. I feel I have been severely reprimanded! (Jenny is laughing now!)

I am thinking this is quite justified as I have got lazy and lethargic so thank you spirit for pointing this out to me. I will do something about it and get myself motivated.'

J. 'Why didn't you tell me - that was the reason you came back - you got told off!'

B. (Bobbie is laughing). 'I found myself back in my chair having been suitably chastised. It was just what I needed - a good kick up the backside!'

J. (Jenny is laughing). 'Well, they're human and, if you think about it, remember I said to you that your guides have their own remit but they can't do their work without you. People seem to think that spirit guides are just here for them. No, it's a two way relationship, a two way partnership.

They have given up their personal progress to walk with you and part of their own growth is achieving their plans *for* you so if you're sitting watching TV all the time, they can't get through so I've always made sure that people understand how this spiritual relationship works. It's necessary that people who want to serve understand that it's a shared job you're doing here.

I also feel that it helps so much to motivate us to do this work as well and now you have the proof! Your guide has actually told you, you're frustrating me because I need to get on with my side of the bargain and you're not helping me. So isn't that a wonderful thing to know?'

B. 'Yes, it is.'

J. 'So many people have looked at me in surprise and told me that they never knew this and of course, until you're taught, you don't realise. It just makes serving spirit that much more enjoyable. We are told that we're never alone and this is just one aspect of it.

We *are* never alone. Everything we do, we do on our side but it's incomplete without our spirit helpers doing the work from their side. It's a shared experience, a shared achievement when we work for spirit whether we're at home, in attunement, in a circle or in our sleep state at night, they can't do it without us and we can't do it without them. It's as simple as that - we're only half of the story so you've had a wonderful proof of that Truth.'

B. 'This morning's attunement began in the usual way. I felt the tingling and the heat. I felt spirit around me but I just could not quiet my mind, it was racing over and over but I couldn't say what about. I tried and tried but to no avail, I just don't know why. Perhaps Jenny will have some tips for me. I'm so sorry spirit.'

J. 'Well, there is a classic answer to that. When people start this course and find it very hard to still the mind, I always say try focussing on one thing. Focus on their favourite place, or maybe on one of their favourite things, focus on a waterfall. Also, if you remember, try and still your mind before you sit. Remember I said you can't attune between Coronation Street and Eastenders! You've still got Coronation Street on your mind and you're wondering what's going to happen in Eastenders so you can't squeeze in an attunement in between.

So there are those two pieces of advice. If you are 'platzing', meaning if you've got a lot on your mind, you've got to make a decision. Either start slowly and focus on one thing or just leave it, don't bother, because you know what you're like at the moment and obviously spirit know what you're like at the moment so there are the three things.

When I attune, I always wind down for five minutes beforehand. I go round the house, I turn off the phones, I plod, I put away, I'm doing my own calming down before I light my candle. Also, I probably do more deep breathing than I need to. I know that even though I've 'plodded' around for the last five minutes, I'm still not settled yet so I do a few minutes breathing even before I start my three deep breaths.'

B. 'OK, right.'

J. 'You're in charge of you. When I teach something practical, although I'm teaching I'm also generalising - giving you the 'gist' of what I mean. We're not all the same but we get to know ourself so well over time. I've got to understand myself. I know that I can't click to 'perform', I need a bit of time, yes?

My mind is disgustingly busy virtually all of the time. I'm a deep thinker so to empty my mind, I need more time. Attunement isn't something that you can 'turn on' like a light. You have to be extremely disciplined. You have to be like a 105 year old Shaolin monk to do that - to immediately switch on - like someone who's dedicated their whole life to meditation and prayer. Our lives here aren't like that so give yourself the time you need.'

B. 'That's true so if I feel that I'm still not ready?'

J. 'Don't do it or try and relax a bit more beforehand. Be kinder to yourself before you start. You've got to find your own formula, you've got to find what works best for you. When I teach you how to attune, I'm saying this is a general way to do things but you can add on, or subtract as long as it proves the most beneficial way for you.'

B. 'It's just come into my mind actually what I could do; go for a walk.'

J. 'Everybody's lifestyle is different. Some people don't have the luxury of time. For some people, 'The only time I have is when I have a bath.' And I've had to say, Ok, if that's the only time, attune in the bath! Spirit would much rather you do it than not do it. So you can't compare a working mum with kids with someone who's retired so finding what works for you is paramount.

It's about being honest with yourself, kind to yourself and not thrashing yourself over attunement. Spirit would rather you left it and had a better attunement a bit later or tomorrow or whatever. You haven't got a gun to your head over this. This is something for *you* - you're not doing it for *me* - you're doing it for yourself, for your higher good and you're doing it with and for spirit.'

B. 'You see this is the problem, I feel I've let them down.'

J. 'Your guides would much rather you got yourself sorted out. You haven't finished this course yet, you're still learning, in fact, we all never stop learning. This isn't just about the course either. This knowledge is for *you*, something that will hopefully enrich you for the rest of your life. That will always be there for *you* whenever you want it, need it or are drawn to it and, as you said, you miss it so perhaps renew the way you do things?

Think about what works or doesn't work for you. Think about the things that you know would make a difference to your life no matter how small that may be, something which will make so much difference to your overall attitude to attunement.

You've got your breathing, you've got your walking round the house or walking around the garden. If you're outside and you're sitting down and it feels wonderful, there's nothing to stop you having your attunement there and then because it's the right time for you. It doesn't mean you have to get up, leave this lovely feeling and go into the house and sit in your usual chair and light your candle, it's not about that.

It's about communing with spirit, being at one with the energies that love you and you can do that in your garden as well in as the room you usually use. As long as you adhere to the disciplines of protection because negativity can be anywhere. When you think of spirit, they think of you. *"Spirit are just a thought away."* Right, let's carry on.'

B. 'This morning my attunement began in the usual way. I felt the tingling and again, got very hot. I was able to enter the silence and still my mind. I felt spirit very much with me but no-one came forward to speak with me and I didn't see anything. That being said I enjoyed the quiet time with spirit just knowing they were there.'

J. 'What month are you in now, you still haven't stopped yet?'

B. 'No, this is 8 January. I began my attunement this morning and experienced the tingling and heat. It seemed to be more intense. I sat in the silence and waited. I asked spirit to lead and I will follow and felt spirit come really close but nothing was said and I saw nothing. I continued to sit with spirit and although I enjoyed feeling spirit close to me I have nothing else to report.'

J. 'Did you think of my words - when the least is happening, the most is happening?'

B. 'Yes.'

J. 'So that was some sort of comfort to you?'

B. 'Yes, I'm glad you said that. And then January 10th, as I began my sitting this morning, I once again experienced the tingling and got very hot. As I sat in the quiet, I felt the energy and began to grow very tall and broad. I recognised the energy of the one I call Daniel. I waited for some kind of communication but none came. I heard nothing and saw nothing then I was once again myself. The time had flown by and I was sitting back in my chair and forty minutes had gone past.'

J. 'So that was really good, wasn't it?'

B. 'Because there was confirmation that he was there, yes. January 12th, this morning I began by sitting, going into the silence and feeling the heat and tingling. I immediately became aware of spirit around me. I felt Daniel step forward and once again I heard and recognised the energy as that of Daniel. The same thing happened as the time before and neither heard or saw anything but during the time that I feel Daniel with me, the time just seems to fly by and before I know it I'm back in my chair and the time is up.'

J. 'And you're always brought round after forty minutes?'

B. 'Yes. Monday, 14 January there's nothing to report. Tuesday, 15 January. I began this morning's sitting with no expectations. I again felt the heat and tingling and I felt spirit draw close to me. I then felt an energy I did not recognise. I felt it was male, shorter than Daniel or Isaac. I asked who it was but got no answer then I was myself again.

Then again, I felt the same energy come in briefly then left again. In all, this happened three times but I did not see or hear anything just felt this energy popping in and out. I was not afraid but I was slightly disconcerted but I did not find out what this was all about and then I was back in my chair.'

J. 'OK. I can see you have more.'

B. 'This morning began with spirit around me and then I felt the same energy as I had felt before. I felt this energy come in, then go, then come in, then go and I asked several times if I could help and who it was and I got nothing. I felt again disconcerted and to be honest I was put out. I felt it was rather rude. I felt a bit cross and then my attunement was over and I was sitting back in my chair.'

J. 'Right, so you've had a repeat, a total repeat?'

B. 'Yes. Before I say anything about my attunement this morning, this is the 19th, I must write down how I've been feeling. I have not been sleeping well for the past week or so. I have been waking up between three and four every morning and cannot get back to sleep. I have also found myself stroking my chin almost as if I am stroking a beard. I don't know if this is connected to the energy that has been visiting. I have started to feel not afraid or anything like that but unsettled.

I have been thinking of cleansing my house. I have done this before. I will discuss this with Jenny. There is nothing really to report although I know spirit is with me as I felt their presence but I neither saw or heard anything. And then I didn't do another attunement then until February.'

J. 'Right and this is when you really stopped?'

B. 'Yes.'

J. 'OK, so now that you've started again, does this energy return?'

B. 'No.'

J. 'I'm thinking that you *did* ask whether you could help which was good but they didn't respond?'

B. 'No.'

J. 'Look, *"Nothing is ever for nothing"* you know that. The things that happen to us make us think but it's often a test. It makes us think and decide what are we going to do about it? One of the things we're all blessed with is *"Freedom of choice, freedom of will."* We all have to make decisions, sometimes they're awkward and difficult and we wish someone could make them for us!

Spirit know that you want to serve and that you want to help, so what choices do you have apart from saying, 'Look I'm here if you need me.' I'm now reminded of the example of when you have a medium on the platform where there is obviously a queue of people in spirit wanting and waiting for the medium to pick up on them.

And then you get those people who just hang around and hang around and the medium might well be saying to them, 'Well, do you want me to help you or not? I know you're there, I can see you but you're not doing anything, you're not coming forward, you're not telling me your name, you're not identifying yourself. What are you, a spiritual groupie or something?' (Bobbie laughs).

If we're all energy and with our own personality, then there are going to be those who need help but haven't quite got the courage to take that next step and come forward. It's like they're sticking their big toe in the water but they're not really ready to step in.

The main thing is that you recognised that something or someone was there and you offered your help, you can't do more than that. Close down afterwards. You've got to meet me half way pal, I can't help you if you don't communicate, yes?

Bobbie, if you're being prepared for the realms of rescue, you're going to get incidents like this and you will have to decide what do to do, what to do with this unpalatable, incoming energy? All you *can* do is say I'm here, do you want me to help you? If you don't come any closer, if you don't acknowledge me, if you don't let me help you, I can't help you!'

B. 'It's a waste of energy, isn't it?'

J. 'So I'm going to say that this energy is like an example of what *can* happen. So in the future, you're going to have to stay strong but you can't be responsible for someone else's decision, yes?'

B. 'Yes. Today is the first attunement for a long while. I began in the usual way, deep breathing and at once I felt the tingling and the heat. The first thing, I cannot say saw, more like a knowing, I felt there were 'fairies' all around me. It was in the forest with the sun filtering through the trees. Then along a path through the forest came a fairy but she was walking and appeared taller. She came and put a crown of small white flowers on my head. She then asked me to follow her which I did.

We came upon an opening which was filled with the most beautiful golden white light. She said for me to walk into the middle of the light as there was someone waiting to speak with me. I did as I was bid and entered into the light. As I got into the centre, Jesus appeared. He just smiled at me and said to allow the light to fill me. I felt the light flowing into me and flowing all around me; it felt wonderful. It seemed to fill me with love, beauty, compassion and so many other emotions but all positive and lovely.

Jesus said to enjoy this feeling and to know that they had not left me but were there always but to know that there are times when they need to draw back. I then felt as if I was being pulled backwards very quickly and then I was sitting back in my chair. It was a very moving experience and I now feel ready to move forward with spirit's blessing. I look forward to my next meeting with spirit.'

J. 'I can well understand how you were welcomed back in such a way because I think what you've been going through and the fact that, mentally and emotional as well as spiritually, you've been taken 360 degrees round on this. (Bobbie laughs). And as you know, spirit are never allowed to interfere with our decisions.'

B. 'No.'

J. 'So when you decided, I miss it, I want to go back and finish the course, I want to carry on because this is really what I'm all about, you got your confirmation in no uncertain terms! Well, you couldn't have had a better 'welcome back', could you?' And when you saw Jesus, did He look and dress the same as he always has or did he look different?'

B. 'He looked the same. If anything, he looked a bit more 'glowy.''

J. 'That's lovely and again, it was like action speaks louder than words. And when He talked about sometimes we need to draw back, I don't know if that means because you have to make your own decisions so that ultimately, you can move forward?

It's a classic scenario and again, it's about growth. We're here on this earth, often all alone, and we've got to walk this life on our own and learn to trust, trust our instincts.

If you're going to work with spirit, you can't walk into the fear, you can't walk into the darkness, you can't serve in any way unless you trust implicitly so unless you have any other ideas, I think that's what is meant by that, that spirit are always here but sometimes they and we have to stand back.

You're the one that has to do it; that's because you're 'the other half' - you're the physical half - they, your guides, can't do it because they're on the spiritual side plus it's your path, not theirs. If you know and trust that spirit are there, linked with you, you can go anywhere.'

B. 'Right! Yes, that makes sense.'

J. 'Anyway, lovely first attunement, wow!'

B. 'This morning my attunement seems to be rather chaotic but I will write down what occurred. For a while there was just the silence but in the silence there seemed to be lettering but I could not make them out. Then I sensed the tall man that I call Gandalf and he said, 'Out of the darkness comes light. Out of the light comes understanding. Out of the understanding comes compassion. Out of compassion comes humility and so it goes on. Out of one lesson begets another lesson.

He then moved my hands apart and placed in them a huge book. He said, 'This is the book of knowledge and this is what we all strive for. This is the knowledge of all things everywhere. When we attain this, we can truly be with the one and of the one, we will be whole.' And then I was seated back in my chair.'

J. 'That was nice for 'Gandalf' to come through. He looks like Gandalf?'

B. (Bobbie laughs). 'He does looks like Gandalf, yes!'

J. 'Spirit speak so eloquently don't they? That was a wonderful message to get. The book of knowledge, have you heard of that?'

B. 'I have heard of the book of knowledge, yes.'

J. 'To me, the Book of Knowledge are the Spiritual Truths and even though we hear a lot of them there are still so many we don't know. I used to say, you've climbed up a high mountain and you think you've done it and it's all buttoned up but once you get to the top, what do you see, another row of ruddy mountains! It's just like that, it never ends and the more you know, the more you need to know.

The Book of Knowledge - it may even be symbolic - but there's always more to learn and it's not so much learning as it's only after you've experienced something do you truly understand. You can't understand anything unless you experience something which is why the more challenges and changes you have, the more you grow, the more opportunities you have to learn. Somebody who does the same thing for years and years, who never ventures into new areas or gives themselves new experiences is limiting themselves.'

B. 'Yes.'

J. 'You get whole nations who are afraid to change. It doesn't just happen personally. It can happen on a massive scale but it's so healthy, it's so necessary because *"Experience is the greatest teacher"* and it must all relate to this Book.'

B. 'Right. This morning during my attunement I saw the one I call Gandalf again. He said to be mindful of my thoughts and actions. He came along a pathway in a forest and by each side of him was a fawn and a lamb. He carried a large staff. Behind him was White Eagle. He was carrying a young tawny owl. Those were the only words Gandalf spoke.

Then White Eagle stepped forward and placed the tawny owl on my shoulder. He said that the owl was to help me to find wisdom in all situations and if I was not sure, to think of the owl and the answer would come. Then they both turned and went back the way they'd come. I got nothing else until I found myself sitting back in my chair.'

J. 'So you got another gift which was another tool?'

B. 'Yes, I got a tawny owl, a young one.'

J. 'It reminds me of the feather slides you wear in your hair.'

B. 'Yes.' (Bobbie laughs).

J. 'Lovely. They're very simple but very effective your attunements with lots of spiritual philosophy. Sometimes people get these great picturesque complex things and you have to pick it all to pieces to make some sense of it but yours are very straight forward. They don't have to be complicated, do they?'

B. 'No.'

J. 'And I think it's also, if I may say, indicative of your path. Your path being true, straight and simple but meaningful - you don't need all the flowery, disguised appendages - you can just go straight to it. It becomes the most effective. Do you understand the way my mind is working?'

B. 'Yes.'

J. 'I'm trying to interpret everything pertinent to you and the forest and the countryside is typically you.'

B. 'Oh yes, definitely.'

J. 'So your 'welcome home', your welcome back attunements are in the forests as well. But I'm moving on from that and it's like Bobbie doesn't need fancy things, it's not what she's about and it's actually not what spirit's about either which, to me, shows how you and your spirit guides are so close because you think and feel along the same lines.

So again, very lovely and very meaningful and by thinking about how simple, true and powerful it was, there's no need for frilly words.'

B. 'No, but if there were too many frilly words, I wouldn't understand it anyway!'

J. (Jenny laughs). 'No, I know but it's a *"Like attracts like"* thing again. It just helps me to understand where you're at, which I need to do in order to try and help you. OK, go on.'

B. 'During my attunement this morning, although I did not see anything, I felt someone speaking to me. This is what was said. 'You are not ready for service yet as you still have much to master. Do not let this trouble you or make you feel that you are unworthy, this is not the case. We work with you even though there appears to be no communication going on.' This was all that was said but I got a feeling I should write down what was said to me when I am actually doing attunements so next attunement, I will do this and see what occurs.'

J. 'Good thinking Batman! OK, that was extremely helpful, to actually have it spelled out to you and also, you've had this before in another attunement where they've said, you know, you're not quite there. I am now going to say that a lot of it depends on you.'

B. 'Right.'

J. 'I was going to say, I disagree but I can't say that! (Bobbie laughs) However, what I *am* saying is that you are in charge of you and I'm reading in between the lines here and I would say that you're *nearly* there. I'm also saying that you're coming back and returning to this spiritual development course with renewed vigour and in doing so receiving all this proof in return in your attunements. What you're getting is testament enough for you to know that you're on your way but *you* need to believe in yourself too.'

B. 'Yes, I think a lot about what they're actually saying to me.'

J. 'You're holding yourself back which is why I say I disagree because you *have* it, you just need to *believe* it!'

B. 'Yes, exactly! Right, my attunement this morning began in the usual way. I felt the tingling all over and I felt myself getting really hot. Nothing happened for a while then I seemed to be on a shore with a boat coming towards me. It was a small boat with white sails. One of them was larger than the other. When it got to the shore, two energies got off. Although I did not see who, I felt male energies.

I recognised these two energies, they were the ones that I link up with. For want of a name, I will say Isaac and Daniel. They walked passed me and as I turned, I saw some steps leading up to what seemed to be a tower. They climbed the steps with me following. They seemed to go up for a long, long time. When we got to the top, they told me to look out and to say what I saw.

As I looked down and around everywhere, it seemed to be like a black sky with white stars twinkling.

As I told them this, they said, that the black was a negative energy that this earth was drowning in. The twinkling lights were those who were working with spirit to bring the light back to this world; the Light of Love. The more light, the more loving this world would become.

Then I was in my home and they said to build a fire in the middle of the house. Then they said to imagine negativity as black fabric, then to start pulling up all the blackness from everywhere in the house, from roof to below ground and I pulled the black fabric to put it into the fire. When this was done, to fill all the space including the garden and down into the earth with a brilliant white light until it formed a bubble of white light then seal it with a golden cross.

They told me that I could use this method for all negativity wherever I find it although I could not use it on people without first asking the soul's permission. Then it was over and I was back around so hopefully now I can begin to help and be of service.'

J. 'That was truly sensational. This is the first time I've heard of a visualisation like that and I want to thank you for sharing that because I think that is an amazing visualisation to have and to be able to use, whenever necessary.

Once again, you're privy to the thoughts of what our spirit guides think of this world. The analogy of the black sky meaning negativity and the twinkling of the stars being the workers, the light workers, is lovely. One doesn't normally look at a black sky and think of that.'

B. 'No.'

J. 'I don't think from now on I'll be able to look at a black sky without thinking like that. It's too late now, I've heard it but it also means that.....you seem to be given *so* many tools Bobbie!'

B. 'I know!'

J. 'I mean before you had a break from the course, your box was filling up with my tools and all the tools your guides were giving you and it just seems like every time you come here you're being given more and more. I think you're going to need a lock up garage or something! (Bobbie laughs). Amazing, amazing! I am so enjoying having you on this course. How did you feel after you had that attunement?'

B. 'I felt a lot lighter, actually. I felt really excited.'

J. 'I don't know whether you realise how *very*, very lucky you are to get all this from spirit?'

B. 'Yes.'

J. 'I hope so because it's almost like an honour to get such lovely.... the words, the tools, the meanings. Spirit's thoughts are shared with *you*, I mean it *is*.'

B. 'I do think it's an honour.'

J. 'Yes, *I* do. I dread to think if you hadn't have come back, I wouldn't be hearing all this!'

B. 'Right and then my last one which was yesterday. During this morning's attunement I saw - and I put saw in brackets - but I don't actually see....'

J. 'No, you sense.'

B. 'Yes, a shining being standing at the bottom of a flight of shiny stairs. He beckoned me to follow so I climbed the beautiful stairs. When we reached the top, we were on like a platform when another shiny being approached and gave the first being a shining robe which he put on me. It was like a long shift with sleeves.

We walked back down the stairs and when we got to the bottom it was all gone and I was sitting back in my chair. I am not sure what it meant but I think they were showing me that to be a spiritual person is like being clothed in a shining light which will help to bring light back into this world.'

J. 'And what was it also - another tool!'

B. 'Another tool, yes!'

J. 'What was the meaning of the tool? Why was the tool given to you?'

B. 'Protection?'

J. 'YES! protection, however, I think there was more than one meaning personally. I think the shiny one came to you to tell you, you attract us shiny beings.'

B. 'Right.'

J. 'I also feel the climbing of the stairs was synonymous with growth. The fact that you climbed to the top means, look how far you've come! The fact that you were given a present - another one - and a message; 'This is what it is and this why we're giving it to you' but I also feel that..... OK, what happens when you graduate?'

B. 'You're given a cloak and a.....'

J. 'Yes, yes, right! I do feel this attunement was one of achievement. Normally when you graduate, you climb up the stairs onto the platform so I'm also looking at this as a 'well done achievement' with this being your personal ceremony.'

B. 'Oh, that's nice!'

J. 'This is what you've earnt; this cloak. This is a cloak that distinguishes you for what you *now* stand for and what you *now* represent. You've earnt it and you can wear it, it will filter out to help you in your work and it will also give you guaranteed protection - if you wear it. Do you get all that?'

B. 'Yes.'

J. 'What an incredible way to end the month! Goodness me. OK, well thank you very, very much for reading all that. I now have to ask you, did you do your homework?'

B. 'I did! My interpretation of negativity. What I feel about negativity is akin to being pessimistic. For example, 'what can go wrong, *will* go wrong' but it is much more than that. Fear is a negative emotion. The more you fear something, the bigger the fear grows. Worry is another negative emotion. The more you worry, the more it grows and the worse you feel.

Greed is the same, like the old saying, 'much wants more.' Whatever it is you are wanting be it money, food, fame, etc. you will never have enough. It is solely based on greed rather than need. Living negatively is really wasted emotions and because you think negatively, you will just attract more negativity.

If you try to turn things into positive actions and thoughts, it is well worth the effort for you see life in a totally new and happier way. Being positive helps you to find the joy in just being. Being negative is really a wasted emotion, it solves nothing and in turn makes you miserable. Trying to find the positive in all things is well worth the effort for it makes us see life in a totally new and happy way.

Being positive helps you to find the joy in just being so if you're feeling down and really unhappy, find the reason for the feeling, for feeling that way and then find a way to turn whatever it is that is negative, into positivity. Then the clouds will clear and the sun will shine again.'

J. 'Brilliant! And you didn't cheat, it all came from your head?'

B. 'It all came out of my little brain!'

J. 'Well, that's brilliant, well done. OK. So now we're going to go straight on to some new material and today our subject is Trance and Rescue. You've done your bit now so just sit back and listen and try and digest some of this.'

Trance & Rescue

Jenny: 'To me, if you are going to do rescue, you will also do trance. This is because in both cases, spirit are taking over your senses, taking over your vocal cords, taking over your 'body'.

I started doing rescue before I was doing trance.

The first time I heard about rescue mediumship, I thought it was the most amazing thing I had ever heard of. I also saw the beauty and genius of being able to help two people by doing one thing; two for the price of one, I used to say. That is, helping both incarnate and discarnate spirit at the same time. I was therefore smitten and I knew, if I ever could, I wanted to do it!

Why, because I've always wanted to help people and this was a unique type of 'work'. You can also see the results of your labours and because you can make everyone's lives better.

You see, when you rescue, you are allowing a lost soul to go home plus restoring the person's life here on the earth plane back to normality.

When I first got involved with rescue work, there was only one way to do it - one procedure - I now know different. We are learning all the time.

When I began my rescue mediumship, it was something done by two people. A medium who would manifest the spirit in question and a corresponding medium whose job was to coax this spirit entity over to the other side. Rescue work was either done in a spiritual circle or at the place where the rescue or 'exorcizing' needed doing.

Since then I have learnt that a rescue can be done by a medium on their own, with two or more mediums linking up and working together even though they all live in different areas and that a medium's participation in a rescue can vary too.

I will tell you about my first experience doing rescue:-

I was working for my brother and one day he called me into his office and told me that his daughter, my niece, was having problems sleeping in his house because she said that there was something there. Did I know anyone who could help? He had obviously been trying to tell his daughter to stop being so silly but she always refused to sleep in her bedroom so he was getting desperate.

Now my brother had never been interested in the spiritual so you can imagine I couldn't believe what I was hearing and I remember sending a thought up to spirit saying, you're kidding me! I saw this as the perfect opportunity for him to understand things better.

Luckily I knew some rescue mediums and they agreed to help. I remember it was a Saturday morning, a taxi picked them up from East London and I just presumed that I was going to stay downstairs with my brother whilst they went upstairs to do the work. But I was wrong! 'You're coming up too.' they explained and so I thought, Oh my God, what's all this about? (Bobbie is laughing).

What am *I* supposed to be doing up there? So I watched as they sorted out and removed the undesirable energies and then, I was told it was my turn and I thought, what do I *do*?

I was told to sit at the end of the bed and to attune, which I obviously knew how to do. After closing my eyes and taking my deep breaths, the first thing that happened was that I started coughing. Everything in my 'blank screen' remained black. I continued coughing and soon I smelt coal and realised that it was the coal that was making me cough.

I thought what's going on, how come I can't see anything? I wasn't unused to the blackness but I wasn't used to the smell of coal and then the coughing turned to tears. Then my medium friend who was in the room with me and whom I was learning from, began talking to me.

When I began to talk back, out came a child's voice and I realised that I was a child and I was crying like a child and I wanted my mummy and it all seemed the most natural thing. I didn't feel pressurised, it was just something that was happening and I couldn't stop it or get out of it. I was just going with it and going through the motions, so to speak.

Then another child came through me who was also crying so there was more than one child. I then saw three children clairvoyantly and they were like urchins. They were dirty and wearing rags and had black all over them which must have been the coal. Then all of a sudden, in the distance, this woman appeared. She was wearing a bonnet and a shawl and I realised it was their mummy and they were all running to her and it was just the most amazing thing to experience.

What had happened was these were three Victorian children that had been left for dead in a coal bunker.'

Bobbie: 'Aagh!'

J. 'So that was my first experience of rescue. I was also in a circle and pretty soon after that I started doing rescue in the circle, again helping children, and I thought I would just carry on rescuing children but these soon became adults.

But why do you need a medium, spirit's power is phenomenal? Surely, spirit can just simply move an entity or a lost soul, just like that? No they can't! This is because their power can be *too* powerful so, in effect, they need a middle man on the earth plane to help them with this.

A higher evolved spirit's energy can harm a lower evolved spirit if they come into contact so it is better for the lower level spirit to be contained within a rescue medium's aura and surrounded with the medium's psychic energy. Spirit are then able to 'trap' them in the light. They can then be taken across without causing any harm. So, they need to contain the lost soul's energy within a medium's aura before transporting them back home to spirit realms.

Before this can happen, lost souls must *want* to go home and so be ready to go home. They must personally ask for help before they can be helped by spiritual guides and their mediums.

Who are they, where are they and what are they?

They are either human or elemental - by elemental I mean that they have a spiritual shape and form but an energy nevertheless - and these spiritual souls or energies have been stuck in their negative thought pattern since 'death'.

When we die, we are normally met and 'taken over' to the 'other side'. Going to the other side is just like walking into the next room, it's as natural as that. We are met by someone we love. We're never alone when we die and we leave the earth plane for home - our real home - which is on a different dimension (of energy) to the earth plane. But some people, for varying reasons, do not pass over and do not complete the move to their new plane of life as planned.

There can be many reasons for this They can be afraid, they can be proud, they can be difficult or ignorant. They can be hurt or angry. They can be in shock having just had a fatal accident. They often don't know where they are and don't know they are 'dead' and now exist on the next level to earth which is the astral plane.

The astral plane is the next energy level after leaving the earth's dimension. When we go home, we travel through the various energy dimensions until we reach our own natural level which equates to the rate of energy at which we are personally vibrating. Remember *"Like attracts like."* The first or next dimension or energy level after leaving earth is the astral plane. The astral plane is very much like the earth plane and can look almost exactly the same.'

B. 'Oh, right.'

J. 'Which is why people who have 'died' but not returned 'home' think they are still 'alive'. The astral plane serves a purpose. It is a place where people that haven't passed over for varying reasons dwell until they come to a point where they feel, I've had enough of this, I want to go home.

Because we are all spirit and our spiritual energy is our mind energy, our mind is the most powerful thing we have and, as you know, our mind will dictate *all* our actions. If you want to pick up that glass of water, your mind will tell you, I want that glass of water, pick it up. Your arm and hand will not go to the cup unless your mind has first told you it wants a drink, so your mind controls everything.

I have explained that there is no heaven and no such thing as hell but your mind *can* still create your own heaven and hell. If you think you are so bad that you deserve to be in hell, you can create that hell for yourself with your mind. Whether it is a dark place and you end up sitting on a rock or wandering around in a dust bowl because you think that is the most awful place you deserve to be in - you see, you *still* have a choice.

Many people who don't pass on to spirit realms come from a Catholic upbringing. They've been indoctrinated from such a young age that anything they do wrong, even their thoughts will mean that they will have to go to hell so someone like me, who stole a tube of pan stick from F.W. Woolworths when I was sixteen, if I was a Catholic and was taught about sin and the consequences, I could still be worried that I would not go to heaven.

So when it came to me dying and passing over, all I could think of was that I stole that stick of make-up so, Oh no, no, no, I can't come with you and I would refuse to go with whoever came to collect me. I had committed a sin and therefore don't deserve to go to 'heaven' so I would end up on the astral plane in a dwelling of my own making. I know this is a very far-fetched example but I am just illustrating an important point here.

So there is nothing anyone can do. If I refuse to go with my mum or my dad or my cat or whoever comes for me, I have to go *somewhere,* don't I? I wouldn't be on the physical plane any more - on the earth plane - I'd be on the next level, the astral. So these people stay in their negative thought pattern on the astral plane until they think, there's got to be more to life than this, I want help? The moment you say I want help or you think, I want help, then help is sought for you. No call for help ever goes unheard by spirit. OK?'

B. 'Yes.'

J. 'So once people realise they need help, when they realise they don't want to be where they are any more or when they get desperate and want to move on, they will naturally ask for help. You remember, always *ask*. Once they have asked, spirit will engineer a way to help them. I have met so many people for the sole reason of just doing a rescue. Here is one example:-

In the year 2000, one of the things I decided to get involved with was mentoring for young offenders. I went on a course in Slough studying with a group of people and was paired up with the only guy on the course called Michael who had done some mentoring before.

When we were coming to the end of the course, Michael suggested that we all go back to his house and practice for our exams.

On the appointed afternoon, we were all seated in his sitting room, his wife was introduced to us and I thought we were going to start talking about the course. What does Michael and his wife start talking about - the things that have been flying around the room and all the noises and the things that go missing! (Bobbie is laughing).

And I'm sitting there thinking, nah, nah, you're having me on, you are having me on! And they're going on and on about the psychic things that are happening in their house and how they bought the house from this lady who had died and I'm sitting on their sofa and I'm saying to spirit, you have got to be kidding, is this what this course has been about, all this hard work I've done? (Bobbie is still laughing).

Has all my studying been about doing a rescue in this house? I just couldn't believe it. They were both talking as though it was something funny and I was feeling *very* uncomfortable because I knew that whoever was doing this was by now desperate to go home.'

B. 'Yes.'

J. 'That's why they were doing it, I *knew* the reason so I casually said to them, wouldn't you like all this to stop? The following night I sat with my guides to see if I could manage to help this woman who had been thrown down the stairs by her husband.

The following evening I phoned Michael and asked him what was the name of the woman who used to own the house and he said I don't know, I've forgotten. So I said, was her name Annie? He replied, ANNIE! that's right, that was her name! Because that was the name I was given so I knew we had been able to help her home.

So do you see what I mean, you never know? When you serve spirit, you are called to help in all different scenarios and in my first book, *'A Medium's Tale'*, I mentioned that invariably whenever I go away and stay somewhere, either in a B&B or hotel, my first night is usually a 'work night'. Spirit bring all the willing lost souls in the area to my room and we rescue them.

I've done this in Llandudno in Wales, in the Dordogne in France, Lockerbie in Scotland and many other places where I've been staying. I've always known that *"Spirit are great opportunists"* so I guess they take their opportunities when they come. I understand that.

At the end of this paper, there is a p.s.

Sometimes, spirit send an electric shock to prevent spirit of a lower vibration getting too near a person on the earth plane. I'm sure you've have had this experience when you suddenly jolt for no apparent reason. Have you had that?'

B. 'Yes.'

J. 'This is beams of white light from spirit who hold an unwanted spirit at bay thereby protecting us from any harm. Sometimes spirit will see an unwanted energy getting too near you and send this light which makes you jump so you now know what this may mean.

Now this next paper is a short introduction to rescue.'

Rescue: An Introduction

Jenny: 'There are many spirits who are trapped within their own programme of thought near the earth plane. This is what is understood as a haunting and they need to be released. Sometimes this can be done from the other side without the aid of a medium but nine times out of ten, to affect this kind of teaching which we call Rescue, a physical medium is needed.

In most cases of schizophrenia, not all, but in most, there is an attachment of spirit. To explain this further:-

Spirit is a term that covers all spirit. We are spirit energy first and foremost. In the spirit world there are good and bad, I would call the bad, ignorant. In human form there are good and there are ignorant people who cause harm.

Sometimes when a spirit passes over, the human being has 'died' and their spirit has been released but the passing is not complete. There are a number of reasons for this. Often, the person has had no religious belief whatsoever and they are stuck in their own pattern of thoughts. They suddenly find they still exist. They go to talk to people but no one hears them, they try to contact people and have little success.

Many people who are sensitive do not realise the dangers if they do not control their 'instrument'. People open themselves up to spiritual influences of all kinds, maybe with alcohol or drugs. Sometimes, if a sensitive here on earth gets disheartened or depressed, he or she can attract a spiritual energy of like mind who is wandering around the astrals and just as the clairaudient or clairvoyant will hear or see spirit, so the uninformed sensitive may begin to hear voices - not always pleasant ones.

There are also spiritual energy forms of the earth - elementals - who are equally good, bad or indifferent. Again, when they see the light in the aura of a sensitive, they are attracted and if that sensitive is open and vulnerable through some of the above causes, then the elemental force, if it is so inclined, so ignorant and of such a low level of evolvement, can also make its presence felt in a most ghastly, horrendous way. So many schizophrenics who are diagnosed as mentally ill are, in fact, not. They are merely hearing the lower orders of spirit.

That is why it is so important for those who are developing spiritually to control their instrument; to be disciplined in protecting themselves. That is why they must attune, to lift the level of their vibration and that is also why the motive for communication must always be pure for *"Like attracts like".*

Over three quarters of people in mental hospitals are either clairvoyant or clairaudient who cannot control their instrument and they are not aware of it. There are people in the medical profession who are coming to understand that there is more than meets the eye to schizophrenia and that there is a spiritual world beyond the physical one that can cause problems.

OK, that was just an introduction Bobbie as there is a lot more to this subject. I'm going to give you these notes now but rescue is something which grows with understanding, it's not something you instantly comprehend.

It's like a puzzle. You have a piece of this and a piece of that until you get the whole picture so I don't want you to get too concerned. Just take the notes. Do you have any pressing questions or is there anything you wish me to explain further?'

Bobbie: 'No, you explain things very well Jenny.'

J. 'Oh, thank you. OK. I want to give you your homework for next time which is to write a paragraph or two on what you now understand about love.'

B. 'OK, I'll just write that down.'

J. 'Now, I'm going to switch the work back to you as we're going to do something extra before we finish today. I want you to pick one of these cards. On the card is a word and I want you to talk about that word for as long as you can! Now this exercise is in connection with trance.

When we work in trance, our minds are 'taken over' by our spirit guides and they are impressed upon. For example, when I teach you, I'll be saying things to you and my guides will also help me. They will show me meaningful symbols, they'll say things, they'll give me cue's and all this aids my talking; it helps give me the information to give to you.

So today you're going to have a trance practical, if you like. By linking up with your guides, we're going to see if you can talk about something for as long as possible.'

B. 'OK.'

J. 'Now, first of all I want you to relax. Next, think about the word on the card and begin thinking about your first sentence - how you would start talking about this subject - and I also want you to ask your guides for help with this too. You start off talking, you think about the first thing you want to say in connection with the word - what is the word, by the way?'

B. 'Silence.'

J. 'So you're going to talk about silence. This is not a test by the way, it's just 'having-a-go'.'

B. 'Have a go!' (Bobbie is laughing).

J. 'Don't be shy. It's just an opportunity for you to link up with your guides and see if they impress upon you, give you cue's, symbols, give you examples, OK? So you're going to work with your guides now and ask them to help you talk about silence.

So take your time, relax, do your breathing, have a think about what *you* want to say and then see if your guides, on your instructions, draw close and give you other things, other pointers, other cue's.

They may do this by actually saying something, they may show you something and you'll think, Oh, I know what that means, are you with me? So it's communication in any possible way and you're going to have a go at this now!'

B. 'Right. Silence is peacefulness, solitude, being alone with one's thoughts. Silence is a way of connecting with your inner self, your spiritual self, with your guides and helpers. Silence enables you to listen, to understand what you're being shown or told. It's getting rid of all the dross and the clamour and just being. That's about all.'

J. (Jenny claps). 'Well done! You see you had a go and you did it! I know it's not nice when you're put on the spot but it's all about testing, it's all about saying OK, I *can* do this and having a go, yes?'

B. 'Yes.'

J. 'I knew that I was going to do trance. I'd already started doing rescue and I knew I was going to do trance as well and I kept saying to my guides whilst sitting in circle, 'No, no, no, no, I'm not ready, I'm not ready, I'm not ready. (Bobbie is laughing).

And then we'd sit again another night and I'd be saying the same in my head, 'No, no, no, I'm not ready, I'm not ready, I'm not ready!' It was like being on the edge of something you knew was going to happen. Then the third time it just went bbbbbbllllllrrrrrrr and it all came out! (Bobbie is in fits of laugher).

And I had *no* choice whatsoever, so I know it's daunting, it *is* daunting and I'll never forget it because I was horrified, I was. You know, I used to almost wet my pants and I used to think, no, I really don't want to go to circle tonight because I *know* what's going to happen! (Bobbie is still laughing; I think she is enjoying this story!).

You know, a man's got to do what a man's got to do and I think my guides were a bit fed up with me so, in the end, it just poured out of my mouth. Then, of course, you get the other extreme. One of the guides who used to speak through me, he used to take his ruddy time and I used to say, for God's sake, start will you! He used to ruminate and I used to be in agony as his energy was making me explode and I used to think, Oh, please, just start talking, just start! (Bobbie is laughing).

At one time, I didn't want to start talking and then it was completely the opposite, I'm in agony here, please start talking will you! You can't win! Oh dear, you've got to laugh, haven't you?

So, that wraps up this lesson so after all that, I think we both deserve a cup of tea?'

Jenny: 'Right Grace, now we've lit our lamps, I need to see what's been happening with you since we last met. I can see that you've got your attunements ready and as I've said before, choose the ones that you think are valuable and the ones you want to share.'

Grace: 'There aren't that many but there's really been a change to the content. They have headings and this particular one I thought I had sat for 10 or 15 minutes but it was for an hour and ten and it was called 'Remembrance' and it was just before Remembrance Sunday.

I have found over the years that if I stop something for a while then I restart again, the format is changed usually for the better so now when I sit in attunement, I feel my cleansing shower begin to fall upon me before I close my eyes. I also feel when the cleansing is complete and when the shower stops.

My prayer now is simple, 'Dear Father, if it be your wish that I see spirit, let it be so. If it be your wish that I hear spirit, let it be so. If it be your wish that I feel spirit, let it be so. I am yours in service, amen.' I feel my angel by my right side, he enters by my shoulder and upper arm, his left wing covers my back in protection. Sonja, my guide, I feel enter my heart chakra then she moves her energy up to my throat. I ask for our voices to be joined when working for spirit.

We lift off amongst the clouds rising higher towards the blue sky. In the distance I see a large white building. We speak, my angel, guide and myself using telepathy. We are approaching the halls of wisdom and learning. I have been here before and have some idea what to expect. We land softly, walking up the white steps together. We enter through this huge entrance. My companions step away waiting for my return. They stand back, one each side of the entrance.

I take the long walk to the very end of the central aisle passing many angels sitting at desks interviewing souls. Last time I visited, I too sat at one of those desks to be counselled and helped in dealing with the passing of my mother to spirit. The angels are not too busy to look up as I passed and we each exchange smiles. I reach the end of the aisle at last and find myself looking up at a great marble monument upon which are cast many names all in gold. I cannot see the top, it passes out of sight and the sides reach away into the distance seeming to curve back on each side; it may very possibly be circular?

I look back at the busy hall behind me and for a second or two, all work ceases. The angels turn towards me and just for that short time I see they wear, each of them, a red poppy. The poppies fade and the hall becomes busy once again. I look down and I too am wearing a poppy, a knitted one my sister gave to me, it is fastened to my clothing.

I turn my attention back to the monument trying to read the names. They seem to be in alphabetical order but using the first name not the last. My attention focuses on the 'H's' - Horace Billingham. As I read the name he is there before me; young, fair haired, slim and in the uniform of a soldier from the First World War. He smiles at me and I asked, 'Do I know you?' He is nodding yes then he is gone.

The 'A's' move forward and become larger - Alfred Jones. There he is, mid to late twenties, wearing a uniform of a captain, on his head a peaked cap. He is slim with dark hair. He has a moustache on his upper lip; just a small neat one. Behind him with its head resting over his right shoulder is a chestnut horse. Alfred holds the reigns with his gloved right hand. I ask, 'Do you know me?' He shakes his head. His lips move and the words in my head are, 'The truth will give you direction.' Then he too is gone.

Red poppy petals start to fall upon my head and my shoulders covering the ground at my feet in a carpet of red. 'They gave so much, never forget.' My tears fall and are still falling as I turn to retrace my steps back to the hall - one of the many here. I feel at peace.

The angels continue with their busy work, they do not look up this time but I know they are aware of me passing. I feel my hands being held very gently. I look to my right, it is my mother, she wears a poppy. I look to my left, it's dad, he also wears a poppy. They walk with me until we reach the entrance. Each of them kisses me on the cheek nearest to them. They smile and step away and are replaced by my angel and guide. We walk back through that wonderful entrance, down the steps. We rise upwards together and I am back in my chair, my face still wet from tears. And I sat..... and I cried.'

J. 'Oh, Grace!'

G. 'It was almost like a release.'

J. 'That whole experience was overwhelming, the content; you can't help crying over. You know, looking at this holistically, you didn't stand a chance *not* to cry because you had everything there. You had the wonderment, the beauty, the emotional ties, the realities, the magnitude - you had the lot! All that happened in that one attunement and again, *"There is no such thing as time in spirit but spirit's time is perfect."* That was a very timely attunement, wasn't it?'

G. 'It was.'

J. 'Yes, I think those tears were very good for you - healing tears.'

G. 'Very much so and to know that there was somewhere to rest just... love for love's sake?'

J. 'But that is all we *are*; that is all spirit is.'

G. 'Yes.'

J. 'OK, I don't think we really need to analyse that attunement, I think it said everything. Right, the next one?'

G. 'This is called 'Soul's Blood' and it took 40 minutes. As I sit under my cleansing shower I know that I am returning to the halls of wisdom and learning. I feel my angel and guide in the usual way and we lift off together and are once again at the bottom of those broad, white, marble steps. We move up them together then Sonja steps aside outside the entrance telling me, I will be met inside. My angel waits with her.

Just inside there's an angel to greet me, it is Aerial. We two have met each other in the past, he smiles and so do I. Linking arms, we start to walk down the big central aisle. Aerial stops a third of the way along just for a second then seems to change his mind and we continue towards the end of the hall. I can see that huge marble wall - the one with the names engraved upon it - and somehow seem to know that the names and purpose will have changed from the last time I stood before it.

We stop just over half way and turning to the left stopping at the fourth desk along. All of the desks, and there are many, are made of polished wood with a seat each side. The empty seats face the front looking towards the marble wall. The angels, and there are one to each desk, sit opposite. Aerial pulls my seat out and I sit in it looking at the empty seat across from me wondering who will sit there. It is Aerial who goes around and sits opposite. We both smile as if it's a little joke used to settle me.

I look around at the other busy angels. They lift their heads and smile then go back to their writing. The desks seem solid but in a certain light, the angels become almost transparent. The chairs opposite appear empty but I know that each chair is occupied; it is not for me to know, therefore to me, they appear empty.

Aerial tells me to just rest and take in what is all around me. He is busy writing. I notice that each angel does not always have the same kind of pen as their neighbour. Some have quills others have pens which are long and made of wood, some pens are short and many angels write with pens of different colours. I also know that opposite each angels are people similar to myself from the physical realm and others from spirit reporting back on their various responsibilities.

I look up at the vast ceiling and see birds flying above me. They appear small because the roof is so high. The carvings are beautiful. Then I see that small angels and cherubs are flying across from column to column sitting on the ledges and having such fun together. My attention returns and I know Aerial has been watching me. He smiles and says, 'You will now be taking lessons with us. We shall be teaching you life skills.' He continues, 'People like you are our Souls Blood.' Then he says, 'That is all for today. You are now able to go back to your earthly home from here and return the same way.'

I ask to return to my guide and angel because we came together and should return the same way if only for today. He tells me to go back to the entrance on my own and smiling, he returns to his writing. Walking back to the entrance, I find my friends waiting outside, we link arms, lift off from the top step and I am back in my chair.'

J. 'Amazing!'

G. 'And when he said - I made a little note in the margin - because I realised afterwards, when he said people like you are our soul's blood, it was his voice and many others at the same time. So I kind of, I can't say I've been doing battle recently but maybe I have been wrestling with things and I found this attunement enormous in itself. It was just overwhelming, that's the word I want. It's not made me unhappy, it's made me think a lot more.'

J. 'It's like the weight or burden of responsibility of this course and what comes with it, how it changes you entirely as you make new discoveries.'

G. 'Yes, I don't mind it.'

J. 'No, what I'm sensing is the burden of responsibility; the responsibility to *yourself* with the knowledge that you're privy to. It's like you can't go back now.'

G. 'No I wouldn't, never will, was never going to anyway.'

J. 'I know, but what I'm trying to say is that even though you'll never be alone, even though there will always be people with you, helping you and guiding you and supporting you, showing you the way, it is still a big responsibility nevertheless. That's what I would feel if I had that attunement. Also, I don't know whether you can understand this, but the enormity of spiritual truths being revealed can make you both fragile and strong at the same time?'

G. 'I've heard your voice many times saying we are *never* alone and that's been such a comfort because I've felt there were times when I needed some comfort because of this enormous thing that has taken place.'

J. 'But you didn't phone me, didn't you think to phone me?'

G. 'I thought about it. I know this is strange but rightly or wrongly, I think at my age I ought to be able to sort it out, look after myself. It doesn't mean that I don't value you very much, I do.'

J. 'No, I understand, you want to manage your own affairs.'

G. 'I don't do it terribly well sometimes.'

J. 'Well, you just take one step at a time. That's all spirit do. They never dump you in it, do they?'

G. 'No, no. no.'

J. 'And remember, you'll never get anything unless you're ready to receive it.'

G. 'That's true.'

J. 'Again, that's the Law; *"No one ever has anything unless they're ready to receive it."* So whatever you get, you know, you're now ready for. OK, you may have to sharpen a pencil or two but you're still ready. So that attunement, you know your guides are being very kind and giving you very straight forward attunements. There's not a lot of guess work to be done there, it's quite matter of fact.

They're showing you, they're telling you, they're doing everything. Sometimes these attunements are like doing crossword puzzles or solving riddles. Everything is thrown into the one attunement and you have to try and pick it all to pieces and work out what they're trying to say - the meaning.

They're not here, spirit are being very straight forward. It's almost as though they're saying it's no laughing matter. We're not going to make a jigsaw out of it. It's time to roll up your sleeves and get on with it!'

G. (Grace laughs). 'I've got only three but they're all relevant to one another. This is called 'Revolving Stream.' I am becoming more mindful of how I open up. More understanding in the care and protection of my earthly body or shell and the damage limitation needed to ensure that I stay strong both physically and mentally in my service to spirit.

I step and move much more slowly when crossing from one world to the other even more carefully when coming back. Proper protection ensures that there is no exhaustion when the work is finished only energy returned both physically and mentally, in fact, a job well done.

This morning when having cleansed, opened and blended with my angel and guide, we stood together looking at the screen. The picture that appeared was of a revolving ring or circle very much like the ones that we watched years ago when the Pathe' News was shown at the cinema. I could read the words easily because they were attached to the circle in an upright position and passed before my eyes at a moderate speed - 'Nothing for nothing' - moving clockwise.

Then, as a question formed in my mind, the words stopped still in front of me then began to turn anti-clockwise. After a very short time, stopping once again in front of me, then once again resuming clockwise. Past, present and future - the answer to my half-formed question - brilliant! That's one thing sorted now to be put into practice and refined. It was as if the floodgates had been opened. Information flooded into my mind.

I made my contract with spirit but became afraid and wanted to go back home at the very last minute but my soul group, guides and the angels persuaded me to continue. This is why I have never felt fully in the physical world, never felt that I belonged and have always felt fearful of what I see, sense, feel and hear. They tell me that the reason I fall over a lot is because for me to walk upon this earth is like walking with bare feet on broken glass; their words. This is why my healing friend entered my life with the skills that she has.

Aerial is the name of my angel and when I asked with my eyes wide open, how could he be in so many places at the same time, he just laughed and said that he could do and did many things - my duty - he called it.

Sonja is my bridge from this world to spirit and I must never go anywhere without her. We move towards the halls of wisdom and learning but many voices spoke together telling me it was time to go back. We three return very slowly. I knew I was sitting in my chair but we remained together while I carefully closed down. I could hear many heavy doors slamming behind me and I can now feel and see rings of energy around my physical body moving up as I open and then moving down as I close.

Also, I've just been told that my husband is my protection and protector.

What they, spirit, were telling me was that when I was born to this world I had made a contract with spirit but became afraid because I came to this world and wanted to go back but I was counselled and I stayed.'

J. 'That makes sense.'

G. 'And that's why I never felt the realness of the physical world for a long time and I have always been fearful. My homework has been hard work this time.

I've always been fearful, fearful of nearly everything but it's gradually leaving me; I can move forward. It's stopped me doing many things in my life just the fear of failing, the fear of what if, the fear of being silly, the fear of being laughed at, all these things. The reason I fall over, I do have a few tumbles and I do fall....'

J. 'Oh, I see, there wasn't one big fall?'

G. 'No, but I do feel very much out of balance sometimes but now I know how to ground myself, I do that but it is very uncomfortable to walk, not so much now but my feet do pain me on the bottom and that is why in some way or shape I have met my friend, she is a chiropodist and podiatrist as well as a healer and she looks after my feet.'

J. 'So, if I may say so, it looks as though you've felt very alone for a long period of your life?'

G. 'I have.'

J. 'Which is also a hallmark of a spiritual person, did you know that?'

G. 'I'm beginning to learn that, I'm beginning to learn, yes.'

J. 'What do they say, *"A spiritual road is a lonely road."*

G. 'Well it is but very rewarding.'

J. 'It also tells me a lot about how you got to 'now', if you like. You've battled on and battled on and battled on, you've had no succour and it must be incredibly..... I just get the impression, rightly or wrongly, that coming to now and being able to learn all this, is like what you've been waiting for, for so long?'

G. 'I've come home.'

J. 'Yes, that's just what I was going to say! That's exactly what I was going to say!'

G. 'And it's a long walk sometimes to your home.'

J. 'Yes, I know that as well.'

G. 'Because you see, that is why when I read your book, *'A Medium's Tale'* it resonated. I thought there is someone who has done or has seen many of the things that I have. I have to find her.

The next attunement is called Feeling Energy. Here we sit and today there are 5 of us. Aerial, my angel, Sonja, my main guide, Innka, my guide who works with me when I paint and Salaman, my scribe. Salaman in Hebrew means Peace.

I have been introduced to Innka and re-introduced to Salaman by Sonja so that I might feel their energies. She has explained to me that sometimes they will work as individuals and sometimes they will work with me in teams of two. I have become used to Aerial and Sonja's energies and now I will become more familiar with Innka and Salamans'.

Just where Salaman's hawk fits into all this, I'm not sure as he often has it sitting upon his left shoulder. There must be energy there but I have never yet felt it. I have asked to be taught the meaning of wisdom from Innka, learning from Salaman, knowledge from Sonja and the meaning of love and protection from Aerial.

They each stepped away when our meeting had reached its conclusion taking care to retreat slowly one at a time. First Innka, followed by Salaman, then Sonja and finally Aerial. I was left on my own and felt rather lonely just sitting in my own energy. It's all good, all learning, working in service.'

J. 'OK. Obviously, this must mean something?'

G. 'I'm not a hundred percent certain what.'

J. 'No, I'm not either to be quite honest. I can't really think of what it means apart from wanting to re-introduce you to your other two guides and wanting you to know that even though they're not there, you're not alone; when they walk away, you're still not alone. Other than that, I really don't know apart from maybe whatever is coming down the track, so to speak.'

G. 'I do feel a great sense of belonging, I know that.'

J. 'Oh, I'm sure, they're very important! They each offer things individually but they offer collectively as well so you're very fortunate to have *all* of them. A lot of people don't have - or certainly don't know that they have - as many spirit guides as you have so that's incredible and not only rewarding but comforting and very special.

I dread to think if I had not met you and not taught you how to attune, I mean you wouldn't have had all this would you?'

G. 'No.'

J. 'So thank God this happened because you're getting so much out of it. OK, next one.'

G. 'Last one. I called it Contemplation but it's not the right word, that will come again. I have opened up and we three are sitting before my screen.'

J. 'Who are we three?'

G. 'Aerial, Sonja and myself. Standing at the edge of the screen is Innka. He is dressed in white robes and a turban. His face changes from a younger man to an older one. The changes happen very quickly in the flash of an eye. The knowing comes into my mind that the choice is mine, his appearance can be whatever is comfortable for me.

Salaman is standing some distance behind Innka, hands clasped before him. Innka shows a card with a picture of a sunset upon it. It is the birthday card sent to my son-in-law several days ago. The card is a print of an original by an artist that I know and respect. If you really look at a sunset, it is made up of many colours which are forever changing as the sun sinks lower in the sky.

Innka looks at me and the words once again arrive in my mind; 'Everything be it good or not so good is part of the greater whole.' I understand the colours in a sunset and sometimes these can be very dark making a marked contrast against the lighter parts which are still being touched by the sun's rays. The life I have here on earth is changeable. Good and bad days, good and not so good choices. This brings balance to my life very much like a sunset made up of many colours painted by a gifted artist. We view what is to hand and act accordingly.'

J. 'I get many things from this attunement. I get a toolbox; it's like I've given you loads of tools and you use them and spirit also gives you loads of tools and you use them too. I also get the more you know, the simpler life becomes - it's a paradox. The more you know and understand, the less you need to concern yourself with.

Another way of looking at this could be just the beauty which a sunset evokes - it takes your breath away. One sees its magnitude and yes, it's forever changing but I tell you this, it is nothing compared to the beauty of the spirit realm. One wonders that if earth is not the reality, how much more beautiful can beauty be? The mind boggles! What is your interpretation Grace?'

G. 'My interpretation is that spirit will never give me more than I can handle. They love, guide and protect me at all times and will always keep me safe. I also feel that they are telling me to be a little braver.

They are giving me proof that I am never alone, not for one minute. I know when I look at a sunset which I do a lot, that they stand with me. The colours are about keeping myself balanced between the two worlds.'

J. 'OK. I also want to draw your attention to the beginning of the attunement when Innka turned from a younger man to an older one and to say that this may have been a demonstration of what I have also been taught which is, *"As you think, so you are."* Because thought is *everything*, because as spirit we exist as just pure thought, pure love, we can do everything by just thinking.

When we are in spirit realms, we communicate with people and the universe via our thoughts and we can also be whoever we choose and dwell wherever we wish just by thinking so Innka was able to show himself to you as both an old man and a young one too.

OK. What about your homework, can we see how you did?'

G. 'The homework was to write half a page on fear and negativity and my interpretation of it. I have been given homework and the subject is fear and negativity. I have my own point of view on most things but this particular subject is rather too close for comfort. Hence the reason it has taken so long to write down on paper. There are two days left before I have to read my essay to my teacher.

It has taken until now for me to understand why there is a difficulty; it is this. By writing about fear and negativity, because do not forget one begets the other, I will have to face my own emotions.

We are all unique. There is not another you or me on this planet or anywhere else as far as we know. Therefore, all of our fear or fears are our own, again, unique only to us.

Fear breeds fear. This makes it contagious spreading out into the world, touching family, loved ones until all around you are affected.

Break the thought pattern. Find one thing to make you happy thus giving upliftment. Carry out one act of kindness, one act of love and you have taken the first step to recovery. Have faith and trust in a positive outcome.

The thought that came into my mind after finishing the above was the Law of Cause and Effect.'

J. 'Thank you. I hope it has helped you in your quest to understand yourself more and also the world in which we live?'

G. 'It has.'

Month 8

Jenny: 'So, this is the first time we've met this year so Happy New Year!'

Grace: 'Happy New Year to you.'

J. 'Were you a good girl Grace; did you have a spiritual holiday?'

G. 'I did.'

J. 'Excellent! Balance should be at the forefront of your mind in everything you do and no more so than when you do this course. You need to have a little rest - a balance - and as far as Christmas goes, your guides, helpers, family and friends, they need a rest too. They also celebrate Christmas, so everybody in spirit tries to stop and recharges by doing other things.

So we're back together now, the beginning of a new year and once again, I want to know how have you been? Are there any attunements you want to read and want to share and is there anything we need to talk about today?'

G. 'I shut my books and I really did rest and although I have been trying to catch up in the last couple of days there are some things - I have done my homework - and I did have one attunement only and then I had gift for Xmas, a spiritual gift.'

J. 'Wow!'

G. 'I have become involved in a rescue and I also think I met an earth angel on holiday.'

J. 'OK, so shall we do one thing at a time so that I can digest each and every one of these. What do you want to start with, do you want to do this as in a timeline; what happened first?'

G. 'I'm such a Virgo I've got to start at the beginning! Some of this I have re-done to cut down on the reading so I can just give it to you in a smaller format but I have to read this to you because I truly don't altogether remember what I did. This is an attunement, the one that I did and it was the 4 December.'

J. 'So this was before your spiritual holiday?'

G. 'It was and, as usual, I've put a heading and the heading is 'Communication.''

J. 'May I ask, is the heading something you've put or is it given you or a bit of both?'

G. 'A bit of both.'

J. 'That's what I thought.'

G. 'It has been on my mind to ask for information from my guides about the communicators necessary on platform work. Our small group consisted of Aerial, Sonja and Salaman and after I'd asked the question, I was shown my brother-in-law's step mother who I understand as far as I know, was very kind to him as a child.

In her later years she had Parkinson's and although my brother-in-law was not related, he too has Parkinson's. I asked my brother-in-law's mother, in spirit, if she could or would give me any information regarding his life expectancy as he has been poorly. She replied saying he would pass in his sleep overnight or in his chair during daylight hours. When I pressed for a little more, she said he would see Christmas. This Christmas or other Christmases, I don't know. Our conversation was finished, there was no reply forthcoming.

I asked if she would show me her light and energy before leaving and she became a shining white orb and then was gone. I also asked Salaman why he was there? He told me to fill my new fountain pen with ink and buy some better paper when this pad is finished.

Then Innka bounced in without any warning giving me a hug which lifted me off my feet, his energy is very strong. He is Indian. He wears a turban, wears long white robes very often and wears a beard. I was then shown myself and my daughters together and given a word, you know I can't pronounce it, P R E V A L E N T. I had to look it up in my old dictionary. It comes from the word prevail and affiliates with having great power and being victorious.

I feel that the later part of my attunement was to bring home to me the strength received from being a loving group where trust prevails.'

J. 'What you're doing is analysing this attunement which is great. What else did you get out of it - dissect it?'

G. 'The original question was about communication and communicators. I have no real wish to do platform work although I have done it as an exercise but I have always found it difficult to understand when you've got past your angel and then your guide and the other members of your soul group if you like.

Communicators would hopefully arrive with a message for someone, not necessarily for you, but for someone you might know and I've always thought, how could you go to people and say I have a message for you, you couldn't? You would frighten them and it's always been in my mind that I have a grey area there as to how this works.

Obviously, spirit wants to get a message across but you have to be very certain who that communicator is. Is this the right person to send a message? You've got to differentiate between the good and the bad, maybe even on the astral plane?'

J. 'OK, first of all not everybody on this course or on a spiritual path is being asked to give out messages, yes? We have to wait to see what our strength of service is. Often people have one main ability, one psychic strength and then they may have affiliated gifts, for want of another word.

Now, I don't want you to be concerned about that too much. I think what we're talking about here is the actual attunement and the fact that you asked a specific question. I know I'm butting in here - I should really ask you to verify more information - but I'm thinking that you actually got an answer to your question.

You entered into a communique' with this lady, yes, and the communique' went backwards and forwards so you got answers to your questions which to me, is amazing and wonderful.

It's like at the end of the year, your last attunement for 2012, you talk about having a present? Well, I think this is a present in itself that you were both trusting each other. You weren't nervous or fearful, you were just going with the flow which is the best way to communicate. You didn't put up any barriers at all, you asked in a positive light and then, I don't know what you felt when you suddenly saw this lady, you just went with it?'

G. 'Yes, I wasn't afraid. I wasn't surprised to see her because the Parkinson's and them each having it, I suppose, it was likely to be her.'

J. 'Why were you thinking of this gentleman with Parkinson's?'

G. 'Well I was thinking my brother-in-law had been poorly. I had seen him recently.'

J. 'Ah, before the attunement?'

G. 'Yes.'

J. 'Well that's even more wonderful, isn't it, that this step mother-in-law had picked up on your thoughts! That's your proof that she was picking up on your thoughts? You didn't expect her to come but when she showed herself, without realising it, you thought it made sense that she was there?'

G. 'And it felt right.'

J. 'Remember the saying, *"There's no such thing as time in spirit but spirit's time is perfect."* So it was timely, yes? We haven't even finished talking about the attunement yet but so far, you've got quite a lot from this. Can you think of anything else you got from it?'

G. 'I can, I've just thought of something now! When I said to you how can you tell if they're the right people, if they're good people and I just told you myself! I saw her and it felt right and maybe that's all it is, a feeling? If you can have a feeling of it being right, by the same token, I would think you would have a feeling that it was wrong, if it were so?'

J. 'Well this is a very big subject actually but if I break it down into 'bullet points'.

You can only receive something similar to yourself. I've told you that our spirit guides and helpers - the people who come through - are on the same wavelength to us so you're spirituality is linked up with people of the same ilk as yourself. You won't be able to receive anything 'higher' because the law of *"Like attracts like"* will prevent this.

Because spirit can read your mind, if you get a message from spirit and you fabricate it and give it out as something different, your guides will know that and they will be disappointed.'

G. 'Fudging - it's called fudging.'

J. 'The point about understanding yourself as an energy as well as a spiritual energy, you come to realise that energy - and spiritual energy - is all around you and therefore there's no hiding place. People forget that.'

G. 'I don't.'

J. 'So you have to be totally and utterly honest with yourself as well as with everybody else.'

G. 'I could not live with myself and someone would be hurt.'

J. 'But it takes all sorts to make a world and people go blindly into this realm of activity - psychic and spiritual activity - with very little understanding which is the whole point of this course, to put bullet points, to dot the i's and cross the t's.

Also, if you do this work, do you realise it comes with conditions, it comes at a price? If you really want to do this, you must do it properly and that means commitment, devotion, integrity; all these things. Some people just brush this aside and then don't get the best out of it.

So to reiterate, not everyone is supposed to be up on the church platform and not everyone is supposed to be giving messages. As a spiritual person on your journey, on your spiritual path who wants to work with those who walk and work with you, communication is of the essence and this course has always been about formulating the best communication you can, trying to find ways to improve it but you can't force or demand anything; it will only come if it's supposed to.

So, when I first heard your question Grace, about communication for platform work, my first thoughts were, I don't know whether you'll need this for platform work? But if you do, spirit will guide you towards this, without hesitation, you will be led if that's where you're supposed to be.

The main objective of this course has always been about service - service to spirit - and as I have said, this is 360 degrees in the fulfilling. It can take any form but you have already agreed what you're going to do before you came here so just be guided for your higher good where you're supposed to be and what you're supposed to do.

At the moment you are finding things out for yourself and what you found out in that last attunement of the year is that you are able to communicate, you're able to ask questions and get a reply with confidence and understand it and therefore you have also been privy to someone else's spiritual journey.'

G. 'Gosh.'

J. 'Which I think is very privileged? She could have said, it's not for you to know, couldn't she?'

G. 'Yes.'

J. 'So that, so far, is what I'm getting. Your last attunement this year ended on a high. It wasn't massive but it spoke volumes and also you've had more people around you than usual and to me, it was almost as though they all wanted to wish you Happy Christmas!

You didn't have your usual two people either side, there were others there too. You had the whole team and because it was your last attunement of the year - and they probably knew it would be - they wanted to capitalise on it, by jumping up into your arms and throwing you off your feet and were doing everything but wishing you Happy Christmas! So to me, it was synonymous with that, do you get that?'

G. 'I do! I do.'

J. 'This is what I'm trying to teach you to do. It's not just saying this happened and that happened, we know about that but can't you see what else happened? Come on, look underneath, look behind, think about it, split it; split the atom?

Try and look at the whole attunement in its entirety, remove the blinkers and see what you were really given. That is what I want to try and get you to do Grace, and you will do it. Look between the lines, the spaces in between, the implications?

It takes experience after experience. It's like the more attunements you have, the more communication you have so the better your link and understanding becomes. You end up thinking or saying, 'You'll never guess what; the penny's just dropped, they were saying this too!' So that's what I'm saying about that attunement so I think there was a lot there.'

G. 'Why I asked the question was because platform work was something I ran away from when I left a circle because I was so anxious, but at the time I did do it.'

J. 'How come you were doing platform work in a circle?'

G. 'Well, no, the circle would meet and then there would be an evening of fledglings.'

J. 'Oh I see, in a church?'

G. 'Well, sometimes, but I did become quite ill and one time we had an evening of friends and family and I didn't know who would be there!'

J. 'But you volunteered to do it?'

G. 'Yes, I had about two weeks of knowing that I would have to stand up and give messages. It sounds amazing when I think about it but spirit started to rehearse with me the week before it happened and I would find myself in the middle of my room at home practising, hearing what spirit were saying and hearing my own voice speak to an imaginary audience.

That night, I sat there and we all had to sit in a row facing the audience and then we would be asked to stand up and I already knew - I was word perfect when I walked in there - and I had all the messages in my head which were repeated and repeated and repeated for that week.

I knew I had a message for someone in that room and when I was drawn to that someone that was the message I had carried with me the whole week and some of them were ten minutes long and I had been holding that in my head and I knew that wasn't the way for me, certainly not at that time. Some people walk in and don't know what they're going to say.'

J. 'Maybe, because you, as a person, are quite pedantic so you needed to be fully rehearsed?'

G. 'I must be. It's hard and I try to get away from it but it occasionally takes me over but it hasn't happened since you and I have been working together. It's taken a back step but I think I was just asking that final question of the year before walking away.'

J. 'It's obviously been on your mind?'

G. 'It has been but after that happened it wasn't there anymore, it had gone.'

J. 'Good. The key is that every experience is beneficial, every experience will tell you something. For example, you can plan to go somewhere and do something and be really excited about it and then afterwards, be completely deflated knowing this wasn't for you at all but you still get answers.

We are taught, *"Experience is the greatest teacher"* so if ever you go back onto the platform, whether it's a one off or regularly, you might have another fledgling evening and decide you want to try. You will then compare how you are now with how you were then but there's no right or wrong thing to do and we always have freedom of choice, freedom of will.

I have always known that platform work isn't for me. I had to do a year of it but then I had to do a lot of things because if you're going to teach you need the experience to go with it. I knew why I had to do my stint on the platform but I also knew it wasn't my forte'; it's not what I'm 'designed for' or what I agreed to do.'

G. 'It's not mine.'

J. 'The important thing is to walk the journey in every way possible as each experience, whether it's on the platform or having an attunement, allows you to take that next step forward - it gives you answers and teaches you, always.'

G. 'Because I knew if I sat in the audience with them later, I knew instinctively that what they were saying was not correct.'

J. 'Grace, if you're a spiritual person, you're normally a sensitive and when you're sensitive you think and feel so many things. Now, in the past, I have been reminded by spirit that I am mentally really critical of others and I am but it's because I am a big thinker and I dissect, analyse and question what people say; I am naturally like that.

I do it because it's the way I get answers, it's the way I measure things. Spirit know I'm like that and when I go 'home' I'll be like that because it's my personality, yes? There's nothing wrong; it's the way you are, you have to be true to yourself, don't you?'

G. 'Yes, I almost test people and then stand back and see what will happen whether it's a good thing or a bad thing. I don't do it in a huge way but then I have something to measure.'

J. 'OK. We're going to have to move on now.'

G. 'Now this is lovely, I've got to tell you this!'

J. 'What is it, it's not an attunement?'

G. 'No, it's a surprise. It's my Christmas present - you're mentioned! My spiritual teacher, Jenny, gave her last one to one lesson on the 28 November. We shall not meet again until early January of 2013. When we last sat together she told me about the connection between butterflies and mediums. Butterflies change from caterpillars which are grubs into beautiful butterflies; it is called the metamorphosis process and is something of a miracle when observed.

We, as mediums, are ever changing and therefore growing in our wisdom and learning. Therefore, we too, are metamorphic. Many books on spirituality often have a butterfly on the cover. The butterfly in my life is called a British Tortoiseshell.'

J. 'How do you know this is your butterfly? Have you decided it's your butterfly?'

G. 'Yes. Back in the January of 2010 it had been snowing heavily for some weeks and on this particular morning, the sun was shining upon my garden and the surrounding countryside making it a winter wonderland.

Walking into an upstairs bedroom, I found in the window a butterfly preening itself in the warmth of the sun. It was just too cold to open the window and let it fly away so I tried lettuce, honey and water but after four or five days of my gentle care it went to sleep for ever.

It was so perfect, it rested on some silk flowers for some months looking as if it would take wing at any moment. Finally, by late spring, I returned it to the garden placing it upon a flower. When I returned to check on it later that day it had gone. This story I had already told to Jenny.

Move forward in time to 2 December, 2012. Walking into my bathroom at 10pm in the evening after several days of gales and rain, with the windows firmly closed, resting upon the soap tray of the shower was, you guessed it, another Tortoiseshell butterfly once again, preening itself.

It was sat upon a duster which I had washed that morning and I had been to check several times to see if it was dry enough to move so I know that the butterfly had not been there earlier in the day and the windows had been closed all of the day.

My husband suggested that I should get my camera which I did. After it fluttered down and rested upon the floor it took its photo call and then flew off and rested on a small side lamp. In the morning it was not there but I discovered it that evening behind a cupboard. It started to move towards the lamp which was turned on by now and when I returned later it was nowhere to be seen.

Move on to Thursday, 6 December. After many searches, the butterfly suddenly appeared downstairs in the lounge window. It was still cold outside and the butterfuly became very agitated banging itself against the glass. It felt right to open the window and although it was grey and overcast outside, our visitor flew straight out flying upwards until I could no longer see it so I have told you that story on the telephone sometime back. Amazing, what a gift, what a gift!'

J. 'And it's also confirmation that everything is right, everything is good and obviously how much you're thought of, how much you're loved; 'Don't forget me!' this sort of thing.'

G. 'Well yes, if ever you needed confirmation, that was it, but you see I got very excited thinking about the connection between mediums and butterflies that I actually rang you and then two or three days later, Oh, here we are again!'

J. 'You hadn't had that happen for a couple of years?" Again, a timely thing, spirit's time is perfect. Very, very lovely and I'm very happy for you as well.'

G. 'Now this one I wrote earlier today so I don't need to read it, I can tell you. This is the rescue that I became involved in.'

J. 'When did this happen?'

G. 'It was on 8 December.'

J. 'So everything has happened within a very short period of time? The attunement, the butterfly, everything is being 'squeezed in' before Christmas?'

G. 'Because we had talked about rescue. I'm just going to tell you this rather than read it because, as you can see, I wore myself out with writing one, two, three pages! It's exhausting but I can tell you.

My husband and I had a dinner to go to at a hotel. We decided to book a room and stay overnight. It was a lovely evening. We booked early and took a room at a special rate and got there at 5 o'clock in the afternoon and the meal was at 7.30 in the dining room. We went up to our room and because it was a special deal it wasn't the worse room but it wasn't the best room and it was towards the back of the hotel.

We went up the front stairs which are in the older part and went through into a newer part and we found ourselves right on the top floor and we didn't even know they had a third floor!'

J. 'And you weren't there for nothing, were you dear!'

G. 'So, we found our way up passed all the important rooms, up to the next floor and then climbed up the last little windy bit to the top floor. Now we were on a little landing and behind us, I suppose, to make it look better, was a floor to ceiling mirror but an old fashioned one with gilt. So you've got the back wall, then about where I was, a little windy stairs going back down to the lower floor. We had to walk with the mirror at our back straight down to the end, we then took a right and we were nearly at the end of this corridor and our room was on the left looking out over the back lawn.

You couldn't go any further, we were right at the end but there were a lot of rooms on the opposite side so you had like an 'L' shape. We opened the door to go in and the first thing we could smell was cigarette smoke. Now they're a non smoking hotel. I walked across to open the windows and it really smelt smoky and I could see a little garden shed down at the far corner.

Now I know that's where the staff go to smoke and eighteen months/two years ago I knew the barman and if I was eating there, because of my dairy allergy, he would make sure that I had a bar meal that was just right for me and if I met him, he would say hello and one day he told me he'd been diagnosed as a diabetic.

Now he smoked and drank heavily and I said to him, well that's going to have to stop and he said, Oh I know, I've been for counselling, I'm going to do this, that and the other. Then a while later, I was in a local pub having a meal and he was there and he was the worse for drink and I knew he'd been outside to have a cigarette and he was so sloshed that he came to see me, got on his knees by the table because he was a big lad, in his middle to late thirties, and he said, I can't stand I'm pissed, and that's not a word I use often, I'm just quoting him. I said, it's no good, you know, it won't do.

After some months, we visited the hotel again and we were told that the barman had died. They found him in the little shed. He'd gone out for a smoke and it was a clot in the leg that moved over the heart and I was really upset for quite a while.'

J. 'So when you went to the dinner, you already knew he had died?'

G. 'Yes, I had known for 6 to 9 months. There was nothing morbid about the room but it wasn't very warm and as we'd already bathed, we thought we'd just get changed, go to the dinner and have a bath in the morning.

After a long night, we were getting undressed for bed about one o'clock in the morning and that room was cold and my husband fiddled with the radiator and it kind of got warm but that room was so cold. Warm in the bathroom but it wasn't anywhere else but I always take a hot water bottle wherever I go, always.

We had single beds so I climbed into my bed with my hot water bottle, my husband went straight to sleep and I got cold and colder and colder and colder. I got up, went into the bathroom, re-filled my bottle, got back into bed, colder, colder. Got up, put my jumper over my nightie, put my socks on, refilled my bottle, looked at the bath and thought, could I sleep in there?

Got back into bed and it was like lying in a bath of cold water and I am lying there and suddenly I had this kind of light bulb moment; this isn't normal, this isn't right? Checking and slapping on protection for all I'm worth and for my husband, it was like something took over and it was very clear.'

J. 'It was as though you're thoughts allowed spirit to begin; the penny dropped?'

G. 'It did, clang! So I'm lying there and it was a cross between my feelings and feeling a vibration, I could hear feet marching passed the bedroom door, lots of feet. The next thing I knew was that although I was still in bed, I was also outside, stood in front of my door and walking passed me, about five abreast, were at least fifty people and they were partly translucent but they were kind of grey and silvery.

And I looked at them and there were men, women, children of various ages, all in kind of Victorian working clothes and you could hear their feet. They went down to the end, took a left - now there was no way to walk round the back - but they could and I could hear them and then, sure enough back they'd come and as I'm watching them, at the front, is my barman!'

J. 'Amazing!'

G. 'And I'm kind of looking at him and thinking as he passed me and I had to almost run to get up in front. So now I'm marching as well and we're marching along together and I'm looking at him and I'm saying, you shouldn't be here, this is not where you should be and he's looking at me and I'm saying, do you know who I am and he answered, yes. I said, do you trust me and he looked very hard at me and he said yes.

Well, by then, we'd tramped all the way round and going down the further side coming back out to come past my room. So we're coming back past my room and I'm saying to him, you've got to find the light, you shouldn't be here and he's asking, where is the light? And as we get to the end to turn towards the little landing, there's the mirror and I know that's where it is!

Top corner, top left hand corner and I say to him, do you trust me and he said yes. I said you've got to walk to that mirror, walk into that mirror and you will go to the light, don't look back. So we get almost to the mirror and he quickened his pace and he was out in front slightly and he was gone.

But I've still got all this lot behind! There was no time to sort anything out so we take a left and walk round again and as we come back past the bedroom door which seems to trigger everything, I'm saying, do you trust me?'

J. 'To all these people as well?'

G. 'And all these voices say yes! So as we turn, there's the mirror and I'm saying, you have to go to the light, go into the mirror. Do you trust me, yes, we trust you, so we're nearly to the end and I stop and they divided and filed each side of me and I felt and saw them pass me and they were gone into the mirror. And then I'm thinking, I better check to see whether there is anyone left over?' (Jenny laughs).

So back round I go, back up towards my door, just as I get to my door, opposite my door, crouching down by the wall is a little lad of about eight years old, Victorian clothes, cap, you know. Then I look across and just past my bedroom door but on the same side as my bedroom is a girl of about ten with her back to the wall. I am pretty sure they could not see one another.

So I just say, you shouldn't be here and I hold out my hands and say take my hand and they each take a hand. I spoke to them because I didn't want them to be afraid. I can't tell you what we said but they replied and I knew they could now see each other. Round the corner we go heading towards the mirror and then, do you trust me, yes, let go of my hands, do you trust me and as we get nearly there I let go of their hands and they're gone!

And I find myself back in my bed clutching my hot water bottle. It took a while to warm up and it started from the feet upwards and I just went to sleep and I slept till the morning.

When I walked out of my door there was space in that corridor because when we had walked to the room in the first place to bring our bags, I had felt I was being jostled and pushed and buffeted and I couldn't think why? There was none of that now and when I walked downstairs and left. I said to my husband, 'We shouldn't be paying them, they should be paying *me!*' (Jenny roars with laughter). So I wasn't afraid.'

J. 'No, well done YOU!'

G. 'I knew what to do because someone needed my help and that was enough.'

J. 'Well, I can't believe there were so many people that had collected there but I have a feeling that...... first of all; well done, well done!'

G. 'Thank you.'

J. 'And there are obviously *so* many people who want to thank you. However, you need to know that they weren't all at the hotel - they were all brought *to* the hotel.'

G. 'Were they? Oh, I hadn't thought of that!'

J. 'They were. You see *"Spirit are great opportunists"* plus this was always something for *you* to do because spirit knew you were ready to do it. They key was the barman. He was going to be the one who led them. I don't know exactly how it works but he was the leader and he was the instigator who was going to fulfil this, not just for himself but for all those in the surrounding areas who were ready to go home.

So they were all brought to that landing because it was all going to happen whilst you were staying there because spirit needed a medium's help and so it was all arranged. It was all prepared so the barman was gathering people, he knew the hotel, it was second nature to him.'

G. 'Yes it was.'

J. 'So it was as though he was saying, look you've got to wait with me, wait with me, so they were all gathered there waiting, so you did quite a lot for the surrounding area!'

G. 'I didn't realise *that* was possible, that other lost souls would come there as well?'

J. 'Yes, what you have to understand is that because there's no such thing as time in spirit, people get attached and don't move on for varying reasons and you were also in an old town. It's changed and been many different things, it's had many different dwellings with farms and churches whatever and it was obviously a great opportunity for spirit and you handled it so well!

You weren't fazed, you took in everything, the way the corridors were running, you heard the noise, you realised, oh, I think I *know* why it's so cold; you suddenly had that eureka moment because there was no other explanation.

And spirit *do* use rescue mediums when they go away - they've used me loads of times in many different places - and my first night is often a 'rescue night' so I'm not at all surprised but they certainly packed the landing, didn't they?'

G. 'They did.'

J. 'And the other thing which was excellent was your knowledge and intuition that there might be someone left behind. Sometimes what happens is that when you have someone go home, one person i.e. your barman, would automatically take *everyone* else with him but this rescue shows us that this is not necessarily the case.

He went off and I think it was the fact that you felt that you wanted do this right? Do you remember when we talked about how pedantic you are, how you mustn't leave any stone unturned and therefore you sensed that there were still people left over, your sensitivity, you picked that up because it was so.

So you actually went back, found out that you were right - which was amazing - and handled everybody yourself and you knew that going through the mirror was the way to go. So all in all, I think you did quite amazingly considering your lack of training.

You're obviously working *very* well with your guides. You're not allowed to do this alone, as you know but it's also testament to the relationship that you have with your guides because to me, it was *very* fluidly done.'

G. 'I don't remember my guides being there.'

J. 'No, you don't need to see them but you won't ever do anything like this on your own, we're only half of it remember? We always have to do things - work - with a spiritual guide so you *never* do anything in your own strength. It's almost as though they were getting it all ready, 'Oh, Grace will be here in a minute....she'll keep going, getting another hot water bottle, then she'll sense it, she'll sense it in a minute.....' and it's all done according to plan; spirit knew how it would all be executed with your help.

Again, it happened at the end of the year so you've had an amazing.... *so much* has been squeezed into the last month of last year! I think you should be a *very*, very happy woman because I know how much this means to you so well done and I'm now echoing loads of thanks from everybody you took home. (Grace smiles).

They were *all* ready because nobody goes home unless they *are* ready. They have to ask for help and your barman had obviously asked for help too but spirit had plans for him anyway. He didn't go over straight away. Spirit knew he wouldn't go straight away; he was wrestling with himself.'

G. 'Yes.'

J. 'He didn't go immediately but that's fine because he's got a job to do before he goes!'

G. 'But that was his way, he was always very good with people and he was always completely sober and professional when he was at work.'

J. 'Yes, well let's move on now.'

G. 'I've got one more thing, I've got more. This was at the last port of the cruise before we came home. We went to a place called Gothenburg in Sweden. It was extremely cold and we weren't allowed on the decks as we came into berth because they were all icy. Although the sun was out and the sky was blue we went into the city but all the rivers were frozen; it was how I would imagine Russia to be. So this is how I see it:-

People must be at the same level of understanding for the exchange of thoughts and feelings. This can happen between people who have met for the first time with different nationalities, different upbringings and so on and so forth but their level of understanding, memories, hopes and dreams are completely connected. Being near to one another in age might possibly be an additional factor in this equation of life.

Whilst on holiday and making a brief visit to Gothenburg in Sweden, I met a lady of approximately my own age. Not younger, perhaps a little bit older but not by much. My husband and I were walking around a very large department store just looking and also to keep warm because it was bitterly cold outside. We had just located the rest rooms which were the only facilities in this area and then realised that in Sweden you must pay to use this facility. My husband was doing his best to work out how much this was going to cost and how to make the machine work.

I had found a place to sit close by and was keeping well out of the proceedings. From out of thin air a lady, about my age and build wearing sensible shoes, trousers and a warm coat went to help him, taking a coin out of her bag and placing it in his hand. I could not hear the conversation but watched the interchange between them. Eventually they began to gain an understanding. The change machine gave change and the lady received her coin back.

She turned to walk away, saw me smiling and walked across. Your husband, she asked? Yes, was my reply. We spoke for a little over five minutes. She said the confusion was because she had thought he was from her native country of Germany. She explained that she had lived in Sweden for fifty years. She was a seamstress and that Holland and Sweden did not like Germans because of the war but that she found by being kind and helpful and by doing her best to get on with people, she had in some ways been accepted.

She was from Northern Germany and asked did I remember the war? I explained that I had been born in 1944, at the end, and that being the last generation we must never forget or let it be forgotten. She said her father had been in the war and that at the time, there was not a choice, you were either in it or you were not. I replied saying that I agreed.

I said that I was going to make sure my grandchildren would understand all that had passed in order to make their world a better place and she said she would be doing and was doing the same.

We looked into each other's faces because by now I was standing for I knew something of great importance was taking place. She touched my hand, I touched her shoulder wishing her a Happy New Year. We both smiled at each other and she returned my greeting. She turned away and was gone.

I will never forget her. Wasn't that wonderful?'

J. 'She just touched you in a way. I don't think you would have bothered to tell the story if it didn't have an impact on you?'

G. 'Oh, so much! It was just two women.'

J. 'I know that when you're going through life sometimes things happen. I *do* know what you mean as I'm now thinking of somebody I will never forget and it's absolutely crazy.

I was in a foreign country, I think it was France, I can't remember but it was in Europe and Sam and I were lost walking down all these different streets and there was this lady walking down and somehow she wasn't a 'normal' lady. I can't explain it. I just knew she'd been planted there to help. I still have no proof, we hardly said anything but that lady was just different!

She was just different and she had grey hair..... Anyone else hearing your story would have said well why have you bothered to tell me this story, what's so unusual about meeting someone who helps you to get the change out of a coin machine?'

G. 'Because the facilities were well off the beaten track you see.'

J. 'No, it was about this lady; what's different about the lady?'

G. 'She never used the facilities herself! She walked back, she never actually turned; she was gone!'

J. 'That was a big clue, wasn't it? Yes, I know what you mean and I know you can't put your finger on it but they made an impression. It's like a footprint on your soul and that's it now, it's in there, it's done! It's a mystery but it's a lovely mystery, if you like?'

G. 'Yes, I said to my husband, I've definitely met an angel because she was so kind.'

J. 'OK, so you had your spiritual holiday and I should imagine it was well received after all that lot! I've just got to hear your homework which you say you've done?'

G. 'I have! Write a paragraph or two on what I have learnt about love? Love for the child: Love is letting go so go try your wings and find yourself. Fly as far as your wings can take you but know this, I will be here if you chose to return waiting with outstretched arms.

For your soul mate: Take part of my heart, hold it, let it give you strength, it is yours. Although to you it may feel strong, it is also a tender fragile thing and can be broken so hold it close until you chose to return it to its owner which I hope will be never.

For the parents who brought me into this world: Thank you for choosing me as your child. Thank you is a small word but it comes from a place within my heart that only you can fill for you have known me all of this life. I love and honour you both.

Love for friends: You lighten my world when I am at my most vulnerable. Your smile gives me the strength to try again against all odds. I will be there for you just as you are there for me. I love you.

Love for love's sake: I love having a body because this one was chosen by me. Sometimes it hurts, other times it feels pretty damn good. My body is my vehicle, it gets me to where I want to be and by the same token, occasionally, where I do not want to be.

It is there even through my many lives, coming into this world brand new, leaving a little weather-beaten, rather like a jacket which has seen much wear yet, in the end, it is just me and my body each of us supporting the other in good and bad times. I trust and love you, you are my best friend.

Because there are different kinds of love.'

J. 'Definitely! That was different! I would just like to make the point that your parents didn't necessarily choose you, *you* chose your parents.'

G. 'Do you think, I've often wondered if it's a two way thing?'

J. 'Yes it often is. It's all planned but your incarnation is the most important because they've already chosen theirs.'

G. 'I understand.'

J. 'So we chose our parents because of what we have to do, what we have to learn but also what we have to teach because we don't just come back to learn, we come back to teach as well but your parents have to also say yes! Do you know what I'm saying? So when you said thank you for choosing me, I just wanted to make sure you realised that it's not always like that, it's more the other way round but with the parents agreeing to it.'

G. 'They have to agree. I kind of thought that when I did it, it had crossed my mind.'

J. 'We discussed this in the workshop. Sometimes part of planning the return to be reincarnated here on earth will include choosing the same family so you may have been your mother's mother at one time or even grandmother, we can take on new roles.'

G. 'And we can change sex as well can't we?'

J. 'That's right, we choose our sex. So I just wanted you to know that it's not just a one way thing. The fact that you, the incarnating spirit, primarily choose why you need to come back and in so doing, you choose the country, the place of birth, the people? Who is going to be mummy and daddy, *why* they are going to be your parents, why they would benefit as parents, what you could do to help them, your time frame? It's all worked out beforehand between you and your guides and soul group. OK.'

G. 'Is that ring you're wearing for spirit? Somebody told me the other day that to wear a silver ring on this hand is for spirit.'

J. 'Oh well, that's a new one on me! Right, for our new material today, we're going to discuss circles.'

Circles

Jenny: 'There are different kinds of circles:-

* An open circle where anyone can attend.

* A closed circle for chosen members only.

* A healing circle dedicated to healing.

* A teaching circle done via trance or by direct teaching, this can be open or closed.

* A working circle used by spirit to work for spirit, hopefully always closed!

Do you understand the difference between open and closed?'

Grace: 'I do and also, do they not take the same position in the circle each time?'

J. 'No, not necessarily.'

G. 'It doesn't matter?'

J. 'No, if spirit are blending the mediums' energies, there is no order - it's collective. OK, to continue, I would say that what we have been doing since we first started here is a closed teaching circle, yes, and what I have termed a development course?'

G. 'Yes.'

J. 'Often the minute someone realises that they are psychic or mediumistic they think they must join a circle. They think this is the glamour or social status of a psychic or medium. They think this is how they can develop the quickest - wrong! (Grace laughs).

Circles aren't glamorous and circles aren't the exclusive way to develop either. I think we have proved this over the last nine months, yes? You do not need to be in a circle to develop. To me, your attunements are your greatest opportunity to blend with spirit for your higher good.

Open circles are very suspect indeed. In a way, I think going to a spiritualist church is like attending an open circle. It requires an immense amount of discipline and spirit work very hard to provide the necessary protection for a simple reason that it is open to all. Many churches are unstructured, unsupervised and undisciplined. Prayers must be said before and after a service as a matter of course and sometimes, they're not.

You may remember when we first met that I mentioned that it was best for me to teach at home because in a way I already have the necessary cover, the necessary protection here at home. Spirit can protect us better here in the home than if we were having these meetings in a public place. Through attunements and positive thought, this house has become our own spiritual and sacred ground attracting positive, spiritual energy back.

A closed circle is always better for obvious reasons but the disciplines still apply. Asking for protection and closing down are the tools you must always apply and never forget. They are vital for your health and safety like wearing a hard hat when you ride a bike or visit a demolition site.

In a healing circle, we allow spirit to use our channels for the purpose of giving healing to others. We leave it to spirit to blend our energies, our vibrations, our auras, our thoughts, our love; everything is utilised for the purpose of giving absent healing to those who need it, whether they are for those in our thoughts or for the world at large.

Spiritual circles are brought together with a great deal of care by spirit which is the difference between a psychic circle and a spiritual one. It is brought into being by teamwork with spirit never by the will of the sitters. It evolves from one or two people sitting together. A third is brought in, then a fourth and then a fifth until the requisite number has been realised.

If a circle is too large then nothing of great import is achieved. Too small, then its work is limited but each person is brought in at the right time.

You see, attunements blend, attunements bring harmony. A circle's harmony is built gradually, slowly as each sitter is brought into the circle. It would prove extremely difficult for spirit to achieve or create the right harmony if a lot of strangers, who probably had little in common, were all brought into a circle at the same time.

When a circle is convened by spirit, the sitters are of like mind and their level of understanding is similar. Some may have a little higher understanding to begin with but the level is regulated because within a new sitter, the knowledge already resides, already exists and only has to be unlocked.

Within a spiritual circle the pathways are the same. The tasks may be different but the pathway is the road of service. The pathway leads to one's spiritual destiny, the pathway leads to the gaining of one's spiritual inheritance. Within a psychic circle, the pathway is usually personal development and not necessarily service.

When you sit within a spiritual circle you do not sit for personal achievement. You are not brought into a spiritual circle for your own personal development, you are brought into a spiritual circle and asked to serve. The whole ethos of a spiritual circle is not demand, is not development, it is service. You do not choose what you are going to do either. You ask, 'How may I serve? How may I best serve spirit and best enhance the work of this circle?'

You sit together to help and support each other. You are brought together of like mind and understanding so that you may uplift each other, help one another and work in total harmony.

In any circle, when you have sat together for some while irritations may creep in. Perhaps one person is not as tolerant as you would like them to be. Perhaps another is not as bright or as intellectual. Perhaps one is developing a little faster than you and you would so love to develop in that direction; a little jealousy creeps in.

Perhaps someone has very strong views and is not afraid of voicing them. Perhaps another is not so strong and you would like to give them a little shake, push them on or wish they would stand firm but you must not give way to irritations.

When you look at them and see their intolerance send them love and help them and maybe say, 'Perhaps it would be better if you tackled the situation this way, etc.' Should they be 'put out' by your suggestion, *mentally* put your arms around them saying, 'I love you and all will be well.'

When you see another person developing a little faster than you, do not be jealous, be happy for them, be glad, give them all the help you can for your turn will come.

But when you sit in a circle you cannot leave everything up to spirit, you cannot depend on them all the time, you have to help yourself too. You have to give, you have to understand, you have to care, you have to be prepared to stand back to let another go forward. There is no room for disharmony for the moment *one* negative vibration finds its way into a circle, it ceases to be spiritual, the vibration has been lowered.

You have to lose yourself, love one another - even the awkward saints and there are many - but with give and take and love, a circle flourishes which in turn will mean that you will too.

A spiritual circle is ever growing, it never stands still. Sometimes you will feel as if you *are* standing still; nothing is happening to you. Continue in your attunements and your dedication. No-one within a circle can develop at the same rate and at the same time. Spirit will work on different people. Each will come into his own at the right time for them; *Trust!*

Now, although you sit for service you *will* develop as it is a by-product of a spiritual circle. However, the circle I am going to concentrate on today is a 'working circle'.

To me, circles evolve. I was always taught that circles are convened by spirit. We do not decide who should join, spirit decides. Why? Because *they* know exactly what each given person can contribute and *they* know what blend is needed to produce the desired effect and *they* know exactly what path each and every one of us in on.

If anyone ever asks you, 'Want to join a circle?' or words to that effect, be wary. If you are meant to be in a circle you will be asked or led in such a way that you know is right, not a casual, 'Why don't you join ours?'

OK, so what do I mean by a 'working circle'? A working circle is a group of people brought together by spirit to work *for* spirit.

A circle is called a circle for the simple reason that it has no head or foot. There is no-one at the top or at the bottom. It is completely equal, completely round just like Arthur's round table. Everyone is equal, everyone contributes their quota, everyone is important, everyone is needed. In fact, without everyone's quota, the circle could not properly function. Again, trust that spirit knows what it's doing!

However, you usually join someone's circle because it is held at their house. It is there that you congregate, they are the keeper of the keys to the circle to whom everyone refers for information about the circle but they are not the head.

As I said, in a working circle each member is utilised for whatever work needs to be carried out. However, because you are being used, you are gaining experience and because of experience, you naturally develop but *only* if your motive was for your higher good. You may remember in my opening prayer, I say, 'Here I am, how may I serve, guide me to the highest for my own good.'

In a working circle you can be utilised for healing, for trance, for rescue or for teaching and helping others by the content of your attunements. But if you do not gain control of your instrument, if you are not satisfactorily disciplined or are uncontrolled, you will be a danger to the rest of the circle.

It is also irresponsible because spirit protects us from their side of life, *our* job is to discipline our instruments on the physical side of life. It is through this teamwork that we are made safe.

To develop the psychic instrument, maybe to progress into mediumship, to sit within a working circle - any circle - demands discipline, demands commitment. No-one ever achieved anything without it. Think of the disciplines and demands needed when training to be good or the best at anything in this life, you still need to put that commitment in!

If the instrument - your mental and physical body - is always open, quite apart from the dangers of an attachment, the sensitive will become drained of all energy, they will become tired which will lead to physical illness. Mental discipline is *so* important, I cannot emphasize this enough.

For a circle to thrive it needs love, joy and beauty within so the work that is done is of the highest. It therefore needs to work on a positive vibration, so positive discipline is therefore a must. Circles and disciplines go together.

All attunement whether done at home or in a circle is better done on an empty stomach. Smoking and drinking will act as barriers to your work or development with your guides and tears or high emotion can actually hinder the circle's harmony and vibrations.

If you sit in a circle and your circle meets say, every week, you do not make excuses and do something else or if you are invited somewhere, you should say, 'I'm sorry, it's my circle night.' A circle takes priority.

Your first loyalty is to your circle, it is your commitment. It is part of your discipline of service because if you do not attend your circle regularly, you cause an imbalance and the vibrations will not harmonise.

If you are irregular in your attendance, it makes the maintenance of that harmony within the vibrations very hard indeed.

A circle's work usually lasts for an hour and each time a member of the circle is given the duty of 'watchman'. This means that he or she must not attune with the others but stay 'awake'. The watchman will usually start the circle with a prayer, bringing everyone round after the hour having watched over the circle.

If anyone speaks during the hour, the watchman will record whatever takes place on an audio cassette. At the end of the hour, each member will relate what took place in their attunement, which can also be recorded. The circle finally ends with a closing prayer.

The candle in the middle of the circle is extinguished after the closing prayer. The work is then finished and the tea, biscuits and chit, chat begins. You must *always* remember to close down before you leave the house.

In a working circle, spirit may be developing you for trance and rescue. You may find yourself needing to draw or write down what is being given to you clairvoyantly or clairaudiently. You may be used for healing or for teaching but whatever is done is always done for your higher good and the good of others.

Basically, you don't have to do anything but:-

* Learn to relax

* Learn to be patient

* Learn to trust

* Learn to be used

* Love and support each other and.... spirit will do the rest!

And don't forget to regularly attune if you're in a circle too!

Not everybody wants to be in a circle but hearing different things about the subject certainly helps with your overall understanding.

To me, the main points of a circle are the disciplines and the knowledge of how a circle works. Achieving harmony, having that commitment and, of course, the love and desire to serve.

We take spirit so much for granted and no more so when in a circle. We think it's like turning on and off a light. If you can imagine, all the mediums - the sitters - have been 'brought on' by their guides throughout the months and years before they eventually arrive at a circle.

Each time, the work that needs to be done is all pre-arranged, prepared and agreed; who is going to do what, etc. So much work is done by spirit beforehand. I'm sure a lot of people don't think of this. They probably think, oh, I'm going to circle tonight I wonder what will happen....full stop!

And remember, *"Like attracts like"* - you will work with those in spirit of a similar ilk to you and obviously only do the work you're capable of doing.

Spirit will even use their influence to close a circle, they will influence a church to be shut down if they think this is deemed necessary; I have heard this happen only in the last month. They will find a way to end or change things, again, for everyone's higher good and to separate the psychic from the spiritual, so to speak.

Spirit are working 24/7 all the time to make those who *do* want to do good able to do so, to be able to serve in the correct way and to teach those who aren't working properly by example; by closing places down.

Another way that spirit will communicate is by heeding a situation if it will not prove beneficial for you. For example, if you're not supposed to be doing something, they will step in, they will make you ill, they will give you a flat tyre, they will cause someone to be late or change an appointment. Again, all for our higher good as spirit always have our best interest at heart.

Our spirit guides are working with us all the time. The sooner you appreciate and understand that, the easier it will be for you to find your way along your journey, to know what to do and also to impress upon others who may not yet understand.

Are there any questions?'

G. 'No, but what I was going to say was when I had the flu, there were so many things that were booked on my calendar and before I had the flu, I wondered how on earth I was going to do it all. And at about the same time as I got the flu, people rang in, stuff got moved, stuff got cancelled and virtually until Christmas, everything was either diverted but I didn't lose out on anything but I was kind of saying to spirit as I didn't know how I was going to do it all!'

J. 'Yes, spirit were definitely influencing things there. OK, so here are your notes on what we've talked about today. I also want to remind you of our Question and Answer session which we will be having in the not too distant future so I hope you have been doing some soul searching and preparing some questions for me?

Finally, your homework, I want you to write down what you feel you have learnt and achieved since you started this course! You obviously need to start compiling a list in order to finish this for next month.'

Bobbie's Attunements At This Stage Of The Course...

Jenny: 'Well, it's lovely to see you Bobbie.'

Bobbie: 'It's lovely to see you as well.'

J. 'Right, we're going to draw right down now, calm right down. Make our energies like you're on simmer - a low light - and then, deep breathing. We've got an afternoon's work ahead of us so get your symbol, get your light up there above your head. Mine is up there - my single flame - which I use as my opening light. I'm asking for our guides to draw close, even though they're probably here already, and when we've done this, we can begin. OK.

So I'm really looking forward to hearing how you've been. I don't really care if it's animal, vegetable or mineral, I'm just pleased to see you! (Bobbie laughs). So, you've been carrying on with your attunements?'

B. 'I have! I haven't got much to report though, it's been very quiet.'

J. 'It doesn't matter, let's see what's been happening and let's see what we need to discuss this afternoon.'

B. 'Right, well the first one since I left you on the 8th was Saturday, March 9th. This morning's attunement was peaceful but nothing occurred. I just enjoyed being in the moment. And then it was Tuesday.'

J. 'But do you always think about what I said? *"When the least is happening, the most is happening."*

B. 'Yes.'

J. 'May I just check, whether there is a change in where you're sitting, what time you're sitting? I know you said there's not much but I just wondered, have you any other information, perhaps a 'knowing' you felt in your attunement? We're going to talk about that.

Also, because you now know about my *"Nothing is ever for nothing"* truth, what has been happening and how long are your attunements now? They went up to forty minutes, are they still forty minutes?'

B. 'Sometimes, yes, sometimes it's thirty. I know when it's finished.'

J. 'Can I ask you, how do you know your attunement's finished?'

B. 'Everything seems to go cold.'

J. 'That's right, because you usually say, I feel the tingling, I feel the heat.'

B. 'Yes, I get really hot.'

J. 'So it is like the cooker - they turn it off!'

B. 'Yes!' (Bobbie is laughing).

J. 'Amazing. That's very interesting to hear. I've never heard it before because people know when they're finished in different ways so this is a new one on me; you've been hot all the time and then suddenly you feel cold and that's your cue; we've finished!'

B. 'Yes. Then it was Tuesday and it was; this morning's attunement was again uneventful so there is nothing to report. The same Thursday, the same on Friday.'

J. 'Right. You make a note of the energies that are coming in and going out, meaning, you record what you sense as in - I sense an energy coming in, it's male, this is someone I know, it's probably Daniel, it's a Gandalf energy, etc. - but when you are in the stillness, is there nothing at all?'

B. 'Nothing, nothing.'

J. 'Sorry, but I wanted to double check that there was simply *nothing* else going on?'

B. 'So Friday was the same and I did put on Friday, this morning's attunement was as before, uneventful. I don't know why but I guess spirit have their reasons so I'll just continue. And then Saturday, the 16th March was the same.

And then Tuesday, 19th March, this morning during my attunement, the one I call Gandalf and White Eagle stepped forward. They told me they are finding it difficult to actually reach me as they realise that I am in a lot of pain. Gandalf said to treat my pain in the same way as they told me to deal with negativity. To visualise a fire, then to draw out from my body the pain, to visualise it as blackness and then put it into the fire and then replace all areas with bright white light.

So I've actually been doing that and I can feel the difference!'

J. 'Wow! Wow! Well, I'm going to tell you something now because it's very apt. I had to help somebody the other night with a rescue and I ended up cleansing their home using *your* given method! I took all the blackness from each room and I made a fire in the middle of one of the rooms. It was like black curtains coming down from every room and I was shoving it on the fire, so I want to thank you for that because I thought, well, I'm going to do that!' (Bobbie is laughing).

That's how I'm now going to replace the energy so I want to thank you because I used that and I found it very effective and easy.'

B. 'Easy, yes, that's how I found it.'

J. 'But to also use this method to remove pain in your body too, that is *truly* amazing, but again, it's the power of thought, isn't it?'

B. 'And I find by doing that, I actually feel lighter. I'm not saying I'm pain free because I'm not.'

J. 'No, but you've had this for goodness knows how long and you know the density of it, the intensity of it and therefore you can compare?'

B. 'Oh yes and it definitely is easier but obviously the cold weather doesn't help.'

J. 'Yes, I know but you need all the help you can get, even this visualisation, very effective. I'm so pleased that you finally got communication. It immediately answered your questions about the silent attunements; so clear and to the point. It was very personal and obviously you weren't surprised by the content of it?'

B. 'No.'

J. 'Have you asked for healing?'

B. 'Yes I *do* ask for healing. I was once told before when I ask for healing, I was told, 'Healer, heal thyself.' So I ask for healing but I do try and do it myself.'

J. 'And sometimes, especially when you're sitting down or you're lying in bed and you're in pain, it's the most natural thing to self-heal because it's part of asking for help. I always say meet spirit half way don't just think, oh, they can do it and especially now that you've learnt that you're half of the partnership - you can't do anything without your other half in spirit. *You have* to do it because otherwise, what are they going to say, 'What am I, your social secretary?' (Bobbie is laughing). You need to be doing things in tandem with your guides because without them, it doesn't happen!'

B. 'No, it doesn't! I mean you can try as much as you like on your own.'

J. 'I think this is a very valid point. People think that they can just ask and it will be done and yes, spirit *do* say we hear, we listen, that no prayer ever goes unanswered, hold out your hand and it will be taken. However, there also is something else and that is, if you're able to be part of that help yourself, you should be, yes?'

B. 'Yes.'

J. 'I mean any Jane or Joe in pain, saying please help me and they don't know what else to do, that is fine but once you have that spiritual knowledge of healing, then you too are responsible. Remember, you're always in charge of you.

Can I ask - I'm know I'm putting you on the spot here - are you able to tell me the difference between Gandalf's energy and White Eagle's energy?'

B. 'Yes, Gandalf's is a lot more firm, it's stronger. I would say his personality, if you can say personality, that's the only way I can say it.'

J. 'So White Eagle is gentler?'

B. 'He is very gentle, yes.'

J. 'Is it just their energy or do they also hit a certain spot in your body; do they come through a certain part of your body? You know, oh, that's Gandalf because of how it feels but also *where* it feels?'

B. 'Actually, I almost see them.'

J. 'So when they draw close, it's a combination of feeling and then seeing?'

B. 'Yes.'

J. 'But you say that you're clairsentient - that you sense it - but you're now saying that you *do* see?'

B. 'Sometimes I do. It's the clairsentience first and then it appears clairvoyantly.'

J. 'That's really interesting so White Eagle is the gentler energy. You see with Grace, her guides come through different points of her body.'

B. 'Oh right!'

J. 'So it's interesting, isn't it? With me for example, a lot of the energy comes through my feet first, always through my feet.'

B. 'I've never really thought about it. I need to think about it, don't I? I need to know.'

J. 'You need to know and you need to be aware. It's like when I started rescue work, I thought there was only one way to do it and then when I carried on, I realised, oh no, this happens too and now *this* is happening! It's all spirit communication.

So it's the same with the energies that are working with you. Your own guides especially have what I call a 'calling card' so you already know or are prepared for who it is. So you know Gandalf's 'calling card' by his forceful energy, yes?'

B. 'Yes.'

J. 'Calling cards - the way your guides make themselves known - can also be different in their manner. For example, when one of my guides comes through, first of all, he takes a long time to come through and secondly, he will then proceed to look around at everyone in the room and therefore, I'm sure who it is - he's identified himself!'

B. 'Oh right!'

J. 'Looking back, it was one of the first things that I was taught to do. It was quite early on in my development and I thought my head keeps moving to the right and then to the left and I thought, I wonder what all that's about?

And of course, a lot later on, that was the way this particular guide who worked with me would come through. This 'calling card' was telling and showing me, 'It's me!'

B. 'Ah, right.'

J. 'Again, *"Nothing is ever for nothing."* They are starting the association in their own way. They don't say, 'Hello, Gandalf here, can I come in?' (Bobbie is laughing) Splash! - 'I'm here!' - like Batman! (Bobbie is in stitches). It's a gradual process.....(Sorry, I can't hear myself talk on the tape now as Bobbie is uncontrollable).

You'd get a fright, wouldn't you if they did that? The other thing - this is a really good point - there are people who are afraid of the spiritual, who are afraid because they think they'll be shocked or frightened.

A lot of people who are actually very gifted, maybe both psychically and spiritually, refrain from taking things forward because their fear stops them; they think they're going to be harmed or hurt or frightened by spirit. They are not prepared to *trust*.'

B. 'Yes, they just think it's an attachment, I know people who are like that.'

J. 'Well, that's the ultimate fear which is *so* misunderstood due to spiritual ignorance but your spirit guides would *never* do that because of their love for you. If you love someone you would never hurt them, would you?'

B. 'No, exactly.'

J. 'And, of course, your spirit guides have known you for donkey's years - even before you were conceived - and it was all agreed how they would come in, how they would present themselves, how they would get to know you. The first signs you have; what is this, why am I feeling this, why is this happening? It's never frightening and also remember, *"No-one is ever given anything that is too much for them."*

So if something happens, it's because you are ready for the experience and spirit know this and are privy to the information. Well, this lady or this man is ready for this, they said they wanted it. They agreed how we would get to know and work together or they agreed, for example, what would be one of their early experiences, yes?'

B. 'Yes.'

J. 'So it's necessary for people to know that spirit don't 'dump you in it'. If you work with spirit, you never get 'dumped' in it. I mean, remember what I said last time we met? That I knew I was going to do trance and for weeks on end I kept saying, 'No, no, no, no, no.' (Bobbie is laughing).

So my guides are thinking, OK, she doesn't want to do it yet, she doesn't want to do it, OK, we'll have to leave it till next time, etc.'

B. 'You've got to be ready really, haven't you?'

J. 'But your spirit guides *know* when you're ready, they *do* know and you have to trust them with this.'

B. 'Right, on the Thursday, I didn't get anything. On the Friday, I didn't get anything.'

J. 'So you're attuning virtually every day?'

B. 'No, I do it four times a week. Three on the same days but the extra one can be on any day I choose. Anyway, on Saturday, I actually did my attunement in the bath!'

J. 'Wow!'

B. 'I was sat at the edge of a forest. Gandalf came along a path followed by White Eagle. He said that animals have a special meaning for me and that I can learn a lot from the animals. Then a fawn came running out of the forest and lay by my left side. Then a lion came and lay at my feet. A big, brown bear came out of the forest and lay behind me. Then a young elephant came and lay on my right side. Then suddenly a rabbit came bounding up and jumped on my lap.

Gandalf and White Eagle turned to walk back the way they came so I got up to follow. The animals got up but stayed in their positions with me carrying the rabbit. White Eagle stopped and came to me and said, 'Learn what these animals have to teach you. Nothing happens without a reason; they have something to tell you.' Then it was all gone and I was sat in my bath. And I will look these animals up in my medicine cards.'

J. 'Good! You can also borrow my Animal Speak book again and I actually think that we should try and get you a copy.'

B. 'Yes, I'll have a look on Amazon.'

J. 'Yes because you've been told about your connection with animals which doesn't surprise either you or me.'

B. 'No.' (Bobbie is chuckling).

J. 'But it will help you so much with pieces of information and it's as though when you're not quite there and then you look something up and you find the one piece of information you're missing to fully understand what things mean.

And I would also, I'm being brave now, I'm wondering actually whether you're going to help people via the animals.'

B. 'Yes?'

J. 'Meaning that the law of the animals is one of the ways in which you, Bobbie, garner information. Maybe in future, when you speak to people, when you're trying to help them, you may get an animal message and that animal may represent something meaningful about that person. Do you understand?'

B. 'Ah, I see, yes.'

J. 'I'm now looking at, *"Nothing is ever for nothing."* Your guides are explaining about the animals so you need to take heed about animals. They are saying this in no uncertain terms and therefore, I'm going one step further and thinking, I wonder whether they're actually saying that this is about the communication, intelligence and the readings that you're going to be given when helping people? I'm not saying that you're going to give readings.'

B. 'No, no.'

J. 'I'm just saying that when we help somebody, where does the help come from? Now, if you work with spirit, this is going to be via clairaudience, clairvoyance - in symbols. Like just now, spirit have just put that meaning, that interpretation in my head, yes?'

B. 'Yes.'

J. 'I'm not going to say it was my thought, I'm going to say I was helped, I was impressed upon, yes? Now, I'm saying that where some people work with tarot, if you get your animal cards, there is a possibility that you will start learning about animals in more depth and it will become almost, excuse the pun, like a second skin!

The spiritual communication, the language, the way you understand what is being shown or given, the way you help people, the way you interpret things, just like a star gazer will read the stars, it will be through....'

B. 'Animals.'

J. 'Yes. Like humans, animals have their personalities, traits, idiosyncrasies. They have strengths, they have weaknesses, do you understand what I'm saying?'

B. 'Yes.'

J. 'It's a totalitarian ideology. It's like each species of animal represents something and I think you may find this very easy. I think you may find this way of working very natural to you. So I'm going to suggest that you don't forget this.'

B. 'No, I won't.'

J. 'Have a think about it and maybe you know, purchase this Animal Speak book or anything that is similar but I wouldn't be surprised - I'll put a fiver on it!'

B. (Bobbie laughs). 'I'm not going to take that bet because I think you're right actually because I've thought of it myself.'

J. 'You have?'

B. 'Yes.'

J. 'So this is like a confirmation?'

B. 'Yes.'

J. 'Well, that is *very* interesting because spirit definitely work that way because it's hanging around, the thought, the idea, it's not going anywhere and then someone pushes it back into the foreground again and you say, 'It's this again!'

Now that is an experience I've had loads of times. I had that, for example, about the workshops when I needed to start doing my spiritual teaching via workshops. I had the thought, the idea, the message but I didn't do anything about it.

Then I met a neighbour in my road and she stopped, got off her bike, and started talking and she was going on about workshops and I thought, Oh, my God, not workshops again! After that, I had a friend for lunch and what does she start talking about?'

B. 'Workshops!'

J. 'Workshops, so I'm now thinking, I've *definitely* got to do something about this now! Do you understand what I'm saying because spirit *do* reiterate things until you say, well, come on then and your spirit guides are saying, 'Well, how many times do we have to bring it up? You *know* it but you're not doing anything about it!'

B. 'And then you suddenly go, Eureka!'

J. 'And your thoughts are, I think I'd better listen to this!'

B. 'Because I always get animals and this has been going on for a long time.'

J. ' Yes, well, I think it's starting to evolve into something that makes sense, something that is very relevant to you but it's becoming more and more obvious what this all actually means because we are all the same - as humans we're no different to animals.

We're also no different to plants, to the river or the wind and everything that is on the earth has a use, it's the law, yes? So why not work with the animals when you help people? I mean they love you so.'

B. 'Yes, it makes sense.'

J. 'And I'm now getting quite excited about this and if I was in your shoes I'd be saying, right, I'm going to start researching and I'm going to start learning and teaching myself. What does a bear mean, what does a lion mean, what does a rabbit mean, yes?'

B. 'I did write it down actually and the only one they didn't have in my cards was the elephant and my own interpretation of the elephant is 'strength and gentleness and determination.''

J. 'And the other thing with elephants is, they never stop moving, they're always on the go and do you know when I learnt that? I learnt that last night!'

B. 'Oh, did you!'

J. 'I learnt that last night watching the TV - that is just uncanny! You're talking about elephants and I learnt something about elephants last night! And what do spirit also say, *"There is no such thing as co-incidence."*

B. 'I love elephants actually, I absolutely adore elephants. I would love to work with them as well.'

J. 'And the other thing as well Bobbie, you could get animals programmes from the library.'

B. 'Yes, I watch all the animal programmes.'

J. 'So you must have learnt something along the way?'

B. 'And elephants are very family orientated.'

J. 'There you go....you're off, we have lift off! No, I think it makes a lot of sense and you know, next year I would probably ask you, are you starting to get these animals as a way of communication? Yes, I think it makes a lot of sense indeed, don't you?'

B. 'Yes, I do, I really do.'

J. 'And it's something that you enjoy.'

B. 'I have a great love for animals and for nature.'

J. 'And also, if you look back at some of your attunements, often animals come into your attunements so this is just growing, isn't it?' And again, it started off quite gently and now you're not just getting the odd bear, you're now surrounded by animals! You're almost like Snow White - she had all the animals come to her.

That reminds me, years ago, I had a neighbour who was animal rescue but her main love was rabbits. One afternoon I gave her some healing and in that healing session, I saw her as Snow White and when she goes 'home' all the animals visit her. I'll never forget that. OK, carry on.'

B. 'That was all my attunements.'

J. 'So, maybe, you haven't had very much but it's a paradox because, in fact, you've had a massive directional message come out of the last one. What may be happening is that you've had the quietness because spirit have been busy working with you; I would say that they're now preparing you for something else.

I am 100% certain the fact that you were getting nothing meant that your spirit guides are preparing you so I don't want you to be disheartened.'

B. 'No I'm not. I just feel that they've got their reasons.'

J. 'Yes and they're saying; Look, we're busy, you just enjoy the silence!'

B. 'And I do actually!'

J. 'I do feel that you're being prepared for something Bobbie but I also feel that this 'animal' attunement that you finally got after all the silences was wonderful and very exciting. I can see by your face that you're happy and it's almost as though you're starting to feel that you've got a purpose.

When you're developing, it's like you're walking and the road is straight and there's not very much to look at. Yes, you can see this and you can see that but what does it mean? You haven't reached anywhere, you haven't reached any junctions, you just keep walking and walking and so I feel that now you've been given something to hook onto and therefore, your road has become more purposeful which also motivates you; you've got a project now.'

B. 'Yes and it's starting to deliver.'

J. 'And the other thing is, we're all here to learn and that's exactly what you're going to be doing over the next few months, you're going to be doing a lot of learning - going back to school - but in a different way because you're also going to be the teacher as well as the pupil!' (Bobbie is laughing). You can ring the bell whenever you want a tea break or school's finished! Alright, so what was your homework?'

B. 'Understanding of love. I found it quite difficult putting it into words.'

J. 'You knew what you wanted to say but you had to work out how to express it?'

B. 'Yes. There are many forms of love but all forms of love, should be, without asking for anything in return. It should be given as Our Father, the Great Spirit gives it to us; unconditionally.

I think the word love is used far too much without any real meaning which is so sad for love is a beautiful thing whether it is for the beauty of nature or family, animals, birds, friends or pets. We can learn a lot from pets, they love us unconditionally and even if they are ill treated, they can still love.

The Power of Love is so strong it can move mountains. To feel the love that spirit gives to us is such a beautiful, moving, all-embracing feeling, there is nothing to compare to it. If only everyone in the world could feel that kind of love and give it freely back, what a wonderful world we would be part of.'

J. 'Well, you said you had a difficulty but I think that is superb, that is gorgeous! That rung a lot of bells for me and all I can say is that knowing you, I'm not surprised you wrote that because I think you've had that very genuine understanding of love for a long time and maybe you didn't even know it?'

B. 'No!'

J. 'But maybe that's why you found it difficult to write it down because it's all around you anyway but no-one has ever asked you to put it into words, yes, so well done, it was really lovely.

OK. There's one thing I want to ask you at this stage of the course because I do ask everybody, can you tell the difference between your voice and that of your guides?'

B. 'Yes.'

J. 'Can you try - I know it's difficult - I don't know whether you're going to be able to do this but I'm going to ask you anyway, what is the difference? We all talk to ourselves a lot as human beings but then, when you work with spirit, you hear them too so are you able to tell me what the difference is?'

B. 'The words are different, the terminology is different. They very often use words that I really couldn't say. They're more.... they're not the kind of everyday language that I would use. With White Eagle, it's a masculine voice, a soft voice, it's not abrasive in any way. It's almost 'sing-songy'.'

J. 'It's almost musical?'

B. 'Yes, yes. I think my voice is quite abrasive sometimes without meaning to be abrasive. His, it's just like a gentleness.'

J. 'That's fine and when things pop into your head, you know when it's them and when it's yourself?'

B. 'Sometimes, not always.'

J. 'That's a very true answer.'

B. 'You know, sometimes I'll have a thought and I'll think, umm, was that me? And then I'll try and work on it and I'll say, no, I don't think that was me.'

J. 'Yes. In your attunements, you've been very lucky to hear what the people who are walking with you are saying to you and sometimes they're telling you quite a lot, so you must have already deciphered.

If we take Gandalf and White Eagle again. You say that you know the difference between their energies and when you feel their energies, the words which come to you, you know are theirs or do you actually feel a different energy when they're talking?

Today you've described White Eagle's speaking voice, does Gandalf have a speaking voice or is it just felt through his energy?'

B. 'I would say it was through his energy, actually.'

J. 'Well that again is interesting. Their energies are different. White Eagle has a sense but you 'hear' his soft voice - whereas you sense Gandalf's voice; firm and strong - very interesting. Thank you very much for helping me by answering that. I know it isn't easy. I know you have to really split the atom and think very hard about it. However, once we have a relationship, we can take it very much for granted, can't we?'

B. 'Yes.'

J. 'Communication just happens. We just see, we just sense, we just hear, we know who it is, blah,

blah, blah but when you're actually asked; OK, explain, it *is* hard, isn't it?'

B. 'Exactly, yes.'

J. 'Now, there is an important issue I would like to mention with regards to our relationship with our spirit guides. To me, part of this relationship is listening and knowing when to say something, what to say and what *not* to say when people are in front of you. Part of the disciplines of working for spirit is being able to help people or, in a lot of cases, knowing when to keep your mouth shut!'

B. 'Yes.' (Bobbie chuckles).

J. 'And I feel we *are* tested on this issue. Some people when they have a 'gift', they tell everybody all and sundry. They also butt into people's lives when no-one has asked them to. Being a sensitive is all about working with your guides, knowing, listening and always heeding their advice. 'No, *don't* say anything, I know what you're thinking but just keep quiet.' So that is also part of development, knowing what to say, what not to say and when to just keep your mouth shut!

The other point is that because our guides know what we're thinking - remember I said that when we go home we communicate via thought - we don't need to talk, we just *know!*'

B. 'Yes.'

J. 'You already do it at the moment anyway Bobbie but when you think of things and when you reflect upon things that have happened, remember that often you're also giving your spirit guides an opportunity to have their penny-worth of say - to respond to your thoughts, yes?'

B. 'Right!' (Bobbie chuckles).

J. 'Spirit hear what you're thinking and they may have something to say about it. So when you need help with something, if you're thinking about a problem, you may get the help you need because you're thinking, what shall I do about this? I need to make a decision, shall I do this or shall I do that and although spirit are not allowed to interfere or make decisions for you, I want you to understand that they *do* help you in their own way without going over the boundary line of making that decision for you.

Often when thinking, you give your guides an opportunity to answer a query so I just wanted to extol the virtues of thought - expect the unexpected!'

B. 'Right.'

J. 'So if you're thinking about something, don't think no-one's listening or no-one can help, that's all. OK, so now we're going to move on to our new material for this month which is about circles. Have you ever been in a circle?'

B. 'Yes.'

J. 'OK. I also want to give you your homework which is quite a big piece this time and it's something you'll have to prepare. I want you to write down what you have learnt and what you have achieved whilst working with me on this course.

So what I advise you to do is to keep a pad open somewhere and when things pop into your mind, just add them on because this is something you're not going to be able to do in one hit, it's something that's going to come to you in dribs and drabs. So, you'll be thinking, Oh, yes, I've learnt that or oh, yes, I've achieved this.

This is very important as it's going to tell not only me but it will also tell you a lot as well.

Also, there's going to be an opportunity for you to ask some questions at the end of the course. The questions can be about something that you've either always wanted to know or things that you suddenly realise you don't know the answer to. I've told Grace to do the same but this isn't a competition! (Bobbie chuckles).

There may be things, that even though you've done this course, you still don't know the answer to, yes? Are you happy with this?'

B. 'Yes.'

Month 9

"Love has many dimensions and an infinite number of expressions - all from one source."

Jenny: 'We're coming towards the end of the course, Bobbie!'

Bobbie: 'I know!'

J. 'There's a lot to do today so we'll do as much as we can. We'll start off by getting ourselves into the right frame of mind and when you're ready, let's start off with what you've been doing since I last saw you.'

B. 'My attunements?'

J. 'Yes.'

B. 'That will be quite quick.'

J. 'It doesn't matter, I am all ears!'

B. 'Right, the first one Monday, 25 March. I did an attunement this morning but nothing happened so nothing to report.'

J. 'Right.'

B. 'Tuesday, ditto. Thursday, ditto.'

J. '*Really?*'

B. 'Saturday, ditto.'

J. 'Never!'

B. 'Tuesday, ditto. Thursday. This morning's attunement was uneventful although I did not see or hear anything, I kept getting the words, 'not yet' running through my mind.'

J. 'OK, I wondered if you have changed anything?'

B. 'I do have to sometimes. Mick gets up; I'm used to him being at work you see, so I did my attunements according to him being at work but now he's at home, I can't judge when he's getting up. So I'm trying to get up early so I can do it before he gets up but sometimes he gets up early and then......'

J. 'So maybe there's something that's at the back of your mind because you're not perfectly settled. You've got this one little door open, this imaginary door open - is he going to get up, is he going to disturb me? You're not completely and utterly settled, are you?'

B. 'No.'

J. 'And that, to me, is like trying to squeeze your attunement in between Coronation Street and East Enders. It's not ideal and you're not at peace. In essence, you're trying to fit a round peg into a square hole and with attunements, do you remember what I said, if it's not working, don't bother.

I think this is a good example of when you're not completely at ease, there's a percentage of you that's on edge and it's not conducive, it's not helping the link.'

B. 'Exactly!'

J. 'So maybe that's why you're getting 'not yet', yes? You must know that spirit *are* aware of your domestic situation?'

B. 'Yes.'

J. 'Your guides are also aware of your diligence, how you *do* want to carry on especially till the end of the course so that we have something to talk about, something to discuss. On the other hand, this course is all about teaching you anything and everything. We don't get straight forward journeys and we don't have straight forward lives. (Bobbie is chuckling).

Life is not like that so this is almost an example, or an opportunity because there's a saying, *"There's no such thing as problems, only opportunities."* This is like an opportunity for me to say it's not a wonder you're not getting anything because things are not right. You're like a cat, one eye's closed, the other one watching for the door.'

B. 'It's like half in, half out.'

J. 'Yes and that's going to prove difficult *but* it also teaches you something. It teaches us not to despair, the will is there.'

B. 'And where there's a will there's a way.'

J. 'There is, don't be disheartened because..... I'm now getting, I know this isn't a very good analogy but sometimes they say that each of us and our lives are like a speck of sand on a beach. Spirit are trying to relate who and where we are as individuals to the rest of the universe.

So this little bit of time that you've had where things are not working, is like a minute percentage of your infinite journey.'

B. 'It's just a grain of sand.'

J. 'It's just a grain of sand in a massive beach and, as you *know,* spirit aren't just with you when you attune?'

B. 'No.'

J. 'Spirit will always take the opportunities to be with you behind the curtains, so to speak, even when you attune and nothing happens, they will be with you, working with you.

Now let's say your husband had a doctor's appointment or something, you could probably safely attune when he was out but since he's at home, it's proving difficult but you're trying to make the best of it.'

B. 'Yes.'

J. 'And what I'm saying - and I'm sure your guides are too - is well done for trying.'

B. 'I am trying to manoeuvre it, so that I can get them in, then if he goes shopping, brilliant because I know he's going to be gone for a good hour and a half so that's brilliant.'

J. 'Yes. When you first started the course, I tried to get you to do things at regular times but with your current domestic situation, that would be stupid. Saying, Oh no, I *have* to sit at eight, I *have* to sit at eight!' (Bobbie laughs). So *now* you've got to grab the opportunities when they come. You're life is not in a normal scenario, so I sympathise but we've spoken about it and so all is not lost.'

B. 'No. OK, that was Thursday. Saturday, 6 April. I'm still getting the feeling of 'not yet' but nothing else and then Tuesday, 9 April. I began my attunement this morning but someone came to the door which utterly disturbed me.'

J. '*OH NO!*'

B. 'It was a parcel for next door! *But*, this morning I managed to do one. Wednesday, 10 April, did an attunement this morning owing to my disturbed one yesterday. I went into the quiet and got very hot almost immediately. Nothing seemed to be happening. I didn't see or hear anything then I began to feel strange.

I find it hard to explain how I felt but then my head felt drawn to the left side and down. I felt old and crippled. My hands were doubled up, like clenched. My back felt bent over with a hump on the left side. I felt it to be a woman, very old. I felt a lot of anger, pain and resentment. I asked, can I help you, what can I do for you? She didn't reply. I just felt this anger and self pity.

I felt sorry for her, she was in a lot of pain. I asked again, can I help you? Then this lovely light appeared and a young girl came forward. She smiled and said, 'Come, grandma, I've come for you. I love you *so* much.' (Bobbie is now struggling to talk, holding back the tears).

The light then seemed to surround them and they were gone and I became myself again. Then I was sat back in my chair. I found it difficult to visualise my waterfall so I just popped into a golden egg and closed down in there.

Thinking about it, what had occurred, I think it was a lesson because *I* am in a lot of pain. I think it was to warn me not to fall into the trap of self-pity and anger and all the negative feelings. I thank spirit for that as I can understand how easy it could be to go there.'

(Jenny now hands Bobbie a box of tissues as she is sobbing).

J. 'Oh Bobbie, I'm *so* sorry you're upset.'

B. 'That's OK.'

J. 'I can well understand why you thought that but I'm getting something *completely* different! I'm getting that you're being prepared for rescue work.'

B. 'Right.'

J. 'And the saying, 'It takes one to know one'. The lady was being drawn to *you* for help because she identified with you. You picked that up, didn't you?'

B. 'Yes.'

J. 'She thought, you're like *me!* But there was a really positive reason for it all, OK. Now, you know we're going to be doing some rescue training soon, don't you?'

B. 'Yes.'

J. 'And I'm so glad that you experienced what you did and I'm so proud of you; that you recognised that this person needed help. However, I cannot interfere with your own interpretation of it because that is exclusively for you.'

B. 'Right.'

J. 'But if it helps you in any way, that's a bonus. All I can say is thank goodness the warmer weather's coming to help you with your arthritis.'

B. 'Yes, definitely.'

J. 'And I think it made up for all the weeks of silence you've had!'

B. 'I do get a lot of silences and then I get something really big.'

J. 'Yes and once again, it was very timely and when you were describing what was happening, I was jumping up for joy that you were feeling *all* the things you were supposed to be feeling when a spirit energy overshadows you - you were becoming her?'

B. 'Yes.'

J. 'And when you do rescue work, that is *exactly* what happens, you become the person you want to help. They can draw *so* close, it's like their energy slips in, it's like an eclipse; it transposes over your aura. You're not only sensing but you're also feeling and that's what happened with this one, didn't it?'

B. 'Yes, I was feeling what she was feeling.'

J. 'Exactly but on top of that, you identified *so much* with her pain and it was almost as though it hit you where it hurt, didn't it?'

B. 'Yes.'

J. 'You were reading personal things into it whereas another person might have just said, I don't know why this happened or isn't it wonderful this happened, I'm so happy I was able to help this lady.

But your tears were like 'double-tears.' Yours were tears of joy that her grand-daughter had come to take her home but also tears of sadness for yourself and also, it was very much like a signpost.

A signpost with signs directing you; if you go that way, you'll go here, if you go that way, you'll go there. It's almost as if you're at a crossroads but it's not a crossroad where you have to make decisions - it's a crossroad in your life - like when you 'cross the Rubicon'.

When you cross the Rubicon, you can't go back, you promise yourself, in future, I'm now going to do this. It's like a personal message of intent. It's like your guides were saying, come on, we've both got work to do, try and put your own pain to one side, yes?'

B. 'Yes.'

J. 'And you *know,* that when you work for spirit, spirit will help you in return. It's like when you attune you are also given healing. If you can sit in that silence, if you can feel that love draw close which I know you've experienced, you come round afterwards and you feel better, don't you?'

B. 'Yes, definitely!'

J. 'Remember, when you give healing, a bit is always left for you but in attunement, so many different things happen in the one sitting. Because you're linking up with people that love you, it would stand to reason that they know what you're going through. You remember the saying I taught you, *"Love, give and give again and all will be added onto you."* So in the giving, you receive, yes?'

B. 'Yes.'

J. 'And that is what working for spirit entails, it's never a one way thing. You serve spirit and love unconditionally but what happens? You get back - without even asking - so I think there's a lot there in that attunement; I feel as though there's a massive bowl full of 'stuff' and I've been scooping out more and more out of it because I now know you.

I know you as a person, how your life has been, how it is at present, what your heart desires and it's as though I want to say, don't forget what this course is *really* all about? It has so much to offer because you don't only become enlightened but you blossom and you feel better, yes?'

B. 'Yes, you do. You *do* feel lighter.'

J. 'And living with the knowledge that spirit are there with you.'

B. 'Oh yes!'

J. 'Suffering is part of life and you wouldn't be human if you didn't say, oh for God's sake, I've had enough of this?'

B. 'Oh yes, I get that sometimes!'

J. 'And I think that is also what you were touching on in that attunement. It really hit home, didn't it?'

B. 'Yes.'

J. 'But, *"Nothing is ever for nothing"* and I *really* think it was supposed to. I think it told you how far you've come. How you're now able to do this type of work. Look how far you've come? *Well done!* And it also told you something about yourself. It was like holding a mirror up to you saying, you don't want to be like *her*?'

B. (Bobbie's laughing). 'No, exactly!'

J. 'And because it's always mind over matter, because *"Mind is king and body is servant"* - you have the wherewithal to rise above it. If you want to suffer, go ahead, if you want to feel sorry for yourself....'

B. 'Go ahead! Yes.'

J. 'But it doesn't have to be that way. Always look to the positive!'

B. 'Always look on the bright side of life. Every time I feel down, that's what comes into my head, that song!'

J. 'It is hard and also, haven't you been gardening?'

B. '*Yes!*'

J. 'And when I discovered that you've been gardening and it was a cold day, I thought, she must be mad!'

B. 'But it was dry! I wanted to get some things in.'

J. 'Yes I know, you were thinking more of that than your arthritis!'

B. (Bobbie's laughing). 'No! I was thinking Oh, gosh, we're all behind, the weather's been awful. I've got to get out there, I've got to get the potatoes in.'

J. 'I know and you were being quite selfless about that because you were suffering so that you could reap the rewards afterwards.' (We're both laughing now).

B. 'That was when my husband *did* help - first time *ever!*'

J. 'Well done, good! Well that was *also* a turning point, wasn't it?'

B. 'Yes! He said to me that was the *first* time I have *ever* done the garden!'

J. 'Well, better late than never!'

B. (Bobbie's laughing). 'Exactly! Well I did point out to him. He said, 'I don't like gardening.' And I said, 'But you like eating the produce that comes *out* of the garden so you can help get it ready by planting seeds in the garden.'

J. 'And I think when it's on his plate and you remind him, well you helped me to do this, I think he'll understand better.'

B. 'Exactly, I can say *we* grew this!'

J. 'And I think that's one of the best things as well because you know, it's all part of how life should be - sharing things.'

B. 'Definitely.'

J. 'It's not, come on woman, that's your job!'

B. 'Yes, and that's how I've been feeling.'

J. 'And that's no good, especially when you get older, you should start doing things together. When you're young and you have your own interests and you go one way and they go the other but then, when you get older, you should start coming together again so I think that was another wonderful thing that happened since I last saw you?'

B. 'Yes and there's another thing I wanted to discuss with you. It was one day last week and I looked out through the window and there's a tree just across and there was a buzzard sat in the tree and he was there *all* day.

He was just sitting there and I was carrying on and I would come back and he kept looking in the window so I couldn't take my eyes off him. So I looked up 'buzzard' and there wasn't 'buzzard' there and I didn't know what family it belonged to, whether it was eagle or hawk?'

J. 'Did you look it up on the internet?'

B. 'No, we haven't got a computer at the moment.'

J. 'Oh, I see, OK. Well when we've finished, I'll have a look and see if we can get a bit further forward on that because if you could find out what family it comes under that would be equally good. And it wasn't in my book that I lent you - Animal Speak?'

B. 'No.'

J. 'OK. Sometimes a guide will appear as an animal; they will show themselves as an animal. I had this when I first started my spiritual road; mine was a magpie!'

B. 'Oh right!'

J. 'Always there. Always, always and I knew that this was not just any old magpie. So I think the person who loves you came as a buzzard and they wanted you to know, in no uncertain terms, that they were there because they didn't leave?'

B. 'Oh, no!'

J. 'And as you say, it was uncanny as it looked as though they were looking right into the house and that doesn't happen every day of the week, does it?'

B. 'It's the first time since I've been there.'

J. 'Yes and *again*, this could denote a new chapter, change. New spiritual guides arrive at the onset of new chapters and when their work is done, new ones come in to see you through to the next chapter. So you see, this buzzard might have shown himself to let you know, '*I'm* with you now.'

They may already be with you in spirit as one person but when they show themselves to you, either physically on the earth plane or in your attunements, they show themselves as an animal or bird or, in your case, maybe a buzzard. So it will be interesting to see whether the visitor comes back again, yes?'

B. 'Yes.'

J. 'What about your sleep state?'

B. 'Nothing yet.'

J. 'OK, I'm sure you would mention this if you had any experiences in your sleep. Going back to your attunements, there is one point I would just like to make and that is maybe, just maybe, the succession of 'nothing' attunements which you have been getting were actually necessary as spirit was preparing you for the 'big attunement' which always follows!

Maybe, it was during those silent attunements, when you kept getting nothing, that the most was being done - just as I teach - *"When the least is happening, the most is happening."* And maybe, this was always the way you agreed you and your guides would work together? So please consider that as well?'

B. 'I will, that's a very good point!'

J. 'Anything else?'

B. 'No.'

J. 'Right, let's continue. Now what we have here are four extra pieces which, in essence, completes the main development course, something I call 'Four Extra Papers!' This is a mix of both old material which I feel is worth repeating together with new subjects as well. So the first paper I'm going to read is called 'General' so we'll start with this.'

Four Extra Papers: General

Jenny: 'The world in which we live today was caused by man's neglect of his own spirituality, of his spiritual being, of his spiritual destiny. It is only now that he is realising what he has done and thousands, if not millions of people are saying that there must be another way, must be something more than this, something more than the physical, something more than I am born, I live, I survive from day to day, I die?

I think we all think that at some point, don't we?'

Bobbie: 'Yes.'

J. 'The Great Spirit is the creative force behind all life whether registered in the plane of matter or the plane of spirit. Do not divide the life of matter from that of spirit. The body of matter is dependent on the body of spirit for its existence but the body of spirit is dependent on that of matter for presentation, *"The Power of the Spirit is the garment of the soul."*

As spirit, you have always existed because spirit is part of life and life is part of spirit. You have always existed because you are part of the Great Spirit which is the life force. You have never had a beginning but you, as an individual, as a separate conscious individual, must begin somewhere, even in the stream of life.

From the time the cells coalesced and formed their union, the tiny particle of spirit has naturally attached itself and begins its expression in our world of matter. Earth parents therefore provide a vehicle through which the life force can be expressed and manifested. If there is a miscarriage or abortion, you have not destroyed the life force, you have merely removed its expression from this world to spirit world.

So most of us are here, as the rich people say, to 'provide an heir'. So our job is to continually produce heirs; well, one of our jobs! (Bobbie is laughing).

We are born of the Great Spirit's Love and it is His spiritual force which dwells deep within us. Our reason is an expression of Him, even the church tells you that we are made in his image, *"I tell you, you are part of Him."*

The spiritual, believe it or not, is the true reality. The material is the elusory, the dream, the image. Do not mistake the dross, the fool's gold for the real treasures and the reality of your existence.

The natural environment of love is light therefore *our* natural environment is light. That is why the heart of man cries out because the darkness does not sit well with him.

It does not matter how much harm or hurt a person has caused, how depraved they are, how stupid, God's Love is unconditional. As our Father, His hand is always outstretched but *we* have to hold out *our* hand and walk back to Him. Even if the steps are faltering, even if we fall many times - it may take hundreds of thousands of years - but no-one is ever turned away.

The way back may be long, may be arduous, may be fraught with obstacles and suffering but there is *always* a way back. That is the beauty of the Law of Karma for it gives everyone an opportunity to put right the things they did wrong. To pay back the debts they owe and even though the debt may be great, it can be paid.

When someone 'dies' and goes home they are whole and they come into the fullness of their consciousness with spirit which is quite beyond what you see in the incarnate body.

When we work together with our spirit guides, we work in trust. When we work together fulfilling the Law and living in love, then the development that is our psychic side becomes the tool of the spiritual and it blossoms and grows beyond our comprehension into a thing of great beauty which can be used for all humanity. It is not our gift alone. It is a gift given to us in trust for all humanity.

Our rock, our foundation is our spirituality that is God. Our strength, our power is the spirituality that is God. Individually we are nothing. Together, bound by His love, we are a mighty force.

Did you understand that?'

B. 'Yes.'

J. 'OK, this second paper is re-enforcing what we learnt earlier in the year about trust and cause and effect.'

Trust + Cause & Effect

Trust

Jenny: 'Trust isn't given overnight. Trust isn't earnt overnight. It is a day by day journey of discovery.

But, if you put your hand out, it will be taken and you will be shown the way and you will prove the reality of spirit for yourself in your attunements. In your quiet moments, open your heart, reach out and you will touch spirit and your awareness, personal to you, will grow.

It does not matter if half of you doubts. In a way that is a good thing because when the reality is proved, it is so much more the stronger.

You see, we are not just thinking in terms of spiritual guides or helpers, we are thinking in terms of the Love of God and that is immeasurable and totally unconditional.

You will have many guides, some stay for longer than others, one or two are with you always. You need them. You are part of a soul group, people whose lives you will touch and who will touch yours. They will help and uplift.

The guides you have are shared between you. It is a family, a wonderful spiritual family. What you have to do is not just *believe* but turn your belief by a leap of faith into knowledge. *Know* they are there for you and in that knowledge, will come your strength.

Cause & Effect

You must not judge a life by just one lifetime. The spiritual is continual, never ending, the physical on earth is only one part.

If it seems that someone is born with a star over them or everything they touch 'turns to gold', the last time they were here, things may have been difficult for them or when things come easy for them, it could even be a test and they are being tested.

There is nothing wrong with an easy life. How one behaves or reacts to wealth, comfort and the ease which it provides is the important thing here. *"What you sow, you will reap."* Whatever you do, you will have to face the consequences; remember the boomerang effect.

Cause and Effect is not a frightening Law. It is not an unjust Law. Cause and Effect makes man his own judge, his own arbiter. At the end of the day, man can stand and look at his life and say, 'There I failed; because of that failure this occurred; because this occurred, I will return and help to put it right.'

From childhood we are brought up to believe that if we steal we are acting against the law. If we go through a red light we are breaking the law, if we maim anyone, etc, etc. *Think* how different the world would be if from childhood we were taught that whatever we did would have an effect, not just on others but on us as well; whatever we did would come back to us?

Cause and Effect runs not just through one life, it runs through eternity.

There are very few people on the earth plane who can look back over their lives with no regrets; regrets are worthless things but the acknowledgement of mistakes are *very* worthwhile and positive.

Therefore, think not how you hurt, think not of the wrong turning you made but how you may rectify the situation, how you may change your mode of being?

We have ecological problems caused by scientists and industrialists who are seeking material gain and proving it is science that is master of the spiritual; that science explains the spiritual. Through their arrogance and their greed they are creating problems which are going to be very difficult to overcome. They are creating an imbalance of nature and matter; it is already happening.

They think that if they make mistakes, it will not affect them during their lifetime and that they will not be here to see it - how wrong they are!

It has been said that, *"The sins of the fathers are visited on the children"* but what has not been understood is that the fathers *become* the children. *They* will be the children who inherit the world they now create - Cause and Effect - you cannot get away from that effect, for we are brought back and we live through that effect.

And here is the Law of Karma. *They* will be the ones who will have to redress the imbalance. It is not an unjust Law. It gives man the opportunity to make that redress. It also gives us the opportunity to grow spiritually through the understanding of making that redress for in serving another lifetime, we take our spiritual journey a few steps nearer to the centre of all things, a few steps nearer to our spiritual inheritance.

And it is not just a debt to someone we have hurt or debts of transgression, we can also inherit joys and gifts through the achievements of another lifetime. If we have given so much in one life then in another we will receive the joys that come from that service.

Karma and Cause and Effect go hand in hand. They are indivisible.

Good one, huh?'

Bobbie: 'Well yes'.

J. 'I really wish everyone knew about this sort of thing. The world would be a different place, wouldn't it?'

B. 'Definitely, yes!'

J. 'Right, this next one is about auras. This is quite heavy Bobbie but I'm going to be giving you this paper so you can go over it and digest it at your leisure.'

Auras

Jenny: 'The aura consists of the vibrations set up by the body.

There are many auras but the ones that are known to our world are the auras which surround the physical body and the spiritual body. All things have auras even things which do not have consciousness within them.

There are five separate bodies being present in the human aura each functioning on difference frequencies, vibrations or wavelengths. Therefore, scientifically, it can be reasonably assumed that these multiple 'bodies' act at varying electromagnetic ranges which exist within the auric field.

We speak of vibration in terms of energy. Everything that exists vibrates, radiates and is active. Everything here on earth, for example, vibrates as it has a component of the earth's energy within it. Matter only exists *because of* spirit and it is spirit that enlivens matter.

"All life is one life" but it has many graduations. Man is more than matter. Man is mind and spirit and there are vibrations which belong to the mental and spiritual life. In addition, there are vibrations which belong to the super-physical life; the life that is beyond the earthly world.

Man can register the vibrations of this life in which he lives *and* the vibrations of that larger life which one day will be his eternal habitat. There is the body of matter, the body of spirit and the vital cord or lifeline in between which I call the 'silver cord'.

I think I said to you in the workshop that when that cord is cut, no amazing doctor or surgeon can bring back a person's life. Also when we are conceived, there are two bodies that are growing, not just our physical body but there is another body that has the silver cord attached to it, but you knew that, didn't you?'

Bobbie: 'Yes.'

J. 'One can accept that spirit is intelligence functioning through electromagnetic energy and that vibrations within the aura are capable of storing and retrieving information as required, just like an audio or video tape.

Your character, your soul, depends on the level of vibration at which the various fields of the aura function. Levels of vibration are largely controlled by the thoughts generated within the mind of the individual through the five senses of the physical body. Frequencies or vibrations within the energy fields affect us both physically and mentally in interacting with each other.

Now Bobbie, do you know that game, the one which has a rod with five silver balls on it and if you pull the outer ball out, it hits all the other balls in the line? Do you know what I'm referring to?'

B. 'Yes.'

J. 'Now this is a good analogy to describe what is happening to each of these bodies. If each of those balls represent a different one of our outer bodies which are each registering at different frequencies and as we go through our daily lives and experience different things; everything that is emotional registers and goes to one body, everything that's mental goes to another body, are you with me?'

B. 'Yes.'

J. 'It's like God's filing system for us, these bodies.'

B. 'Ahh.'

J. 'They all exist outside of our physical body so that if you were very gifted you could look at someone and see all their other bodies emanating from their physical body and each one of those bodies is responsible for its own subject which means that when we die and our life is played back, we use these bodies to retrieve information.

So, just like we're recording this lesson and when I want to hear it, I rewind it and play it again, our lives are replayed to us when we die in order that we can judge ourselves and it uses *these* bodies which have been storing information about everything that has happened in our lives. Clever?'

B. 'Very, very clever!'

J. 'God thought that up! First filing system ever! The aura of the etheric or vital body is closely connected with the nervous system and collects most of what later manifests as ill-health of the physical body, holding fast to poisons put forth by the lower mind of man by wrong thinking, wrong eating and wrong living.

If energy fields within the aura continually react to each other, we can then perceive the manner in which our character, our soul, is developed.

So you take everything that's happened in your life and you get the final equation. The total sum of all these bodies equals our character - our soul - which is continuously developing. The more we experience, the more it's shaping us, like the recent experience you had with the old lady in your last attunement.

To me, that was very pivotal. It taught you something, it made you think, it also made you decide about how you felt about yourself. Now that, to me, is a 'biggie.' That is something that I believe one of your bodies is going to store.'

B. 'Right!'

J. 'Because that really was raw, wasn't it? It was an amazing experience for you and it made you think, it made you cry - and it was *very* personal so that was an important one for you.'

B. 'Yes.'

J. 'OK. Attached to the physical body is a certain form recognised as the body elemental. This is not an evil thing. It has its place in the evolution not only of man but also of the lower forms of life. When questioned how it is that when man is in a physical body, the pull to evil seems so much stronger than the attraction and aspiration to good, the answer is in this body or 'desire' elemental which is very strong in most men. I'll explain this in a minute.

Elemental energies are neither good nor bad but they *can* be used for ill. Man can use them for the benefit of self and the destruction of anything that stands in his way.

Man has to learn in the course of his evolution that the higher self, which is only partially in evidence in most of us, must gain complete domination over the body elemental *but* the body elemental is also assisting man in his evolution, acting as a kind of ballast which keeps him tied to earth and I quote, *"You all feel this pull but it is not to be regarded as evil for it forces growth of the spiritual of God-consciousness which we all come back on earth to unfold."*

Now I'm going to try and explain this to you.

We have an elemental body which is the next true body after our own. This has two properties, two uses. Number one, it helps keep our feet on the ground so we're not, for example, like people flying in space, so when I say it acts as a ballast, it holds us to earth.'

B. 'It grounds us.'

J. 'It grounds us, exactly! But it also acts as a test. It makes us decide whether we want to go towards the bad or towards the good but this is all part of evolution because we can't understand goodness until we understand bad.

Spirit gave me an example of this when I lived in High Wycombe. My son Sam was having his dinner in the kitchen and on the worktop was a knife. I actually experienced a pull to use that knife on Sam and I felt absolutely shocked. But then spirit told me *this* is what we're talking about; this is the 'elemental pull'.

Remember, I said earlier that this is more prevalent in men? So I think what God is trying to get us to do is to reject that pull - to negativity - and pass through it. So when I talk about, *"Out of the bad, comes the good"* - it's about rising up through the 'badness', rejecting it and saying, '*No!* I'm not going to do it.' And in doing this, you draw nearer to the higher planes. Do you understand?'

B. 'Yes.'

J. 'So in effect, we are all tested, 'Are you going to use that knife or are you going to stand firm and reject the opportunity to use it?' And that's also how we learn, we learn via contrast. It's as though our consciousness is also our own personal barometer which teaches us what is right and what is wrong.

So our elemental body is helping us to stand firm on the earth, on the other hand, it's testing us, are we going to follow the pull of that elemental energy because it's so easily done? It's like talking negatively, it's so easy to criticise someone and find fault with them. It takes a little bit more effort to praise them.

Also, if you're unhappy, it's easier to do nothing about it, to just wallow in self-pity. It's harder to do something positive, to push yourself and take that positive step out of your negative situation. It's that sort of negative, elemental pull you're up against. The negative comes free! You don't have to work at it.'

B. (Bobbie is laughing). 'Yes!'

J. 'It's much harder to reject something and say, No, I'm not going to give in, I'm going to make my way in another direction and reject all these easy things which have been thrown at me. So do you understand now what this elemental body is doing and what elemental energy is responsible for?'

B. 'Yes, I should imagine you need it.'

J. 'You *do* need it or you wouldn't have it otherwise. Yes, it has a *very* important function and, of course, you're rewarded if you manage to reject it and turn towards good, you are rewarded in return. It's like fighting your way through a thicket or fighting your way through depression. Resisting anything that is negative and coming out the other end; you are rewarded with a positive outcome. OK.

So we all feel this pull but it is not to be regarded as evil for it forces growth of the spiritual of God consciousness.

A *psychic* medium does not communicate with spirit, they draw from the earth's energies and from other people's energy. A *psychic* medium will read auras. They can get quite a lot of information from someone's aura because it is their spiritual fingerprint, their spiritual blueprint. Everything you are, everything you have been, everything you hope to be, is registered within your aura.

A psychic medium will often tell you the colour of your aura; you have a beautiful blue one or pink one, however, they are seeing the aura of the moment.

The aura is many colours but it is forever changing, it is never still. Your moods colour your aura. Progress, where you have come to in life, colours your aura but it is forever changing. If you look at the aura of a new born baby it is mostly blue. As the child grows so the aura changes in colour. An aura will often turn grey and disappear completely two or three days before a person dies because the soul, the spirit, is preparing to pass.

Psychic mediums tire very quickly because they are reading and drawing energy from *you*; there is no spiritual communication. A psychic medium will *decide* what to say - a spiritual medium will be told. When spirit 'see you', they only see your aura; they don't see you in fishnet stockings and suspenders!

(Bobbie is in fits of laughter).

An aura is like a sponge and absorbs so much from the earth's atmosphere and that which is around you but spirit vibrations can be as polluted as the earth's atmosphere. Don't think the spirit world is all clear and refined and beautiful? There are different dimensions, levels and clarity in spirit as well. If you are undisciplined and allow your aura to expand and your light to shine, you are likely to pick up unwanted lower level spirits.

This is why when closing down or after healing, I advocate pulling the gold through all your psychic centres, your chakras, as it cleanses and protects you. Cleanse your aura after communication as you can pick up people's depression and if you are a healer, their headaches, aches and pains, etc.

One day all the colours of our aura will blend into one and be totally translucent like white or mother of pearl.

As we work towards our spiritual attainment and spiritual progression, we imagine and work in gold because it is the colour which is protective of highly evolved spirit which we all hope to be one day.

So that was quite interesting?'

B. 'That was *very* interesting.'

J. 'I know there's a lot to digest but when you get your head round it, when you can see it simply...'

B. 'It makes sense, yes'.

J. 'And, I think it makes you see the genius of things? Everything that's happening to us is being recorded but it's all used to help us judge ourselves so everything we have, even though we don't know it and see it, is helping us - it's all positive - it's all good. Even a bad thing is a good experience. It's amazing isn't it?'

B. 'Yes.'

J. 'OK, this is the last paper. This is about higher consciousness and again, hopefully, I'll try and explain some things so you understand.'

Higher Consciousness

Jenny: 'What happens to our higher consciousness when we come back and incarnate onto the earth plane?

Many people have this idea that you leave your higher consciousness in spirit when you return to earth and it is left suspended in mid-air in the spirit realms until you go back and pick it up again! (Bobbie is laughing). The truth is, your higher consciousness it is always with you.

You see you have several bodies with you which, in turn, amount to a number of vibrations around your physical body. Your higher self or the higher consciousness is the outer and last layer and the furthest away from all of the bodies surrounding your physical body. It is the most difficult to reach because it is also the most refined of all your bodies - sometimes called the celestial body.

So that makes sense; the furthest to reach is the more rarified?'

Bobbie: 'Yes.'

J. 'So, in essence, the more pure you are, the more you will radiate towards your higher consciousness. You have a number of vibrations emanating from your physical body which are all part of you and you have your aura which also emanates from your physical body both of which we've discussed?

When our physical body is about to die, our aura gradually fades, which we've discussed, the etheric body is left which is sometimes called the vital body.

You have an astral body, sometimes called the emotional body. You have a mind body, sometimes called the mental body and so on until you reach the higher consciousness which is the most spiritual of all.

So to recap. You've got your physical body first, then you have the etheric, the vital body. Next you have the emotional body which is sometimes called the astral or elemental. Then you have your mental body and then last of all, your higher self so that's the order.

So this higher consciousness stays with you but it exists on another vibration which is why you cannot see it but it is part of you. You cannot divorce yourself from it but you have to *raise* your vibration to reach it - to access it - because it is the highest, the furthest one of all. When I speak about raising your vibration, it is intended to reach this higher consciousness.

Can I ask you Bobbie, what do you think I mean when I ask you to raise your vibration? What is it I'm saying, what is it I'm asking you to do?'

B. 'To go deep inside.'

J. 'No, I'm asking you to love more.'

B. '*Right!*'

J. 'The more you love, the more you raise your vibration because love is *everything*. The more you love, the more pure you are. Your spirit guides know *how* you love, the quality of your love, how pure your love is. If I say to you, 'I love your cardigan.' My guides will say, 'Jenny, you're lying, you know you don't like that cardigan!' (Bobbie is laughing).

Do you understand what I mean? You can't fool spirit. Your spirit guides know *everything* about you so you can't lie because they connect with you mentally. For instance, you can't say I love when you don't mean it, do you understand?'

B. 'Yes, I do.'

J. 'So when I ask you and teach you to raise your vibration, I am asking you to be a better person and to love more. To love without question, to love without any strings attached and the more you can do *that*, the quicker you can reach your higher consciousness.'

B. 'Right!'

J. 'To continue, so when I speak about raising your vibration, it's intended to reach this higher consciousness, this last refined body of yours.

It explains the manner in which communication works because you have to go through *all* of these 'bodies' to reach your higher consciousness. In the same way as you have to raise your vibration to reach the spiritual realms, it is the higher consciousness to which the higher realms of spirit communicate, remember *"Like attracts like."*

So the *more* you can love, truly, honestly, the more you will attract those who truly and honestly love, yes?'

B. 'Yes.'

J. 'If you are not willing to raise your vibration, you are then only communicating through the etheric body and through the astral body which are the spiritual 'bodies' closest to your physical body. Therefore, you are communicating with spirits who only vibrate on those lower levels. That is why you have some mediums who do not operate at a particularly high level of understanding. Their communication may be excellent but they are only communicating with spirit on those lower levels; they are not the guides which operate on a highly evolved vibration.

People get deluded. They think if a person has amazing psychic ability then that is the be all and end all. It just means they have a gift but how highly evolved are they? Who do they work with, who is giving them this information? The people who will be giving them the information will be on the same level as them, no higher, because *"Like attracts like"* is an immovable, imperishable Law - you cannot change it or destroy it. So if they have a big ego, if they are greedy - whatever negatives they possess - they will limit who they attract, won't they?'

B. 'Yes.'

J. 'But it doesn't mean it will disturb their psychic ability so, you know yourself, you can go into a church and oh, isn't he wonderful, isn't she incredible but you don't really know them do you? You don't know who they 'mix' with - in spirit?'

B. 'No. That's true, that's *very* true!'

J. 'So this puts things into perspective?'

B. 'Definitely and explains things as well.'

J. 'Which is what this course is all about. This course is done month by month because you can only digest a bit at a time but since we're nearing the end now, it's hopefully all coming together into a full circle. You're now looking at things more holistically because you're own understanding has grown over the past year, yes?'

B. 'Yes.'

J. 'And so this is why these four papers are reserved to the end. It's almost as though it's all being wrapped up in a bow and it's being presented back to you and you're now beginning to relate what you've learnt to the outside world and to your own experiences.'

B. 'Definitely.'

J. 'And, you're also starting to 'file' things better?'

B. 'Yes!' (Bobbie laughs).

J. 'When you understand it, you know what to do with it!'

B. 'Yes, exactly.'

J. 'Good! It is having the desired effect, so I'm pleased.

So, a medium's communication may be excellent but they are only communicating with the spirit guides who are very close to them, they are not necessarily spirit who operate on a highly evolved vibration.

You can have someone who is very gifted. Their psychic ability is amazing but their spiritual knowledge and understanding is not and your guides will only be attracted to your spiritual understanding. The more you love, the more you raise your vibration, the more you attract those higher spiritual beings.

The aura is the only one which fades and dies because it is no longer needed, no longer necessary. The etheric body can last for a while. Sometimes the ghosts which people see are the etheric bodies of people that are still intact - it's this 'double' or 'carbon copy' body but it doesn't have any life in it - it's a shell. We're often shown that ghosts move and live and...'

B. 'Walk through walls!'

J. 'Yes, whatever, but they are in effect, an 'empty' energy. So these etheric bodies are not spirits because the spirit, the spirit life, has left and withdrawn from that 'physical' body. It is spirit which enlivens so without this, there is no life.

When the spirit withdraws, it is that higher consciousness which stays. The etheric will stay for a while as an empty shell - the ghost - and then dissolve. Some people stay within their astral body; they do not move from the astral body through to the higher planes. They can dwell within the astral body but the etheric is just like a shell and is a complete 'carbon' copy of your physical body - a complete copy of you.

After you are conceived, you are not just growing as a physical body you are also growing this 'carbon' copy etheric body as well.

So once the physical body has died, the etheric becomes a shell which can stay for a while. The higher consciousness and the mind are enlivened by the spirit as is the astral. The astral body will stay so if you have someone who is stuck at that level of understanding, at that level of consciousness, they will remain and grow within the astral body upon the astral plane, they will not move on to the realms of spirit.

And this is what you're going to learn more about when we do our rescue training.'

B. 'Right.'

J. 'The astral body will exist upon the astral plane and this is where people dwell when they don't go 'home' so they stay within that 'body'. So they discard their physical body. They will discard their etheric body - their carbon copy - but if they don't go home to their loved ones when they die, they have to stay within their astral body. If they remain within their astral body, there's only one place they can dwell and that is on the astral plane, on that dimension which, as I've already mentioned, is very much like the earth plane. Once again, "Like attracts like".

This is about people who don't go home to spirit when they die. The astral plane is the next level after the earth plane and people who do not go home reside on that astral level, within that dimension and can grow in knowledge and understanding on that level until they are ready to move on.

Once they say, I don't want to be here anymore, I've had enough of this place, there must be more to life than this? Then spirit make arrangements, usually through a medium, and they are taken home to their designated spiritual home in spirit realms.

As you go through the realms of light, you no longer need all those bodies and eventually you will just have your higher consciousness.

I think I started explaining during the workshop how you do not need your physical organs in spirit - you do not even need a body - you exist as pure thought but it is very hard for us living in a finite world to understand infinite situations and processes but I can assure you everything is gradual. Remember, *"Like attracts like"*, *"As you think, so you are"* and you have all the time in the world.

So that's it; the main bulk of the course!'

B. 'That was *really*, really interesting.'

J. 'Good, I'm pleased!'

B. 'It really opened my eyes to things.'

J. 'This last lesson?'

B. 'Yes.'

J. 'That is *so* good to hear because it is the culmination; of everything making sense.'

B. 'Yes, it all comes together.'

J. 'I'm really pleased that it's done that for you because that's what I was hoping.'

B. 'I've really enjoyed this afternoon, it's been brilliant. You explain things so well in easily understood terms. None of this high-faluting language! Thank you!'

J. 'You're very welcome.'

Jenny: 'Grace, I was just thinking that normally I would come into a room and there would be a whole load of people going, chat, chat, chat and the first thing I would say would be, OK, let's stop now, let's stop the chat, let's settle down, let's calm down but I don't have that with you! (We both chuckle).

So let's take a deep breath and light our lamps, get ready for this session and hopefully our guides are already here to help us make these few hours a profitable, beneficial and achievable afternoon. So on this cold February afternoon, I hope you've got some things to tell me?'

Grace: 'I have.'

J. 'Good, so you take over the proceedings now.'

G. 'I have spent a few minutes looking at our last lesson which I found really interesting.'

J. 'Circles - you enjoyed it?'

G. 'Yes, very much so.'

J. 'This course is giving you a bit of everything. We don't go into great depth because that's a whole new type of learning but that's where the questions come in. Not everyone will join a circle because circumstances may change and they may not join a circle for quite a few years but I'm glad you found it interesting.'

G. 'Very much. I have questions later because I'm reading your first book for the third time and I started again with more knowledge and understanding which takes me deeper.'

J. 'Yes, it's like when you see a film for a second time you think oh, yes, I didn't realise that but now I do. You can't help it because every day you're older and wiser and more experienced. We learn things without even realising it.'

G. 'Yes and then it comes forward at the appropriate time.'

J. 'Spiritually, yes.'

G. 'I read the book you left me, The Boy Who Saw True, and there were lots of things but one thing took to my heart more than many things within the book was 'love thy neighbour as thyself.' We see it as I must love that person as much as I would love myself but if you realise that we're all connected, when I'm loving myself, I am loving them because we're all from the same, all interconnected.

So if you offer up a thought, that thought goes up to the universe, it's there, it's always going to be there. So if you love someone as you would love yourself, it's not seeing them as a separate entity, they are you and you are they.'

J. 'I think this comes back to when someone is giving you a problem. You remind yourself of that principle and it helps, which is why I always advocate feeling sorry for them. If you find yourself having negative thoughts towards a person for whatever reason, it's not going to help to feel negative so I find the solution is to feel sorry for them using the 'Father, they know not what they do' mental approach; it helps when dealing with this.'

G. 'Yes.'

J. 'I certainly don't go around loving everybody per se'. It just helps me when I have a problem to be reminded, like what you said, we're all from the same, we're all spiritual brothers and sisters, we're all part of the bigger picture; it helps us deal with some of life's obstacles.'

G. 'Because it was as much my fault, I had never thought it through until I read that, I had read it but I hadn't understood it and it was just like, Ahh, the light's come on! I now understand everything, that's what I strive for, is to start to *really* understand.'

J. 'But you can't rush knowledge and understanding, it comes into its own when you need it.'

G. 'Yes, but I *so* love it.'

J. 'I don't often recommend books but that book, to me, was very uplifting, enlightening, very informative and funny too. A true story written by a little Victorian boy. You couldn't help but love him, feeling all the things he went through and it was lovely to walk with him and experience all those things. It was like layer upon layer because then *you* experienced all the things he experienced and learnt all the spiritual knowledge that he garnered over his formative years.

Yes, it had some hidden gems that I thought were definitely worth putting forward now I know you better. I wouldn't have loaned it to you if I didn't think it would teach you at least one thing.'

G. 'It made me smile.'

J. 'Oh yes, it made me laugh actually, many times!'

G. 'And it was this overall feeling when he was a little boy having always seen 'lights' as he called it - it was so much a part of his life - he thought, well everyone sees what I see and then quickly realised that not everyone did and at a very young age began to choose who he spoke to. He didn't understand his sister and he didn't understand so many things but it was nothing to do with that, it was just this lovely feeling.'

J. 'It was so humane, we've all had it, we've all been there. It reminds me now of my very, very first school when I had to sing hymns. I was four and yet I knew I was Jewish and I had to sing about Jesus and I thought, what am I supposed to do? And my mind was going like the clappers thinking, what do I do, what do I do, what do I do?

And the solution was, well, just shut your mouth when you come to the Jesus word and I pleased everybody then! Even as a young child you have a conscience that you wrestle with, you can't sleep at night especially with a mother like *he* had! (Grace is laughing). OK, so that's that, so are we going to hear some of your attunements?'

G. 'Yes and the rest I will speak to you about later; it's odds and sods, I have more than usual. I haven't as many attunements but I feel that they're special.'

J. 'Quality rather than quantity.'

G. 'Absolutely. I did ask spirit would you please not give me so many so that it would give me more time to discuss what is here. I just didn't always feel that I needed to sit. It wasn't that I didn't, there were times when I just sat very quietly and I just felt the energy.'

J. 'I think this might be mainly because this course teaches you a lot via attunements and I also need you to do these in order to be able to help and teach you.'

G. 'Yes, I understand. First attunement of the New Year, this was on the 10th January. My angel and all of my guides plus Sister Sunshine - I felt each of their energies enter my body.'

J. 'Who is Sister Sunshine, we haven't heard of her before?'

G. 'Have we not? I'm sorry. She suddenly arrived. She takes care of my osteoporosis - my bones. She enters through my back because they all enter from a different way, from a different angle and feel different and she's a nun. She wears a long robe and she wears a headdress.'

J. 'A wimple?'

G. 'No, it's long. It's very gracefully folded but it comes over the face, a little way and then it hangs down on each side.'

J. 'And how long have you had her, how long have you known about her?'

G. 'Well, she's new, she's arrived whilst I've been doing the course.'

J. 'Oh, excellent! Sorry Grace, who named her?'

G. 'It was a joint decision. I looked at her and I knew and it was also this feeling of warmth as if the sun was warming my back.'

J. 'OK. So you named her by what you saw and felt?'

G. 'Yes, I did and she smiled so I felt that it was the right way forward. I felt each of their energies enter my body. They told me that they were re-enforcing Jenny's words to me and that I must start to use the power of my mind - that was the key - then I would start to move forward.

I asked was the mind stronger than the body or the other way around? Their reply was, 'Mind and body, body and mind - they were both equal, each to the other.' My angel and guide said that was enough for today and then I asked Innka to step back but he would not go nor would any of the others. Aerial told me to close down. They were going to stay to support me with my new venture. Aerial was protection, Sonja, communication and heart, Sister Sunshine, strength and healing, Salaman, writing and imagination, Innka, fun and activity.'

J. 'So do you know what this new venture is?'

G. 'No.'

J. 'Right, so what you're saying is, when you heard what they said - you obviously heard it clairaudiently - I presume you weren't surprised because you had a feeling that you were going to have another chapter. I feel you already knew it when they said it so, yes, a new chapter!'

G. 'It wasn't a surprise; it was unexpected but not a surprise.'

J. 'What I would say is that I disagree with mind and body being equal. Mind is always king and body is servant so I wonder whether....'

G. 'I did take note. One had to be there for the other, that's how I saw it, how I felt it.'

J. Yes, I am thinking spiritually here. I think both of you were thinking literally, maybe, in a well-being situation; what is more important in well-being? What should you look after or what should you protect, etc, etc. In that case, they are equal because you have them both and you need both whilst you are on the physical plane.'

G. 'Yes, if you took away equal, I mean because I put it down as I hear it but sometimes you do get the odd grey area if they give you a lot and I'm trying to write it down. If you took away equal and put support; each supports the other as one cannot manage without the other. In this world, you have to have your instrument in order for the mind to go whatever.'

J. 'And the mind will tell the body what to do. I think we'll just accept that there is a case for equality in mind and body, or supporting definitely, but as far as the normal spiritual reference to mind and body, your mind is your spirit and it is that which enlivens your body and will live on even when your body no longer exists.'

G. 'My feeling was that I never saw it as one better than the other or a gentle battle, I saw it as one has to have the other in order for you to do the things you need to do.'

J. 'Especially on the earth plane. OK, so that was a gentle but good introduction really to the year, wasn't it?'

G. 'Yes, It was. I didn't have another - I'm not making excuses - it has been quite a difficult month to find a quiet time so I tried to make use of it when I could and if I knew I had a period of time that would not be interrupted. So this is the 24 January and it has a heading which is 'Truth.'

For the first time I did not call my angel, there is no need, for he is with me always, I will never have to call him ever again. I can feel his wing covering and protecting my back. My screen has begun to look more stage-like. It has red velvet curtains each side and a matching pelmet across the top, all are trimmed in deep yellow cord.

Sonja walks forward coming from the centre back. She moves in a gliding motion. She is wearing a long white robe. On her head is a long veil held in place by a golden band. She stands bathed in light at the very edge of the stage. She steps off moving to my left side. I feel her energy touch my heart then the warmth moves up to my throat. Her energy always enters from the front.

Salaman and Innka are together moving as from a great distance, becoming larger as they draw closer. They reach the edge of the stage, stepping off and moving towards me. Salaman stands just off centre on my right. Innka sits cross-legged on my left. Sonja speaks saying we are to discuss choice and Innka and Salaman have arrived together to show me they are equal as guides.

I ask where is Sister Sunshine? Then I see her walking from the back of the stage as if from a great distance. She reaches the front of the stage taking up position at the very edge. She does not step off but sits on a chair on the left hand side. I ask her why she is not coming to stand by me and she replies that it is not necessary at this time.

She also tells me that I am well but should relax, drop my shoulders and stretch my neck and not to forget.

Sonja now continues telling me that my choices are mine alone, no-one else's. That everyone should make their choice or choices independently, that I should remember all were equal and very much connected, each to the other. We must remain true to ourselves.'

J. 'OK, so was that an experience where you didn't prompt your guides yet they still came?'

G. 'Yes.'

J. 'It was a different scenario with the stage and that was good that you actually did the exercise that I asked you to do?'

G. 'But you hadn't asked me then - I had the date of your email - which made me smile when the email came and I questioned it.'

J. 'Cool! So your guides, me and you were all thinking in tandem?'

G. 'We must have been!'

J. 'No we were! We were, because they knew what I wanted to ask you because as I said to you, I had forgotten to ask you and it had niggled me to such an extent that I thought I've got to send Grace an email about it! So I ended up emailing you maybe two weeks after I initially thought to ask you to attune without promting your guides.'

G. 'Which made me smile when I realised that this attunement was something different.'

J. 'Well, so far we have a new chapter and choices which go hand in hand, don't they? Have you got anything else to say about that attunement?'

G. 'They are mentioning the quality again of being equal. They're also mentioning the connection each to the other. They're kind of reiterating what I know but possibly could have forgotten. I feel I'm sort of being prompted to just look at what I already know and remember what I already know so that I can use it.'

J. 'And I'm also getting that when you're on a new chapter you have to feel confident about yourself. So, I think there is a justification in going over things again, just to remind you about this, just to remind you that. Just before you fly off, don't forget this, don't forget that. I think it's very natural so I'm getting a re-enforcement here.

You're going to have some changes, you're going to have to make some choices but always remember where you've come from and what you've learnt, etc. because, you may go off excited!'

G. 'It's very easy to do.'

J. 'Also, when you grow spiritually, it's always step by step, layer by layer and I mentioned when I first met you that you always have to build on solid foundations so you're hearing that again, OK.'

G. 'On the 31st January, it was a new way of attunement.'

J. 'And that was you not prompting or creating a scene? You were going into the blackness, the nothingness, looking at your empty screen, so to speak. How did you find this?'

G. 'I have tried once before and I had, I said, felt scared but I wasn't scared. I felt a little, I believe, quite controlling, which works against me sometimes and I actually didn't let myself go anywhere. I got up and made a cup of tea and went away. But I thought about it then for a day or two and then came back and felt perfectly at peace then to be able to do it.'

J. 'Can you remember how you did it or not?'

G. 'Yes, I did it by imagining a spot, focusing on the spot so that I still had to have something to just make sure my mind didn't wander away, just to sit in the quiet. It was just a spot almost like a shadow in front of my eyes and every time my mind would go, I would bring it back and then, after a while, you just don't need the spot.'

J. 'That's interesting because when people find it difficult to go 'blank', which a lot of people do, I have suggested that they just focus on one thing, maybe choosing their special place or something specific, focusing on that one thing until they drift off, without knowing it. So that's exactly what you did. You decided to focus on something and you *did* drift off, excellent!'

G. 'The only way I could do this in attunement is to imagine a spot in front of my eyes. This calmed my mind. Within a couple of minutes I found myself watching shadows of native hunters passing before me. They were dancing, bending forwards then drawing themselves upright only to bend forward once again.

It was as if they were dancing in front of a backdrop of flickering orange lights; sunset colours. I could see grasses and jungle-type bushes and trees, some of them in front and some behind the moving men but they were all in silhouette - it was black and so were the clouds.

Because I felt they were all male as I watched, it seemed to me that this scene passing before me was also all around me at a short distance away, about ten feet approximately. There was the sound of drum beats. I was aware that throughout the whole attuenement, I remained sitting in my chair.

As I watched the scene that was ever changing but still following the same pattern, I felt a pain at the back of my neck at the top of my spine then a clear blue white light, very focused, passed through me from the back of my neck and out through my throat and lighting up all before it. The beam of light cut through like a laser touching the moving dancers, it focused for a second or so and then continued to slice onwards cutting through to show a blue sky beyond - a portal.

My wish was to go there to escape and so I did still sitting in my chair! I felt feedom; I could go anywhere, do anything that I chose. I heard a man's voice say, 'Fly little bird, fly.'

J. 'So you've had proof of the power of the mind?'

G. 'Yes, it was so calm in that place.'

J. 'It seems synonymous with how you live in spirit. When you dwell in spirit everything is mental, *"As you think, so you are."* You can go somewhere in a flash, be with someone in a thought because thought is what connects you. So as you think, so it happens which is why you can create everything and communicate with everybody by that one power of thought which is why it is 'king'. So over to you now, what did you get from this?'

G. 'I felt I had a glimpse of heaven or whatever that place might be. I felt I went there and I didn't finish writing it down because it's so clear in my mind and I went through that portal and I was on a grassy bank and it was very soft and gentle and there were white clouds in the blue. The sun was shining from the back and I could hear the birds singing and I just looked across and there was perfect peace there.

I didn't feel alone, I didn't see anyone else but I knew there were other people - spirits - they were there but I hadn't gone far enough to see them, it was just a glimpse.'

J. 'So may I ask you what the difference was from that experience and other experiences you've had in past attunements where you've been in places, was it exactly the same?'

G. 'No, it was *very* clear, *very* brilliant, *very* focused and I had this feeling of calm, there's nothing to do, you are here, this is where you are meant to be.'

J. 'You actually gave me a clue when you said I haven't written it down as I remember it, it was *so* clear. When you have this type of experience, they are, without a shadow of a doubt, true spiritual experiences. With true spiritual experiences, you can recall them years and years afterwards and those experiences are in a league of their own.

If you think that we're energy and we all live in a certain dimension. There are many, many dimensions, some we may have been in, some we may have yet to be in and I think that particular attunement illustrates how you can be in a different dimension. You started off in one dimension and then you went into another dimension whether you passed through other dimensions to get from one to the other, possibly, yes, but the clarity of your destination was undoubtable, wasn't it?'

G. 'It was real.'

J. 'I was going to say real; I was waiting for *you* to say that word!'

G. 'Where we live - the earth plane - is not real.'

J. 'Exactly!'

G. 'When you've been there, this is just a shadow.'

J. 'Exactly and that is what I was next going to say that the earth is not the reality. We think it is but it isn't, so maybe this attunement was illustrating what 'reality' really is. 'Grace you think this is real, your garden is wonderful, the birds sound lovely, the colours are amazing - you have no idea! We're going to give you a window into reality' - which I think is what it's all about?'

G. 'Yes, I feel that is exactly right.'

J. 'Yes and I also think it's wonderful that you were able to see, feel and experience *how* they took you there - through that laser light - because often people don't have that. They have maybe first step, second step, they don't know how it's done but *you* were privy to almost scientific, spiritual information! 'This is how we do it Grace. We come through the back of your neck..... and we use this blue light, etc.' Do you know what I'm saying?'

G. 'I do.'

J. 'So you were *very*, very lucky to have that.'

G. 'I felt blessed, I felt honoured to go there.'

J. 'Exactly and I also feel that spirit *know* you won't take it for granted. There are so many people, for example, maybe on a psychic level, just spewing out 'stuff' having no idea how they get it. You know, I personally haven't had things like that, I haven't known how spirit have got me from my chair or bed to being a bird in the countryside, I don't know *how* they do that, I just went through the motions but you were actually *shown* - I think that's amazing, that's *really* amazing.'

G. 'It was so clear and then, after thinking about it, the light going through here and through here, that's really communication, this is the chakras of communication. But it was a real sharp pain enough to get my attention almost like a little electric shock, if you like but not uncomfortable.'

J. 'No, I think if you looked into this further and further, if you went into other forms of mediumship; materialisation, physical phenomena, etc. you would understand that it's the spiritual scientists and doctors, *they* are all making all this possible.

So yes, someone made up that recipe of the laser so you could have that experience and it may be an old recipe that they used or a special recipe just for you, I really don't know but you had the experience and you had it at the right time for *you*.'

G. 'I also knew that was as far as I could go.'

J. 'And again, I'm thinking that you accepted what you were being shown and it was obviously night time as the dancers were lit up by the sky and maybe you thought they were African natives?'

G. 'Yes, they didn't really have clothes - feathers - but it was all very much in silhouette; it was only their movement that let me see.'

J. 'And when you went into that new place, into 'reality', describe again what you saw, you said it was blue sky?'

G. 'The thing I could see before I started my journey and I went through with a whoosh, no noise, it was very smooth.'

J. 'It was almost like an astral travel of some sort, wasn't it?'

G. 'As the thought came into my mind, I would like to go there, I was there. I felt and saw clearly. I felt myself go through the darkness and then I was just looking at something else completely, I had gone somewhere else. The previous vision was still continuing but was not for me.

I found myself on this gentle bank looking down over other rows of banks with green grass so bright, *so* bright, the sky was *so* blue and the clouds were lovely, the clouds you look at sometimes, the magnificent ones. There was also the sun on my back, very gentle warmth not burning and I could feel a slight breeze, there was a breeze as well and I looked across this countryside and I felt the presence of - and it was almost the feeling of - look at this with us, let us *all* look at this.'

J. 'And as an artist, you naturally take in colours so am I right in saying the vibrancy and the colours were beyond normal earthly colours, they were different?'

G. 'Very clear, it was also a feeling of being just in the right place, where I was meant to be. I had no wish to do anything other than be there, I wasn't even wondering what might come next, I was just very happy and very calm, extremely calm. It was very lucid, it was very quick. I heard the voice say, fly little bird, fly and I was back and I didn't return in the same manner (with a whoosh) all that was gone, I was back here.

This one was on the 3rd February, also the new way of attuning. It has a heading which is 'We Make Our Own Peace.' I have a picture to show you later, I haven't turned my computer off because on there is a picture which I need to show you.

I took a photograph of a field of corn a few years ago and it is my screen saver of choice and it will stay with me for a little while until I feel drawn to change it. When looking at it, I am taken back to that day. The sky was blue, the sun shone, the birds were singing and the butterflies were everywhere. There was a slight breeze and because it was later in the day, the heat was much gentler.

So here I am, walking on my own through the corn letting my hands, one each side of me, trail lightly across the tops of the ears of grain. A voice in my head speaks. It is a man's voice and he says, 'We make our own peace, Grace.' Yes, this place has a peacefulness to it. Hard to find in the physical world. We get swept along and find very little rest for our minds and bodies becoming unwell as a result.

Then I see my friend Iris who is in spirit, walking directly towards me. Her hands are also brushing the tops of the golden corn. She was my daughter's mother-in-law and she and I were very good friends. We both had a common aim, looking after our grown up children and their daughter Poppy.

We draw closer looking into each other's smiling faces and greetings are exchanged. Then I see my mother approaching. She is wearing her red dressing gown. As mum draws closer, Iris begins to fade, still smiling, her expression saying, until next time.

I ask my mother, 'Do you know Iris, she was here, have you met?' My mother says, 'No, I never saw her.' She continues saying that if you're on a different level, the energies are not compatible so they cannot see each other.

She speaks to me telling me that it is time for me to find my perfect peace or as close as it can be. She also tells me that I need to change the wording of my sentences, not a lot, just tweak them a little bit and it will make a great difference to my life and it will also help me find my peace. Then I remember the man's words being very similar - Find my own peace - and my mother telling me to change the way I formed my words, just slightly.

I remember asking Iris - this was before mum came along - had she met anyone I knew and she said, 'Yes, Elsie!' and that Elsie had visited her in the spirit hospital during the early days of her life in spirit. But, of course, she would. Elsie was the one who took her to the Light, helping her to cross over.

Mum asked me to sit in my chair a little while longer, telling me she had to get back - busy, busy, busy - that's my mum. That was it.'

J. 'I am trying to figure out if you're doing an attunement in a new way where you just go blank and wait to see what happens because, when you closed your eyes, the field of corn, similar to the one on your computer screen, was there?'

G. 'Yes, I didn't focus on there, I was there instantly.'

J. 'That's fine, I just wanted to check.'

G. 'Sometimes because I think it, I don't always write it. I should but sometimes it's almost as if I had.'

J. 'I know what you're saying because we discussed this when you first started. That we must dot our 'i's' and cross our 't's' when we communicate which is why I do sometimes rewind a bit and re-ask you a question so I know exactly how it occurred because you started off saying, I'm doing my attunements differently now and, as far as I can see, I quite like what is happening with you doing your attunements differently, what do you think?'

G. 'Yes, new experiences.'

J. 'Yes and it also teaches you that you don't need to *do* anything because spirit are there, the most important thing being, to *follow* your guides, not the other way round. They know what's best for you, they always do things for your higher good and you've now also learnt that you don't have to see your guides to know they're there.

So coming back to this one, what did you gauge from this attunement, what do you think it was all about?'

G. 'My mother's much more at home in the spirit world and she's certainly more informed about things than she was.'

J. 'You mentioned her dressing gown?'

G. 'It seemed perfectly natural!'

J. 'Exactly, you said she was 'at home' and to me, wearing the dressing gown was a statement - I'm comfortably at home!'

G. 'She could also explain to me that they too had places they couldn't go to, that there were levels that it wasn't their time to move forwards to and it has left a question in my mind - which I will never know - as to which level are Iris and my mother in relation to one another?'

J. 'But does it matter?'

G. 'Not really.'

J. 'I think you were privy to another piece of information that they both have a different soul group and you will accept that, won't you?'

G. 'I will.'

J. 'So I think it was lovely that you got confirmation of that. That you actually had it verbatim, that you were told; No, I haven't seen her, we're not on the same level, so that's brilliant!'

G. 'So matter of fact, so natural as if I'm seeing the spirit world now as.....what it's telling me all the time is....Grace, it's real, don't ever doubt for a moment that this is an illusion, earth is over there.'

J. 'Earth is the illusion.'

G. 'Yes, it's a shadow of what can be and will be.'

J. 'But this earth is all we know when we're here and we think this is real and it's real enough for us and we love it all the same.'

G. 'Yes, we do.'

J. 'And we should do because it's spirit given, you know. It's a planet that's been given to us to learn and experience and we should never take it for granted either but.... there's much more where that came from!'

G. 'It's our school here, our university, our college - we have to come here to move forward.'

J. 'OK, so your mum felt at home arriving in her dressing gown and I'm saying, yes I agree with you, what else? You were told about the levels, what else did you get from that?'

G. 'I heard about the levels. You brought it forward yourself as in, you need to tweak your sentences, you need to speak slightly differently. I always say this thing about dotting 'i's' and crossing 't's' but I don't always remember to do it.'

J. 'Do you think Iris and your mum are saying the same thing but in different ways?'

G. 'They are.'

J. 'Do you understand *exactly* what they are referring to; is it to be taken literally?'

G. 'There's always another meaning.'

J. 'That's what I'm saying; I'm asking, do you understand what they mean because I'm sitting on the fence here, I'm not diving in and coming to any conclusion myself at the moment because I don't know your life.

This is something that your conscience has been prodding you about, what is it? You have to choose your words? Is it to do with somebody you're dealing with in particular, is it generalising, do you know what it is that they're referring to?'

G. 'Well it made me smile because the one thing that came to my mind, occasionally, I often feel that I need to speak to you in a slightly different way.'

J. 'ME?'

G. 'Yes.'

J. 'Oh, OK.'

G. 'So that you understand me.'

J. 'Is it my deafness? Why just me?'

G. 'That was one of the aspects that crossed my mind that it might be a part of it because you can cause a great deal of confusion to yourself and others if you don't think before you speak, if you become over excited. If you start to ramble and I have been thinking about that quite a lot over the past weeks that I am inclined to think rather than say. Think a bit, say a bit and then, of course, the thinking bit leaves a gap. I think that I have filled it but I haven't!'

J. 'No because you've gone through it all but you haven't actually said it and that is quite a common thing for people to do because we talk to ourselves, we talk a hell of a lot to ourselves! (Grace is chuckling).

And therefore when people don't understand what we're saying or take us the wrong way, we can't understand it! We think, but I've already said it! So you say it again and the person will say, 'Well, you didn't say that the first time.'

However, I'm thinking that spirit wouldn't actually say something unless there was something in particular that they were referring to. Grace, this is the point I'm getting at and it's normally your first thought - your first thought is usually the right one. So when they said this, did you know what they meant? Is it something ongoing, is it something personal, is it something to do with your dyslexia, what it is, what are they referring to?'

G. 'The only thing that came to mind at the very beginning was teaching.'

J. 'Teaching, right! So maybe this is to do with the new chapter? Maybe you are going to hopefully pass all this onto other people which is what *I've* always been all about - 'making more me's' - and they're saying, right, you need to watch this?

You need to practice, practice talking. Practice listening to your voice, not in your head but hear the words you say out loud. Are they what you want to convey or have you missed anything?'

G. 'I hadn't thought of that.'

J. 'Maybe, in future, spirit want you to practice hearing yourself talk to other people because if you are going to start teaching, and this can be done very naturally, you know, you don't have to buy a building and set up, pay rates or anything, it's not done like that.

It's initially done by you setting an example by just being yourself and then, believe me, spirit will send you the people you're supposed to help or supposed to teach, you won't have to go looking.

So, you may now have some information about your new chapter, about everything that you're now learning and about why you took this course in the first place? And the one thing that they want to draw attention to is the way you speak and your long term habit of talking to yourself but not conveying your exact thoughts to other people.

You missed a bit and you think, well *they* know because I've gone over it and over it, they know, but again, you're taking it for granted that they know. You always need to check whether the listener understands?'

G. 'Yes.'

J. 'So that could be something major! You know, from now on, listen to yourself talking when you talk to other people. Maybe, you say a couple of sentences, you listen to their response and you might say to yourself, No, I've got to verify this bit, I've got to justify this bit, yes? And knowing you, you are a very pedantic person anyway which is why, I'm convinced, they gave you that rescue with the two children still unaccounted for!'

G. 'Yes.'

J. 'I meant to say that to you. That was for *you* because only *you* would go back and check - have I missed anybody out? Most people would have thought they've all gone now. Oh no, Grace's not like that, she's very pedantic, she will go back and double check, so *do* that when you speak - double check.'

G. 'Of course! Of course.'

J. 'That's the way you are so it shouldn't be too difficult. What you should start doing is having that echo, you know, instead of just talking per se', when you talk, listen to your voice, listen to what you're saying.

The other thing is that when you teach, you must set your command of communication, your command of the English language at the same level as those who you have in front of you.

So in future, if you *do* teach anybody, you will need to quickly evaluate who you have got in front of you and direct your language to equate their level of intelligence so you know that you can be completely understood. Don't talk above their intelligence - otherwise they won't understand what you're saying and it will all be a complete waste of time.

OK. I have four more pieces of new material to give you today and these are no less important than everything else. They reiterate things but there is also some new material here too.'

After reading Grace the Four Extra Papers:-

G. 'Instead of 'General', I'd call your first paper, 'Food for Thought!''

J. 'Maybe I should change it!'

G. 'Also auras were something which fascinated me from the very beginning and which started me on this path. I loved that paper on auras.'

J. 'Did you? It *is* heavy in places but if you understand that we're all an energy and everything is feeding information and also, if you recall in your last attunement with your mother saying, I haven't met her because we're not on the same level, it is pure confirmation of what we're talking about!'

G. 'There is something I want to mention. I woke up in that 'in between' place between waking and sleeping. I heard it, I felt it and words were, 'Love cannot dwell where anger abides because anger burns like a fire' and I'm thinking that is *so* beautiful, the words are so beautiful it could bring a tear.'

J. 'Was that recently?'

G. 'Yes, it was last week or so.'

J. 'Again, that to me, demonstrates who is with you because, you wouldn't have had that from someone on the lower astral plane, now would you?' (Grace chuckles).

Month 10

Jenny: 'Well Grace, it's a special date today. It's the thirteenth of the third, thirteen and this looks like being our last lesson of the course. You've been battling away since last May and it has come round really quickly.'

Grace: 'It does seem a long time since we started and yet it's like we're starting off again!'

J. 'Yes, I know what you mean. It's like, *"When one door closes, another opens"* - it's that sort of feeling, isn't it?'

G. 'It's quite exciting, it's like a springboard.'

J. 'Yes, so now I'm going to remind you that we need to close our eyes, light our lamps, calm down, still the mind, breathe deeply and evenly and ask our guides to join us - not that they're not already here - and then we can begin. So how have you been?'

G. 'I've had a very busy time since I saw you last.'

J. 'That's good, keeps you out of mischief! 'Busy-ness' is good for the soul. Lazy person; no good. Being busy whether actively, mentally, physically or spiritually; to me, all those things are healthy considering we have so much to do whilst we're here. I always say, whatever comes into your mind, do it; it hasn't come in for nothing, yes?'

G. "Nothing is ever for nothing."

J. 'That's right! So let's start as we always do by hearing your attunements.'

G. 'They are in a different format. I've found that because I couldn't always remember the finer details and that means a lot to me sometimes because I think it's all in the detail so I have started to do it on the computer.'

J. 'OK. Do you write or type it up when you've finish your attunement? Do you write it down immediately or do you wait?'

G. 'If I can, I do it straight away but it's not always possible so then I'll write a few notes on a piece of paper just to remind me, that seems to work. It's a different way of doing it but yes, it's good.'

J. 'I've never asked what you do but with me, I think I'd probably worry that I'd forget so I'd probably want to write it all down when I came round from my attunement.'

G. 'I did that for a long time and I'd put it in my file which took me a long time but I find sometimes you can't help but be interrupted so you have to write a few notes but that's not always the case, it depends. If I feel that I'm not going to be interrupted then I'll carry straight on.'

J. 'OK, so let's start off with what you're attunements have been like since we last met?'

G. 'I find them different whether it's the method of doing them, they seem clearer and more pulled together.'

J. 'So what have you changed, have you changed anything because you say the method? Has the method changed now, have you changed something?'

G. 'I quite often sit and wait to see what will come but occasionally I feel that I have to go and sit with my guides because we haven't perhaps been together for a little while, I will gather them together; it's like seeing old friends, catching up.'

J. 'So what you're actually saying is, when I asked whether you would do a test and not ask them to draw close - just to look at your blank screen - you were doing that but sometimes you revert back to asking them to draw close; is that what you're now saying?'

G. 'I just feel it's polite to go and have a word.'

J. 'Oh, Grace you *are* funny! Your spirit guides are always there, they never leave you.'

G. 'I know.'

J. 'In this 'at-one-ment' there is no wrong way. It is just a simple blending of soul with soul, spirit with spirit, energy with energy. Also, *"Spirit are great opportunists"* they will *never* miss an opportunity to be with you. Sometimes you know it, sometimes you don't, either way, it's all good! There's no bad, there's no negative about anything, really.

In trying to understand everything you say, I will pick up on *everything* in order to justify what you actually mean because it helps me with my responses, yes?'

G. 'Sometimes *I* don't know what I mean until you stop me, then I take a step back and look at it. I understand it but there's a different way.'

J. 'Yes, there are! They're many ways to crack an egg and also spirit never do just one thing either so when we learn, it doesn't matter if we're learning Spanish or engineering, we have our own thoughts and then the teacher will give us others, so it's no different.'

G. 'No. When I sit and wait, I don't look for the screen, it's there. I have my headings and this one is, 'So, every day is a school day.' Today I sat and waited. Sonja, my guide started to come forward then I asked her to go back, explaining that I was attuning in a different way. She became transparent and I could no longer see her.

Then it came into my mind to scan my own body which I did. Starting from the feet, working all the way up feeling where there was any tension or pain, scanning each part in turn, remembering to really feel the inside and the outside of my instrument.

When I reached my head, I waited. I was sitting under a large tree. I felt my back resting against the trunk and looking down. I saw that my legs and feet were straight and also resting upon the ground. My hands were loose in my lap. It was autumn with red and golden leaves spread around me. Then the landscape changed, it was winter. The ground had a covering of snow, the sky was grey in colour promising more snow to come.

Quickly the seasons passed before my eyes; spring with sunshine, rain and new growth, summer with hot sun, blue skies and abundant bright flowers. The thought came into my mind that all things come and go, there is no need for reasoning, it is the order of things.'

J. 'And I get the cycle of life and that everything is cyclic - there is no beginning, no end.'

G. 'It has balance. It has its place. It is as it should be. And it gave me a great feeling of being in the right place at that moment.'

J. 'But I think, if I may say so, you're always in the right place.'

G. 'Yes but I had the trust to know because you have to trust it. No matter how clear cut it is in front of you, there can sometimes still be a question.'

J. 'So did you have a question, after that?'

G. 'No, I didn't. I didn't, I felt that everything was as it should be and I had the understanding that although all things pass, that was how it is. Spring and summer, winter and then we're back to spring, one follows the other in a circle. That it's continuous.'

J. 'But that's very much a spiritual analogy. To me, when you understand, when you *truly* understand who you are, what you are, why you're here; then you understand that you will have many springs and many summers and you understand that winter has a purpose.

It's as you said, one needs balance, one needs renewed energy, one needs to be 'born again' and in the winter of death, the spring of life which follows brings renewed optimism and confirms that you haven't actually died at all!'

G. 'I also wondered if I was being told that I was more rounded now?'

J. 'Yep, that's your interpretation - I can see that, definitely - but this isn't for me, Grace. I only put things to you but you know yourself. *You* have the best relationship with your guides and don't forget your first thoughts are normally the right ones. So that was a lovely attunement.'

G. 'The next one is Amy, my little granddaughter and these thoughts came to me this particular morning.'

J. 'Were you in your attunement or before?'

G. 'My attunement finished at approximately eight thirty a.m. but what I didn't realise when I finished at about eight-thirty that morning was that it was at eight-thirty when they were wheeling her down for her heart operation, I didn't know.'

J. 'So it was very timely?'

G. 'I have been sitting in attunement, my thoughts were with my granddaughter waiting for an operation to mend her small heart. There is always another child who needs help and Amy's has been cancelled a number of times during the past few days.

I asked and received help from my angel Ariel who placed his wings around my body taking the weight of my jumbled thoughts and prayers. Sonja came, placing her hands upon mine and I felt their warmth. Innka and Salaman stood a short distance away. I knew they were there to support me in my distress. Words were not needed just kindess and love, this I received.

I knew that the life contract Amy has chosen cannot be changed or it will interfere with her continued growth in the spirit world. However, my own heart aches when I see and feel the pain of my daughter and son-in-law. There is also Timothy, her brother to consider and even their dog, Searcher, who knows that something is different. Francis, my other daughter, is chief baby-sitter for both Timothy and Searcher and has her little girl Poppy plus her husband to attend to.

My own husband does not show his feeling easily but I know how concerned he is. We have no alternative but to wait and pray doing it all in love, Amen.'

J. 'It *was* an attunement?'

G. 'Yes and I could feel Sonja's hands on mine, I could feel them. I could feel my angel's wing that is usually half way across my back, completely wrapped around me this time and it gave me such comfort. I had tears on my face and I came round at just that moment so afterwards I thought that we were all there for her at just that moment.'

J. 'I'm now getting, 'All is known.'

G. 'They know?'

J. 'Yes but the fact that you wanted to draw close to spirit and the fact that they know what you and your family have been going through and all the things you think and say rises up to be the priority above all things.'

G. 'It's true. It's been a very muddled week and I didn't sleep properly, I don't think I have for eighteen months but as soon as it was over and she then came out of intensive care, I started to sleep and now I sleep much better.'

J. 'Yes, everyone holds their breath, don't they?'

G. 'With the best will in the world, knowing that everything is at it should be, you still hold your breath.'

J. 'Yes you don't take life for granted.'

G. 'No. The next one is called 'Inner Calm'. I sit at the top of a cliff overlooking a river. Opposite me is a much higher cliff with an arched entrance at its base into which the river, pale green in colour, flows. The water hits against the rock before flowing out of sight into the dark void. It is a lazy river just finding its way to the sea.

My eyes are drawn to the blue sky above. There are birds flying on the air currents drifting in circles. I watch a large bird and my gaze, magnified, is looking into the eyes of an eagle. We exchange looks, we are as one, no fear on either side.

I am back sitting on the ground watching the water. I can see a small yellow flower growing on a low ledge to the right of the tunnel into which the river flows. My gaze is once again magnified so that up close, I can see it has five petals, a brown centre and a fine red line at the base of each of its petals. The line makes a red circle around the brown centre. The petals start to multiply until there are twelve in total then, just as quickly, there are only five once again.

The sun is warm upon my back and I realise that I have been in this place all day listening to the sound of the water and the song of the birds. Time to go home but just a minute, I *am* home.'

J. 'So what was your interpretation of that?'

G. 'I felt that I was there because I required peace. I felt I was there to see the bigger picture. The river, lazy but still finding its way, getting to where it should be. The birds up in the sky and this gaze of mine that was taking me up so close although I was still sitting on the ground. I felt that I was drawing nearer to something. Making the journey, without fear, just drawing near to something that ordinarily I would not have wanted to have got close to; an eagle.

It was the eagle's eyes, we just looked at one another; we were the same. We were part of the same energy. It was all perfectly alright and quite safe. And the same for the eagle as well as myself, it wasn't just about me, we were both pure energy.'

J. 'Reciprocated?'

G. 'Yes, exchanged. We were there for one another, supporting. And then I was back on the ground and I was watching and suddenly, from something so magnificent, I was looking at a tiny, simple flower; a little yellow flower. And I remember thinking yellow is gold, gold is good, gold is protection, gold is cleansing - I didn't write it but I remember it. And then I was looking at the five petals and then it became twelve and I thought, the twelve disciples and then I looked at the red circle and I thought everything is held together by blood.

Blood within the body, the blood line, it is the very thing that gives us life just as water does but on a different level. Red is for courage, red is for drawing yourself up and going forward no matter how you might feel about it, taking that step and then another step and drawing closer each day to something and not being afraid.

And then I was back in the sun and I felt so protected and so loved and then I thought about going home but then I thought, no, I *am* home, this is home, I don't have to go back to where I live, I can come here whenever I want.'

J. 'I profess I don't get as much as you from that attunement apart from that we're all energy and we're all one, the bird and the flower and the water and the sky and it's all the energy that we have ourselves. So whereas some people will say, Oh, I've always wanted to live by the sea and they don't really understand why they say things like that. It's just the pull of energy that you get and the beauty of the sea and it all comes back down to love.

The love energy that you exchanged with the eagle; that he is the same as you and he knows it and the growth of the flower when you look at it, the love you give it enhances the flower and makes it grow. The fact that you were right to feel that it was so wonderful, you felt like you were 'in heaven' and that this is where you need to be but then you quickly realised that you can be in this place any time you want - because it is *within* you.'

G. 'Yes.'

J. 'And in a way, those of us who have spiritual knowledge and understanding are so blessed to be able to recognise and go 'home' whenever we want. To understand that we're here to surmount the challenges of our earthly path, that this is balanced out by the comfort and assurance and the knowledge and understanding that we are so blessed, because *we* are *all* things and always will be.

So I think it's come naturally after that last attunement as if to say you can come here whenever you want. Nothing will touch you but you also have to come to the point where you understand *why* everybody's here, which you do as well; you understand it.'

G. 'Yes.'

J. 'Yes, a lovely attunement and very poignant and a gift especially for you - for your appreciation and understanding.'

G. 'I don't have too many. The next one is 'Balance'. This morning, just sitting and waiting, almost straight away off to my right, I see a sun, very red in colour with the rays expanding out all around the central globe. A young child would see and interpret the image in this way when painting a picture.

The sun disappears and instead I am now looking at a plain wooden table. The table is small and in the centre is an orange. It has two green leaves at its top finished off with a small stem. Then the leaves and stem are gone and I am looking at just the orange. I find myself having an internal conversation with myself. What should I do with the orange, maybe eat it? I do not like the taste of oranges; that narrows it down a bit. A small shudder follows. I really do not like the smell or taste of oranges.

Perhaps the orange has some say in the matter, it might be happy to be eaten? That may be its role or it may wish to give pleasure by being admired. I hear a man's voice telling me to pick the fruit up using my right hand then let it roll back into my flattened palm. The voice continues, 'When it becomes motionless, it is balanced.'

I ask the man, 'Who are you?' He replies saying, 'I am source, I am balance, you have your answer.'

J. 'Well, that was *very* different wasn't it? So, explain to me what else you thought about this attunement?'

G. 'I thought the colour orange was quite important. I also realised that I was seeing a round sun and a round orange so there was this shape thing going on and it was a sun such as you would see as a cardboard cut-out and it was the way things disappeared and then were different.

It was an orange, the next thing the stem was gone and you'd have just the orange alone. In fact I was, as I say, having this internal conversation with myself; am I supposed to eat this orange, I don't like them?

So maybe it tells me that just because I don't like something or someone, it doesn't make them bad or difficult? If I don't like them, that's about me, it's not necessarily everyone else's opinion on things, or life or the way we are? An orange can be eaten, looked at, admired, rolled but the voice told me that when the fruit became motionless after rolling down my arm, it was where it was meant to be so a circle is a sort of balance, doesn't have a flat bottom but no matter which way it turns, it's still going to be the right way up.'

J. 'What about the fact that you take a dislike to something or someone, that it will teach you something?'

G. 'Yes, that's good.'

J. 'We're very much opinionated, aren't we? We're very much, 'Don't like that.' 'What's wrong with it?' 'Dunno, just don't like it.' We're very quick to judge, aren't we?'

G. 'We are.'

J. 'I'll never forget I used to be like that until I met this woman, and boy, was I wrong about her! I was *so* wrong and from then on I would never prejudge a person because it taught me that you can't tell a book by its cover. I was always quite sure of myself but this one person, when I got her totally wrong, I thought, that's it, I'm never going to do that again.

Even though you don't like it, it doesn't mean to say that it can't help you, can't teach you, can't give you something. So don't discard the things you don't like because sometimes the lessons in life, the important lessons in life, are the ones to do with what you don't like.'

G. 'You always remember them.'

J. 'They're there for a reason, again, *"Nothing is ever for nothing."* The roundness, again, I come back to the cycle of life again - the sun; the enormity of it and what it provides - and the orange is also providing something. I think that if you look even deeper, this earth provides simply *everything* we need but it is raped and used and abused for man's gain.

Everything in this room is from the earth and, I guess you could split the atom again and again with this attunement, couldn't you?'

G. 'You could.'

J. 'I must admit I don't agree with red meaning courage, which you said of an earlier attunement, I actually feel that orange is for courage. I think in your last attunement you said about the red and the petals?'

G. 'The blood.'

J. 'But I find your interpretation incredibly interesting Grace and food for thought!'

G. 'The other thing I would say is the orange in the chakra is about feelings and emotions and I think that's very much in there.'

J. 'Yes, I think you may have a point there and all your attunements have been so colourful just as an artist's should be!'

G. 'With all the colour, I've got a little short one now. This is called 'Look to the Light'. I am looking at a darkened space, square in shape. There is an entrance and all is silent. Through the entrance comes a small ball of white light; it probes the darkness. The darkness pushes the light back with a firm strength at the same time, I hear a whoosh. The light disappears for a moment, then returns as if on the rebound. The darkness, once again, pushes the light back and I hear the whoosh noise.

The light returns just as quickly as before, only now it is in the form of a ray of light. It returns gently, softly without a sound. It slides to the entrance, trying a different approach. The light slips under and around the darkness and before the darkness can plan an escape, it finds itself held in the gentle but firm grip of the light. The darkness is absorbed becoming part of the light. There is a feeling of completion. I find that very interesting.'

J. 'Very unusual as well, so come on, interpretation please?'

G. 'The light will always win over the darkness.'

J. 'True.'

G. 'Always, always, there's no competition. The darkness can try every which way it wants to, the light will always win. It will find a way of almost helping the darkness to become light. It's also about positivity and negativity. Positivity will always be the leader and the winner.

It's about love. It's about fear. It's about using love to overcome all that is negative and you can't always do it up front. Sometimes you have to regroup and slip back in through the back door and work from a different angle because people don't always want to be told what they should do.

You have to stand back and it's almost like, if you get up very early when it's sunrise and the night is going and the sun comes up with the first few rays, it creeps along the ground so softly if you watch them and eventually, the day is there and the night doesn't even notice that it was fading.

And I just feel that it's about trust, knowing that if you are prepared to do your best and put in the time, to learn, to move forward, to never discard anything as being useless, to always pick it up and look at it one more time because in there, there's something for you. Nothing's for nothing!'

J. 'That was a great feedback. I also can't help but get positivity and light for your granddaughter Amy. I feel that her name was attached to this attunement in some way? That it was a reminder for you - even though you know it - it was still worth reiterating. That there is always light there, there is always positivity no matter how dark something may seem, you *know* that the positive and the light in the darkness will prevail, will win?

I'm not saying that the whole attunement was about Amy but I do get a connection with her in this attunement with your spirit guides saying, 'This applies to Amy as well.'

G. 'Yes.'

J. 'But the very simplistic and mighty attunement that it was, refers to *so* much that it could fill a whole book!'

G. 'It could, couldn't it?'

J. 'Yes. That something as mighty is worth reiterating but your analogy of it was lovely, very simple but it's like, one thing spoke a thousand words so even though it was little, it was a lion of an attunement!'

G. 'I've got two left. 'The Path.' This morning I asked God when saying my opening prayer, if I might link with my guides. It has been some time since we sat together either in attunement or conversation.

The guide who revealed himself was Salaman and he was showing a much older image of himself. He was wearing a beautiful, long, golden robe trimmed with red. It reached down to his matching slippers. On his head was a tallish headdress with fringed sides that framed his face, these touched his shoulders and was also in gold and red. His hands held a scroll and a long wooden pen or pencil. He dropped the scroll onto the ground and it started to unroll. I could see that it was about twelve inches wide and covered with writing.

Looking at me and seeing the question in my eyes, he said, 'This is your path, your life. Which way should you be facing?' I could easily see the one end, it was not very long but the other end stretched away into the distance. I looked at the end closest to me thinking to myself, if this is all that I have covered, it's not a lot!

I turned around looking behind me at the long end of the scroll but chose the shorter end. Salaman asked me if I was sure and I said, 'Yes.' He smiled. The scroll moved sending the shorter end out of my sight. I looked behind me; I could not see either end. I realised that I had covered a lot more than I had first thought.

Salaman asked, 'Are you going to stand upon your path or watch from the side in fear?' 'Stand upon it!' I said firmly. 'Then stand upon it with courage and move forward with grace' were his words. I asked, 'Is that it?' 'For today.' said Salaman with a smile, then he was gone.'

J. 'That's great. I loved it! I really loved it and you describe what they're wearing so beautifully and you can see, you can envisage it all yourself. Very spiritually metamorphic. A typical spiritual lesson from an elder. It was wonderful, I thoroughly enjoyed that! Thank you for sharing that. That was really lovely.'

G. 'I think they get better as I go along.'

J. 'No, no, there's no good and there's no bad. It was just; when I teach and I listen to people's attunements, it's like I'm in a library and I'm reading or listening to *all* these stories - I'm the lucky one. Have you got anything to say about it?'

G. 'I thought it explained itself very well. I often wonder where I am on the path of life. If I am 'trundling' along at the right speed, where I've got to and how many times I have to come back to complete what I've neglected or not understood - all of those things - and when he dropped the scroll and it rolled and the one end only went a short distance and the other end went much further, you could take it both ways you know?

You could look at the long end and think, Oh, I've done all that, I've only got this little bit to do! But I didn't see it that way. I saw it as just a little bit that I had covered with a lot more to follow and I think I got it right because when I chose the shorter end, even though it was going to take me longer and I had much more to do, it suddenly moved and became more balanced.

I had covered a lot more; it was almost like a test to see if I was willing to work that hard to make up lost time or follow my path no matter how long it took, no matter how many times I had to come back, I chose the shorter end because I wanted to get it right.'

J. 'Don't forget that we often don't change our personality. You're a very principled lady, Grace. You set yourself quite high ideals and one of your characteristics is that you're not happy unless you get it right so I really don't think that you can do any better than you're doing. I think you're knocking yourself for want of splitting hairs, if you like.

Do you remember the story I told you where someone had climbed up a mountain and they were very happy that they had reached the top and were feeling really pleased with themselves with what they had achieved and then they looked over and saw yet another range of mountains?

I don't want to dispel the myth or disillusion you or to spoil anything for you but it's ongoing; it's the circle again. I really don't think there is a short bit or a long bit!'

G. 'No.' (Grace is amused).

J. 'It's like what we often get told about; 'living in the now'. If every day you do your best, what *more* can you possibly do? If you must know, spirit only ask that we do our best and nothing more. Spirit will sometimes say, 'If you help one person in your life, your life has been worth living' and, of course, we generally exclaim, that we want to help *more* than just one person!

So we *do* expect so much of ourselves and I think, once again, a beautiful attunement, georgously presented and a real mental crossword which can say and mean many things.

I can't see you being complacent Grace, you're not like that. I think the scroll was there, not to test you but to confirm that you're on the right path. This is your path and you're doing just fine whether you look at the short end or the long end - it's A.OK! (Grace is chuckling).

Because spirit *know* you - they know you *so* well - and I'm laughing because it's as though I'm getting that your guides are saying, aren't we lucky to have someone as diligent as Grace as our partner on the earth plane.

There are many people who aren't half as diligent as you, who do not take their path seriously in any way, shape or form and your guides now join with you in saying, we're a brilliant team, aren't we? So I think everyone is very happy and *you* should be too.'

G. 'Thank you, thank you, I have one more and that was this morning. Quite amazing, it's called 'The Beginning'. I cleanse, open up and wait sitting with my eyes closed. Even though my eyes are closed I can tell that it is daytime. There is a pale lemon light shining on my face. I open my eyes and see that it is early morning. I hear a buzz in the distance; it is getting louder.

A large bumble bee comes into view flying along just going about its business, it passes turning to look at me. My goodness, it has a face and an expression just like a cartoon character! It disappears into the distance. The sun is getting stronger. The pale lemon light has become more of a yellow in colour, it has more depth. It's going to be a beautiful day.

I continue to sit, my back against a rock. It's very comfortable here but I see someone walking towards me, it is Salaman. He is dressed in a simple white robe and is bare-headed. On his feet are brown leather shoes with straps around the ankles. He carries a bundle of white paper, the breeze lifting the leaves into a fan as he walks. He also has a long wooden pen which has an old fashion nib.

'Did I call you?' I ask. 'You must have' he replies, 'because here I am.' He begins to explain saying that the paper is not for me but is symbolic; it means news of a book. A book still in the early stages, I will be part of this book and will be taking an active part in its launch into the world.

'So is there more?' I ask. 'Oh, yes, much more' he tells me. 'You must learn to be brave and know now is your time to work for us.' 'What will I be doing?' 'Well, painting and drawing, of course!' He smiles and is gone.'

J. 'Ah! OK, so tell me more - elaborate on this - what your thoughts were, what your interpretation was?'

G. 'Well, I started at the end and worked back to be truthful because the only book I could think of was *your* book. It was the only one I could think of. As far as I know, I'm not anywhere near a book that's being written other than yours and I think he was telling me that if you could write a book that included things about me, I could stop procrastinating and get on and do my bit as well and start by going back to doing my painting and drawing. What was I waiting for? I could do it.'

J. 'So my question is, do you feel that your drawing and painting has taken a back seat?'

G. 'It has done for the last, at least twelve months that I know of.'

J. 'So that fits, doesn't it; you put this course first?'

G. 'Yes.'

J. 'And it's almost as though he knows you're coming to the end of this course so what are you waiting for girl! There is nothing now to stop you and also, it will be very interesting Grace to see the calibre of your work now?'

G. 'I think it will have changed.'

J. '*I* think it will have changed too! When people come on this course, I say that you will never be the same again not because I'm blowing my own trumpet but because learning changes you. You can't unlearn. You can't say I haven't heard it, I haven't read it, I haven't understood it, I haven't thought about it, I haven't experienced it.

A year on, you are a different Grace whether you like it or not and I think that having done this course and having experienced everything that comes with it, you will now put *your* 'pen' or paints to paper and feel and see the difference; I'm sure of it.'

G. 'If I have to say one thing about this course and there are many, I now don't have to keep going back to the spell-checker. I started to write and it was hard work to begin with but it's got easier as I've gone along and I have thought of words that I would never have used and wondered how to spell them and waited a moment and then I've seen them and then I've just known what to put down!

I think the bumble bee is me buzzing along, going about my own business but actually doing what a bumble bee should, what Grace should do.'

J. 'Dipping here and dipping there and in my view anyway, bees are one of the most cherished and under-rated insects ever. Without them we wouldn't have the world we have now, we wouldn't have the food and flowers we have.

The humble bee - I can't praise it enough - and very slowly, it's circulating amongst the population just how amazing they really are. How we should encourage them and help them because they do so much for us and maybe that is your role too; that you're going to be doing so much for us and for spirit - sowing seeds?

I also felt that Salaman was bringing you the tools, the paper, the pencils; a lot of it. There wasn't just one sheet was there?'

G. 'Oh no, the wind lifted it and it just went up like a fan.'

J. 'Exactly! He's giving you a window into your next chapter! I, myself, can't wait to see what sort of work you're going to be turning out.'

G. 'I'm quite interested. I'm really quite interested myself.'

J. 'And also, isn't it wonderful that you're given encouragement? That your guide actually tells you, come on, roll up your sleeves, let's get down to it girl. Wonderful motivation because sometimes with motivation, we have to wait for it, we have to wait for inspiration, aspiration, motivation when we're creative; we can't just switch on the light and do it.'

G. 'No, you can't.'

J. 'Whether you're writing songs or drawing or poetry or whatever it is you're doing. I also feel and this is a 'p.s.' I feel that this course also has something to do with your artwork because I also feel that your attunements are so artistic. They are beautiful, like a snapshot, like a piece of art in themselves and I just wanted to say that I see a connection between your attunements and your artwork. That one can help the other, that one can inspire the other, that one can motivate the other. I just feel some sort of connection there.

That you've come to the end of the course and yes, you know you can attune anytime for the rest of your life but I also feel that there is a role that your attunements might be playing in your artwork? I don't know what role that is but I think it's there. There's a significance; something you didn't have when you were painting before.

You never had your attunements when you were drawing or painting and now you've got this extra something that I think will be coming in handy, put it that way. Do you understand?'

G. 'I do.'

J. 'OK. So that's all your attunements. I thoroughly enjoyed them.'

G. 'Thank you.'

Questions & Answers

Jenny: 'So we now come to whether you have any questions that you want to ask me? Am I going to be up for the task, that's what I want to know?'

Grace's Questions...

Grace: Q. 'Well, the first one I think you've answered today which was about my higher self. Is it part of me, is it part of spirit, is half of me left in the spirit world? You've just covered it all! Whether part of me that is left in the spirit world when I am also in the physical? So you've answered that question.

Q. And then this one I think pertains to that? I often hear people talking about the 'Christ Consciousness' and I am a little uncertain as to what that means. Is it a Christian belief? Is it a belief that comes with going to church?'

J. **A.** 'I, personally, don't know the answer to that but I would guess that it stands for everything that Christ stood for. So using my logic and common sense, rather than my intelligence, I'm going to answer that the Christ consciousness is an embodiment of what the Nazarene stood for, so it's His teachings. What he explained would take you nearer to God. So it's the way you think, the way you live your life, the way you are and I personally feel, that it's not necessarily a Christian thing either.

Remember, the Nazarene was a Jew. He came back for a very specific purpose and His spirituality speaks across the whole board as he said the same things as Allah, Muhammed, etc. Whether the Christian religion wants you to have Christ in mind when you are doing things, I don't know but that's what I think the Christ consciousness means. I hope that's a fair answer?'

G. 'It's a very fair answer. It feels right. This is, I don't know whether you call this an incidental but nevertheless, it interests me.

Q. If someone was doing platform work, just out of interest or giving a reading to someone or sitting in circle and they received these things and start to give a reading but it's not for that person. It's for someone perhaps sat to their right or their left or behind them - they call it 'crossing over', I think. Then you say all these things about the person who's asking the question but it's not meant for them, you

---

are actually finding out about the person who's sat maybe just in front of them.

How do you know if there's something wrong? I mean you can ask yourself the question. You should be able to think in your mind, this doesn't feel right, this is not correct?'

J. 'Is this from the medium's perspective or the listener?'

G. 'The medium's.'

J. **A.** 'Right. Well, to start with every medium is different. Every medium works with spirit in a different way, every medium doesn't always give what they themselves are given. I can't speak for everybody but all I *can* say is that if a medium is picking up an energy, some mediums have more proof because of the way they work with their guides.

So you can have a medium, for example, who sees spirit and who are linking up with them in a room giving a message, the medium will be attracted to somebody but then they notice spirit standing behind that person or to their right or to their left so it all depends on the accuracy of the medium's relationship with their guides.

OK, let's re-wind. One of the things that people think is necessary is proof of survival and this *is* necessary but proof of survival for survival's sake, to me, is a misnomer. When spirit are in a public place, I am confident that they are there to touch someone's soul, they come in a positive light for a positive reason.

I cannot answer your specific question directly. All I know is that spirit want to help, they naturally want to serve, they want somebody's life to change for the better every time their influence is felt.

If somebody is in that room or in that church and they want 'something', they may have gone not knowing why. They may attend because they want a message but it may end up being something else which touches them and they leave having learnt something, having been touched by something.

I, personally, am not interested in whether a medium makes a mistake or not or goes to the right person or not. My whole ethos - what I am being impressed upon - is to serve in any which way that will effect a positive outcome so my answer to you could be a rude one!

It could be; it all depends on the medium and their relationship and what they get and what they say and what they make of it and whether they've been given 2+2 and made it 22, I can't answer that.

All I *do* know is that spirit will always work in love and even a medium who may not have a very spiritual reason for serving, maybe have an ego, maybe in it for fame, money but still *they* are learning too - we are all learning. But I know that spirit will never miss an opportunity to help somebody and therefore, from the moment that evening starts to when it finishes, please God, something positive will have been accomplished.

I know I haven't fully answered the question but there's my answer!'

G. 'No you have, because whilst you were speaking to me, I got the answer and as you say, whether right or wrong, it will touch someone in that room so get rid of your ego, it's not all about *you*.'

J. 'Psychic and spiritual development or mediumship, is very personal. It's a language; the communication, the relationship which you have formulated with your spirit guides is specific to you. Yes, they may work with other souls, other people but the relationship won't be the same as the one they have with you. So when you talk about the medium doing something, providing that medium is doing the best and serving in the best way possible, they can't do any more than their best, can they?'

G. 'No.'

J. 'And hopefully, whatever you do, you learn from it. I remember when I was on the church platform, it was excruciatingly painful and I didn't want to be there but I knew it was part of my path and this was my next challenge and this is what I had to do but I read myself the riot act afterwards. I criticised myself, I split myself into pieces, I challenged myself, I wasn't happy with my performance but I did it and that was the main thing - I did it!'

G. 'It's almost like a rite of passage.'

J. 'The whole of our path is like a hurdle race.'

G. 'You're right!'

J. 'You have to overcome this and then you run a bit and then the next hurdle looms ahead. So then you run a bit more and then the next one comes but everything can be overcome by loving and doing your best. And that's it.'

G. 'Thank you, you've answered my question.'

J. 'Is there any more?'

G. 'A couple which do not fit in with anything particular but which came to me this morning and I thought, if there's anyone who can help me, it's you.

Q. I know that when we pass, we go wherever we're meant to go but I have one long abiding fear of being buried alive. Of people thinking you're dead or passed and you're not. Now, I've put it down to watching too much Hammer House of Horror!'

J. 'Oh, you silly billy!'

G. 'This is years ago, as a teenager and it goes away and I forget about it. And then I opened the paper the other day and there was a double page spread of the worst stories possible and I should have shut it and not looked but I did and suddenly it was back, nipping at my heels and I'm thinking what if?'

J. **A.** 'OK. I've got two answers to this. You've heard of *"Like attracts like?"*

G. 'Yes.'

J. 'If you constantly worry about something, if you're always thinking of negative things, you *will* eventually attract that same negativity back to you.'

G. 'OK.'

J. 'It's a law. If 'bad' things have happened to people sometimes it's because they've made it happen themselves. They were *so* worried, they actually created the very scenario they were worried about so my advice from now on, is to close it!

Imagine this particular 'worry' of yours written down on a piece of paper. Crunch it all up and sling it on the fire and burn it. I do not want that scenario to be in your head any more. Do you understand?'

G. 'OK.'

J. 'So that's the first thing to do. Secondly, what this course must have taught you is the strength and value of *trust*?'

G. 'I was going to say that.'

J. 'So whatever happens in your life you have God to call on and your guides to trust. No cry for help ever goes unanswered, ever!

The third thing I want to say is that I feel, that as humans, we all have a built-in safety mechanism and a cut-off mechanism for when we cannot cope with something anymore. At that point, we naturally cut off, we pass out, we faint. I do not feel that anybody in the whole universe, no matter how horrific they may appear to be in pictures, suffers unduly as I feel that this mechanism is there for everybody.

People will only endure the pain that they must suffer, no more. Once it goes beyond that point they become unconsciousness so I always feel that this 'law' is permanently and automatically in practice. I have never read about it. It is something between me and my teachers, something that I have come to understand, my own personal assessment.

So there are three responses to that question:-

* No more thinking about it - chuck it away, it's in the past. It's not going to raise its ugly head again because it's a nonsense. It's a childhood thing and you've grown up. Chuck it out!

* Understand that you always have help when you need it and it's there for you always, 24/7. Your thoughts are their thoughts. *"Spirit is just a thought away."*

* Understand the Law, that *"No one is ever given anything that is too much for them."*

G. 'I had that said to me when I was in hospital and the vicar came to see me and I was very surprised because I never went to church and there he was. It was a bad day and I had more pain than I ever had in my life and I remember him sitting by the bed and looking at me and saying, "God will never give you more than you can bear" and I've always remembered that, always. Now, I've another question.

Q. How would you withdraw from a circle if it suddenly became or felt too inappropriate in some way, how would you withdraw from that circle - gracefully?'

J. **A.** 'Well, I can speak from experience on this one because I have done that myself. A long time ago, I started feeling that the circle I was in wasn't the same as it was when I joined and every time I went, I was feeling the same thing - that negativity had entered the circle. There were people in the circle who were letting the rest of the circle down and I was always taught that if one bit of negativity enters the circle, it ceases to become spiritual.

So one evening I waited for everybody to leave and I had a word with the keeper of the circle, the person whose house we were in and I just told her the truth. I just said I'm really sorry but this circle has changed. It started a little while ago and it's not getting any better and so I can no longer be part of it because it doesn't represent what I feel a circle should stand for.

In my particular case, the person that I spoke to agreed with me and said that she had felt the same so it was not too hard for me.

But I think that in every conceivable situation you cannot argue with truth. The truth is just the truth and that's all there is to it and no-one can argue with that. You're not a bad person, you're an honest person, you're a *"To thine own self be true"* person and when you're on a spiritual path, *especially* when you're on a spiritual path, you *are* tested. You're tested by spirit in many, many ways.

It comes in ways that you least expect and I've always thought that *"To thine own self be true"* is very necessary because we are all individuals, on our own individual path and we always have to do what we feel is right for us.

Yes, it may take a bit of courage but the truth should be the most easiest of things to explain. There are always very gracious and respectful ways you can talk to people. You don't have to discuss things in a hurtful or nasty way, no matter what you're talking about or to whom. So that's my answer.'

G. 'Thank you, that's great. The next one is.

Q. How would someone who thought they were empathetic protect themselves from being overwhelmed by the weight of information when in a room full of people?

If you are feeling all different kinds of emotions within the room, by that I mean both positive and negative emotions. The thing one wants to do is fix it and make it all better, put a bandage on those wounds that cannot be seen. However, it may not be for us to fix things. People have to walk their own path. It may be that by trying to help we are interfering with free will and by doing so, making ourselves unwell at the same time.

We know how to place our protection or closing down symbol above our head and pull gold through our body which usually does the job in most cases. My feeling is that there might be another way to close down, stopping all these emotions from spoiling our evening and making us feel unwell for the next few days?'

J. **A.** 'You answered a lot of your questions yourself; send love and loving thoughts. Ask spirit, 'Help this one please.' but never forget why we're all here - to walk our own individual path and to surmount our own personal difficulties.

Remember the quick ways I taught you to close down; Stepping into a golden egg, stepping into a golden sleeping bag, closing an imaginary umbrella into your solar plexus. Be disciplined and mentally respond there and then in a positive way.

As you grow wiser, as each spiritual truth is understood, so you become stronger, more disciplined and more at peace with yourself, with the world and the people in it. You already know that you are never alone, that each of us have our personal guides and helpers who walk with us and that everyone is facing their own particular hurdle right now - that IS our path!

Love conquers all and is then easily dispensed.'

G. 'Thank you for that. There's just one left.

Q. Something I don't do very well but I'm learning and that's speaking up for myself but doing it with care. When I'm bending over backwards not to offend someone but going down the road of doing something that is not making me happy.

So instead of struggling on and still doing it, because there's always a crunch somewhere along the line, I now speak up and say, you know, it's not for me or I don't feel comfortable. And sometimes I come away and I think - this is very recent mind you - I hope I haven't offended them but my sister-in-law always says this one thing - I have to be true to myself.'

J. 'So have you not answered your own question?'

G. 'Yes, just be true to yourself. I did, didn't I!'

J. **A.** 'Yes, and we spoke earlier about a path having hurdles and that we're tested and life isn't about standing still. Life isn't about being all 'rosy in the garden' either. Life is about learning and you can only learn from challenges and the best way to learn is to put you in a difficult predicament and then you have to challenge yourself, you have to find the will, the wherewithal within, to rise above the challenge and that's how we grow.

If there's nothing challenging us, we're not growing and we all have to grow. We begin as a baby and we carry on growing just like a seed, just like the plant, the flower, the tree, we have to grow. So we need those awkward predicaments and challenges to make our choices, to test ourselves and to grow.

When we have our difficulties, these come at the right time in our lives - the hurdles - they come in order that we can also question ourselves and our self-respect in the hope that we will be true to ourselves. Sometimes we may even lose out as we often have to take a step back in order for us to take a step forward, a test in itself.

This particular philosophy I have always visualised as 'a sling'. The stone in the sling is pulled backwards but when it's released, it will travel further forward than it would normally have gone. So by taking a step back, in humility, you can actually achieve a greater reward.

We all have many challenges in life. They actually begin with the family! Our family is put together for us, not just as a loving unit but also as a challenge and often that's why you will hear spirit say, *"Put your own house in order first."* A lot of people turn their back on their family to help other people leaving their family still needing, still wanting and that's the wrong way round.

This is done because family difficulties are so hard but they're hard on purpose. They are hard because some of the difficulties we face, we have specifically come back to learn how to overcome - family difficulties, family obstacles. It's not easy but it was never supposed to be easy but whether it's family or work or money or domestic, we have to learn to overcome these problems, we can't grow otherwise.

We would just vegetate and we would not fulfil the purpose of our incarnation either and we have to try and achieve this otherwise, when we 'die' and the time comes for us to 'go home', we would be very, very disappointed in ourselves.'

G. 'My husband is not the easiest person in the world. It's like being a bird in a cage sometimes and after a while, I sit in my cage with the door shut although I'm perfectly capable of opening it. So I came out of my cage, I looked at my husband and I realised that a lot of the obstacles that he'd put in my way was because he was afraid that I would do something without him and move on; not leave him but just change. So I started looking at him with love and I just put all the love I could think of into everything I did and it was like a miracle - he changed - it worked!'

J. 'There are so many little things happening that collectively mean such a lot and they all build up in the back of your mind and they won't go way and you're constantly trying to find your way through this fog of a situation and then suddenly, you'll do or change one thing and you know, every little helps!

It doesn't matter if they're pigeon steps as long as you're making a 'forward' move. It doesn't matter how big or small the steps are as long as you're going in the right direction, then there's hope.'

G. 'And he's taking a little bit more interest in the things which are spiritual. He's actually listening to me now - I don't talk about it too much - just a little now and again but he actually stops and pays attention so it does work this 'love' thing.'

J. 'Relationships are always very challenging. When you have an interest that your partner isn't interested in, I think it all comes back to balance again. As long as your life is balanced. As long as you respect one another, as long as you have the decency to let them have a piece of their own enjoyment without feeling threatened that what you enjoy isn't going to override their love for you.

And it does come back down to love. If someone loves another, they want them to be happy, they want them to be surrounded by the things that they enjoy, it's a selfless thing. Love is completely and utterly unselfish and puts others before yourself because you want the best for them.'

G. 'It's like a beautiful bandage. If there's a bit that hurts, you smooth it with love, put that 'love' bandage on that place, it gets better - if you want to use a metaphor.'

J. 'Yes, it all comes back down to love. I remember, I start off this course by saying, 'There's only one thing you need to learn about spiritual development and that is 'love'. You don't need to do this course at all because that is it!' I think we've come a full circle? We began with love and we've ended with love and I think that's a really lovely way to end this course.'

G. 'And sometimes we just have to do the journey!'

J. 'Oh, we *always* have to do the journey, we don't have any options but I just think we're so lucky to be privy to some of the spiritual Truths. We're so lucky because they enhance our lives. They make the going easier and make everything look more 'glowing'. I will always be eternally grateful for what I've been taught.

I couldn't have progressed without it. It's been my rock, my hand, my sun, my shadow. Spiritual Truths, the spiritual Laws, this knowledge and ultimate understanding - it's been everything to me. It's helped me to become the person I am and to achieve what I have. I can't speak highly enough of it really.'

G. 'It's changed my life. I have the understanding to move with it now. My thoughts at the beginning of this course; I knew what it was and I understood it to a certain extent but not the depth that I do now and have the trust. There were always things that seemed to just contradict one another all the time and I hadn't got the knowledge to unravel it. It was just like a big ball of wool that had many ends that needed to be joined up so I could understand it and I've had that with this course, most definitely.'

J. 'Brilliant, brilliant!'

G. 'Thank you.'

J. 'No, thank you for staying with me and for giving me the opportunity to walk with you this year because I've thoroughly enjoyed it and you have given me, I think, as much as I may have given you so I think it's always a two-way thing.

You challenged me, you've made me work, you've made me think, you've made me come up with answers, you've made me think how best I can help you and when you meet somebody new and they begin something like this, you have no way of knowing where it's going to lead and what you're going to explore and discover along the way.

So I've thoroughly enjoyed it. Thank you so much Grace.'

G. 'And we met, didn't we, across the table and here we are again.'

J. 'But I know this isn't the end, this is just the end of this chapter.'

G. 'Yes, the end of what has been a wonderful journey. I have a friend now who has been my teacher and is now my friend and who will stay my teacher and my friend.'

J. 'We still have the rescue training to do so we're not quite done yet!'

Bobbie's Questions...

Jenny: 'OK. Bobbie. It's time to test my wits! You now need to ask me your questions and we'll see if I'm clever enough to answer them!'

Bobbie: **Q.** 'Right! When I talk about 'seeing', I don't actually see as we know it but it's not totally feeling either. Can you explain to me what's exactly happening?'

J. **A.** 'Well, just like we talked about having these five 'bodies', you have your senses and these senses - if you are growing spiritually - are also growing. They're like antennae 'catching' things, picking things up.

Now these senses are psychic but you need them for spiritual growth, you remember *"The psychic is a tool for the spiritual."* You can't grow *spiritually* without these psychic tools so if you have a sense, which you do; you're operating a lot on your clairsentience sense, aren't you?'

B. 'Yes.'

J. 'But you also have a clairvoyance sense which is like a third eye. Now I can't tell you how they put this package together in you, your senses are unique to you and the relationship that you have with your guides - how they're working with you - is also unique but you just have to accept that you are able to sense, see and hear within your own psychic ability; I cannot dissect it. (Bobbie laughs).

I cannot give you a mathematical equation - that plus that equals this. All I can say is that it's unique to you. You've earnt it. You agreed to have it and you live and work with it but it can change and it can grow. There's a saying you can never 'unlearn'. If I teach you something, you can't say, 'No, I didn't hear it, I haven't learnt it!' You can't stuff it back!'

B. (Bobbie is giggling). 'No, because it's there!'

J. 'Because it's now there - too late Ethel - it's out there! So from your childhood experiences you have grown with knowledge and understanding which is pertinent to you. What you have 'sussed' out, what you have concluded and obviously, *now,* you're not the same Bobbie who came to me a year ago, are you, you've grown?'

B. 'Definitely!'

J. 'So your senses have grown too. I cannot be definitive in my answer. All I can say is that you are fortunate but you have also earnt all your 'gifts' too and not just in this life but over many lifetimes. So how you register things using your psychic ability can be a combination. It's like a receipe. You can have eight ounces of clairsentience and four ounces of clairvoyance.' (Bobbie is in fits of laughter).

J. 'I don't know how it works but I personally don't think you really need to know. Together with spirit you're both operating on the frequencies which equal your personal relationship. OR perhaps you would like to think of it as this?

You and your guides operate together on certain frequencies which are unique to your personal relationship(s). Like, for example, both of you are tuning into 981FM or 2020 longways when you work together! Now these frequencies or stations may be shared with other people, but your relationship is unique because each of us are unique, totally and utterly unique, which makes each and every one of us special in our own right.

And because spirit is infinite, there are an infinite number of frequencies for us and spirit to use and to tune in, connect and work together. I guess that's as near as I can get to explaining it. So does that help answer your question?'

B. 'Yes, Right. I think you've already answered this exactly when you were talking about my last attunement.

Q. What does it mean and what is happening when I feel myself changing? i.e. getting taller, bigger, fatter,etc.?'

J. **A.** 'So you now know that it is the spirit which is eclipsing your aura; it's coming into your 'space'. Their energy is eclipsing your energy. You can say overshadowing for want of another word.

What is happening is the lost soul's spiritual energy is being impressed upon you and the depth of that impression, again, depends on one's ability, on one's psychic ability. Your guides have been working with you and through this unique relationship, the two of you are able to perform, if you like, certain spiritual tasks. In other words, it's how well they have managed to train you and how well you have responded. You are now both reaping the fruits of both your labours.

Never forget that we are an energy and all spiritual and psychic work is based on energy of some kind so it's a combination of both yours and your guides energy which make things happen.

We can't do it alone. OK? So they want you to experience this 'overshadowing' for example, if you're being prepared for rescue. This is what you need to start experiencing and you need to get used to feeling like this. You need to understand why it's happening. It doesn't happen just for nothing. It happens so that you will be able to work with spirit and help them. You need this particular ability in order to fulfil a particular purpose - your part of the job.

They can only do so much from their side of life. They're hoping that working with you, you can help complete the tasks involved, yes?'

B. 'Yes.'

J. 'But in that attunement, with the old lady, I feel that you were being asked to help but also being tested. Spirit were giving you a real example, a real job to do. It wasn't just a test run. This was an old lady that needed to go home and your spirit guides *knew* that *you* Bobbie, as a developing medium, was the perfect person to help her. Especially as she related to you, as the two of you had such similar ailments which, in turn, helped you to identify and empathise with her and so help her in the manner you did. So there were many, many things in that one attunement.

You did a rescue. You experienced somebody that needed your help and you felt her with every fibre of your being because she overshadowed you so closely, so you now know that you can do that! But, in truth, your spirit guides had also been working with you long enough to know that it would be a success.'

B. 'Yes.'

J. 'So in a way, it was also like a present! Your guides were in essence saying, 'Do you understand Bobbie, that you can do this now? This is what we've been doing with you behind the scenes, this is how well we've done!' The present was finding out something about yourself and how far you've come in your development.'

B. 'Right. The next one is.

Q. I know you cannot cleanse people without the soul's permission but can you cleanse houses and things without permission?'

J. **A.** 'Of course you can, yes and we'll be going through that when we do the rescue training because when you've finished a requested rescue you should also cleanse the home.'

B. 'Right.'

J. 'Sometimes I get asked, can you check this home out. Maybe someone's moving, they've had a previous experience and they don't want to move into a home if it's got a bad energy so this is a personal request asking me for help. But as a matter of course, whenever you do a rescue on a place or a home that's been brought to you via 2nd, 3rd, or 4th parties, you should always finish by cleansing the house or building.

It goes without saying when something or someone has left. It's like when you move house, you clean the old one before the next person comes in and that's what we do when we rescue somebody from a place whether it's a house or building, we make sure that we give it a good cleansing over before we leave.

But I think you're actually talking about whether you can help somebody without them knowing?'

B. 'Yes.'

J. 'And if you're aspiring to good, then I would say yes, because you only have their best and higher interest at heart. You're doing it in love. If you're working on a love vibration, it's like saying a prayer for somebody. Now you don't ask someone, 'Can I say a prayer for you tonight?' do you?'

B. 'No.'

J. 'You're thinking on a positive love vibration and you would be doing the same if you were helping someone by cleansing their house, wouldn't you, so I think the answer would be the same - you don't have to ask permission to do good.'

B. 'Right.'

J. 'And if you're implying that the person whom you want to help doesn't agree, favour or embrace spiritual matters, then the best thing to do is to just help them without telling them.'

B. **Q.** 'Right! So that leads actually onto the next question which was about absent healing?'

J. **A.** 'Absent healing, yes? Before I go to bed, I ask spirit to use me to help others less fortunate than myself. I don't know who they are. I don't know which country they live in - I don't need to know. All I'm saying is, I want to help those less fortunate than me so use me whether in Syria, India or wherever.

And if someone I know, who I love, is going through a bad time, just like saying prayers, I will send them healing, I will do anything for them, even if they don't agree with my spiritual understanding because it matters to me.

I'm not saying what they think is right and what I think is wrong. It's my intent and I trust it and I know if I ask for something, it will be given because I've earnt that trust with my guides as I've served them.

We've been working together for a long time, we know each other well. They know I would never, ever do anything other than for someone's higher good.'

B. 'Yes, you definitely wouldn't want to harm anybody.'

J. 'No, so when you have a scenario where you want to help somebody but they don't approve of your, I'm going to say, beliefs. The spiritual is a belief rather than a religion. It's a knowledge and an understanding but it still has to be believed to act on, so it is a belief, yes?'

B. 'Yes, but it's more than that.'

J. 'It's more than that providing you're doing something for a higher good be it animal, vegetable or mineral. If you want to help someone and you're concerned, they don't need to know because if they did know, they might get upset so it's best to do it in your own home, via your own thoughts and your own prayers.'

B. 'Yes.'

J. 'Your own positive love energy - send it out to them - whether it's clearing their house or helping them or healing, it doesn't matter, you go ahead.'

B. **Q.** 'World Healing?'

J. **A.** 'The same, it's exactly the same. It's all a loving energy, loving thoughts. When we exist in spirit, we exist as pure thought so your thought is real, that's why prayers are heard, whatever they are, they're heard. So if you're asking for anything in love, it will be heard. It doesn't mean to say that you need to know the outcome but you are contributing your 'quota' of positive love towards it. 'Take my energy and use it positively' - that's basically what you're saying when healing.'

B. 'Right.'

J. 'When we work for spirit, that's what we're doing whether it's healing, rescue, whatever! We're saying 'use my positive love energy to make a positive difference', yes? So whether it's for your family or whether it's for someone you don't know, or for a country crippled with famine or war you can make a positive contribution. Do you remember what I said about closing down at night? I said if you don't want to be used, say so, because you've already given your permission.'

B. 'Yes, I do do that.'

J. 'So, when you sleep, you're going to be used anyway unless you say otherwise but sometimes we want to ask for specific things and that is equally fine and so it doesn't matter what you're asking for, it's your motive that counts, isn't it?'

B. 'Yes it is, as long as it's with love and pure?'

J. 'You go ahead whether you want to help a country or an individual or just leave it to spirit to decide what to do with your loving energy either way, you're making a difference.'

Response To The Development Course
What I Have Learnt & Achieved

Jenny: 'So Grace, are you ready to reveal what you think you have learnt and achieved since last May?'

Grace's response...

Grace: 'Yes, I hope this is what you wanted of me because I don't always think as everyone else does so here goes:-

* I am less afraid of things I do not understand.

* I work very hard at being less judgemental.

* My faith in spirit wisdom is stronger.

* I try to look at misfortunes and mistakes as lessons.

* Turning negatives around so that they become positives.

* Trying to live my life in love - this is a hard one.

* How to open up and close down properly.

* Remembering to say my opening and closing prayer.

* My spelling is much improved.

* I have become a better listener.

* When fear leaves you, everything and anything is possible.

* Finding my connection to spirit and being able to maintain it.

Is that what you meant?'

J. 'Perfect. It's to do with what you feel you have achieved and learnt. There's no right or wrong answer; it's personal. It's a précis which is what I wanted. It's a hard task which is why I asked you to begin making a list earlier on because the answers don't come all at once. You suddenly realise oh, that's what I've learnt, that's what I've achieved but you know, they are excellent examples and it is what I hoped for you, so I'm a very happy bunny!'

G. 'I also have my written response to this course, would you like it?'

J. 'Of course! Thank you. Why don't you read it out?'

G. 'OK, It's got a heading!

'Light your Candle'

I had a near death experience in February 2000. It changed me in many ways and I have no doubt that there is something beyond this earthly life. I became a Reiki healer, read spiritual books and joined groups in the hope that understanding would follow.

Then a friend offered to loan me a book and when she placed it into my hands, little did I know how much my life was about to change as I opened its pink cover. I liked the layout and the style of writing. It told a story and answered many of my questions. The author was Jenny Martin, she lived locally and my friend knew her!

Soon after, the three of us met for lunch, Jenny looked across the table at me and said, 'What am I going to do with you?' and after that, 'When can you start?' My life was about to change - again. The teacher had arrived and the pupil was ready.

Light the candle. I was to hear those three words many times during my course of lessons with my teacher. She always asked after my health and requested that I tell her of any problems that might have arisen since we had last met. She made sure that I understood her method of teaching and told me that I could telephone her if help was required.

My lessons continued over the next few months and I grew both in spiritual knowledge and wisdom. I know now that I have a soul and that it does not die, we just change lives carrying on in this world or the next. It is our choice.

Jenny's words of wisdom are going to stay with me for the rest of this life, helping and guiding me along my path. My mantra will be the one she taught me:- 'If all things are done in love, we need nothing more in our spiritual tool box.'

My knowledge of living a spiritual life is ever growing and I have gained a new confidence. However, I am still learning; that will never end.

Jenny is now writing another book about spiritual development. I look forward to reading it and recommend her first book with the pink cover called *'A Medium's Tale'*.

Grace. April 2013.

How I Met Jenny And What She Has Done For Me

I had been in circles before but they were mainly geared towards mediumship and although I didn't know what I was needing, I knew that mediumship was not for me, so I asked spirit to please send me a mentor, someone who could help me discover my purpose.

Then one Sunday morning I went to a spiritualist church I sometimes go to. A friend named Annie came over followed by a lady I didn't know. I looked at her and I could see fairies all around her and when she turned towards me, I could see her as a fairy. Annie introduced her and it was Jenny.

After the service there was general chatting and I heard someone say to Jenny, are you a medium? Jenny replied that she was and the person said, 'Oh, I must come and see you work.' Jenny replied, 'I don't do platform work.' As the conversation continued, I heard Jenny say that she did rescue work.

A light went on in my head and I thought this is it, this is my mentor. My friend, myself and Jenny arranged to meet in town for a coffee where I learnt that Jenny taught workshops to help people find their spiritual path and purpose. Naturally, I signed up. I thought, 'Yes, this is for me' and it was.

Since being taught by Jenny, I have learnt so much. I could write an epistle about what Jenny has taught me but I'll spare you that. Suffice to say, I have learnt more than any books or anyone else could have shown me.

The thing that makes Jenny a brilliant teacher is her sincerity and belief and commitment to what she teaches. She taught me to understand that being spiritual is far more and far deeper than just connecting with spirit, it is a way to live.

* I am now more aware of my thoughts and actions as to what impact it could have on others.

* That happiness is a state of mind and comes from within and cannot be bought.

* To face fears and negativity and to overcome them.

* To view people and the world in a more loving, compassionate way.

* To love people who have done wrong, for that is their journey and it is not up to us to judge them.

* Jenny has also made me understand that caring for and loving oneself is not vain or selfish, it is necessary. If you cannot love yourself, how can you love another?

* I have come to realise that working with spirit is a partnership, it is a two-way street.

* That trust must be built up on both sides for as spirit teach us, they too are learning.

* That our guides are always there for us, not telling us what to do but guiding us to what is best for our higher good.

* That they will always help us if we ask, although it may not be in the way we expect but guaranteed, it will be for our good.

* That if during communications with spirit you don't seem to get anything, that your guides are there working hard behind the scenes.

I could go on and on but that is just a little of what Jenny has taught me.

Jenny is the most kind hearted, trustworthy, honest, loving person I have ever had the privilege to meet and I am very lucky to be able to call her my friend. Thank you so much Jenny. Don't ever change as you are a beautiful person inside and out.

* I feel that since meeting Jenny I have grown in many ways. I know I have become more tolerant, more compassionate, more loving - a better person.

Bobbie. 2013.

Rescue Training Day

"How can you appreciate the light until you have known darkness."

Jenny: 'Well, good morning ladies!'

Grace & Bobbie: 'Good morning Jenny!'

J. 'We are back altogether. We started altogether and we're finishing altogether - just the way it should be - and now I'm going to have to lipread both of you!' (Grace & Bobbie are laughing).

Even though we've finished the main development course, these extra sessions - the rescue training - is something I usually recommend to people who are interested and to those I think may become involved themselves.

Right now, I think it's an opportunity for you both to find out more about what rescue means - certainly what it's meant to me. I have worked with spirit doing rescue for quite a few years now so I'm delighted that you both have agreed to take up my offer.

So welcome back to my humble home. I'm going to start off this morning by playing a recording of a rescue that I was involved in very early on in my 'mediumship'. This is a recording that I would normally play in Month 7, however, I decided that it would prove more beneficial to use it for our training session.

So we're going to begin with you listening to an example of a rescue done in a circle which takes place one evening in October 1999 and involves myself and Carol, one of the other circle members. To help you differentiate between the two people talking on the tape, Carol is the one who is doing most of the talking and who is helping me, who has got the lost soul with them. Alright, so have you both understood all that?'

G. & B. 'Yes.'

J. 'OK. So I'll just switch the tapes and off we go.'

(Grace and Bobbie now listen to the following recording of a rescue done in a circle):-

CAROL. 'Hello there, there're people here to help you, can you hear us?'

JENNY. (High pitched moaning sound).

CAROL. 'Can you hear us, are you in pain?'

JENNY. (High pitched moaning continues. Jenny can see clairvoyantly a battle field of soldiers with a long-handled wooden cart in the foreground piled high with dead bodies and soldiers in red, blue and white uniform).

CAROL. 'Try to relax. Try to relax, try to take deep breaths. We're here to help you.'

JENNY. (Moaning sounds settle slightly).

CAROL. 'What's your name?'

JENNY. (Moaning becomes less frequent).

CAROL. 'Can you give us your name?'

JENNY. (Desperate voice with an foreign accent) 'Antoine. Antoine, my name's Antoine.'

CAROL. 'Your name is Antoine?'

JENNY. (Almost as a cry now) 'Antoine!'

CAROL. 'Try to relax Antoine. We're here to help you. We're here to get some people to help you. Can you look around? Can you see anyone? Can you tell us where you are?'

JENNY. (Still crying out) 'Oh, the army, the army - everywhere! Help me! Help me! Save me! Lord, please save me!'

CAROL. 'You're already with the Lord, Antoine. Can you try and relax.'

JENNY. 'Oh, the army!'

CAROL. 'Look up, look up Antoine. Don't look around where you can see the army, look up. Can you see some nice lights, some bright light? You're not in the dark any more and you're not surrounded by all those people in the army. You've gone on to a much, much better life, Antoine.'

JENNY. (Crying continues) 'Oh, they kill me! They kill, the soldiers kill me! The army kill me!'

CAROL. 'It's only your body that's killed Antoine. The real you, the inside of you has gone to another life. If you can look around, if you look up, can you see any light?'

JENNY. 'It's all dark here.'

CAROL. 'It's all dark?'

JENNY. (Cries) 'All the light has gone out, no light in here.'

CAROL. 'No light? There will be a light, just keep looking. Do you know what year it is Antoine?'

JENNY. 'It is eighteen..'(voice trails off).

CAROL. 'And if you were going home, would you go home to your mother, your father, your wife, who would it be in your family? If you just look...'

JENNY. 'My family went during the war, the Napoleon.....' (Antoine is exhausted. Jenny can now see clairvoyantly a man on a horse on the horizon flanked either side by soldiers on horseback and wearing a hat like Napoleon).

CAROL. 'The Napoleonic war? Your family... if you look around you, someone from your family or your friends, will come to meet you. Just keep looking and try to keep calm. Can you see anything yet, Antoine?'

JENNY. 'What am I looking for.....I don't understand?' (Antoine is fragile).

CAROL. 'The person you wish to see, that if you were going home, would be there to greet you.'

JENNY. (Antoine's voice falters) 'Can you stop the pain? Oh please God, can you stop the pain!'

CAROL. 'I'm not God but God will be with you.'

JENNY. 'OH!' (Antoine lets out a cry as he re-lives his death by bayonette).

CAROL. 'Look up Antoine, look up Antoine, look around you. Can you see anything, can you see anyone? There are a number of people here and they're all praying for you, for your family to come to take you, to get rid of the pain. Can you see something? I think you can see something there or someone - a person or a light - you're much calmer?'

What can you see Antoine? You will feel peace, completely at peace, the pain will go and you will be relaxed.'

JENNY. 'I can see the light.'

CAROL. 'You can see the light? Can you go towards the light? Is the light coming nearer to you? Keep looking Antoine. Keep being relaxed and feel the peace. What do you see?'

JENNY. 'I see my wife.'

CAROL. 'You see your wife? Go with your wife Antoine, go to the peace and go to the Light.'

JENNY. 'How do I go to her?'

CAROL. 'She'll be coming to you. Is she coming closer and closer to you now? Reach out to her Antoine with your mind and your soul.'

RECORDING FINISHES.

(Antoine was taken by Jenny's spirit guides to join his wife and they would both return to spirit realms).

J. 'So, is that the first time either of you have been involved or listened to a rescue, not including the ones you have had yourselves during the course?'

B. 'It's the first time I've heard one, yes.'

G. 'Yes, it's the first time I've heard one.'

J. 'OK, as I said, this was done a long time ago when I was still learning this sort of thing. Every rescue is unique, is different. With this particular one, you've probably guessed, it was during the Napoleonic Wars and when I went into that attunement, the first thing I saw was the wagon, the wooden cart, with the long wooden handles with all the dead bodies and I saw the uniforms so I obviously knew this was taking place in a war.

I could tell by the uniform that it was that era but it wasn't until I saw the man on the horse in the distance with the hat on, which was Napoleon's hat, that I knew that we were in the Napoleonic war.

Antoine had been bayoneted and in those days they had the swords at the end of the guns, didn't they?'

B. 'Yes.'

J. 'And when I go, 'Oh!', it's when Antoine is re-living his own death. When people don't pass over, they often keep re-living their death and that is how when you help with rescue, you're able to work out who or what it is you're dealing with as you are privy to the details surrounding their death.

So with Antoine, his fear or whatever reasons he had, prevented him from passing over and returning with whoever originally came to take him home. He therefore stayed in his negative thought pattern re-living his death surrounded by the others on the battle field which I was able to see clairvoyantly.

And I could see the colours of the uniforms, the blue and the red and the cream, you know, I can remember it now. And do you remember what I explained to you, when you can remember something so vividly years later, that that is the hallmark of a true spiritual experience because our own memory fades.

So if you can remember things, like I'm sure both of you have had experiences whilst you've been working with me that you can recall even now and you can remember everything about it?'

G. & B. 'Yes.'

J. 'And that is a hallmark of a true spiritual experience because, during that experience, you're in a frequency, a dimension which is rarefied and refined. It's like the reality rather than where we live here which is the shadow, are you with me?'

G. & B. 'Yes.'

J. 'So as you can see, his wife came for him but it took a while, it took quite a while. So I've started off quite aptly, I think, with an example of a rescue so that at least you've been 'there' and witnessed it. Have you got any questions?'

G. 'Two! Where is this 'in-between' place, you have the astral plane?'

J. 'That is it! It's the next level after earth. The next level after earth is very much like the earth plane and just as I explained to you about the different bodies which we have, so equally we have the different dimensions in spirit. The next dimension after the earth plane is known as the astral plane.'

G. 'Are there any levels within the astral plane?'

J. 'I don't know. I have no idea, no idea whatsoever. It's a good question!'

G. 'Also, and I'm sure there's a very good and reasonable explanation, he, Antoine, would have been at the time that the event happened, speaking, I would think?'

J. 'Yes and no! *"There is no such thing as time in spirit"* but Antoine still thinks it's the present.'

G. 'But it is given to you in a way that can be understood by all?'

J. 'Yes.'

G. 'And how does that occur?'

J. 'Because if you want to help someone, you have to deal and manage with the tools that you have.'

You might as well know, that there are lots of rescues where one doesn't have a clue what I am saying. I am speaking foreign languages and the person helping me with the rescue cannot understand what I'm saying either but I will understand them and I will nod or shake my head or something and the job will eventually get done.

It's like where there's a will, there's a way, yes? And don't forget that we mediums are only half of the help - our spirit guides do the rest.'

G. 'Right, yes.'

J. 'This particular rescue, I was obviously ready to do it which is why spirit gave it to me, *"Like attracts Like."* It was always supposed to be done in the circle - I was in a lovely circle for a long time - so the people there were true spiritual servants.

Also, Antoine can't be helped until he's ready - until he asks for help - so he will remain in his negative thought pattern and, don't forget that, *"There's no such thing as time in spirit..."* so even though we're talking about the eighteen hundreds or whatever, the Napoleonic wars, it....'

G. 'It was like yesterday.'

J. 'Yes, in a way. Antoine didn't know how long it had been and he probably thought the war was still going on - his mind will dictate everything. So this morning I will teach you how we identify what year we're dealing with because sometimes, you will have a person talking and you haven't got a clue who they are, where they're from and you have to learn how to ask the right questions in order to help them.

So this is what the training is all about, OK? The more examples you have, the more you will begin to understand what serving as a rescue medium means, yes?'

G.& B. 'Yes.'

J. 'It is as natural as any other service, being a nurse or being a teacher, it's just learning how things are done. Not only learning but more importantly, understanding, because when you speak from strength, you then find the tasks much easier but we're just beginning today.

There's no deadline. I'm opening it all up today. I'm going to teach you, explain what I mean, give you examples, and later when you do the role play and read the 'rescues', you'll take on the mantle of those people yourself so you really start to get underneath it. Is that OK?'

G. & B. 'Yes.'

J. 'So this first paper is called 'Rescue Mediumship' and even though I'm going to read it to you, I'm also going to give you your own copies to follow in case you want to make some notes whilst I'm talking.'

G.& B. 'Thank you.'

J. 'One other thing, I just want to remind you that these are my original course notes I wrote with spirit's help years and years ago, so some of the content might not be applicable to you but it won't affect the teaching of it.'

Rescue Mediumship

Jenny: 'I would like to give you some general information on rescue work which will either reinforce what you may have already heard or be new material but whatever the case is, this will provide you with a broader picture before we start the actual training.

When we first started this 'development' course, I told you that everything we were going to be doing came down to one thing; 'the relationship'. The relationship you were going to forge with your guides and with those who walk with you. I said it was a partnership, I said it was teamwork.

Nowhere is this teamwork more defined or more important than when helping with rescue mediumship. Spirit call it 'teaching' for that is what is being done. Teaching the ignorant, showing them there is a better way and bringing them across, out of the darkness of our world where they are trapped and into the world of spirit where they can be taught and helped and allowed to progress.

Rescue work takes many different forms. Sometimes we do not need a medium to help. If there has been a disaster such an air crash or a ship sinking or a train crash or even an earth quake, spirit would have been privy to the incident before it happened so they move in their multitudes for there are a great many souls in the spirit world who do this work.

They manifest in a manner in which the people who have suddenly passed away can recognise and relate to. For example, they will arrive as nurses or nuns, as ministers or as members of the Salvation Army but it will be somebody appertaining to their era in whose presence they will instantly feel reassured, feel calm and at peace in the knowledge that help is now at hand. Whatever happens, it will be someone with whom the sorrowing and the troubled can identify and respond.

Now, I want to give you an example which is also a true example. You will, of course remember what happened on September 11? Not knowing how I could possibly help, that evening I sat and attuned - I believe this is relayed in *'A Medium's Tale'* - and I got two things from that sitting.

First of all, I found myself looking at part of a large aeroplane. One of the wings was right up close to my face. It was as though I was Pinnochio and had grown a wing for a nose. I didn't see the whole plane, just the wing and surrounding the whole of the wing, were people clinging on with their hands. Their bodies were dangling down as though all their fingers were stuck to the wing whilst in flight.......... and everyone was smiling.

From that one attunement, it was if I was being shown and reassured by spirit that all these people from that awful day, were going home and because these people were smiling, they knew they were going to be alright, they knew they were being helped and all would be well. Do you understand?'

Grace & Bobbie: 'Yes, yes.'

J. 'It was symbolic, whether I was helping them in my attunement it didn't matter, this is what I was given and I was glad, it was my proof.

Now straight after that I found myself in an office, high up in one of the towers and I saw a man busy working on his computer despite what was happening all around him. I remember watching this man typing when suddenly, a fireman came through a door running and shouted, 'Get the hell out of here!' and the employee said something like, 'I'm just finishing, I'm nearly finished' or words to that effect. (Grace and Bobbie are both laughing).

And, you know, this fireman was really cross, re-enforcing just how serious the situation was. So this, to me, was another message from spirit. This man had already died but the way spirit chose to help him was in the guise of a fireman, which, of course, adds up because the whole tower was on fire, so again, do you see what I mean?

It re-enforces this paragraph when I talk about spirit arriving in different guises? Do you remember the Potters Bar rail crash? There was a big train crash at Potters Bar station. Now I think seven people died in that crash and I was told then that spirit came as Salvation Army or something similar but it's the same, because when you have an accident, it's not a normal passing is it?

When you're nearing your time, you remember in the last papers I read when I talk about the aura - the aura fades, it turns to grey and disappears completely just before a passing - so spirit know way in advance when you're going to die, when you're coming home. Do you remember the saying, *"You may weep but we rejoice, a friend is coming home?"*

B. 'Yes.'

J. 'Again, in *'A Medium's Tale'*, I talk about being shown what was happening in spirit whilst I was on the phone to a medium friend of mine. She was crying as her best friend was really ill with cancer in hospital and whilst I was on the phone, I was shown a white road lined with people and children were walking down the middle of the road scattering rose petals from their bowls or baskets. Spirit was, in essence, taking an opportunity to tell me that, actually, we're already getting ready for her return!

So just like people are born in all different circumstances, people pass in all different circumstances too. Each pregnancy is different, I mean this is the uniqueness which is us so we don't all 'go home' the same way.

A couple of years ago there was a friend of mine whose mother-in-law had recently died and she was in a wheelchair and I was on my computer and thinking about this lady when suddenly spirit showed me how she passed!

She was in a field sitting in her wheelchair and there was a thin stream running right across in front of her with a short, narrow wooden plank to aid people across to the other side. I saw an elderly lady standing on the other side of this stream and I saw the mother-in-law get up from her wheelchair and walk across the narrow wooden plank to her mother! So that was how that woman passed over! Do you understand?'

G. & B. 'Yes.'

J. 'It can be any situation. You know, I've even heard of a farmer's cow coming for him! (Grace & Bobbie chuckle). Because this was his favourite cow and that was just what he wanted, it was his nearest and dearest. So this is what I mean, it can be anything and everything so when we help with rescue, this is how broad based it can be. This is not something where I can say, this is what happens because each one is unique.

So the more I teach you today, the more examples I give you, the more you will understand. When people have not 'died' in a 'natural' way, maybe they've died in an accident, in an earthquake or one of these awful things, spirit know in advance that this is going to happen and they bring in all their rescue re-enforcements, an army of people, and because I've already explained to you the thought principle - *"As you think, so you are"* - spirit can 'turn' themselves into a Salvation Army worker in full regalia or the Red Cross just by thinking; all you have to do is *think it*, and you *are it!*

You often hear or read, 'An angel came.' An angel can be anybody! They don't need to have wings to be an angel.'

G. 'That's right.'

J. 'So when someone passes over suddenly through a great trauma, they are confused, even those who have an understanding and a knowledge of an afterlife. You know if you were to suddenly bump your head or be knocked over, you can be confused or lose consciousness for a while, the same applies to people coming round in spirit. They too can be equally confused.

It would be spirit's job to help these people across so they are met. They are never on their own, they are not left to find their own way but brought lovingly to the light and into spirit by those who do this work. I think you understand this now?'

G. & B. 'Yes.'

J. 'However, it is not always possible to reach everyone. You know that you can get into a negative frame of mind and you also know that when you become negative, that is when your spirit guides have great difficulty getting through to you.

It's as though you've built a wall around yourself and you're not allowing help to get through because negativity is real, it's not just a word! It's an energy which takes shape and form and nowhere will you learn this more than when you do rescue. You will learn exactly what negativity means, OK?

How often do you hear people ask, 'Where is God when I need him? Where is spirit when I'm down? Why don't they help me when I'm crying?' Because, you have wrapped yourself in *so* much negativity, you can't even hear them and you can't see them either and spirit cannot get through until there is a chink in that negative armour which now surrounds you.

A cry for help; then spirit can push, they can come in. Your guides can then chip away at the negativity but it is still very difficult for negativity is like a thick, high wall. So, that's where the trust comes in,

I teach you to trust.

You know, when I'm having my own problems, I don't want to build up negativity around me to stop the good happening. I want to say, 'Come on in, all ye positives!' (Grace and Bobbie are laughing).

So I turn that negative thought into trust. You never know, I may end up better off than when I started? Whatever works for you, but don't build the negative around you because you're shooting yourself in the foot, you're not allowing the people who love you to help you, OK?

So there are many people who die in such a frame of mind. People who commit suicide, for example, you really cannot get more negative than that. Then there are people who have had an accident but who had been depressed or miserable before that accident. They, in turn, wake to a spiritual consciousness in a negative frame of mind.

Their thought pattern is steeped in negativity. They cannot hear spirit calling, they cannot see spirit coming. The light which spirit bring actually frightens them and they run away. In this situation spirit need a medium. You will remember I said that if spirit manifested in all their Light, it would actually hurt and harm the deceased person - the light would blind them.

Do you remember I made a comparison with the Bible story of Paul on the way to Damascus where he was stopped by a blinding light, a spiritual Light but he was physically blinded by it as it was so highly evolved?

In the same way, when spirit draw close to those who are ignorant, who have wrapped themselves in negativity or who are ignorant of the afterlife - maybe those who have walked an earthly road steeped in crime and darkness with all the negative emotions of hatred, bitterness and vengeance - it is difficult to draw close without frightening or hurting them.

Spirit then need a transformer, they need a medium, they need somebody who is strong enough to trust, that in the service they are giving, they are protected, and one thing you will learn when doing rescue work, spirit always promise - NOT A HAIR ON YOUR HEAD WILL BE HARMED - and after working with spirit for all this time, I can also give you this assurance.

If you say, right, I want to help, you will have loads of protection. I have never, ever been harmed, I have been doing this for years and what they say is true so there's nothing to be personally frightened about. All the protection is given. So in this manner spirit and the medium can work together to help a soul who is lost return to the realm of spirit.

But the relationships which you two have been building with your spirit guides whilst with me are also the building blocks to do other spiritual work, not just rescue. This is why you need to know them, you need to trust them, you need to have that wonderful, loving relationship with them because if you want to serve, you will in your own way. There is so much work to do that spirit are crying out for people who want to help.

There are many different ways of working as a rescue medium. Some work merely by hearing and seeing and talking to the entity or the lost soul and by moving him or her across.

Some mediums take the spirit entity within them - within their aura - and a physical partner talks to the lost soul and explains to them where they are, what has happened, bringing them to an understanding that they are 'dead'. We have had an example of something like that on the recording earlier on.

When people exist on the astral plane, they don't even realise they have died, they think they are still living. There is nothing to tell them otherwise as everything seems the same, remember, the astral plane is similar to the earth plane.

What is so frustrating is that no-one will give them the time of day because these 'dead' spirits want to talk to people and get themselves known and heard and that is why a lot of the spirit souls who need help often disturb people in houses because how else are they going to be helped unless they make a fuss?'

G. & B. 'Yes.'

J. 'A lot of people have said to me in the past, why do they have to do this *so hard* or *so loud*? And I always reply, because if they didn't, you wouldn't take any real notice, would you? You would just carry on with what you were doing. Eventually, it will become, 'You are *not* listening to me - knock, knock, knock - I'm here!' Hopefully, you will discuss this with somebody and eventually the situation will find its way to the ears of a medium like you or me to help. Do you understand?'

G. & B. 'Yes.'

J. 'Spirit then bring relations, friends, people the lost soul has known. In this way, the spirit entity is encouraged to move across and he or she moves across in love and is cared for both by spirit and by the spiritual members of their family or spiritual friends. That is the lovely side to rescue mediumship as it is so enjoyable to spirit and to us when a soul who is lost finally arrives home.

However, there are other times when spirit need our help because a spirit entity on the astral plane has been causing problems or causing trouble. Now if you remember we said just now that the light of a highly evolved spirit can actually damage or harm an entity especially those on the darker levels. The psychic energy of a medium forms a barrier which allows spirit to retrieve a negative entity from the medium's body and back to spirit.

I said body but what I really mean is the aura for the departed spirit will draw so close to the aura of the working medium that it will often feel as though it is within the physical body itself.

Now both of you have felt yourself 'turning into somebody else', for want of a better phrase, haven't you?'

G. & B. 'Yes.'

J. 'And it sometimes feels as though the dead spirit is actually inside your body but they're not. I often describe this as something very much like an eclipse - it's an eclipse of their energy over your energy. Their energy covering your aura which is so lifelike that you feel that you are turning into somebody else. However, you need to know that although you seem to be taken over, having these different mannerisms, gesticulations, thoughts and feelings, they are *not* in your body. They are just within your aura and as mediums, your sensitivity is so excellent that you can actually feel that person and this is exactly how it should be because how can you help them if you don't know them.

So the lost soul dwells within the aura and not actually within the physical body but this can sometimes be quite challenging, sometimes unpleasant but at *all* times, the medium is always extremely well protected.

This is a warning:- THIS WORK SHOULD NEVER BE ATTEMPTED UNLESS YOUR GUIDES ASK YOU TO DO IT. You don't just trot off and help out if you hear about a haunting. YOU NEED TO WORK WITH GUIDES WHO KNOW WHAT THEY ARE DOING.

If you're going to be working within a rescue capacity, you've been working with dedicated rescue guides for a long time. It will not have been just any spiritual guide. Just like I'm teaching you now, the spirit guides who are helping me have had to learn too, so you're both in the profession, so to speak. Remember, *"Like attracts like!"*

B. 'Oh, right!'

J. 'You would be amazed at how much work is done on spirit's side of life and spiritual guides need to specialise in this type of work too.

FOR EVERYONE'S SAKE. THE PROTECTION YOU NEED IS INCREDIBLE - YOU LITERALLY WALK WHERE ANGELS FEAR TO TREAD.

And this comes back to what I always say at the beginning of the course:- 'When I'm finished with you, your channel is going to be thick and strong, like polished steel - you're going to be *so* strong!'

Now, why do I want you to become strong? Because I want you to progress as much as possible. I want spirit to be able say, 'Right, Bobbie's up for it, Grace's up for it, she's ready now, come on, let's give her this to do!'

And the stronger you are, the more you will be able to help spirit and this strength is built over time and over many experiences. Do you remember I said to you that in the beginning I used to help rescue children and I thought I would just carry on rescuing children. As I progressed, I got stronger and stronger so the people who needed help were more and more in need and their situations were more and more daunting. *"Like attracts like."*

Nowadays, I'm given all the shit, because there ain't many people that can deal with shit! (Grace and Bobbie are both laughing). But also remember, that *"No-one is ever given any more than they can cope with."* So I often get the horrible ones but, you know, OK, someone's got to do it!'

B. '*They* need help.'

J. 'Of course they need help, equally and even more so. And remember, sometimes when you're helping with rescue, you're also helping the person who has been suffering on the earth plane too.

So highly evolved spirit cannot go into the dark without the risk of damage but they *can* transmute the light through a medium and give them all the protection and through that teamwork, they can pull the soul across but if you go in your own strength, you will get into trouble.

So I know you've both had a personal example of rescue; you've both experienced doing a rescue and on both occasions, you had your rescue guides working with you. It was all planned - what they were going to do, the timings - you remember, spirit's time is perfect? '

B. 'Yes.'

J. 'So, it was all written on the wall, so to speak, and your spirit guides knew you'd cope and you probably, without realising it, practiced it and practiced it in your sleep state, yes, until the right time, 'Lights, camera, action; it's going to happen!' (Grace and Bobbie laugh).

Now as you now both probably realise, it is *most* important that you always ask for protection when you work with your guides. So that is why, from day one, I taught you about protection. The first lesson I teach you is all about protection, is it not?'

G. 'Yes it is.'

J. 'And I keep reiterating it and re-enforcing it. Why? Because hopefully, it will become second nature, like brushing your teeth. But, more than anything, it is *most* important that you employ your protection routine when engaged in rescue work because it is not like any other work; it is in a class of its own, and you are always dealing with negativity of some description.

Sometimes, you could be asked to help just a normal person who has lost their way. On another occasion, you could be dealing with something heavier and maybe more sinister, you just don't know but you won't be given a situation unless you're ready to deal with it, unless you have the required strength and ability to help, yes?'

G. & B. 'Yes.'

J. 'If a soul is merely wandering and is very gentle and just troubled, then, yes, you will be able to talk to them and your spiritual helpers will be able to help that soul across.

No-one can tell you how to perform this kind of mediumship. I can give you my experience, my advice and the training to start you off but *you* as a spiritual medium are unique. Your guides know you better than anybody and it is to them that you go for advice and help whenever you need to.

Ignorant souls are not only in buildings, homes or other places, spirit entities also follow people. You as sensitives have a beautiful bright aura. It shines like a Belisha beacon in the darkness of this world. The souls who are lost are often roaming about and wandering in the negative darkness of their world.

When they see your light, it is like a magnet and they are drawn to it hence the importance of closing down. I have not made a big issue of closing down and discipline for nothing.

You could end up with an attachment to your aura and then you *will* have problems. If you work with spirit, if you do as you are told, if you think and work in the positive, if you maintain your disciplines, if your rescue mediumship is in partnership with spirit, then you *will* be protected.

You will know what is required of you from your guides, from your helpers and if you are sensible, you will do it, you will work with them. If they say this is not for you, it needs a more experienced medium, do not tackle it. They do not say these things for fun or to put obstacles on your path or to hinder your progress. They do it because they *know* that at this point in time, you are not ready for that particular task.

If you are to become a rescue medium, if that is your road of mediumship or part of your service of mediumship, always ensure that you ask for protection. Never assume that it will be given automatically. Again, spirit have to abide by the law too. They are not allowed to interfere. You have free will. If you choose to do something in your own strength, your guides cannot come in and take over so always remember you have to ASK for protection. It is *so*, so important.

Rescue mediumship is beautiful as well as rewarding but it is specialised work for both medium and guide.

Finally, you can afford *no* fear for if it is this path you have agreed to tread, you will see many dark, very strange looking things. If you are gifted with clairvoyance, it can be quite frightening to see these things but you cannot afford fear for fear is negative.

A malevolent, ignorant entity is negative. It feeds on negative power. If you are frightened, it will feed on your fear. What is the answer? Some people are afraid of the dark. What is the answer? The answer is to TRUST.

Know your guides, know with whom you work and most importantly, know that above all, they work in the strength of the Great Spirit. It is *His* Power, His Love that flows through them. It is His Power they draw from, no-one else's. Once you are assured of that, you need have no fear because this is the greatest power in *all* the universe; the creative force.

There is nothing greater, nothing more powerful so if your guides stand in His strength, so do you. You know that nothing can harm you. You do not have to think, or hope, or pray, you KNOW and you TRUST. That is the knowledge you must have as a rescue medium.

Once you have gained that understanding, once you have placed that trust with those with whom you work, you can go into the darkest places of the metaphorical hell and *nothing* can touch or harm you.

Are you now ready for the training?'

G. & B. 'Yes!'

J. 'There was quite a lot in that paper?'

G. 'Yes, there was.'

J. 'But rescue is no small thing. That is why you need a separate day to start learning about it. It's 'meaty', it's challenging but it's also very logical and sensible and easy to understand once you have all the pieces in place. Then, when you really understand it, you think, I can do this because it's no longer daunting, it's the most natural thing to do - to help.

It's just like helping someone that's fallen down or helping a blind person cross the road, it's nothing more than serving but in a different way which I find really intriguing. I think people who do this sort of work are kind of special because it's not everybody's cup of tea. It's like a specialised job, you need to train and learn it as well has having the ability to carry out the tasks involved. It's not your usual run of the mill job.

The fact that you're doing such a great service and if you think, if the boot was on the other foot and *you* were trapped in the darkness or trapped in your own negative thought pattern or suddenly realised, I don't want to be here, I want to go home, I want to be with my loved ones, wouldn't you want to be helped by someone?'

G. & B. 'Yes.'

J. 'So you've got that incentive, that motivation and it's a selfless thing but it's also a loving thing. So yes, you know, you need to have your wits about you but eventually, the fact that you want to help and the fact that you love, overrides all your apprehensions because you work in that positive love and you say, 'OK, let's do it!'

Right, so is there anything you want to say or shall we continue with the training now?'

(Grace recalls what happened recently when she, her daughter and her granddaughter, Amy, visited a local M&S cafe.)

Apparently, the family chose a corner table at the very back of the room and Amy was put in the corner against the wall next to Grace. After a little while, Amy became extremely restless and uncomfortable and made a point that she wanted to leave the table. So seeing this, Grace eventually suggested that she go and join her mother in the queue for food.

Upon returning with her mother with a tray of food, Amy was still not happy and refused to go back to her seat in the corner only becoming more settled once they had left the cafe.

G. 'Jenny, she wasn't being naughty, just very uneasy. She became more herself once we had left.'

J. 'What I have often found is that people who have an interest in the spiritual and have wanted to learn more, some of these people often have in their family, children or grandchildren who they now realise *also* have a sensitivity or psychic ability.

To me, this is not a co-incidence, because there's no such thing as co-incidence, there's no such thing as a mistake, it's because *they,* the older family members, are meant to be there for the younger ones, yes?'

G. 'Yes.'

J. 'You don't say anything, you just carry on with your lives but there is a 'strand' of you that is reserved for that special part of them. There is a latent connectedness that you have with them and you may never speak about it or suddenly, in the future, things may happen and you will be there for them - someone they trust who they can talk to about this part of themselves. It is up to you to decide how to help them or pacify them or soothe them or share with them or to support them.

Also, I've always thought that a grandparent/grandchild relationship is *very* special. I've always been very conscious of my feelings about this, it's like no other. As you know, we all have different relationships with different people in our lives and strangely enough, I haven't even experienced this for myself. Once again, it's just a theory of mine.

Sometimes a child will confide in a grandparent; 'Don't let mummy know, don't tell daddy' because they sense that you're on their side, they sense that grandma will know what I mean, yes, and I believe it's a special relationship that is always meant to exist.

So I'm not surprised that you had an experience with your granddaughter because, in a way, it's almost like the beginning. It's like you've identified something and you'll just keep it under your hat, it's not going any further. It's just something you've noticed and you think, umm, very interesting!'

G. 'Yes.'

J. 'You're just going to 'watch this space' so to speak but it's like a warm feeling that you know she's going to be fine, as long as I'm alive, she's going to be fine because I'm going to be there for her should she ever need to speak to me about the 'spiritual' or should she have another experience, which needs your support in the future.'

G. 'We've had a couple before this which is probably why I took a second look but ooh, two months ago, perhaps a little bit longer, I went there, her mother said, 'Amy has a question for you grandma.' And I said, 'What's that?' 'Grandma, what are angels?'

J. 'Yes, so it's started hasn't it?'

G. 'Yes.'

J. 'But when you told the story about what happened in the cafe at M&S and the rescue?'

G. 'It wasn't even a rescue but it was just something that I thought, just a minute, there's more to this, there is more and it was so simple to make it right.'

J. 'Yes, but I'm getting that there *is* a lost soul in M&S!'

G. 'Possibly, I hadn't thought!'

J. 'Corner - when you mentioned that, well, that is what I got straight away and I thought it was what you meant actually because often a medium will retrieve someone hiding in a corner?'

G. 'No, it didn't occur to me!'

J. 'I think that Amy was probably 'picking up' something which may have been a lost soul?'

G. 'She didn't like it!'

J. 'I'm sure she didn't. He or she is sitting or waiting in the corner waiting for their cup of tea or whatever and they haven't gone 'home' yet and that's it, end of story but they will eventually, something will happen.'

G. 'Well I am hoping that when I said, 'Go to your mummy.' I'm hoping that perhaps the lost soul also went home.'

J. 'I don't know whether it could be done that easily but you just don't know. Spirit may have seized the opportunity there and then, anything is possible. However, I think the important thing here was that Amy started to feel better, yes?'

G. 'Yes, well a lesson learned.'

J. 'Yes! It was also a good experience for you wasn't it?'

G. 'Oh yes! I will always think now you've told me that.'

J. 'When you visit a house or a pub for instance, you can almost feel the 'corners' sometimes?'

B. 'Yes.'

G. 'Because energy doesn't move in a corner.'

J. 'Exactly, it's just like you would imagine, a corner is where it collects!'

B. 'It's funny isn't it because I've always wanted to live in a 'round' house!'

J. 'Yes, I know someone else who's always wanted that too.'

B. 'I would love to live in a lighthouse. I just think there's something about them, no corners!'

J. 'OK, so now we're going to go on to our next piece which is called Rescue Mediumship Training and once again, I'll give you this paper so you can make a note of anything whilst I'm reading it.'

Rescue Mediumship: Training

Jenny: 'Rescue mediumship, what is it?

* It is when someone agrees, consciously or sub-consciously to be used to help those who have 'died' - passed over - to the other side, to spirit world.

* To help those who have been dwelling on the astral plane who are now ready to pass over to the other side.

* To help those discarnate beings - spirits - who have attached themselves to someone incarnate, someone on the earth plane, who now need to be led to the other side thereby freeing both the earthbound spirit and the discarnate being from this attachment.

Do you understand?'

Grace & Bobbie: 'Yes.'

J. 'There are also possessions which are more serious - when a 'dead' spirit has now taken over the thinking and mechanics of a human on the earth plane - but this involves additional and more specific handling and is not what I teach or usually get involved with either.'

G. 'Is that a separate thing altogether because I can see where there could very possibly be, in ignorance, a lot of damage done?'

J. 'Oh indeed but you hope to stop this before it goes any further. With a possession, it is normally so serious that it completely takes over somebody and I don't think we're ready to talk about this at the moment, I think we should deal with the business in hand.

Rescue is a service you are rendering. It is an exclusive form of mediumship, not performed by a great many mediums. In the orthodox church, something like this would be called exorcism - freeing evil spirits - but as I have said before, I have been taught that there is no such thing as evil, only ignorance.

There is no point, in my mind, training you on how to help with rescue until you understand what you are doing and why you are doing it.

So Bobbie, why do you think you would like to do this kind of work?'

B. 'It must be awful for these souls to be stuck, it is so sad so if I could help them to go back to where they're supposed to be.'

J. 'Good! Grace?'

G. 'I cannot think of anything worse than re-living something over and over again and not understanding why this was happening to you and just waiting for a sign, a hand, anyone to say, 'Do you trust me? I can help you. Do you trust me? I will help you.'

J. 'Thank you. The souls you will be helping home could really be anywhere - land or sea. They could be in and around a home, a workplace, a public place or anywhere else but always on the astral plane; even those who have long been buried.

When I say it could be any of those things, I mean that if people need help and they are re-living their situation when they died, re-living their death, they could be *anywhere*, couldn't they?'

G. & B. 'Yes.'

J. 'So they could be in the water, up a mountain, they could be right there in their home and they haven't budged and they ain't gonna budge!'

B. 'No!' (Bobbie is laughing).

J. 'They could be in a person's house, someone who is very similar to them; a depressant, an alcoholic, a drug user and they have found comfort by just being near them. 'Hey, gimme one of them, will you?' They can be in pubs because they want a drink - can you imagine how many lost souls are in pubs?'

B. 'Yes, jam-packed, I expect!'

J. 'Lining up at the bar; 'What about *me!* What about *me!*'

B. 'Why doesn't he listen to *me*, I want one!'

J. 'So, yes:-

   * They have either never left the place where they 'died' having been stuck in their negative thought pattern and have therefore not passed over.

   * Perhaps they have been wandering and stayed near to someone's bright light for comfort, familiarity, company, subsistence in order to feed their addiction to drink, drugs, money, insecurity, etc.

   * Or they may have actually cried out and sent their pleading thoughts for help. Spirit will find the right situation where they can be taken to the other side often with the help of a spiritual medium.

Do you remember I talked a bit earlier about people getting disturbed in their homes by all sorts of things? They could be woken up in their sleep perhaps. They then tell somebody about it because the experience was quite daunting, quite alarming. That begins a chain of events - similar to 'Chinese whispers' - where someone tells someone else, who in turn tells someone and, eventually, it finds its way to the ears of someone who knows a medium.

As I have explained, people can remain on the astral plane for as long as they don't want help. They don't go home and they stay where they are until suddenly they think, 'Do you know what, I don't really want to be here anymore!' or whatever the reason is.

They may cry out for help or they may want their mummy, whatever it is and it is at *that* moment when spirit will start to organise the 'rescue'. How this is done, how they organise it, can take any shape or form.

One of the ways this process of help begins is with somebody being annoyed and telling their friend who then tells their friend who then decides, actually, I think I should tell Flossy because Flossy goes to a spiritualist church and it goes on and on until it reaches somebody like us but spirit will always find a way to help.

As I reflect in *'A Medium's Tale'* and, as you *now* know yourself Grace, a lot of the places I've stayed in for a holiday, the first night is always a 'work' night! (Grace and Bobbie laugh). Spirit will know, 'Because Jenny will be there! Grace is staying the night there! Alright, we'll do that one then!' (Bobbie is in fits of laughter).

It may sound funny but, *"Spirit are great opportunists"* - they will *never* miss an opportunity and you can imagine how many people haven't passed over? You know, there's work every day and every night so yes, let's get a few more done.

Everyone is allowed home even the most wretched. All they have to do is say, 'Help me' and they can take the first step back. OK.

Being Used For The Purpose Of Rescue

You may already have started to be 'used' for rescue, perhaps in your sleep state, do you think this has happened to you? Can you both give me one example when you think you've helped with a rescue? Bobbie, I think you've done one recently?'

B. 'Yes, the old lady.'

J. 'So, for Grace's benefit, can you explain, was it in an attunement?'

B. 'Yes.'

J. 'And you just went with it and realised, after a while, what was happening?'

B. 'Yes, I just went with it. She needed help and I asked, could I help her and eventually her granddaughter came and took her back home with her.'

J. 'So, you've now actually been involved and I was *so* delighted for you. You were just sitting there minding your own business and suddenly you were turning into that old lady, weren't you?'

B. 'Yes, she came with such anger, resentment and self-pity and I could feel all the things she was feeling.'

J. 'Amazing, wonderful!'

B. 'It was very sad really.'

J. 'Yes, but you did it! You realised what was happening which was the best part, you didn't just go 'DOH!' and ignore it or close down with fright? (Bobbie laughs). You realised what was happening, you took control and started asking her whether you could help her which was brilliant. You saw it through and finished the rescue waiting until someone came for her. Absolutely brilliant, well done!

Now for Bobbie's benefit, let's hear your recent experience Grace. Little précis please as it's very long.'

G. 'I'll make it short. We had an evening at a hotel just before Xmas and there was a dinner so we chose to stay overnight and when we'd gone up there originally to take our bags, I could smell cigarette smoke and because they're non-smoking now - all of them - I couldn't understand why so I opened the window.

It was still daylight so I looked out of the window to the back and there's a little wooden shed right in the bottom corner where the staff go for a cigarette.

There had been a young man, probably in his late thirties, who had been a diabetic, had various things wrong with him who was the barman there and we had talked over the years about him getting treatment, but he died.

After dinner, we came back upstairs, got into bed but it got colder and colder, my feet were so cold. I had never been so cold; I thought I was in a wet bath! So I put my socks and clothes on but felt no better and I'm lying there thinking what on earth's going on?

It's now the early hours and I could hear feet. It was almost like I could see through the walls, all these people trampling down outside the door and, at the front, was this young man.'

B. 'Oh right!'

G. 'So they would go down, round the corner and then I would hear the feet and they were going by again. So, clairvoyantly, I went out, through the wall, through the door, just slipped out as they came by and I said, 'Where are you all going?' Nobody seemed to know and there were some children, grown-ups and the children had mob caps on; they came from a much older time.

I just said, 'Do you know me, do you trust me?' 'Yes, I trust you Grace.' And I said, 'Well, you have to find the light.' So off we go and I'll just cut it short. At the end of this particular corridor where the steps came upstairs, was a big mirror and I *knew*, just in the top corner, was the light and I was saying, keep watching, keep walking, I can't go all the way with you and he went and they all followed him through the mirror.'

B. 'Oh, lovely!'

G. 'So I thought I'll just nip round and make sure there was no-one there and there were a couple of children left!'

B. 'Aaagh!'

G. 'So, I took their hands and we walked round the corner and they went too!'

J. 'So now *both* of you have had an experience of rescue; your own kind. Maybe not your very first one Grace as you had that gentleman with the snake neck remember, but now you're each going to build on your own rescue experiences.'

G. 'And they're all so different, absolutely poles apart!'

J. 'Yes, they are, and they'll carry on being like that. As rescue mediums, I believe we start off by helping children and as our experience, knowledge and understanding grows so we move on to adults, but I may be wrong.

What Happens When We Are Being Used For Rescue?

The spirit entity or lost soul draws close and/or enters the medium's channel or aura before being transported back to spirit realms.

The 'passing' spirit is now contained within the medium's aura which acts like a designated 'half-way house' as well as a safe haven for all concerned. The medium will have asked for protection and will work with their spirit guides 'performing' the rescue until the lost soul is met by someone and taken 'home' - even if it is by their favourite animal or pet.

What Happens With Rescue In A Circle?

We need the help of two mediums when performing a rescue in a circle:-

* Someone whose channel can be used for the 'teleportation', whose aura is strong enough to accommodate the lost soul. The medium will often take on the personality and mannerisms of the passing spirit as they draw nearer and enter the medium's aura or channel.

* Another medium is needed to verbally offer guidance and help ensuring the spirit a safe passage home.

And in the audio tape I played you earlier, you have that example; of one medium doing one job and one doing the other.'

G. & B. 'Yes.'

J. 'I must confess that I don't know which role is the more trying. I think the person who 'does the talking' has probably the hardest job but we'll talk about that later. I think the medium who takes the lost soul within their aura may have the easier task as they just need to go with it and co-operate with the help given.

The medium who is coaxing the lost soul home has the hardest job because they have to work out and deal with so many anomalies:- Who is this person, where are they and why are they there? Is this a man, a woman, when is all this taking place, how can I help them? So many questions!

This is why you need the training because you need to understand all the different things you need to ask in order to help, so, yes, I think it's easier just sitting there being able to 'perform', like you did with the old lady, Bobbie?'

B. 'Yes.'

J. 'And after a while, this role could become more like a second skin. Oh, here it comes, another one's coming through and you just wait to see who it is this time and what's going to come out of your mouth!

Let Us Go Through A Typical Rescue 'Scenario'

We're now in a circle and let's just say that you two lovely ladies decide to meet once a month for an hour to do this work, OK?'

G. & B. 'Yes.'

J. 'So what we're going to do now is go through what would happen if you two did work together. A circle - two people is adequate - you don't need loads of people, certainly not to do this type of work.

The circle will be in attunement with one sitter being watchman, that is, staying awake and watching over the other. Eventually the watchman is aware of unsettlement which gradually increases. The audio tape - if wanted - is switched on to 'record'.

If we go back to the recording you listened to earlier, there were six or seven of us in the room in that circle. The moment one of us made a noise, the watchman switched on the tape to record what was about to happen.

The medium being used as a 'channel' has gone into trance because you can't do this work without it affecting your senses in some way. However, each medium's working relationship with their guides is different so it goes without saying that each medium's trance state may also differ.

There are many levels of trance. I personally don't agree with people going into full trance; I think this is dangerous. I actually like to work with my guides and know what I'm doing. I like to *know* that I'm doing a rescue. I realise that I can't 'get out' of my trance state but I *know* what I'm doing and I *know* when it's finished and that I'll 'come back' to being me again.'

B. 'Yes, you like to lead*?'*

J. 'Everyone has their own opinion on this but this is just mine.'

G. 'I don't think I'd like to go off and not know what I'm doing.'

J. 'OK, so we both feel the same but some people profess that the 'best' ones are the ones who go out into complete trance but I really don't think it matters. I don't think you're graded, I think it's the work you do which counts.'

B. 'As long as you're accomplished at that.'

J. 'Exactly! As long as you do your disciplines and work with protection. It doesn't matter whether you're 'asleep' or 'half asleep' or not asleep at all! So to recap, I'm just saying that the medium has gone into trance and when I say trance, it's their level of trance, OK.

You will definitely feel a change in yourself. For example, this can feel like a shot of anaesthetic, like you are going numb or your heart chakra will starting throbbing. Your stomach may feel queasy or your head will ache in a certain place and any of these feelings may affect different parts of your body.

You may feel a certain energy rise through your feet and up your legs or your limbs or hands may get pins and needles, however, at the same time, you are also aware of activity going on elsewhere. So you may feel lots of different things often at the same time.

Do you remember what happens when you astral travel? You feel fixed to the bed or the chair but suddenly, you're going off somewhere but you know that you're in your bed or the chair but you can't get up and move because you're just going with what's happening. So it's like a two-way energy. Your mind is telling you that you're in your chair at home but it's also saying someone needs my help and I have to trust that this is the way it will affect me.

It's quite incredible really. Don't ask me how spirit do it because I don't know!

At the same time you start to feel this change; your clairvoyance will often begin to roll - this *may* happen. Again, it all depends on your training and ability working with your guides - they use the strengths you have, yes?

You, Bobbie, are very much a clairsentient person, you sense a lot but you also see and hear as well. Grace, you can equally see, hear and sense but your 'sense' Bobbie is particularly strong but you have your other senses to go with it.'

B. 'As a back-up.'

J. 'Whereas with you Grace, you seem to have an equal proportion of strengths meaning all your senses seem to be just as good as each other. I don't think there is one predominant sense except, of course, your 'art' sense, if I may call it that, which is amazing and very strong but your proportions are different to Bobbie's, do you understand what I'm saying?'

G. 'Yes.'

J. 'It's like a pie and the way it's divided up and having got to know both of you, I find it fascinating seeing and understanding how you're working. I'm being taught as well by the examples you give me so I'm the lucky one here!

So your clairvoyance will often begin to roll as you start to watch the pictures being shown to you which will lead to the events, time and place where the lost soul has been waiting in their negative thought pattern.

So often you're given a clue where you are by what you see. You may even get to understand more - like Grace did when she saw the children wearing mob caps - she knew immediately *who* they were *when* they were living.

Hats are one of the *best* ways to tell you who you've got in front of you; I'm a *great* hat girl!' (Bobbie laughs). A lot of the people whom I've helped have worn hats and it tells you so much because with clairvoyance, their clothes tell you so much - they are big informants. For example, are they regal or are they peasant, what age in history is this? So clothes tell you *so* much.

So when you have the clairvoyance like I did with Antoine for example; this is a cart, I've seen this kind of cart in history books and it's got dead bodies on it. This is a war and I recognise the military uniforms and I know I'm not in England and this isn't twentieth century either, etc. etc. Do you understand what I'm saying?'

G. & B. 'Yes.'

J. 'And then - Napoleon's *hat* - what a give-away that was! (Grace and Bobbie are both laughing). As the 'channel' medium, you are able to work out where you are and often *who* you are.

Sometimes you will have a sensation in the stomach, again, it may be anywhere, but this sensation will really prove that you are being effective in what you are doing, so you should be pleased about this. So when you have a sensation, instead of being afraid, you should be pleased!

It's like what I said to you Bobbie about wearing the magnet for your arthritis. Remember I explained that after putting the magnet on, you may get a reaction happening to your body. Don't think this is a bad thing, it's the magnet trying to work out where it has to go and what it has to do.

The feelings or sensations you're getting tell you the magnet is working and should be regarded as positive! Well, with rescue, it's exactly the same.

You might experience an ache or a dull sensation. It may be a sharp pain but that is all part of you being overshadowed and recognising what this lost soul was feeling; their pain, their handicap. You might not be able to feel your legs - they might not *have* any legs - which is exactly why you can't feel anything yourself! Do you see?'

G. & B. 'Yes.'

J. 'You get the clairvoyance and then you get the clairsentience - what they are feeling - so a picture is building up. You may start to weep or groan or moan or say things. Suddenly, sounds or words start to come out of your mouth and you may not have any warning that this is going to happen.

You may suddenly be talking or crying and again, this eclipsing of their aura over yours as you are *becoming* that person and experience some of the feelings they had when or before they died. You are now beginning to understand what they went through or what situation they found themselves in.

Everything is thought, isn't it?'

G. & B. 'Yes.'

J. 'So what *they're* thinking and feeling is transposed to what *you* are now thinking and feeling, however, right now you both need to be reminded that:-

SPIRIT HAS PROMISED THAT ANYONE UNDERTAKING THIS SERVICE WILL NOT BE HARMED; 'NOT A HAIR ON YOUR HEAD WILL BE HARMED'.

With the onset of the noise and commotion coming from the 'channel' medium, the other sitter in the circle now knows that a rescue needs to be performed. The 'channel' medium - the one who has taken the negative energy within their aura - realises that they 'have become someone else' as the spirit is now contained within their aura.

So this medium now has a rough idea what is going on from how they are feeling and the pictures which have been shown to them clairvoyantly now settle down to one scene. I remember one of you had this rolling of clairvoyance where you get picture after picture after picture and you think, oh it's this, and then the picture goes away and then another appears and you think no, it's this and then that picture goes away and so it goes on?'

B. 'Oh yes, I had that!'

J. 'And you think, will you just settle down into what picture it's meant to be! It's like showing the whole album, quickly. So, for example, you see a village with a deep well and you think, oh, it's this and then that goes and then you see a forest or a horse - something completely different. This is something I used to have a lot so expect that too, just go with it!

Eventually things will settle but you need to understand what can happen whilst you're in a trance state. Especially you Bobbie, as you've already had this running of pictures and spirit may work with you in a similar way to how they used to work with me, I don't know for sure.

So eventually, the 'channel' medium settles down to one 'screen' as I put it, yes, and things are now taking shape and you might have details about the person who is 'with you'? Whether they're a man or a woman? Whether they're young or old, maybe their age? You may even see *who* they are?

You may now, because you're looking at a 'picture' clairvoyantly, know *where* they are, because you can see it, yes? They may be in a dungeon or in a dark place. They may be down a well or in a forest clearing or on one of those tall ships on the high seas. Whatever your screen is telling you together with what you're feeling, what you're sensing, the rescue picture is building up, isn't it, like painting by numbers?

You will also learn more from the clothes they are are wearing, the places or buildings you can see or even the objects in the picture - even if you're not that well informed in history - you'll be able to guage and have a rough idea what time in history this is taking place or that this is not in modern times. So the questions:-

   * Who, where, how and why have they been stuck..........need to be answered.

With Antoine from the audio tape, for example, 'where' was on the battlefield so that's *where* he was and where his negative thoughts kept returning, stopping him from moving on.

How did they die? Were they murdered, did they drown, were they killed in action, did they die in an accident, were they hung, were they in a fire? After a while, all these things will become apparent.

In a way you see, feel, smell.... everything and you two are both capable of doing that - you've both already done it!

You may start speaking and it is not your voice that's coming out of your mouth but someone else's which *also* tells you something about this person. You may start talking like a cockney! (Bobbie laughs). Or you may sound very 'poash'!

You may come out with garbled nonsense, a foreign language or be crying like a baby or little child but what comes out your mouth is also telling you something, isn't it? It may even conflict with what you're seeing but what comes out of your mouth is the truth.

You may suddenly realise, Oh, it's *not* this, it's *this!* Because remember, you're only looking at your 'screen' and deducing for yourself who you *think* this person is but what's comes out your mouth is proof of who is really with you.

What The 'Talking' Medium Needs To Do

Now, if your role is that of the other medium, the one who is doing the talking and helping this lost soul home, you have a lot of work to do but initially, you have to establish:-

* Who it is who needs help; who needs rescuing?

* Is it a man, a woman or a child?

* What is their name and how old are they?

So this 'talking' medium will need to start asking lots of questions because in order to help someone you don't know, you must also build a trust and bond with them so, in essence, you have to become their best friend, and saviour, almost from the word go.

The suffering soul is not going to talk to you if they don't trust you and they won't allow you to help them if they don't feel you're on their side, OK. So I'm going to teach you how to build that trust because you won't be able to help with rescue unless you understand and can put this into practice.

So, the 'talking' medium needs to establish straight away *who* this is! *Who* is this person talking, crying or groaning? You begin by gently asking them questions about themselves and waiting for the answers - it may take a little while to get these answers.

Once you know a bit more about *who* needs help, you then need to establish:-

* *Where* they are?

They could be anywhere, in a cupboard, in a castle, at the bottom of the ocean - where are they? You can't help someone unless you know *where* they are!

And then the next step and more importantly, you then need to find out:-

    * When they died?

You need to ascertain how long this person has been 'dead'? This is because someone will be coming to take them home and if this lost soul 'died' recently, then some of their family or the people close to them, won't be coming to fetch them as they'll still be living!

It's no use asking a young child, for example, to look through the light for her mummy or daddy if this child only died, say in the sixties, as her parents are probably still alive. Do you understand this?'

G. & B. 'Yes.'

J. 'So one of the most difficult things you will have to do once you have built the confidence and the trust is not put your foot in it - you still have to tread carefully and *always think the situation through*.

So when you finally ask, 'Who would you like to come to take you home?' and they say, 'My mum.' You can't automatically tell them to look through the light for their mum if there's probably no way her mum will be coming!

So you're manoeuvring, treading carefully whilst doing lots and lots of thinking. You may say to yourself, I'm sure of this fact and I'm sure of that fact but I'm still unsure about a couple of other things so maybe I need to ask another question but you must *always* 'play safe'. So you can now see how the 'talking' medium has to work very hard and, added to this is, they don't have the luxury of time either!

So the questions you will be asking yourself are; what do I still need to know, how do I find this out, what question do I now need to ask, how shall I put it, what do I still need to know? You mind is going like the clappers to establish a full picture of this person and their situation - all the pieces of the puzzle - in order to responsibly guide them back home.

And again, you can't ask an intelligent question to a child, can you, so you have to word it to make yourself understood. All this will become natural, the more you do this work, the easier it becomes. That is why we're going to do the role play after this so you get an idea of the sort of things you need to say.

Above all, you need more than anything, to gain:-

    * A rapport with this person in order to find out *all* these things.

You need to befriend them and gain their trust before you can get this information so the first thing you do is learn how to put them at ease. How to calm them down, how to make them realise that you're specifically there to help them even though some of them swear blind that they don't need any help! 'What do you want? Why are you here? Leave me alone!'

Not everyone *wants* to be helped or is going to be easy to help. Some of them are so stubborn but spirit know they have asked for help or are ready to return home.

A Typical Communication By Mediums During A Rescue

Once the 'channel' medium becomes animated in a circle, the 'talking' medium will usually respond by saying:-

* 'Hello! Can you hear me?'

The 'channel' medium who is being eclipsed by the lost soul will not always be able to speak or answer straight away. Sometimes it will take a bit of time to coax them into speaking so the 'talking' medium will often have to repeat the question.

Also, the 'channel' medium will be in a trance-like state so it's not like how we're talking now in the fullness of our own consciousness.'

G. & B. 'No.'

J. 'In other words, you've got two differing levels of consciousness so you have to allow for this. It's like downloading computer material or when a reporter in the UK is talking to someone in Australia for example, you have to allow time for the communication to get through. The 'channel' medium will have to digest the question and then find a way to physically answer, this can take a little while.

So you have these two mediums, one is doing one job and one is doing the other. They have to work together but they will be using different skills when playing their role. Hopefully, if the two of you worked together, you would both be able to perform either role, taking it in turns which role to play.

However, which ever way you decided to do it, the more experience you have, the more you will understand what is needed but you have to begin somewhere and even though you both have already had one or two experiences, I'm now building on that, yes?'

G. & B. 'Yes.'

J. 'You'll be given loads of information today - like building 'rescue boundaries' or sketching the outline - so that you'll think, right, I'm starting to understand. It's like a colander, you'll only retain so much information today.

I'm also going to give you a book to take home and you'll be going over it and over it. Rescue work is not something you can just snap your fingers and get right, that's why it is intense. It takes a lot of effort and even now my guides are saying to me, 'Tell them this, tell them that!'

G. 'I realised that I was trying to do both roles at the same time, therefore, sorry.'

J. 'No, no apologies, you did absolutely the right thing, you were doing it all on your own remember. What we are learning today is how you work with rescue in a circle and this involves two people each taking on a different role. But this is exactly what today is all about? You need to have the experience and to question, that's how we understand things and perfect.'

G. 'It clarifies a lot although I knew it.'

J. 'Each medium will work in their own way with their guides. You don't have a gun to your head to learn this, I'm trying to help you broaden your understanding. So to recap, the person who is doing the talking will usually begin by saying:-

   * 'Hello, can you hear me?'

The 'channel' medium may not be able to answer straight away so the medium who is asking the questions will have to be patient.

If they don't get a response, they should either repeat this question or ask another basic question as, initially, they need to focus on achieving a response as well as an acknowledgement from the 'channel' medium confirming they understand they are being spoken to. They may even end up saying:-

   * 'Can you nod your head if you can hear me?' or 'Can you give me a sign that you understand me?' or 'Don't worry I'm here now, take your time. Can you hear me *now?*' It's almost like you're bringing someone round from a coma, think of it that way, yes?'

G. & B. 'Oh right, yes!'

J. 'It should be natural. They are human and you are human. They are not anything different to you, they're just in a different place to you so you treat them like you would a patient, a friend, whoever.

OK. So the 'talking' medium might then say:-

   * 'Hello! I know you're there.' And then re-assure them by saying, 'I've been waiting for you, I've been waiting to help you.'

This should put the lost spirit completely at ease and will hopefully confirm that this is someone I can trust. Saying, I've been waiting for you is very re-assuring, yes, so now they may continue by asking:-

   * 'Hello, will you talk to me? I've come to help you.' And introduce yourself, you say, 'My name is Bobbie, my name is Grace, can I help you? Don't worry, you're going to be OK, I'm here now. Can you tell me your name?'

So you're gently talking, building the trust whilst trying to get them to respond as you need information about them in order to effect this rescue and help them home.

If they're crying, calm them down. Tell them there's nothing to worry about now. Tell them that they're safe with you. That nothing more can harm them, that nothing more can hurt them.

Now if you're clever, you *could* say:-

 * 'What's the matter?' or 'Why are you crying, tell me?'

This question will hopefully give you the first details you need of *who* they are, perhaps *where* they are and maybe their age. Maybe they'll respond in a little meek voice, 'I'm lost!' and straight away you've found out that this is not an adult, this is a child!'

G. & B. 'Ah, yes.'

J. 'So now you grab that first bit of information and start building - is it a girl or a boy? How old are they? So continue asking more questions which will help you get more details. By asking:-

 * 'What's the matter, why are you crying?' You may get even more details than you hoped for. Whatever they say, this will help you identify more about the person who is crying.

If they haven't told you their name, ask them again and give yours again just to re-enforce that you're on first name terms. Remind them that you're here to help them. Ask them how old they are as you need to communicate with them at their level of understanding. You also to need to work out whether their death was relatively recent, remember their parents may still be living.'

G. & B. 'Yes.'

J. 'If they're a child, you need to speak in very simple, basic terms so, yes, you *need* their age. The spirits coming through will normally be distressed but talk to them as though they were any stranger you met on the street and eventually, by gentle persuasion, they will start answering.

Grab every bit of information you can get and use it to build a picture and ask whatever questions you need in order to ascertain who you have in front of you.

If, for instance, they shout, 'I can't breathe!' Ask them where they are? They may be coughing. Ask them, 'Is it smoke?' They may say, 'I can't move!' They may be stuck, maybe in a hole - ask them, where they are? They may re-live the events leading up to their death again and again but you will get your information from this.

Eventually, you start to get a picture as they become more relaxed in your company so they might even start giving you bits of information as to why they are distressed. Listen to what they are saying, grab the details and respond by asking the relevant questions to find out more and more whilst bringing relief to them at the same time.

If they died in a fire, you can put it out with water. If they are cold, you bring a blanket. If it is dark, you bring a lamp so these responses will become automatic. You will soon remember the tools you can bring to make these people feel a lot more comfortable.

So, once you know they're cold, you respond by saying, 'I'm going to bring you a blanket to make you warm. There, is that's better, I've wrapped it all around you?' whilst stating with confidence, 'You're getting warmer now, aren't you?'

This is the *most* important aspect of rescue because *everthing* is thought. You can talk to them, re-assure them and make their thoughts *real.* You can say, for example, 'I've put the blanket around you. You're much warmer now, *aren't* you? You're a lot warmer now, *aren't* you?' The very *thought* of the blanket and they will feel warm! Remember, *"As you think, so you are."* The *thought* of the blanket makes them warmer!

So, for example, if they died on top of a mountain, they've now got blankets, hot drink, whatever you bring or want to give them to make them feel better - AND THEY WILL! They soon start to change, begin to feel as though they are really being rescued! They start to feel more human, if I can say that! Their trauma is withdrawing.

They may be thirsty so you bring them some water and you can say, 'Here you are, I brought you some water, it's lovely and cold, drink it!' And so mentally they feel themselves being refreshed by the water you have given them because you've told them what it is and so they begin to revive.

It's all thought. *You* have the power, through your words, to overshadow their negative thoughts and feelings and make them forget about their death; they forget they were shot, murdered, drowned, hung - they forget it! They now start to concentrate on the present and the rescue. Are you getting this?'

G. & B. 'Yes.'

J. 'OK. Very often, because the lost soul has been existing on the astral plane in their negativity, they will be:-

    * Cold;   Ask them, 'Are you cold?'

    * In darkness;   Ask them, 'Is it dark where you are?'

Find out *where* they are and what they need; you won't be able to help them unless you know the conditions they are in so ask the right questions. If they're cold, tell them you're going to make things a lot warmer. Also, work with your guides and ask them to send them the warmth they need; a blanket please, a warm fire.

BUT, if they have died in a fire, the *last* thing they want is fire to make them warm. I've made this mistake and that's why I'm mentioning it. Whilst I was learning, I was helping someone and it was dark and I said, 'Oh, I'll bring a nice fire for you.' And they screamed and screamed, 'No! No!' And I suddenly realised, you silly thing, they died in a fire, they've had nothing but fire, so the last thing they want to see is *another* fire!'

G. & B. 'Oh right, yes.'

J. 'It helped me learn and I've never forgotten as it was such a good example. I made a mistake but a very worthwhile mistake so you've got to make sure you don't make things worse! You've got to keep focused on the job in hand.

So, ask them are they getting warmer and if they say yes, say, 'Good!' Keep re-enforcing it. If they are in the dark, tell them you're going to bring a lamp or a torch or whatever you think is needed so they will no longer be in the dark.

Your guides are there so ask them to help you, you're not working on your own, remember. NEVER FORGET you are working with your guides ALL THE TIME and that you are only half of this rescue process - the physical half.

Hopefully, you will get a reply and you will now know their name, how old they are and how they died. If not, ask them more questions.

If you cannot tell what age in history they come from, ask them who is on the throne at the moment? We need this information as someone must come to take them home. I've already mentioned that you need to make sure you suggest an appropriate person will be coming for them. Finding out what century they lived in, when they were born or who was on the throne, will immediately tell you what age they lived in.

Obviously, if they are a small child, you can't ask them big questions like this; they're not going to know who is on the throne!'

G. & B. 'No.'

J. 'But if you're helping an adult, yes, OK? With Antoine, easy-peasy, the Napoleonic war - anyone can come - they'll all be dead by then!

So you now ask them, wouldn't they like to go home? They don't want to stay where they are! Ask them who would they like to see? Tell them someone is going to come and fetch them, so who would they like to come to collect them; to take them home? Once you know who this lost soul is, where they are and how they died, you are now ready to prepare for homecoming. Have you got a question Grace?'

G. 'I have actually. What if they were adopted and had no mummies or anyone, who would be likely to bring them home?'

J. 'This is Grace, she's so amazing, she's always thinking. That is also fine. You might as well know right away, there is someone called Rosa. She is a gypsy - someone who I have worked with in spirit - but she has a responsibility to the children. So she always comes for children who have no mummy or daddy; and she brings children with her too.

So if you have a problem with a child - write this down - there is a lovely lady and she is very pretty and she wears lovely gypsy clothes, you can see her can't you Bobbie?'

B. 'I've drawn her!'

J. 'Oh, gosh! I forgot, so you *have!* So Rosa will come for these children. So, if you ever get stuck with a child with no-one to come for them, think of Rosa and remember to say, 'Now there's a *lovely* lady who's going to come and she will be bringing some children with her for you to play with.' Just be natural, just think what that child would want.'

G. 'I could ask Elsie? I know she is with children. She is in my soul group painting and is with children in the picture.'

J. 'Great! If you think that would work because you're dealing in love, aren't you?'

G. 'Yes, thank you!'

J. 'And it's your thoughts, so if you think of Elsie, Elsie will think of you, that's the way it works.'

G. 'Because she took Iris home when she couldn't find the light.'

J. 'Grace, there are no perimeters, no restrictions. The idea is to do your job, to make it happen. If you think that's the way forward, then do it!'

G. 'You've given me food for thought.'

J. 'OK, but Rosa will *always* come for children.'

G. 'That's nice to know.'

J. 'But also don't forget, that spirit have known and planned each rescue well before it arrives at our door. They already have it in hand by the time we do our bit, so we are the culmination of all their preparations and that again, is re-assurance that when you ask for protection, you are safe and well protected when doing this work. Remember, we can only see to the horizon but spirit see much further on.

OK. So where are we now? Sometimes these lost souls that we've helped don't understand that they're 'dead' so you may need to explain this. It can be an awful shock to them when they find out so you have to tread carefully.

One of the ways to tackle this problem is by asking them who is on the throne? For example, you could say, 'There's something I need to tell you, Maisie.' or Bob or Charlie or Fred. 'Victoria isn't on the throne anymore. It's not 1868 either. I don't mean to shock you Fred but it's now 2013. What does that say, Fred? Doesn't that tell you something? Fred.......you're dead!'

(Grace and Bobbie are now in such uncontrollable laughter that we cannot continue. So I switch off the tape and decide, enough for one morning, let's have some lunch!)

J. 'So ladies, let's now carry on where we left off. As the 'talking' medium in this rescue, you continue to befriend, re-assure and help this lost soul in front of you. Together with your spirit guides, your job is to help get them home.

I don't think it really matters that you're thinking of one home and they're thinking of another as eventually, it's going to be one and the same so there's no need to be specific as to where 'home' is unless, of course, it's the way your conversation is going or it's necessary, maybe because they're not getting it!

For example, sometimes you get people who resist help even though they want the help! Always remember, you wouldn't have this person unless they said they were ready but sometimes they're being difficult, sometimes *very* difficult and things aren't flowing very well! (Grace and Bobbie laugh).

You may have to repeat yourself and take a few steps back before you can go forward again. You may have to justify or coax them, yes? Just like in human nature, you get all sorts of people.

So to continue, you're explaining to them that you want to help them return home and often, it's natural to ask them *who is* at home because, hopefully, one of those people will be coming to fetch them?

So, you ask, 'Who would you like to see?' Ask if they would like to see their mother, their father, grandmother, whoever? Now, if you have someone who you know has 'died' within the last thirty or fourty years, it may very well be one of their grandparents who comes for them rather than their parents as the parents might still be alive on the earth plane. So in these situations, suggesting a grandparent is the safer option here.

You explain that someone is coming to fetch them and that if they look hard, they will see someone and you begin by encouraging them to look for a light and to start searching, as the person in spirit will be coming through the light. That is where home is, home is through the Light.'

G & B. 'Right.'

J. 'You don't go through darkness to get home and, as you will see when we do the role play, you ask them, 'Can you see the light, can you see a light shining?' Some of them say, 'Yes, the sun!' So OK, that's a good start, you say to yourself!

Never let them know that you're mind is racing and working ten to the dozen to pull this off. Mentally, you will be working hard to keep the conversation going and making sure you always say the right thing at the right time. You'll be thinking what can I say, what can I do, which is why it's hard because you're in charge of getting them home, aren't you?'

G. & B. 'Yes.'

J. 'So it's quite a responsibility and you're having to take in everything plus work out what they can cope with, what they can understand, avoiding all the pitfalls, yes, and don't bring a fire to warm them if they've died in a fire! (Grace and Bobbie are chuckling).

So to recap, once you've got their trust and you've calmed them down, you start talking about 'going home'; it's always about going home because 'home' is much better than where they've been and *you* know what home really means but *they* think it's just their house.

So now you begin the homeward stretch and start explaining to them about the light, and you encourage them to look for the light, because you tell them that the person who's coming for them will be coming *through* the light. So you might say, 'Look for a light, start looking and see if you can see someone?' You always re-assure them that someone will be coming, so say, 'Keep looking! Can you see anything? Can you see them yet?'

This often happens really quickly. They see the light and then they see someone from their family or whoever, it's brilliant, it happens so quickly. Other times, it may take longer and you have to keep at it and you will need to coax them, again and again.

However, you usually know when the status quo has changed, when something has happened and when they have seen someone as their demeanour changes. They may go quiet or their face may appear transfixed; you can see just by looking at the 'channel medium' that something has happened.

So you pick up on that and when you think someone has turned up, you'll probably get a reaction from the 'channel' medium. They may start smiling, they may start crying, they may say, 'Good God!' It could be anything, yes? (Bobbie is laughing).

It all depends who you have with you. The reaction might be, 'Mummy, mummy, mummy!' Every rescue is different so it can be anything but you now think hallelluya, I've done it! Or rather, we've done it because you mustn't forget it's teamwork, it's always a joint effort between you and your spirit guides.

So eventually, you get a reaction because they've seen someone and obviously, it's such a relief and the love they feel is just overwhelming, I mean you often end up crying yourself and now you're on the homeward straights so you say, 'Go on, go with them. Go on, take their hand. Go on, you're safe now.' Or perhaps, 'Go on, they're going to make you a lovely cup of tea! Go home for some tea!'

You can say anything which suits their situation, anything that you think they'll love. Don't say go home for a drink! The pub's over the road or something like that. (Grace and Bobbie are both laughing). Keep it clean!

Having said that, I have had to take somebody to a pub because he was being *so* difficult and wouldn't co-operate and it was the only thing I could think of to move him forward.'

B. 'Oh right!'

J. 'Yes, that was the only way to get him to shift, he was SO obstinate. I had literally run out of ideas and couldn't persuade him to move from where he was so I ended up saying, 'I tell you what, do you fancy a drink?' Straight away, he cheered up, so mentally, we 'went' to the pub and so the person who was coming to take him home obviously met him there - simples!

Remember it's all thought, his mind took him there so it doesn't matter does it as long as you get the job done. Nothing else was working so it was just a case of 'good thinking, Batman' - I reckon a drink will do the trick - and it did!

So moving on, eventually someone comes through the light; the mother, the father, an animal, Rosa - it can be a horse and carriage - anything. After this, the channel medium who has had this person within their aura, will start to feel the relief as they now feel a withdrawal of the lost soul's energy.

Let's say the channel medium has been crying at the sight of seeing the family approaching her protégé. The crying will cease and it's almost like a balloon deflating and so you know that the passing has been successful because all those 'feelings' are leaving you.

So the lost soul has joined their family, their guide, their dog, whoever, and with the trance now being lifted and the anaesthetic wearing off, the channel medium can now open their eyes because you always start off doing rescue with your eyes closed.

I just want to say that there came a point in my own mediumship where I began doing rescue with my eyes open but for a long time they were always closed!'

B. 'Yes.'

J. 'Yes, I'm saying this especially to you, Bobbie! You remember how you started off doing your attunements - with your eyes open!'

B. 'Oh yes!' (Bobbie is chuckling).

J. (Jenny looks at Grace) 'Madam here, was doing all her attunements with her eyes open!'

B. 'I was!' (Bobbie is laughing).

J. (Still talking to Grace) 'Then, all of a sudden, it hit me! Bobbie, do you close your eyes when you attune? No, she said. That's why I'm saying; then you open your eyes!'

G. 'I was wondering where that was all going, what have I missed?'

J. 'Yes! So, the 'rescue' is now over. Job done, well done, everyone! Often, you will get a thank you or a God bless you! Or sometimes, even later on, you'll suddenly hear a thank you. It doesn't necessarily have to come straight away but either way, the work is *very* rewarding.

I can tell by looking at you both that you're taking all this on board and understanding how wonderful it must be to do this sort of work, so yes, it is *very* rewarding.

Right! Some bits and pieces to put on the end here:-

   * Just like attunement, always do this work on a relatively empty stomach. Again, the clearer your channel is, so to speak, the better.

   * Sometimes you *do* feel things the spirit felt when they died but it is just a 'shadow' of what they felt themselves.

   * Sometimes the 'channel' medium's face will change. Again, the overshadowing and sometimes it's not a very pretty face either! So don't be vain about this, it doesn't matter what you look like so don't get self-conscious, that's what I'm trying to say. You know, if you look more like a criminal.....'

B. 'As long as you get the job done.'

J. 'Exactly! *We* know what you look like!

   * Speak loudly and clearly to the 'channel' medium.

However, you will get to know the person or people you're working with in your circle and you'll develop a comfortable rapport between you.

Grace, you've got a beautiful quiet voice and if you're not getting a response, it may be that you need to speak up. Bobbie, your voice is quiet husky and of a medium tone so I don't think you'll have any problems.

   * Only one person in the circle should be talking to the 'channel' medium.

OK, this is a good point. Let's say you were in a bigger circle. I want you to know that spirit will only ever have one person working at a time. I used to be *so* frightened when I felt someone coming through - that someone else had something too - and that they were going to start talking at the same time as me.

It used to *really* bother me because I couldn't stop the spirit from coming through. You know, I was thinking, I can't stop it! I hope someone isn't going to say something because I'm just about to say something!' (Bobbie is laughing).

It wasn't funny, but now I know that spirit will only work with one person at a time in a circle, yes? If someone is getting something that doesn't interfere with the rescue or the trance then that's fine, it is between them and their guide but verbally, you will not get two people doing a rescue or trance at the same time. Spirit would *never* do that. They will only do one rescue or trance at a time in a circle. It makes sense doesn't it?

But when I was learning, I was really worried about that. I didn't have the knowledge and understanding that I would have later on.

The other thing which I need to say - because I don't know what's going to happen to you guys in the future - but let's say you had a bigger circle and let's say, Grace, you were helping Bobbie. Bobbie had a lost soul who came into her aura and you Grace, were watchman, and you were doing the talking to help the lost soul home.

Now let's say Grace that you got stuck, you just froze, you know, like stage fright and couldn't continue and that does happen.'

G. 'It's happened!'

J. 'Well it *does* happen which is why I want to talk about it. It's happened loads of times, especially when I had my own circles and the people who were working in the circle suddenly got stuck! So the best thing to do is for someone else in the circle to then take over and continue the conversation, yes?

Let's say, the three of us were working and you Grace, got stuck for words when helping Bobbie and let's say, the spirit needing help was called Alice. I would see that you Grace were suddenly lost for words so I would naturally introduce myself and take over.

I would say something like, 'Hello Alice, my name's Jenny and I'm a friend of Grace. I've also been standing here with Grace waiting to help you.' or 'I'm a friend of Grace and I'm here to help as well.' Someone else in the circle must naturally take over because the person who needs help *now* is the circle member who's frozen up!

And the lost soul Alice, might reply by saying, 'I didn't know you were here!' and you could reply, 'Oh yes Alice, I've been here all the time in the background but *I* can help you now.' You talk as though you were talking to anybody, yes? Just a simple explanation is all that is needed.

So you gently relieve the circle member who's got tongue-tied and finish it off for them. So that's a very good way to help if someone gets stuck. Do you understand that?'

G. 'Yes, yes, I do, I was just.....my brain runs off and I was just thinking well, OK, the person's got stuck, frozen for want of a better word. You've given it what you consider a very quick, reasonable amount of time. You know it's not going to rectify until you eventually start to talk but what quite often happens to people who are frozen, they suddenly unfreeze, then what happens?'

J. 'Well, they would have to know their place, they couldn't then re-enter the conversation, they would remain silent and listen. Also, the medium in the circle who has now taken over, would have held up their hand signalling that they would now take over from the 'frozen' medium. If the spirit entity doubts this new person, they can re-assure them, 'Oh, I'm friends with Grace and we always work together so can you tell me, etc, etc.' and continue with the questions.

This is why I'm discussing this particular scenario because you have to expect the unexpected. I am trying to think of all eventualities. Your first cause is to your lost soul, you have to protect them but you are also in a human circle and have to always do your best. The people in the circle would need to know beforehand, that in the event of someone getting tongue-tied, this is the procedure we follow.

If you had a rescue circle every month and you had four people who sat with you every month, you would teach or explain this is what we will do if anyone gets tongue-tied.

You must both remember, today is just the beginning. You're not going to learn every single thing I teach you about rescue or anything else right away. It's a day by day or month by month experience and maybe, over a period of time, you'll be emailing me and asking me questions until you feel you've got a stronger understanding.

People getting tongue-tied is a reality and you need to know what to do.'

G. & B. 'Oh yes!'

J. 'Spirit would never 'dump you' in it and never forget that we are just half the exercise, half the procedure. We are being used to effect a rescue, *but* spirit *also* want us to have experiences so that we continue to grow in our awareness, strength and understanding.

You may feel you're qualified to climb a mountain but it's not until you start climbing that you realise just how much you know, just how much you're capable of and just how much you need to learn. Without the attempt, you won't learn anything, certainly not about yourself.

But in addition to all this, I feel, with confidence, that whatever role either of you are playing, you would take things step by step. You're both intelligent enough, humane enough and you care enough to be able to think of something which would help someone in all situations and you're going to get lots of examples later when we do the role play.

Here is another point. Sometimes you sit with a circle of people and it ends up being a rescue circle because the mediums present have this ability. You're not aware of this to start with but your strengths come out in the circle.

So let's say the two of you sit for an hour, you would take it in turns to be watchman - one of you would have your eyes open - whilst the other would go into attunement. You may even decide to split the hour and change places after halfway or maybe to switch places every month but whatever plans spirit have for you, they will take the opportunity whilst you're in circle.

So let's say Grace, you're watchman. Bobbie may start off doing some trance and it's recorded and then the next thing you know, the trance stops and someone starts to come through, so then you've both got to work together to effect a rescue, Yes? And then there might be nothing - no vocal work - and spirit are using you both for healing.

When I had my circles, I would take the last five minutes for *all* of us to attune together, including the watchman, and this was often a very beautiful experience for all of us to blend with spirit together and we all felt the love and didn't want it to end.

You also need to be reminded that initially, when a new circle is convened, a lot of blending needs to be done. Spirit may have a lot to do to harmonise and prepare all your energies for working. You may just get one rescue because they're busy blending the energies for the rest of the hour; you always have to trust spirit with this. They know what's best for you and the circle. Also:-

   * Have a pad and pen next to you in case you find a guide wants to talk to you clairaudiently.

As I've mentioned earlier, if you record what happens during your circle, you can then play it back and talk about it afterwards which helps you learn and share your experiences and increases confidence.

Eventually, with time, you may begin to help people on the earth plane who are having negative things happen in their home. 'Rescue' situations may also land 'on your doorstep' which usually means that spirit needs *your* help. I want to go through some extra points to help you deal with these situations yourself.

So before you can help someone here on the earthplane with problems they're having at home, you need to find out some relevant information, namely:-

   * The address and type of property where this negativity may be present?

   * The names and rough ages of the people living there?

   * The problem(s) they're having and who is being affected by this and how?

   * What is surrounding the house, e.g. Woods, a railway, a cemetery, a flyover,etc?

You need these details so that you can be as specific as possible when asking spirit for help.

Once you have the above details, you can then sit in your circle, or, if you are experienced enough, on your own and have this information written down in front of you.

You then need to do the following:-

* When you open up and after your prayer, you ask for your 'rescue guides' to draw close as you need their help to effect a rescue.

* You then ask spirit to help you *specifically* with this problem and outline the information you have managed to obtain so that there is no doubt who the rescue is for and where.

* After the rescue(s) have been done, you then need to cleanse and cloak the house in protection before closing down.

The cleansing can be done by mentally visiting each room in the property and imagining the walls covered in golden light. I often visualise throwing all the windows and doors open to let out the negativity, followed by allowing the sun to shine through and cover the complete house or building and then asking for the place to be sealed and protected with golden light.

You must also allow two or three days for all the existing negative energy to disperse into the ether which means that things may not be restored back to normality straight away but take a few days at the most; energy doesn't just vanish instantly, it dissipates and drifts away.

There is another way to cleanse houses and property which Bobbie's guides revealed in one of her attunements recently. This is where you imagine negativity in each room as black curtaining. You make a fire in one of the rooms and strip the black curtaining from each room whilst throwing it on the fire which both burns and cleanses.

OK. There is something else I would now like to discuss. Remember we talked earlier about mediums being in deep trance?'

G. & B. 'Yes!'

J. 'And I said that my own views were, that going into trance is fine but I personally want to know what I'm doing so I don't want to go too deep.'

B. 'So do you make that clear to spirit?'

J. 'Well, that's just what I was going to say next! If necessary, you can say to your guides that, in future, you don't want to be taken over to such an extent if you feel that your trance is heavier than you would like it. Remember it's a partnership.

You have to work *with* them so you have to say, 'This is too deep.' You know, it's like when you have your attunements and they may be working on your head and it may be a bit painful. You then have to say, 'No, no, this is too painful, not so hard please, can you ease up a bit?' If you don't tell them, they won't know will they?'

G. & B. 'No.'

J. 'So it's the same with the trance. When we talk about people going into trance, I have been horrified to hear stories of people walking out of the room and leaving the sitter in trance because they haven't come round!'

G. 'Really?'

J. 'Really and not just once! I've heard several instances of this.'

B. 'You're joking?'

J. 'No, I am *not* joking! I was horrified to learn that this poor person was left in trance whilst the other members of the circle got up, left the room and made themselves tea or whatever. So, we need to talk briefly about this because that is *not* on. You should never, *ever* leave someone in trance.'

G. 'What was the watchman doing?'

J. 'Exactly! Well done Grace. No, these people didn't have a watchman, they probably don't know what a 'watchman' is. There must be loads of people in circles who don't know you need a watchman - everyone just shuts their eyes, some may not say prayers or even ask for protection.'

G. 'Was it a development circle?'

J. 'I don't know what kind of circle it was. All I *do* know is that you don't walk out and leave someone in trance so I am going to explain what needs to be done in a situation like this.

Let's say you two are sitting, Bobbie is in trance and she is not coming round when she's apparently finished. You, Grace, have to gently talk to Bobbie and get her to come out of her trance.

Now, just like a doctor or nurse bringing a patient round after an anaesthetic, you would say, 'Bobbie, Bobbie, can you hear me Bobbie? Come on Bobbie, you're finished now. Come on, time to wake up, open your eyes now' or words to that effect. So you must never leave a sitter who has been working unattended. They must always regain full consciousness.'

G. 'Oh right. I'm so glad you said because that was what I was coming up to.'

J. 'So don't close the circle until everyone has come round. And, of course, when you close the circle, you say your closing prayer, you close your chakras down but there again, I feel there's no point closing down your chakras after the hour because you're going to carry on talking about what has happened during the evening. So I always advocate closing down at the front door before you leave the house.

Right, I've done enough talking! *You're* both going to be doing some work now as we're moving on to the 'Role Play!'

Rescue: 'Role Play'

Jenny: 'Right ladies, rescue role play! This is the last part of our Rescue Mediumship Day.

Years ago, a good friend and circle member offered to produce a typed transcript of every rescue and healing circle we had sat in over a 3 year period so each paper I give you depicts the words of an original rescue. I have chosen a variety of straight forward situations as examples to help you learn more this afternoon.

As I have explained, each rescue in a circle involves two people. One taking the lost soul within their aura - the 'channel' medium - and another who is helping them to pass over, the 'talking' medium. So here is your first paper. Tell me who are the two people working on this rescue?'

Grace & Bobbie: 'Susanne and Jenny.'

J. 'OK, so both of you decide which person's role you're going to play and we'll start. I suggest that you change roles with each rescue you read in order to benefit from this role play session. Are you ready? Off you go!'

Role Play: 1.

Grace: 'Hello, can you hear me?'

Bobbie: (Sobbing).

G. 'Are you cold?'

B. 'Mmmm.'

G. 'OK, I'll wrap you in a blanket. Can you feel it getting warmer a little bit? Can you talk to me? What's your name?'

B. 'Abigail.'

G. 'Abigal. Where are you Abigail?'

B. 'In a dark place.'

G. 'In a dark place. Don't cry, we'll bring you some light, can you see the light? We have a lantern, just have a look? I'll wave it in front of your eyes, can you see it? Alright, so that's better. You are warm now and you can see the light and we are all here, ready to help you.'

B. 'Who's here, who are you?'

G. 'My name is Susanne and I have a friend with me and we are all here to help you. How old are you?'

B. 'Eight.'

G. 'You're eight. Oh yes, how have you come down into that dark place?'

B. 'I was pushed!'

G. 'You were pushed?'

B. (Sobbing).

G. 'Oh don't cry, we are all here, are you hurting anywhere?'

B. 'My hands are tied up.'

G. 'Your hands are tied up. OK, look here, I've got my knife.'

B. 'AHHH!'

G. 'Don't worry, don't worry, no, I'll put it away. Don't cry, don't cry. It's gone, it's gone. I'll untie the knots, don't worry. Can you feel your hands now, move them a little bit. OK. Alright, calm down, calm down. Move your hands, alright, we want to take you home now. Where do you want to go?'

B. 'My mummy.'

G. 'You want to see your mummy. OK. Have a look over there? Can you see a bright light? We brought a bright light for you, a *really* bright light and it is coming closer, can you see someone in there? Can you see someone, slowly coming towards you?'

B. 'I see a lady.'

G. 'You see a lady. Oh right, I think that lady is waiting for you. She loves you very much. Go, go. Give me your hand and we walk a bit closer. Come with me and all our friends are there as well. Look, who is it, do you know the lady? Come with me, look she's holding her hand out to you. Take her hand, she loves you very much, she will take you home.'

B. 'And my aunty too!'

G. 'And your aunty is there, isn't that wonderful! They are both waiting for you, go with them.'

B. 'Thank you.'

G. 'Go to the Light, bless you.'

The End.

B. 'Ahhh!'

Jenny: 'I thought we'd start off with a child. Now you see the example of the knife?'

G. & B. 'Yes!'

J. 'It was silly but Susanne learnt from that. Now, Susanne is German so whenever Susanne is working on these rescues, I can hear her German accent and the way she speaks. We all have our own way of helping and talking but the knife was a 'no,no'! Just like the earlier example of bringing the fire, yes?'

G. & B. 'Yes.'

J. 'But it doesn't matter because you soon realise your mistake and Susanne did and so untied it with her hands and I thought the lady was Rosa coming, whether it was or not I don't know or remember - this was way back in 2004 - but her aunty also came, so it was a success, wasn't it?'

B. 'Oh yes!'

J. 'So that was your first one. Do you see how it will become more practical and natural and all my talking this morning will hopefully begin to take shape? Ready for the next one?'

Role Play: 2.

Bobbie: 'I'm here, I'm here, don't worry. No more crying, I'm here now. No more tears, I'm here for you. My name's Jenny and I'm with you. What's the matter, I'm here to help you?'

Grace: 'I want to go home. (Sobbing) I want to go home.'

B. 'OK darling. I'm going to take you home. I'm going to find someone to take you home. Can you tell me your name?'

G. 'Sarah.'

B. 'Sarah. Who do you want to come to fetch you Sarah, Mummy or Daddy?'

G. 'Mummy, Mummy!'

B. 'OK, darling. Sarah, are you cold? Is it dark where you are? I'm just going to make it lighter for you. I'm going to bring a beautiful bright light so you're no longer in the dark. It's coming, it's coming. Here we are, you're now surrounded by the light. Is that better Sarah?

(Sarah nods). Good! Now, go through this light, you're mummy's going to come for you, hopefully, your mummy will come but someone will come that you know. Look out for them, you'll know them.'

G. (Sobbing).

B. 'Can you see her? Go on then darling. Go on then, you're safe now darling, go on.'

G. 'Thank you.'

B. 'God bless.'

The End.

Jenny: 'Now she didn't say very much.'

G. 'Who Donna?'

J. 'Yes, Donna and I were doing this rescue. Donna 'had' the little girl within her aura but I was also reading her body language, yes? You have grab whatever you can and if you don't get much you have to keep going as long as the person is OK, is not frightened, is not going backwards. You have to keep progressing with your charge.

And this is an example of where you didn't really get much information but with a child, you might not.'

G. & B. 'No.'

J. 'And because of who she was, I couldn't grill her with questions. It wouldn't be fair, would it? So this is an example of having a *child,* having to run with whatever you *can,* keeping the proceedings going. As long as she's no longer crying, eventually, you can tell that things are moving. You just get on with it and your guides will do the rest. Alright?'

G. & B. 'Yes.'

Grace: 'Hello, hello, can you hear me? Hello, my name's Donna and I'm here to help you. Can you tell me your name? It's OK, take your time.'

Bobbie: 'I'm cold.'

G. 'Aww! I'm going to put a blanket around your shoulders to warm you up, here it comes, I'm wrapping you in it now. There you are, that *is* warmer isn't it? That's much better. What's your name?'

B. 'Michelle.'

G. 'Michelle, where are you Michelle?'

B. 'I'm in a dark place.'

G. 'In a dark place, are you stuck somewhere, are you hurt?'

B. 'I just can't see anything!'

G. 'You can't see anything?'

B. 'Nothing!'

G. 'Have you hurt yourself? No?'

B. 'I don't know how I got here.'

G. 'Don't worry, don't worry, you are safe now. I'm going to help you. I'm going to shine a nice light to make things a bit more comfortable for you and you don't hurt anywhere Michelle? No, no?'

B. 'Just can't see nothing.'

G. 'Don't worry darling, you're safe now, I'm here to help you, don't worry, don't worry. I think we need to get you home, don't we?'

B. 'I want to go home!'

G. 'Go home, that is a very good idea. Michelle, can you tell me darling, who was on the throne, have we got a King or a Queen? Do you know? No?'

B. 'I don't know.'

G. 'You don't know darling, don't worry. How old are you Michelle?'

B. 'Eight.'

G. 'Eight, is that all, only a little 'un, aren't you! Aww, and do you go to school?'

B. 'I'm not that little!'

G. 'No, but you are a young girl aren't you? Do you go to school Michelle?'

B. 'Sometimes.'

G. 'Sometimes you go to school, sometimes you don't go?'

B. 'I don't like it!'

G. 'You don't like it, what don't you like about it, your teacher?'

B. 'She doesn't like me.'

G. 'She doesn't like you? Oh, I can't believe that, you're lovely, you're lovely! Oh, I don't believe that, they just haven't got to know the real you, have they?'

B. 'No.'

G. 'No, don't you worry. Is there a lot of children go to your school?'

B. 'No.'

G. 'No, not many. And do you have any brothers and sisters who go to school with you?'

B. 'Tom.'

G. 'Is he your brother?'

B. 'Mmm.'

G. 'Is he bigger than you?'

B. 'Mmm.'

G. 'Yes, and what sort of things do you learn at school, boring things?'

B. 'Reading and writing.'

G. 'And when you do your writing, do you use a pen or do you use chalk?'

B. 'Chalk.'

G. 'Chalk, you use your chalk, well right that's OK. We're going to take you home now. Now then, I expect you..I think you might quite like Mummy to come and get you?'

B. 'My mummy!'

G. 'Mummy? Yes, definitely mummy. Well, we are going to shine this really big light and it is going to light up the whole place and make you feel much more comfortable. Here comes the light now. It is really nice and bright and if you look through it very carefully for me, like a good girl, you are going to see someone coming to take you home. Good girl, keep looking.'

B. 'Sure?'

G. 'I'm sure; she's on her way. Keep looking.'

B. 'My friend!'

G. 'Your friend's coming, she'll take you home.'

B. 'She's got her best dress on.'

G. 'Oh, especially for you!'

B. 'Ribbons in her hair an' all.'

G. 'Oh, lovely, look. You go with her darling. She'll look after you, you're safe now darling. God bless you.'

The End.

Jenny: 'So that was different again, wasn't it? Donna had a hard time with this one. It was like getting blood out of a stone as she was only able to get information 'on the drip' so to speak. It took quite a while but she managed to eventually find out what time in history it was once she found out about the chalk; that was her big clue!

So do you see how she's *always* re-assuring her, don't worry, don't worry, you're safe, the continuous reassurance, especially to a little girl? And it didn't matter that she asked about the king or queen. It wasn't a hard question, it was a natural question; sometimes little girls know about kings and queens so she either knew or she didn't.'

G. & B. 'Yes.'

J. 'The main thing was that she thought her mummy was coming and we all thought her mummy was coming and then her best friend came! So that was brilliant wasn't it?'

G. 'It was like the early nineteen hundreds. My dad used chalk.'

J. 'So that just goes to show, expect the unexpected!'

Jenny: 'Here's another one. I'm doing the talking and Lesley is the one who has the negative spirit within her aura.'

Bobbie: 'Hello, I was waiting for you to ask for help?'

Grace: 'Well, no-one is getting me out of this house, I'm telling you that now. They keep coming and keep going.'

B. 'Why don't you want to go with them?'

G. 'I'm not going from this house. I've always lived here and I'm not going nowhere, no matter what or how many of you come. You keep coming and I keep telling you, I'm staying in this house!'

B. 'Have you ever thought that it might not belong to you any more?'

G. 'That's what they keep telling me. It's the only house left, all the others have gone and I'm staying where I've always been, in this house!'

B. 'By the way, I must be very polite, my name is Jenny. What's your name? Are you going to be polite too?'

G. 'Alice.'

B. 'Alice, pleased to meet you Alice. What happened to the other houses?'

G. 'Knocked down.'

B. 'What bombed down or knocked down?'

G. 'Knocked down.'

B. 'Why is yours still here then?'

G. 'I'm not going nowhere, that's why!'

B. 'Do you imagine the house is there or is the house really there?'

G. 'Well it's here, I can see it!'

B. 'What about the other houses?'

G. 'No, all gone, rubble.'

B. 'Well, how come your house is the only one there?'

G. 'Because I stayed and I said, I'm not going nowhere.'

B. 'Well, what would you say if I said to you, that the house was demolished too. That it was just your imagination that was keeping the house there. There really isn't anything because I'm standing next to you and I can't see a thing! I can't see a brick, I can't see a roof tile, I can't see anything. So what would you say to that?'

G. 'No! No! That can't be right!'

B. 'Well, I can't see a thing, I can't see a thing. I can't see a door, a window, I can't see a path, I can't see a garden. I can't see a gate, I can't see anything Alice.'

G. 'Well where's my house gone then?'

B. 'Your house was demolished with all the other houses.'

G. 'Well why am I still here then?'

B. 'Because you really shouldn't be here.'

G. 'Well, where have I got to go now? I've got no house!'

B. 'You've got to go to your *real* home.'

G. 'Well, I haven't got another home have I? Where's my house!'

B. 'Listen, if you'll be calm Alice, I will tell you where your real home is and where I'm going to take you to.'

G. 'You know, I just feel so cross about this. Where's my lovely house?'

B. 'Alice, Alice, who was on the throne the last time you were in your house?'

G. 'Oh Victoria, everybody knows that!'

B. 'Well, Alice, I've got a bit of a shock for you. Victoria's no longer on the throne. Do you know who is on the throne now?'

G. 'Her husband's dead.'

B. 'Yes, Albert died and Victoria stayed on but she died in 1901 but it is now 2004. What does that mean Alice, if it's now 2004 and you thought Queen Victoria was still on the throne, what does that tell you?'

G. 'Well, how did I get here?'

B. 'Because you have been stuck here. You haven't wanted to leave a house that wasn't there anymore. You were so attached to your house that you wouldn't leave it and I am trying to tell you for the last time, you must go home... to your *real* home.'

G. 'Well look, my house isn't there now, all there is is rubble, so where has it gone?'

B. 'Well done Alice! It has been knocked down with all the other houses.'

G. 'Well, where have I got to go now?'

B. 'You are coming with me, if you trust me?'

G. 'Well, where are *you* going?'

B. 'With you; you're coming with me and I'm coming with you and we're going to go to your real home and your real home is where the light is. And if you go through the light, you will get picked up by somebody that you will know instantly. They have also been waiting for you, not just me but someone on the other side; the other side is your spiritual home, because we never, ever die Alice.'

G. 'I'm going to have a house there then?'

B. 'The actual house that you want, the actual house that you have been dreaming of, the actual house that you have always wanted but you *must* let me take you there.'

G. 'Where's my family?'

B. 'They're coming now, they're coming to get you. If you look through a big bright light that I have asked to be sent to you. It is coming, it's coming, it's getting brighter and brighter; you look very hard now Alice.'

G. 'Oh, I can see Fred in the kitchen, that's my kitchen! That's much nicer, it is all bright. Oh, the kids are there! All the kids are there, how did I get there?'

B. 'Go to them now.'

G. 'Can they see me?'

B. 'They can see you, they are waiting for you, they've got the kettle on.'

G. 'Can you take me? I'm not sure.'

B. 'Go to them Alice, go to them. Go to them now while you've got the chance, go on now. Bye, bye Alice. Bye, bye.'

The End.

J. 'Alice was also hard work. I was tearing my hair out and if she says where's my house one more time, I'm gonna hang her! (Grace and Bobbie are laughing).

Again, an example of when things are *not* going your way and you're banging your head against a brick wall and you're thinking, 'What can I say!' But even if it's pigeon steps, you keep on and on trying to get somewhere. You can't be cross with them but as you see, I won't stand for anyone being rude to me either.

So we'll go on to the next one. Claire is the one who's doing the talking and I'm the one who has the spirit within them.'

Role Play: 5.

Grace: 'Hello, hello, can you hear me?'

Bobbie: 'Mmm, help me lady.'

G. 'Hello, my name's Claire.'

B. 'Help me lady.'

G. 'I'm going to help you. I've come to help you.'

B. 'Help me lady.'

G. 'I'm going to help you. Are you hurt? Where are you hurt?'

B. 'Please!'

G. 'Calm down, take some deep breaths, try and take some deep breaths. Calm down, I've come to help you.'

B. 'I can't feel my legs.'

G. 'Are your legs trapped? Try and calm down, I've come to help you. I'm going to help you. Are you trapped? Are you under the ground?'

B. 'It is all dark here.'

G. 'It is all dark. OK. I'm going to bring some light.'

B. 'Can't feel my legs!'

G. 'OK, I'm going to help you. I'm going to move the things away from your legs. I'm going to take all the pain away. All the pain is going to go from your legs. Can you take some deep breaths for me, try and relax a bit.

Take some deep breaths. I'm going to take all the pain away from you so that you begin to feel healthy again and there's no pain in your body and the feeling in your legs is going to come back. Can you take some deep breaths? That's right, calm down. Would you like to go home? Can you tell me your name?'

B. 'Tom.' (Coughing).

G. 'Tom, I'd like to get you home. Do you think you can walk now or will I have to carry you?'

B. (Coughing).

G. 'Do you think you can walk with me?'

B. 'I don't know.' (Coughing).

G. 'Let me help you up. Can you feel the fresh air coming, it'll take the cough away? Breathe in some fresh air.'

B. (Coughing).

G. 'Have you got soot or smoke?'

B. (Coughing).

G. 'Breathe in the fresh air, Tom. Can you feel the wind blowing now?'

B. 'My legs are better, lady.'

G. 'They're better?'

B. 'Better, lady. My legs are better now.'

G. 'Good! That's good Tom. Listen, I'm going to take you home now. Come with me and I'm going to bring some light for you.'

B. 'I live in Eastern Street.'

G. 'You live in Eastern Street? That's a good help.'

B. 'Number 22.' (Coughing).

G. 'Number 22, I can take you there now. Come with me and I'll take you home. If you look to the bottom of Eastern Street, I'm going to bring some light. Would you like some water Tom for that cough? Here you are then, I'll pour some water for you, take some nice cool water. Is that better?'

B. 'Yes.'

G. 'Look down the street for me, can you see a light, a beautiful light is coming. A golden light is coming, look into the light Tom and someone is going to be there.'

B. 'Oh my brother, my brother!'

G. 'Your brother?'

B. 'Yes!'

G. 'He's come to take you home.'

B. 'Ta, lady.'

G. 'You're welcome.'

B. 'You're clever!'

G. 'I know!'

B. 'Thanks ever so much.'

G. 'You're very welcome Tom. Go with your brother. God Bless you.'

B. 'Bye.'

G. 'Bye, bye.'

The End.

B. 'Aaah, that was a nice one.'

G. 'Yes.'

Jenny: 'That was an example of where they were being helped with the pain and everything. If you tell them what you're doing, the lost soul will also *feel* what you're doing too. So you take the weight off and as you heard, 'My legs are better now.' He drank the water; he felt better. Whatever you say, you make it happen but you have to keep thinking, what can I do, what shall I do?

You see how it weaves, depending on who you have in front of you. You put yourself in charge of that individual and work out what you need to know because you have got to help them and they may not be saying very much.'

B. 'Right.'

J. 'Again, it's the personality of the person who is coming through and also each rescue medium will work differently as well. When I lived in the Forest of Dean, I had someone working with me and it was *so, so* simple! She told you everything - what was wrong, where they were - even the inside leg measurements! (Bobbie is laughing).

With her, you didn't even have to ask any questions, she just told you everything! Where she was, what her name was; you see, everybody works differently.'

G. & B. 'Yes.'

J. 'OK, this is the last one. This one is Susanne and me and Susanne is doing the talking.'

Role Play: 6.

Bobbie: 'Hello, hello, can you hear me?'

Grace: 'Yes.'

B. 'My name is Susanne, I have been waiting for you. Are you in pain?'

G. 'Yes.'

B. 'Alright, I'll take the pain away.'

G. 'My legs, my legs!'

B. 'Yes, can you feel the pain going? Slowly, I'll take the pain out of your legs. It's going, it's going, can you feel it going? Getting better, getting better. Now it has gone! Where are you?'

G. 'You are very good aren't you. How did you do that?'

B. 'Well, I have a little help.'

G. 'You had a bit of what?'

B. 'I had a bit of help.'

G. 'Thank you very much.'

B. 'My pleasure, where are you?'

G. 'I'm, um, I, you're not going to believe this.'

B. 'Oh, I'm sure I will.'

G. 'Have you ever known anyone being buried and they weren't really dead?'

B. 'I have heard about it, yes.'

G. 'Well, that's me!'

B. 'OK and I'm here to help you.'

(Grace interrups the role play)

G. 'Nothing is ever for nothing!' (This is Grace's worst fear)

(Role play continues)

G. 'What are we going to do now?'

B. 'What I'm going to do now? Do you not want to come back up again with me and get out?'

G. 'Come back up where?'

B. 'Well, to the light.'

G. 'Sure!'

B. 'OK, now, I'll lift the lid, are you in a coffin?'

G. 'Mmm, I don't know really, I'm just....'

B. 'You're just buried. I'll start digging, I think that's a good start! I'll start digging and my friends can help me to dig a big hole. Can you see a bit of light, a bit of light coming in?'

G. 'Yes.'

B. 'Alright. OK. They're helping me to dig around. Give me your hand, I can...

G. 'I'm out now.'

B. 'OK, you give me your hand.'

G. 'Were you in with me?'

B. 'Yes, yes of course. I'm with you and I was in there and now I'll get you out. OK, up you go, OK?'

G. 'I'm up, I'm up!'

B. 'Yes, yes, alright. So can you see, I'll show you a wonderful light which is as bright as the sun. Can you see that? It is warm, it is bright, lots of light. Can you see someone in the light? Have a good look, can you see someone?'

G. 'Who is supposed to be in the light?'

B. 'Well, do you want someone to come and fetch you home?'

G. 'Oh yes, I don't know my way home now. I don't know where I am.'

B. 'OK. I'm with you and someone will come through the light and take you home.'

G. 'Good!'

B. 'OK. Can you see someone coming? Have a good look.'

G. 'I'm looking!'

B. 'Yes, can you see, I can see someone.'

G. 'Can you, who is it?'

B. 'I don't know. Is it a friend of yours, you tell me, you recognise the person? Can you see?'

G. 'I can't see them yet.'

B. 'You can't see the light?'

G. 'Oh, I can! Hang on, hang on, hang on, hang on, hang on!'

B. 'You can?'

G. 'Oh, ha, look! Ha,ha, they've brought the horse and a wagon! Oh my God and supplies! I'm not going to go hungry!'

B. 'No, you're not!'

G. 'Are you coming with me?'

B. 'Yes, of course I'll come with you.'

G. 'What's your name again?'

B. 'Susanne.'

G. 'Oh, Susanne! Come on Susanne, you come with me. I'm very, very grateful.'

B. 'We'll share the carriage.'

G. 'It's not a carriage, it's a wagon.'

B. 'A wagon, yes, well it looked like a carriage.'

G. 'And the horse isn't fast, you don't mind do you?'

B. 'Oh no, no, I have a long time.'

G. 'Oh good! Come on then Susanne.'

B. 'OK, hop on.'

G. 'We'll go home together. I'm *very* grateful.'

B. 'Alright, off we go. You give the signal. Bless you, we're going to the light now.'

The End.

Jenny: 'Well, we never knew the name of that person.'

G & B. 'No.'

J. 'We never knew how old they were or what age in history but the rescue was done, do you see?'

G & B. 'Yes.'

J. 'Now you don't get chastised if you don't ask them their name or their age; what I'm trying to say is, the way it happens is the way it happens. I always say there's no wrong way to do a rescue. The main thing is that you start and you complete the job. So that was an example of where there was no name, no age, no time in history and unfortunately, it was a circumstance that Grace doesn't really like, but nevertheless, she kept going too!

So do you think you know more about rescue than you did when you came in this morning?'

G. & B. 'Yes, definitely!'

J. 'It's beginning to take shape and form and you now understand the two roles I was talking about, the two roles which are needed to effect a rescue in a circle?

It doesn't matter right now whether you will work together or whether you will do work on your own or both, the main thing is that you understand rescue per se'. What it entails, what it means, why you're doing it, the different ways you can help, the different responses you might get.

So these are just examples, there are many more I could share. There are two brilliant ones in *'A Medium's Tale'* - I don't know if you remember - each one a gem but we do not have the luxury of time today but you can borrow them whenever you like.

You will get all kinds of people stuck in their negativity. Gentle ones, rude ones, grateful ones, stubborn ones, old dears and little 'uns but treat them all as 'real' people just as if they were standing right in front of you.

Always speak their language so they understand you, as you need to befriend them early on and earn their trust so they will co-operate with you and answer your questions. They need to know you have their best interest at heart.

I don't know how your rescue guides are going to work with you but the basic principles apply. Everyone who comes through is ready to go home as they have already asked for help. They have all been stuck in their negative thought pattern and a lot are distressed having re-lived their death over and over again.

Each rescue will differ depending on who they are, where they are, how they died, how much pain they're in, etc. but *everyone* needs help to go home - through the light - and the people who come for them can be anyone; often a nice surprise!

Remember, everything is thought and with rescue, you are in charge of their thoughts and deeds. So when you say, 'Come on, let's get some fresh air' they will sense and feel the fresh air. *You* can *make* it happen, you can make it real and with the help of your guides, remember, you have the weight of spirit behind you.

Also, as I said before, there is no wrong way to help with rescue. Your rescue guides are with you each and every step of the way, helping you and putting the thoughts and words into your mind. You are the physical half of the partnership. You are helping out from the physical side of life and I *know* that at least you two, will always do your best. I am confident of that.'

The Last Pages

Dear Reader

This is a true, honest and faithful account of my year teaching Grace and Bobbie spiritual development which has added another dimension to my life.

The 'have-a-go' trance, which Grace initially performed in Month 7, never came out on the tape so we did it again when I visited her home a few months later after the course was finished. I now leave you with this:-

'Guidance'

'Guide with heavenly hands

Guide me on my path

Help me walk my path with strength

Guide me through the good times and the bad

I know you'll never leave my side.

And when I falter, I know you're there

And if I should fall, I know you will catch me.

I see your angels, I see them watching

They walk with me all the time

My helpers, your heavenly host

Taking me ever onwards.

And if my path should meet another

And that we might walk together side by side

Because one can never walk the other's path

But we can walk together as comrades

Until once again, we part and go our separate ways

Only to meet again later.

Because always we meet those we are meant to meet

Those who help us, those who chose to guide us

Those who are ever present

I ask they walk with me, I ask they help me

I ask that they uplift me

Even when I feel low, I know they are with me.

And to you, at the end of my life, in this world

To be there in your heavenly arms

To feel your arms around me

To see your heavenly light.

Dear Lord, I beseech thee

Ever guide me, ever forward.

Amen.'

Jenny: 'So this is the new Grace? Can't you see how you've grown? Well done, well done!'

Author's Note:

The word 'spirit' is used so much in this book and because we are in conversation, this word is often used to denote different things depending on the context of the sentence. Here are some examples to help:-

(i)   'Spirit' invariably refers to our spirit guides and helpers. e.g. Working for spirit., spirit are still with you.

(ii)   We say 'in spirit' when referring to the spirit realms, as opposed to the earth plane.

(iii)   Often (i) & (ii) both relate to spirit. e.g. Thinking about spirit., learn more about spirit., the world of spirit.

(iv)   'Spirit' is also an energy. e.g. Spirit is infinite., Spirit Power., your spirit.

(v)   'Spirit' can also be a combination of (i) & (iv). e.g. Channelled from spirit., attracts spirit of like mind.